TAX REVOLT

TAX REVOLT

SOMETHING FOR NOTHING IN CALIFORNIA

Enlarged Edition

David O. Sears / Jack Citrin

Harvard University Press Cambridge, Massachusetts, and London, England 1985

10 9 8 7 6 5 4 3 2 1

Library of Congress Cataloging in Publication Data

Sears, David O.
  Tax revolt.

  Includes bibliographical references and index.
  1. Real property tax — California — Public opinion.
2. Tax and expenditure limitations — California — Public
opinion. 3. Tax and expenditure limitations — United
States — Public opinion. 4. Public opinion — California.
5. Public opinion — United States.   I. Citrin, Jack.
II. Title.

HJ4191.S4   1985   343.79405′4   84–25233
  ISBN 0–674–86836–6   347.940354

Preface to the Enlarged Edition

This is a welcome opportunity to assess the meaning of the popular rebellion against the prevailing fiscal regime in California some time after the initial electoral dust has settled. The reverberations of Proposition 13 in California, in other states, and in Washington, D.C., resulted in a historic halt to the onward march of governmental expansion. Responding to the voters' mood, officials at all levels of government shifted from reform to preservation. How to live with less became the order of the day.

In analyzing the dynamics of public opinion leading up to the vote on Proposition 13, we concluded that the people wanted something for nothing. Tax relief was the fervent desire of the majority, not dismantling the structure of public service built up over three decades of growth. Proposition 13 owed its success to an unusual conjunction of economic and political factors — rapid inflation in the real estate market, a fiscal structure that automatically translated this into higher tax bills, generalized frustration with the size and competence of government, and the failure of state leaders to produce a plan for property tax relief. Once the fiscal reins had been slipped around their necks, public officials had to cope with the problem of meeting the continuing demand for services with revenues limited in supply by legal restrictions, electoral pressures, and economic recession.

We have written a new chapter for this paperback edition, briefly reviewing how government responded to this fiscal stress and tracing the interplay of public opinion and public policy in the aftermath of Proposition 13. The main conclusion is that the tax revolt in California led neither to the millennium promised by its supporters nor to the apocalypse predicted by its detractors. There has been a decline in the tax burden and in the size of government, which has aligned policy more closely with public opinion as it was expressed at the time of the passage of Proposition 13. But officials also have succeeded in preserving the core of existing programs, even in the face of complaints by the most ardent tax rebels. The public has in turn perceived these changes in policy rather clearly, and the intensity of discontent about the level of taxation has faded. Nevertheless, the underlying ambivalence in attitudes toward the proper role of government continues to prevail.

Our research suggests that this pattern of policy and opinion change is the rule in other states and in the federal context as well. There is a political logic to cutback budgeting in the present climate of opinion: the golden rule is to preserve as much of the programmatic status quo as possible without raising general taxes on individuals.

The aftermath of the tax revolt has shown that public opinion and elections do matter. Government remains constrained by the complex pattern of beliefs that we describe. Today, budgeting is more than ever controlled by the vagaries of the business cycle, and new programs must be carefully marketed. Howard Jarvis's unique moment in the California sun has had lasting effects. It is our hope that the additional chapter clarifies the nature of these consequences and the reasons for them.

We want finally to acknowledge the assistance of Donald Green in the preparation and analysis of new data and the usual efficient help of Carolyn Drago and Tony Kenney in the preparation of the manuscript.

Preface to the First Edition

We began this project as the Proposition 13 campaign struck gold in California. The victory of Proposition 13 appeared to us to be a watershed event in the history of California's politics, potentially marking the end of an era of strong commitment to building a public sector large in scope and high in quality. It triggered a chain reaction of protests against taxes and public spending at all levels of government in America, and this tax revolt challenged the long-run trend among industrialized democracies everywhere for government to increase the size and scope of its activities. In America, the national repercussions have now led to an historic shift in spending and tax policies. But as we began to probe the intentions of California's voters it was unclear whether the tax revolt of 1978 was more than a momentary pause in the steady movement toward the assumption by government of responsibilities once held by family, religious, and business institutions.

Our inquiry mainly focuses on the attitudes of individual voters and how these influenced their choices on ballot measures proposing to limit taxes and government spending in California. Our approach to the meaning of the tax revolt, therefore, is to assess directly the motives of the general public. What did the people want? What were they rebelling against? And how do they feel about the results of their rebellion?

This concern places our research in the tradition of survey-based studies of public opinion and voting. We do not pay systematic attention to a variety of other analytic approaches to the tax revolt that search for causes by comparing the political institutions, fiscal climate, tax regulations, spending policies, or demographic composition of the locales in which protests against taxes have variously succeeded or failed. Others are mining these lodes, and we have benefited from the results of their efforts, but our own study has a distinct preoccupation with the dynamics of the attitudes and actions of individual citizens.

We deal primarily with California, but move at the end to selected comparisons with other states and to the nation as a whole. As the largest state California is of course politically important in its own right. But it is also socially, economically, and politically heterogeneous, affording the opportunity of studying a fairly representative subsample of the nation's population. Too, the tax revolt in California has had its ups and downs, providing the occasion for analyzing the public's mood in dynamic rather than static terms. Finally, California has the reputation for being a political harbinger of things to come, a reputation that the elevation of Ronald Reagan and the implementation of his Jarvisite program seem to confirm.

We are indebted in many ways to Professor Merrill Shanks of the Survey Research Center of the University of California at Berkeley. As director of the center when our project began, Professor Shanks was instrumental in obtaining funds for the study, and he has led the development of Berkeley's innovative system for computer-assisted telephone interviewing, which we used for our Tax Revolt Survey. As co-principal-investigator of the tax revolt study, he collaborated with us on instrument design, data collection, and preliminary analyses. His own final analyses and conclusions from this study will appear in a separate report, along with data he has collected in subsequent nationwide studies of public preferences concerning taxes and governmental spending.

This research was supported by a generous grant from the Hewlett Foundation, to whose president, Dr. Roger Heyns, and board of trustees we express our deep gratitude. Final data collection costs were covered by supplementary support from the Survey Research Center's current director, Percy Tannenbaum. The data analysis and preparation of the manuscript were supported in part by funds from the Biomedical Research Support Grant and Academic Senate at the University of California, Los Angeles. We were also fortunate to have at our disposal the facilities and resource of the State Data Program at the University of California, Berkeley, including its valuable archive of Mervin Field's California Poll data, and the Data Archive of the Institute for Social Science Research, University of California, Los Angeles.

John Foley generously provided access to the data from the *Los Angeles Times* Poll.

We also wish to thank the staff of the Survey Services Facility at the Center for their careful administration of the Tax Revolt Survey. We are especially grateful to the many anonymous and unsung respondents in this survey who gave their valuable time for our purposes. They may have been mad as hell, but they consented to tell us why. Tom Jessor bore almost all the responsibility for executing the data analysis, and did so with exceptional intelligence, patience, and good judgment. Margaret Baker, Ilona Einowki, and Libbe Stephenson helped greatly in unearthing and analyzing a variety of state and national polls. The material on the history of the tax revolt in California included in Chapter 2 owes a heavy debt to the research and advice of Frank Levy. We also greatly benefited from careful comments on the manuscript by Thad A. Brown, Walter Dean Burnham, Donald R. Kinder, Richard R. Lau, Susan Fiske, and Steven J. Rosenstone. And finally, Carolyn Drago converted more illegible draft into clean copy in one year than any person should be forced to do in a lifetime. We are deeply and permanently grateful.

Contents

1 Introduction 1

2 The History of the California Tax Revolt 19

3 Opinions about Taxes and Spending 43

4 The Vote and the Tax Revolt Schema 73

5 The Social Base 96

6 The Pro-Revolt Interests 111

7 The Anti-Revolt Interests 142

8 Symbolic Predispositions 163

9 Proposition 13: The Peculiar Election 188

10 Putting the Pieces Together 207

11 Comparisons and Implications 225 ⁻

12 The Legacy of the Tax Revolt 243

Appendix 279

Notes 283

Index 309

TAX REVOLT

1
Introduction

People are understandably readier to demand services from government than to pay for them. Resistance to new or rising taxes is as old as government itself and has punctuated American history from the very beginning. But in the late 1970s a new wave of popular protests against the rising cost of government erupted in many of the world's industrialized democracies. This book seeks to establish the boundaries of this ongoing tax revolt, its causes, and its likely future.

The steady expansion of the welfare state in both Western Europe and North America after World War II both reflected and reinforced rising aspirations for equality and security. Under the conditions of slow economic growth, inflation, and unemployment that have persisted since the energy crisis of 1973, however, the financial burden of ever higher government-protected minimum standards of income, health, nutrition, and housing has become controversial, and conservative complaints about the stultifying effects of the enlarged public sector have gained in support.

The results of the Danish general elections in 1973 dramatically exemplified the popular backlash against rising taxes and public expenditures. The newly formed Progress party campaigned for the abolition of the income tax and curtailment of the powers of the "wasteful" and "arrogant" civil service and won an astonishing 23 percent of the vote. A few years later, the Social Democratic parties of Sweden and Norway, architects of generous "cradle to grave" welfare systems, were cast into political opposition after more than three decades in office. In 1978, Britain elected as prime minister the Conservative Margaret Thatcher, who dedicated her government to cutting individual taxes and promoting the growth of private enterprise at the expense of the public sector.

The election of Ronald Reagan as president of the United States marked a watershed moment in this international trend toward governmental retrenchment. Mr. Reagan campaigned against "big government." Once in office, he proposed and Congress quickly passed budgetary changes that resulted in far-reaching cutbacks in social programs that had developed over the long period of Democratic political dominance beginning with the New Deal. The victory of the Socialists in the French presidential and parliamentary elections in 1981 shows that the movement to the right was not universal and that the previously mentioned electoral changes partly reflected antagonism toward incumbents, whatever their political coloration. Nevertheless, it is undeniable that the desirability of established welfare systems and the weight of the citizen's tax burden are salient and divisive issues once again.

In the United States, the current movement to limit the fiscal authority of government began by aiming the weapons of direct democracy at state and local officials. This phase of the tax rebellion reached its apogee with the passage of Proposition 13 (the "Jarvis-Gann amendment") in California in June 1978 by a margin of two-to-one. Two longtime toilers in the tax-reduction vineyards, Howard Jarvis and Paul Gann, managed to place on the ballot and lead to success a radical initiative that amended the state's constitution so as to reduce property taxes sharply and to restrict their future growth. It soundly defeated a rival, more moderate measure (Proposition 8) developed by the state legislature and much of the state's liberal and centrist political establishment. Proposition 13 ushered in an era of plebiscitary budgeting in California and spawned a variety of imitative proposals in other states. In national politics, the success of Proposition 13 prompted leaders in both parties to speak in more fiscally conservative tones. The Republicans went further, and made Howard Jarvis's message the centerpiece of their 1980 presidential campaign: eliminating bureaucratic waste would make it possible to cut both taxes and public spending without the loss of valued services, and less government would enhance both the personal freedom and the personal finances of citizens.

Proposition 13 promised substantial tax savings to property owners and gave all voters a chance to strike a blow against officialdom. Its overwhelming victory resulted, as we shall show, from the economic anxieties and opportunities created by the tax structure in California, and from the accumulated mistrust and resentment of government at all levels that prevailed in California as well as nationwide. California's tax rebels won another campaign in November 1979 with the passage by 74 percent to 26 percent of Proposition 4 (the "Gann amendment"), which placed a limit on the allowable annual growth in state and local government appropriations. But in June 1980 the voters spurned their erstwhile hero, Howard Jarvis, and rejected Proposition 9, his proposal to cut the state's individual income tax rates in half, by a margin of 61 percent to 39 percent. At this apparent reversal in popular feeling, commentators turned from speculating about the genesis of the California tax revolt to explaining why it had run its course.

The recent events in California provide the raw material for a case study of the nature and underpinnings of popular preferences on taxing and spending issues and the significance of these attitudes for the future course of government social programs. The size and variety of California's population and the strength and diversity of its economy make the tax revolt there worth studying in its own right. Beyond this, moreover, the evidence of numerous surveys points consistently to the similarity of public opinion in California and in the rest of the nation. There is a widespread tendency among Americans in and out of the Golden State to desire simultaneously lower taxes and increased government services. It is not necessary to hold the view that California is representative or, alternatively, that it is the vanguard of the future, to believe that the motives and decisionmaking processes of voters there are widely shared.

Because Propositions 13, 4, and 9 enabled Californians to decide tax rates and levels of public expenditure directly, we can analyze voters' intentions and the meaning of their choices in a context relatively free of the muddying influence of the many other issues that come into play in partisan contests for executive and legislative office. And because the referenda, with their different outcomes, were held within a short period during which the public's basic values changed very little, the tax rebellion in California provides an unusual opportunity to explore the interplay of changing tax structures, government service commitments, and campaign events in determining the public's choices.

Alternative Images of the Tax Revolt

What stimulated the latest outbreak of protests against taxes in so many American states and localities? And how did voters choose their stance on proposals to cut taxes and limit government spending, with some emerging as fervent advocates of less government and others as staunch defenders of the public sector? No one disputes that the passage of Proposition 13 reflected at least a strong collective preference for lower property taxes. But this consensus dissolves when observers describe the intentions of voters in more precise terms. The many interpretations of the tax revolt can be crudely distinguished according to the relative weight assigned to economic self-interest versus broader political and cultural values as determinants of how people voted.

Economic Theories

Economically oriented theories predominate in efforts to explain the revolt. Almost everyone has some personal economic stake in matters of taxation and public expenditure: we all pay taxes and receive, or fail to receive, benefits from public spending.[1] Some pay more or receive less, to be sure, but everyone could potentially calculate a personal price for the bundle of goods provided by government and then decide if the price is too high. When a referendum or election gives voters the chance to make this decision explicit by asking them to vote on a proposal to limit the fiscal powers of government, they could conceivably calculate the tradeoff between taxes to be saved and services to be lost and then act on the basis of this personal "bottom line."

So, for example, it is argued that the rash of defeats for proposals to raise local-government revenue by bond issues in the early 1970s simply reflected the downward movement of the business cycle.[2] During periods of economic growth when real personal income is rising, citizens are likely to be sanguine about the growth of the public sector. When times are hard and individuals must retrench, they expect government to do the same. From this perspective, the current movement to reduce taxes is a natural reaction to the prevailing recession in the world economy. What is more, tax revolts are bound to be quite regular occurrences, tides of discontent whose ebb and flow are the wake of macroeconomic performance.

This idea is restated forcefully in Michael Boskin's identification of concern over "the *total* tax burden and the *aggregate* amount of government spending at all levels" as the main cause of the tax revolt in America generally and the passage of Proposition 13 in particular.[3] He argues that between 1973 and 1977 inflation and rising taxes resulted in the absence of any growth in real disposable income per worker in the United States; government spending soaked up virtually the entire increase in Gross National Product during this period. This shift in the balance of spending power between private individuals and government agencies, he claims, generated discontent among voters. And their unhappiness was reinforced by the conviction that inflation, for which government gets blamed, rather than unemployment, was now the main economic evil. Unless people acquire a new taste for spending on public rather than private goods, therefore, according to Boskin, demands for reduced taxes should persist as long as the growth in personal incomes remains sluggish.

Where Boskin emphasizes the total amount of taxes paid as a cause of current protests, others argue that what matters is the degree and rate of change in specific taxes. Harold Wilensky argues that the tax revolt is most intense where the government relies on highly *visible* taxes for funds and where these taxes increase steeply and suddenly.[4] Before people rebel, they notice that their tax burden has become much heavier. Since the property tax is notoriously visible, Wilensky's hypothesis seemingly accounts for the passage of Proposition 13 in California, where property taxes rose sharply and inexorably between 1973 and 1978, and of Proposition 2½ in Massachusetts, another state with disproportionately high property taxes.

In the years leading up to Proposition 13 there had also been a steady increase in the share of the local tax burden in California borne by individual homeowners as against owners of commercial property. Some observers have speculated that anger at this inequity was the underlying source of support for Proposition 13.[5] Indeed, George Break suggests that the vote for Jarvis-Gann indicated support for a tax *shift* rather than a tax *cut*, that people were not so much unhappy about the level of government spending as about who was providing the revenues. At first glance, this argument better explains the contrasting outcomes of Propositions 13 and 9 than the hypothesis that the overall tax burden is crucial. The argument is less successful, however, in accounting for the fact that even renters gave Proposition 13 a relatively high level of support.

We explore these variations on the general theme that high taxes produce tax revolts by using survey evidence to connect the individual's perceptions of his tax burden, both in general and with respect to specific taxes, to his stance on Propositions 13, 4, and 9. As Chapter 6 shows in detail, the more convinced the voter was that he was paying too much in taxes, the more likely he was to support any and all of these measures. Even a voter whose dissatisfaction centered on the property tax was disproportionately likely to support Proposition 9, which was aimed only at the state's income taxes. However, as the defeat of Proposition 9 implies and as our survey data bear out, support for a proposed tax cut varied with the amount of savings one anticipated. Concern for one's personal bank account, whether motivated by fear that taxes were devouring it, greed for the chance to add to it at the expense of the public treasury, or both, strongly influenced the course of the tax revolt — but clearly more than this was involved.

In November 1978 there were tax or spending measures on the ballot in thirteen states. In states where taxes were lower than the national norm, proposals to cut property taxes along the lines of Proposition 13 sometimes passed (in Idaho and Nevada) and sometimes failed (in Oregon). In Michigan, where taxes were high by national standards, the Tisch amendment, which called for large reductions in both state income taxes and local property taxes, lost by a three-to-one margin.[6] In November 1980, six states had measures limiting property taxes on the ballot; these lost everywhere except in Massachusetts.[7] Measures to limit spending or to require special legislative majorities for raising taxes were more successful: a combined boxscore for 1978 and 1980 shows seven of nine such proposals passing.[8]

These results, along with public opinion polls that found approximately two-thirds of the public preferring a balanced budget at current levels of taxation to reduced federal taxes, have caused some observers to argue that the roots of the tax revolt lie in negative reactions to the spending side of government policy rather than the taxing side. American government has grown dramatically in the last half-century; total government revenues constituted more than 25 percent of GNP in 1978 compared to only 11 percent in 1929. In the 1960s and 1970s government spending rose steadily at the state, local, and federal levels. Between 1969 and 1975 the annual increase in the spending of all states was 12.4 percent, for all local governments 11.6 percent, and for the federal government 10.3 percent.[9] Ironically, the growth of government slowed in the 1975–1979 period during which the protests against taxes and spending reached a crescendo, but even in these years it kept pace with or exceeded the increase in GNP.[10] This increase in government spending was, if anything, accentuated in California, where state and local taxes as a proportion of personal income reached 16 percent in 1977, compared to 12.1 percent for the rest of the country, and where direct per capita general expenditures for state and local government were 118 percent of the national average.[11]

Changes in the pattern as well as in the amount of government spending preceded the recent protests. As state and local government budgets expanded in the 1960s and 1970s, the expenditures devoted to activities whose benefits are available to everyone, at least in principle, declined relative to what was spent on services with specialized constituencies. Nationally and in California, universal services such as police, fire protection, sanitation, parks, and local schools received a diminished share of public funds compared to welfare, health, and higher-education programs, which have more restricted clienteles. For example, between 1956 and 1976, nationwide the share of state and local government spending devoted to local schools fell from 30.4 percent to 26.5 percent, while the share devoted to public welfare rose from 8.6 percent to 12.3 percent of total expenditures and the share devoted to higher education rose from 4.8 percent to 9.5 percent.[12]

According to the "spending side" interpretation of the tax revolt, the average middle-class voter, presumably made aware of these trends by direct experience or by the mass media and mobilized interest groups, had by the late 1970s learned that he was paying more, but for services used by others. From this perspective, the victory of Proposition 13 in California and the election of President Reagan represented protests against what government was *doing* as well as what it was *costing*. Unfortunately, we know little about the accuracy of popular beliefs concerning the distribution of public spending. But the public's apparent consensus, revealed repeatedly in public opinion surveys, that government should maintain or increase the activities that make up the bulk of its expenditures does run counter to this anti-spending theory of the tax revolt.

— A third economic interpretation, already hinted at above, holds that anxieties generated by the overall state of the economy rather than feelings about particular taxes or spending programs motivated the tax revolt. Inflation is singled out as a particularly significant factor. An inflationary psychology encourages people to buy now since everything will almost certainly cost much more later. This belief and the accompanying resentment over the prospect of not being able to attain one's promised due—the home, second home, college education for one's children, or vacation abroad—is thought to enhance the propensity to sacrifice public expenditure in favor of private consumption. The obvious counterhypothesis is that the coexistence of high rates of both inflation and unemployment prompts people to demand more government protection to arrest their slide into the economic abyss. Our own evidence, while not definitive, does not suggest a central role for such factors, however.

Political Theories

The theories outlined above treat the tax revolt as a considered response to genuine economic grievance. In these accounts voters soberly calculate the personal costs and benefits of particular proposals to limit taxes or public spending and then act to maximize their resources. By contrast, what we for convenience label political interpretations view the tax revolt as a symbolic protest against broader targets. In other words, while voters might rationalize their choices as based on financial need (or greed), reactions to the tax revolt more truly express long-established values and deeper passions than are engaged by campaigns over seemingly technical fiscal measures.

One widely held hypothesis is that the tax revolt gained support in the late 1970s because it provided the opportunity to give vent to accumulated feelings of disaffection from all levels of government.[13] The statistics of declining confidence in government beginning in the mid-1960s are by now very familiar.[14] For example, the University of Michigan's biennial national election surveys show that in 1978 only 30 percent of the public said they trusted the government in Washington to "do what is right" all or most of the time, compared to 76 percent in 1964. In the same period the proportion of the public regarding most government officials as competent fell from 69 percent to 41 percent. Moreover, this rise in political mistrust was an across-the-board phenomenon manifesting itself in all demographic, partisan, and ideological subgroups of society. Thus proposals to cut taxes or limit spending were readily supported as convenient clubs with which to beat victims ranging from "wasteful" local bureaucrats to national politicians responsible for Vietnam and Watergate, and opposition to such proposals may have been muted by the tendency of even people who had a personal stake in their defeat to share in the general disenchantment with government.

The California electorate's gratuitous rejection of Proposition 8, the "official" alternative to Proposition 13, indicates the strength of public antagonism toward the political class.[15] Proposition 8, after all, only promised a cut in taxes. But Proposition 13 explicitly and deliberately slipped a fiscal noose over the heads of legislators and administrators. In the words of Howard Beale, the evangelical newsman in the contemporaneous movie "Network," and Howard Jarvis, Proposition 13 would send them a message from "the people" that "We are mad as hell and we're not going to take it any more."

We shall argue that the tax revolt in California, particularly in its early phase, incorporated important elements of a populist crusade against the established political and economic institutions in the state. The campaign for Proposition 13 began as a grass-roots movement led by men on the political fringe. Opposed by both political parties and by both corporate and labor leaders, Jarvis and Gann were able to mobilize latent antigovernment sentiment into passionate support for their cause. In this they were helped by the inept, if not provocative, actions of important public officials. Whatever mass character the tax revolt possesses, then, appears to be largely a function of generalized political cynicism.

Other politically oriented explanations have emphasized the role of partisanship and political ideology in shaping reactions to the tax revolt. A fundamental difference between the Democratic and Republican parties, of course, is in their stands on the government's role in economic and social affairs. Democrats, who typically advocate an expansive role for the public sector, were in power in both Sacramento and Washington during the later 1970s. Thus it would be surprising if attitudes toward the tax revolt were unrelated to partisan identifications. Its successes in California did partly reflect hostility to the incumbent administration, which foreshadowed the Democrats' national defeat in 1980.

Understandably enough, Governor Jerry Brown preferred to see the victory of Proposition 13 as the reflection of a change in the ideological orientation of the California electorate. Support of "small" government and opposition to public spending for social programs are leading elements in conservative political philosophy, so it seems plausible that the tax revolt was stimulated by a more far-reaching shift in political outlook. The population may indeed have moved toward favoring private solutions for social problems, and away from the redistributive policies that resulted in increased allocation of tax revenues to the poor and minorities. Quite predictably, we do find that conservatives are consistently more likely than liberals to support initiatives to cut taxes and limit government spending. But this is not to say that the electorate has moved rightward on all issues. Indeed on the most prominent economic issues, the public generally held constant through the 1970s.[16] And even among self-proclaimed conservatives, only a minority favor reducing most state and local government services. Diehard conservatives by themselves could not have passed Proposition 13 or elected Ronald Reagan.

In this vein, liberal intellectuals such as Walter Heller and Robert Heilbroner view support for Proposition 13 as derived not from genuine philosophical conviction but from the mean-spirited desire of the affluent to punish the disadvantaged groups that are the main beneficiaries of government services.[17] More specifically, they view the attack on high taxes and public spending as a thinly veiled form of racism. Blacks, they argue, are perceived as the undeserving recipients of special attention from government. The perception is that, to help blacks, government imposes forced busing and affirmative action; yet they continue to swell the welfare rolls and fill the prisons. To limit the fiscal authority of government, therefore, is symbolically to put racial minorities "back in their place."

The attitudes and impulses we have isolated as potential causes of support for the tax revolt all appear as elements in what James Q. Wilson has aptly described as "Reaganism." This outlook expresses a deep-seated resistance to prevailing cultural trends for whose spread government is blamed. According to Wilson, Reaganism opposes both the unrestrained right to personal self-expression and the idea that government should strive to perfect society and regulate all aspects of human affairs.[18] Traditional institutions such as the family, the church, and the local community rather than the state should constrain social behavior; traditional values such as thrift and individual initiative should hold sway in the economic realm and be allowed to bring their just rewards.

In California this ideology has appealed most strongly to the predominantly Protestant, frequently fundamentalist white middle class with origins in the South or Midwest. Once in straitened circumstances but now comfortable, if not always prosperous, its adherents are highly protective of home and property, and they blame government and the courts for fostering permissiveness and secularization. From their perspective, the tax revolt is a movement of social change as much as an economic policy, a crusade to restore the cultural hegemony of threatened values and to reverse the onward march of government spending that only favors the grantsmen, social engineers, and malingerers.[19]

The two classes of explanations of the tax revolt — economic and political — are representative instances of the two leading hypotheses concerning the causes of all political opinion and conduct. By clarifying the nature of support for the tax revolt, therefore, we hope to contribute to the ongoing scholarly effort to develop a general theory of voting behavior.

Analytic Issues and Strategies

Like other mass protests, the current rebellion against high taxes doubtless draws its support from disparate sources. Moreover, the reasons for its support are likely to change according to the character of specific ballot measures and the course of the electoral campaign. In California, for example, an uncertain contest was transformed into a landslide victory for Proposition 13 because of an upsurge of support following the announcement of projected increases in tax assessments in Los Angeles. The ranks of the tax rebels swelled even further after the passage of Proposition 13, as the movement for fiscal limitation became the repository of new discontents. Opposing tax reform became tantamount to attacking motherhood, the flag, and other symbols of national virtue. Similarly, reactions to the personal impact of rising property taxes understandably had a stronger influence on the outcome of Proposition 13 than on Proposition 4, which advocated a lid on state spending rather than reduced taxes per se. And the vituperative exchanges between Howard Jarvis and leading politicians before the vote on Proposition 13 were bound to arouse and focus antigovernment sentiments to a greater degree than the mild, virtually invisible campaign over Proposition 4. Thus, while people apparently held fairly stable preferences concerning what government should do and how much it should cost, the link between these attitudes and voting behavior varied with the nature of the proposed fiscal reform.

Most previous efforts to disentangle the sources of support for the tax revolt have employed evidence about aggregate trends in tax rates, government spending, public opinion, and electoral outcomes to make inferences about the motives of individual voters. We too wish to test hypotheses about the determinants of voters' choices, to track ups and downs in popular support, and to compare the basis of support in California and elsewhere. But we rely on surveys that provide direct information about the beliefs, circumstances, and actions of individuals. Specifically, we analyze the California Tax Revolt Survey, a half-hour telephone poll of California residences that we designed and that was conducted just after the special election on Proposition 4 in November 1979; the continuing series of California Polls conducted by the Field Institute; and a variety of national polls.[20]

The initial task of this investigation is descriptive: we need to know precisely how people felt about the tax revolt, and beyond that, what they believed more generally about their tax burden, government services, and the performance of government agencies and officials. In addition to the cognitive underpinnings of attitudes toward the tax revolt, we describe the pattern of popular attention to and participation in this movement. An important conclusion is that supporters of the tax revolt tended to be more active than their opponents. Proposition 13 won not only because of a favorable distribution of public opinion but also because its advocates were an unusually intense and mobilized group.

When we come to treat these matters more analytically, we will concentrate on three classes of dependent variables. First and foremost, we will focus on the determinants of *support for the tax revolt*, particularly in terms of attitudes toward the three initiatives proposed by Howard Jarvis and Paul Gann that appeared on Californians' ballots from 1978 through 1980. We want to know what contributed to the formation of an *issue public* for the tax revolt, in terms of issue salience, high levels of information and opinionation, supporting attitudes about government spending, waste, and taxation, and cognitively consistent thinking about all these matters. And we will explore the determinants of active *participation* in the revolt, both in terms of voting turnout and other forms of political activism.

Schemas and Tradeoffs

We will develop a number of analytic themes. One concerns how opinions about the tax revolt are packaged; that is, to what extent do anti-tax, anti-spending, anti-government beliefs form a tightly woven cluster such that someone who holds one of these positions holds all of them. We shall use the term "schema" to refer to this coherent structure of beliefs. This concept is in vogue among social psychologists, who define it as a set of interconnected cognitions about an event, type of person, sequence of behaviors, or value preference. A racial stereotype is a kind of schema, for example. Or, it is likely that some people have a schema centering on "government" whereas others have beliefs about government that are isolated from one another.[21]

Determining the extent of schematic thinking about the tax revolt is significant because whether one holds a highly organized set of beliefs about an object influences the way one processes new information about it and the consistency of his actions toward it. This is true because a schema can be matched in template fashion to external patterns of stimuli. The schema operates as a control mechanism that governs the evaluation of incoming information. So, for example, the sharp rise in property tax assessments just before the vote on Proposition 13 neatly fit the "Jarvisite" schema about the unresponsiveness of government and especially its insensitivity to individual citizens' onerous taxes; presumably the impact of this event was less powerful on those whose views about their tax burden and the quality of government were unconnected.

Learning about how opinions about the tax revolt were packaged helps in evaluating the frequently heard claim that decisions on how to vote on proposed tax cuts or spending limits are based on computation of the tradeoff between paying less (or more) to government and getting less (or more) out of it. This conceptualization of the voter's decisionmaking process assumes that people recognize the connection between taxes and services and realize that their choice on a particular ballot proposal is likely to impose a sacrifice. To be faced with a tradeoff means that one feels conflicted—that one desires both to pay less and to receive the same or increased services. The number of citizens forced to "trade off" and the balance of choices among this group are thought, particularly by economically oriented theorists, to be the crucial factor in determining the outcome of referenda on bond issues, tax reform, and public expenditure. In seeking to identify the conditions under which particular tradeoffs are made, the California Tax Revolt Survey asked respondents to resolve the conflict between their stated goals of decreasing taxes and maintaining government services by choosing among alternatives such as increasing selected taxes, redistributing the pattern of public spending, and pruning the number of public employees. This approach provides a classification of outcomes of people's subjective cost-benefit analyses.

The assumption that the average voter is a super-rational actor who calculates marginal changes in his wealth or the value of his property and then maximizes these assets is hardly warranted by the host of empirical studies that show gaps in the public's information about prominent political issues, let alone the intricacies of public finance and real estate.[22] Nonetheless, investigating the nature of subjective tradeoffs allows an assessment of two competing images of the electorate in California. Some observers took the massive victory of Proposition 13 as proof that its supporters were foolhardy gamblers willing to risk severe disruption in the public sector in order to relieve a cash-flow crunch that could have been offset.[23] The opposite view is that voting for 13 was a risk-averse strategy that provided protection against certain large increases in property taxes without posing more than a vague and distant threat to the supply of public goods.

Self-Interest

It is commonplace to assume that voters are essentially egocentric, that a person's politics depends upon his personal circumstances and how the proffered choices impinge upon them. The model of a risk-averse citizen simply posits one approach toward estimating one's self-interest: future benefits are discounted and immediate costs avoided. By contrast, the notion of "retrospective" voting holds that in deciding what is the self-interested choice people weigh most heavily the economic results of the recent past, presumably on the assumption that this at least is known whereas promises about the future are straws in the wind.[24]

Demographic characteristics — race, age, income, and so forth — are frequently used to indicate where a particular individual's self-interest lies. And some scholars employ a broader definition of self-interest so that voting for what is expected to benefit a category of people to which one belongs, even if not oneself, qualifies as a self-interested act.[25] But however one defines self-interest, membership in a demographic group is a very insensitive index of the personal or even collective impact of a given policy. Members of any given group usually have a variety of crosscutting problems, values, and interests. And the strongest enthusiasm for the group interest need not be found among those with the largest personal stake in an issue. For this reason we rely on more direct indicators of self-interest such as the amount of anticipated tax savings, public-sector employment, and the personal use of government services in assessing the influence of self-interest in the California tax revolt.

We have already noted the rapid inflation-boosted growth of the total tax burden during the 1970s and the longer-term growth in the size and responsibilities of the public sector. With so much money being pumped out of taxpayers' pockets into government, and with so many people dependent upon government services and employment, self-interest seems such an obvious motive for supporting or opposing the tax revolt that it may be wondered why we study its role at all. We do so because prior research in a variety of contexts has found self-interest to have only weak effects upon the mass public's political attitudes and behavior. For example, being personally affected by busing for school integration is not a significant influence on whites' attitudes toward busing. Nor did personal racial threats in a variety of areas of life influence whites' support for Los Angeles's first major black mayoral candidate.[26] And economic misfortunes, such as unemployment, inadequate health insurance, or simply worsening financial status inspire neither support for remedial government policies nor opposition to the responsible political authorities.[27]

The tax revolt, however, provides a context in which self-interest may play an unusually powerful role. The potential outcomes of the various ballot measures were posed in monetary terms; information, always in dispute to be sure, abounded about what one would gain or lose. In California, the numerous interests at stake in Propositions 13 and 9 had vociferous spokesmen who posed the issues in terms of how people would be personally affected.

Symbolic Protest

The third general theme in recent research on the causes of individual political behavior is that people respond to issues, events, and electoral contests in terms of long-standing predispositions such as ideology, party identification, nationalism, or racial prejudice.[28] Research shows that these general attitudes typically predominate over self-interest as determinants of electoral choice in partisan contests, reactions to race-related issues such as busing, preferences in foreign policy, or attitudes toward law and order.[29]

The general theory here is that such basic predispositions are acquired in response to preadult socialization (and occasionally early-adult resocialization), and then are triggered later in life by political symbols that resemble those present earlier. Presumably the early socialization involves conditioning of specific affects to specific stimuli; for example, of strong negative affects toward "welfare" or "blacks." In adulthood, related stimuli evoke the same emotional response; for example, confronted with a candidate who advocates more welfare spending, the voter will have a strong negative response.

To elicit these symbolic predispositions in adulthood, therefore, an event must present the triggering symbols. The imagery of the tax revolt evoked three symbolic predispositions—party identification, liberalism-conservatism, and racial prejudice—that underlay historic cleavages over the proper size of the public sector and the degree to which government should assist disadvantaged groups. In this sense, the tax revolt called forth a replay of enduring divisions in American political life.

The tax revolt also portrayed itself as a movement of "the people" against a punitive government. Howard Jarvis often compared Proposition 13 to the Boston Tea Party, hoping, in our terms, to mobilize support for his tax propositions on the basis of widespread cynicism about government in general.

Class Politics and Mass Protest

Our statistical analysis of the influences of self-interest and symbolic attachments in the tax revolt has relevance for the broader question of the role of social class in American politics. Where economic self-interest functions as the primary political motive, electoral alignments are likely to form along class lines and distributional issues are likely to assume importance. It is generally agreed that in the United States, by comparison with most other advanced industrial societies, social class plays a minor role in political conflict. Appeals to class consciousness on the part of politicians are quite rare, and partisan cleavages reflect the division between capital and labor indistinctly at best. Where students of European politics can devote themselves to explaining the rise and fall of socialist parties, scholars of American history must account for the absence of a significant class-based political movement.

As Richard Hofstadter and others have argued, "status" politics have played an unusually predominant part in American history.[30] This term re fers to a situation in which the central political issues revolve around a particular moral code or set of cultural values and the social prestige of the groups that embody these, rather than the allocation of tangible economic benefits among discrete occupations or income groups. Status politics has a strongly moralistic tone: the struggle is between the "right" way of life and an evil alternative. In these circumstances, conflict tends to become highly emotional and an all-or-nothing affair. Splitting the difference between the good and the morally odious is difficult to contemplate. Race, religion, or ethnicity tends to structure political division, and people in similar economic circumstances find themselves rejecting the positions self-interest might dictate and adopting those to which their primordial loyalties lead.[31]

A fundamental cause of the lack of importance of organized class conflict in American politics is the persisting legacy of what Louis Hartz called the Lockean consensus: the commitment of most citizens to an individualist ethos that celebrates the rights of the citizen against the state and holds that unfettered self-effort in the economic realm produces both prosperity and social harmony.[32] The permeation of American society by this ideology of economic individualism, which emphasizes the virtues of the free market and private property and regards one's level of economic success as an accurate measure of one's personal effort and worth, is distinctive. According to Wilensky, this is an important part of the reason the United States has been slower and more grudging than other rich countries in the development of the welfare state. While adherence to the "success ideology" is more widespread among the upper economic strata whose interests it promotes, it does find support throughout society, and it contributes to political support for measures that cut taxes and public spending.[33] The main beneficiaries of government programs, by contrast, lack both a political party organized in their interest and a well-articulated ideological defense for their position.

If the consequence of the tax revolt is to impose serious deprivations unequally—for example, if, as many predict, the impact of tax cuts and budgetary reductions turns out to hurt the poor and help the rich—class-based reactions to the movement for fiscal limitation may become more widespread. So far, according to our surveys, the demographic profile of the tax rebels is relatively flat; support for the tax revolt came from almost every social group in California.

Howard Jarvis led a mass protest that resembled in important respects earlier upheavals in American history such as Prohibition. Proposition 13 was something of an anomaly in the recent history of largely unsuccessful anti-tax referenda in California. And it owed much to a late surge in popular support that swept people of diverse economic backgrounds along in a frenzied mood. The collective impulse was populist in that it was hostile to established institutions and complex legislative answers to rising taxes. Anger at government boosted people's willingness to adopt a "meat-axe" approach to Califor-

Figure 1.1.   Analytic scheme.

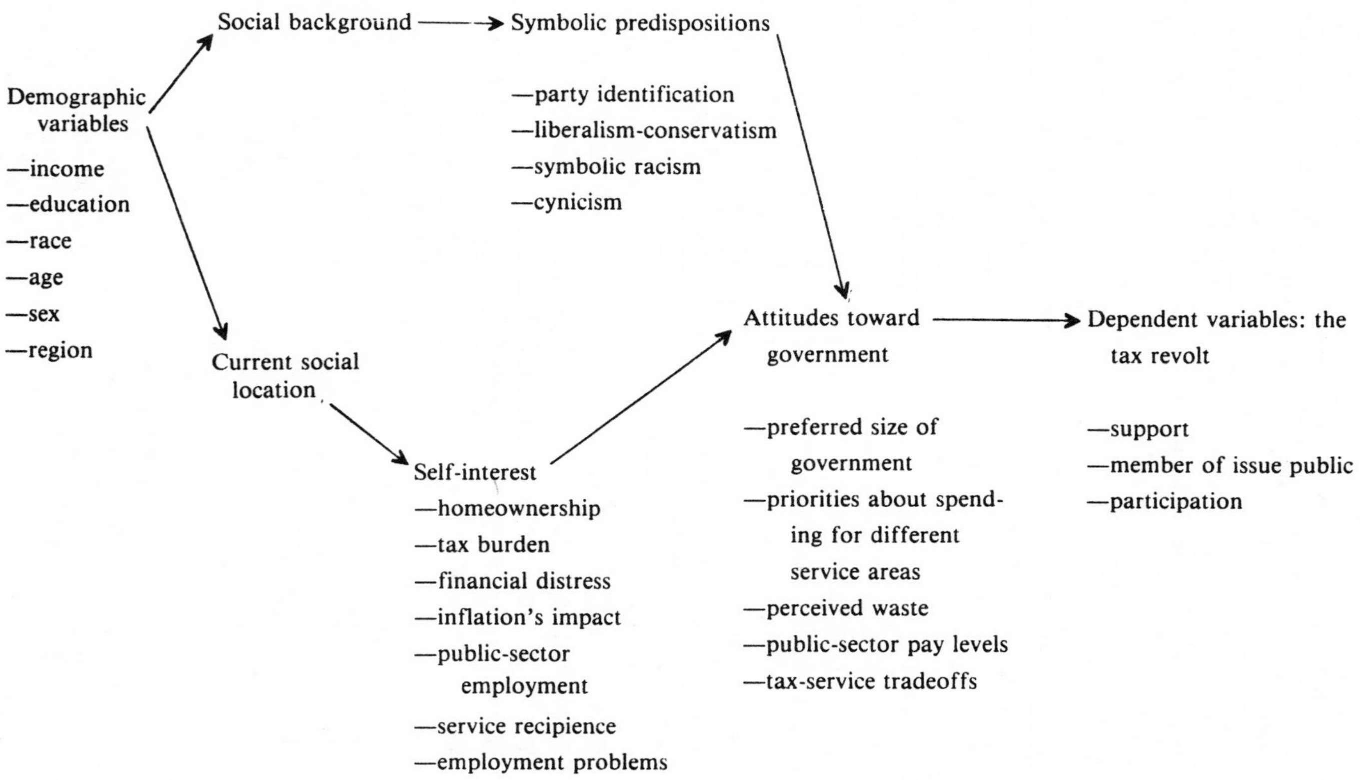

Social background ——→ Symbolic predispositions

—party identification
—liberalism-conservatism
—symbolic racism
—cynicism

Demographic
variables

—income
—education
—race
—age
—sex
—region

Current social
location.

Self-interest
—homeownership
—tax burden
—financial distress
—inflation's impact
—public-sector
   employment
—service recipience
—employment problems

Attitudes toward ————→ Dependent variables: the
government   tax revolt

—preferred size of
   government
—priorities about spend-
   ing for different
   service areas
—perceived waste
—public-sector pay levels
—tax-service tradeoffs

—support
—member of issue public
—participation

nia's property tax system that was reminiscent of Henry George's proposed Single Tax or the "funny money" schemes of Social Credit. The urge to make sure "they" could not go on extracting money from "us" with impunity and the fragility of the party system in California made it easier for this feeling to be rapidly given organized expression. Thus, to the extent that the tax revolt represents a symbolic protest of a frustrated populace against remote institutions or unwelcome changes in cultural values, it exemplifies a persistent pattern in American politics. The pull of economic interest is overshadowed by the push of deeper passions in determining individual choice, but the resultant reallocation of benefits may solidify pre-existing inequalities.

Overview

Our analysis treats support for and participation in the tax revolt as the principal dependent variables, or "effects," to be explained. Figure 1.1 portrays these at the end of a hypothesized chain of causal links in a nonrecursive model beginning with a person's location in the social structure, which we treat as a crude indicator of both early socialization and current self-interest, moving to more direct measures of relevant symbolic predispositions and economic circumstances, and then to beliefs about the role and performance of government, which we view as the proximate causes of support for (or opposition to) the tax revolt and of participation in it.

In fleshing out this "model" statistically, we encounter two distinct questions. One is how to account for variation in support for the tax revolt. Multiple regression analysis provides the familiar tools here, indicating what variables account for the maximum amount of variance and the relative influence of each predictor, say self-interest or racial prejudice, in dividing people into supporters and opponents.

The second question is more directly political and asks why did the side of the tax rebels win (or lose); that is, what accounts for the aggregate distribution of support versus opposition. This question can be addressed by considering which side was most advantaged by the crucial predictors that account for the variance among individuals. For example, residential status was a powerful predictor of support for Proposition 13; homeowners were more likely than renters to vote for it. The fact that almost two-thirds of the voting public in California were homeowners therefore strongly advantaged the Jarvis forces. But this anticipates the end of the analysis. We should begin with history, and with the events leading up to the California tax revolt.

2

The History of the California Tax Revolt

Attempts to use the intiative process to reshape the tax structure have a long history in California.[1] Before 1920 the electorate rejected several proposals to tax land, and between the two world wars initiatives seeking to impose a gasoline tax and a personal income tax were also defeated. In the 1960s a number of proposals to limit or cut the property tax rate failed to qualify for the ballot; containing the fiscal powers of government was not a salient political issue.

Proposition 13

The seeds of Proposition 13 were planted in 1965 when it was revealed that elected tax assessors, most notably Russell Wolden of San Francisco, were receiving "campaign contributions" to "review and adjust" assessments on business properties. Spurred by the outcry over this scandal, the legislature passed a bill (A.B. 80) in 1967 that required communities to reassess all property at 25 percent of market value within three years and then to conduct subsequent reassessments with sufficient frequency to keep the ratio intact. The immediate result of these reforms, neither anticipated nor intended by voters, was to increase the assessment for homeowners. For despite the special treatment of some commercial properties, business as a whole had usually been assessed at a higher ratio of market value than single-family housing.[2] The application of the uniform ratio of 25 percent to all property therefore meant that homeowners had to assume a greater share of the burden if the overall level of property tax revenues was to be maintained. And, because residential property tends to turn over more quickly and assessors employ sales prices to establish the market value of "similar" properties, shortening the reassessment cycle also added to the relative burden of homeowners vis-à-vis business. In addition, A.B. 80 transformed property tax assessment into a nondiscretionary, administrative function. In the 1970s, as a result, "political discretion could not act as a buffer between homeowners and inflation."[3] Increases in the assessed value of a homeowner's property automatically appeared in his tax bill.

The property tax increases engendered by A.B. 80 quickly led to a ballot measure calling for relief. Philip Watson, the Los Angeles County Tax Assessor, sponsored an initiative in 1968 requiring that property-tax revenues be used for "property-related" services only and that the state government relieve the burden on homeowners by assuming the responsibility for such "people-related" services as education, health, and welfare. More important, it provided that property taxes could not exceed 1 percent of a property's current market value.

Watson's initiative, like most subsequent efforts to reduce property taxes in California, can be viewed as a populist insurgency against the state's political establishment. In a pattern that was to become familiar, Watson's ballot measure was opposed by the leaders of both parties, including then-Governor Reagan, who argued that slashing property taxes would necessitate increases in the income and sales taxes to pay for valued government programs. And at the same time the governor and the state legislature moved belatedly to head off popular discontent about rising property taxes by sponsoring a constitutional amendment that exempted from taxation the first $750 in the assessed value of an owner-occupied home. In sum, the yin of the voters' anger over high taxes and their accompanying urge to limit the fiscal powers of public officials elicited the yang of elite cooptation and dire warnings about declining services. In this case, the precursor of Proposition 13 lost by a margin of 68 percent to 32 percent and the more limited tax relief measure supported by officialdom passed with 54 percent of the vote.

In 1972, a second effort by Watson to use the initiative process to reduce property taxes suffered a similar defeat. Proposition 14, "Watson II," went beyond its predecessor in specifying increases for the state sales tax, liquor tax, cigarette tax, and corporate income tax. This measure also proposed a uniform limit on per-pupil expenditures for local schools. Quite clearly a "tax shift" measure, Proposition 14 was attacked by state leaders from both parties and by a curious coalition of the tobacco and alcohol industries and public school employees. Once again, there was an "establishment" response, S.B. 90, which increased the homeowner's exemption to $1750 and placed limits on city and county tax rates.[4] And once again, during a period of only modest inflation in home values and public optimism about the state's economy, voters would not risk cuts in public spending and opted for the slice of tax relief prepared by the state's leaders rather than the loaf cooked up by Watson and his followers.

In 1973, Governor Reagan proposed an amendment to the state's constitution to limit the size of the public sector. Proposition 1 would have limited the annual growth of total state expenditures to the increase in state income, tightened the limits on local tax rates imposed by S.B. 90, and required a two-thirds legislative majority for state tax bills. Six years later the central elements of this measure reappeared in Proposition 4. The governor argued that embedding the spending limit in the state constitution was the only sure way to reverse the steady increase in the size of government. His opponents, who included the state's Democratic leaders and the public employees' unions, replied that such a limit would either force renewed reliance on the property tax to fund services or result in unacceptable cuts in public programs. On this occasion the vote was closer, in part because the antispending cause was personally led by a popular governor with aspirations for national office, but by 54 percent to 46 percent still another fiscal-limitation measure failed. And in 1976 neither Philip Watson nor Paul Gann could collect enough signatures to place property tax initiatives on the ballot. Clearly, the success of Proposition 13 must be viewed as a dramatic swing in the fortunes of the anti-tax movement.

Inflation

If reform provided the germ for the revolt against taxes, inflation was the carrier that spread it throughout the body politic. The boom in California real estate beginning in 1974 caused property taxes to soar as the procedures governing assessment ensured that rising values were registered in tax bills. By 1977–78 property taxes in California were approximately 52 percent above the national norm. Inflation also contributed to the rise of other state taxes in California, and just before the vote on Proposition 13 the overall per capita burden of state and local taxes in California was exceeded only in Alaska, surely a special case, and in poor benighted New York.[5]

Property taxes, however, were the dominant issue. As the prices of single-family homes in California exploded in the late 1970s, real estate was the topic on everybody's lips. People thrilled as news of what others paid testified to the increased value of their own homes or bemoaned their bad luck in not being "in" the market. The talk turned angry, however, when it became clear how much had to be paid for the homeowner's newfound, if unrealized, wealth.

Prices for single-family homes in the San Francisco area grew by an annual rate of approximately 18 percent between 1973 and 1978, and prices rose even faster in the more populous Los Angeles area.[6] (Indeed, prices continued to rise, albeit at a somewhat slower rate, until 1981 when unprecedentedly high mortgage rates helped force a leveling off.) The average rate of growth in assessment was similarly high, reaching 28.9 percent per year in San Bernardino County and 30.1 percent per year in Orange County for the 1973–1977 period.[7] To take a dramatic example of the effect of such rapid inflation in housing values, the property tax bill on a home purchased in Los Angeles for $45,000 in 1973, when the average selling price was $39,600, would have risen from $1160 in 1973–74 to $2070 in 1976–77, an increase of 80 percent over three years. In short, property taxes in California escalated rapidly in the years immediately preceding the vote on Jarvis-Gann. Moreover, because of the two-to-three-year reassessment cycle, many people experienced this increase in one painful bite. And those yet to be reassessed waited in fear and trembling for the blow to strike them.

Numerous homeowners thus faced abruptly higher property tax bills without a corresponding rise in their incomes, or at least with a much more gradual rise. Proposition 13 sought to alleviate this problem permanently. Once passed, it would: (1) set the full cash value of each property at its cash value in 1975 or at the time of the property's last sale, whichever came later; (2) limit the annual increase in a property's assessed value to 2 percent as long as it was retained by the same owner; and (3) limit the combined property taxes of all jurisdictions to 1 percent of full cash value. Since property taxes in California averaged about 2.6 percent of market valuation in 1977, the Jarvis-Gann initiative had a ready constituency.

All California state taxes grew rapidly between 1975 and 1978: while personal income grew by 23 percent, total state taxes rose 40 percent. The largest increase was in personal income taxes, which shot up by 48 percent between 1975–76 and 1977–78, compared to the 34 percent growth in receipts from the general sales tax and 17 percent from the inheritance tax.[8]

Inflation was an important factor in the steep rise in taxes. As money incomes rose, California's sharply progressive income tax subjected some residents to the tax for the first time and boosted others into higher brackets. Thus, income tax payments increased more rapidly than incomes; indeed, from 1973–74 to 1977–78 the average state income tax paid per $1000 of personal income increased from $16 to $27, or 65 percent. The state treasury enjoyed an "inflation bonus" of an estimated $4.5 billion in income taxes. This bonus contributed to the surplus that figured so prominently in the funding of local services after Proposition 13 passed.[9]

Thus the tax revolt in California erupted in the context of a high and rising level of state taxation. People did tend to single out the property tax as particularly unfair; in 1978, 60 percent of homeowners in California stated that the amount they had to pay in property taxes was inequitable.[10] But Proposition 13 probably also appealed to those who did not pay property taxes by requiring that *any* new taxes be approved by a two-thirds majority of the state legislature. Survey data indicate that anger about high taxes was growing throughout the nation. For example, in 1963 the Harris Survey found that 49 percent of the public believed their taxes were too high; by 1976 fully 72 percent felt this way.

Growth of Government

In campaigning for Proposition 13, Howard Jarvis repeatedly decried and ridiculed "big government," and his complaints about the growth in taxes, government spending, and the number of public employees were echoed in other states where contests over fiscal limitation took place. In Chapter 1, we described the overall rate of growth in state and local governments. Here, too, California exceeded the national norm. Beween 1973 and 1977, state and local government expenditures per $1000 of personal income in the state were 8.2 percent higher than the national average. In this same period, expenditure in California grew by an average of 11.2 percent a year, and the state spent more than the national norm for both the widely popular fire and police services and the much-despised welfare programs.[11]

Growth in the number of public employees and in their compensation are tangible evidence of how government has expanded. Between 1949 and 1979, employment in state and local government tripled nationwide, making this the fastest-growing sector of the work force. In California, too, employment in the public sector outpaced growth in the private sector. In 1978, state and local government employees made up 14.7 percent of the state's civilian work force, almost double the proportion (8 percent) that prevailed in the early 1950s, and the number of public employees per 1000 residents exceeded the national norm by 12.7 percent.[12] Thus, the rhetorical sallies against a bloated bureaucracy seemed to have statistical backing.

Political Disenchantment

The growth of government, which, following the end of the Vietnam War, was largely the result of expansion in health, education, welfare, and pensions programs, occurred during a steady fall in the public standing of political leaders and institutions. The loss of faith in the integrity and effectiveness of government cut across all traditional class, racial, religious, and ideological boundaries. It can be clearly seen by tracking the five questions appraising government that have been included in the University of Michigan's biennial election studies since 1964 (the government can be trusted *only some* of the time, is run for the benefit of a *few big interests*, includes *quite a few* crooked administrators, is staffed by *many* incompetent officials, and wastes *a lot* of tax money). For every aspect of national government, the proportion of unfavorable opinions rose substantially between 1964 and 1978, regardless of which party was in power. Indeed, the *average* proportion of such negative answers doubled—from 30 percent in 1964 to 60 percent in 1978.

The erosion of confidence in government was spawned after 1964 by racially tinged civil strife and the war in Vietnam. From 1970 to 1972 there was little overall change in public attitudes, but Watergate and economic recession renewed the downward slide. The public's opinion of government stabilized somewhat with the inauguration of President Ford and with Jimmy Carter's brief honeymoon, but in 1978 the White House itself started to worry about an emergent sense of national crisis and malaise.[13]

As the next chapter will show in more detail, these cynical sentiments were widely shared by Californians and clearly put opponents of the tax revolt at a disadvantage. Indeed, many defenders of increased government spending shared their antagonists' negative image of government. Public officials under attack by Howard Jarvis had to explain the growth in their budgets as the result of inflation or federal regulations, not waste. They blamed local tax increases on the procedures imposed by the state legislature. But these justifications had heavy going, since there was no deep reserve of trust and goodwill for public officials to call on. The state's political leaders faced a hostile climate of opinion as they attempted to head off the uprising that culminated in Proposition 13. But it is also clear that they badly bungled the effort.

Legislative Impasse

In 1968 and 1972 California's elected leaders responded to the threat to government revenues posed by the Watson initiatives by reaching bipartisan agreement on more limited forms of tax relief that proved acceptable to the electorate. The need to deal with the problem of rapidly climbing property tax bills was apparent by 1977, but on this occasion state government failed to meet the populist challenge. This failure to respond to demands for property tax reform contributed importantly to the disillusionment that stimulated participation in the tax revolt; in fact, Jarvis and Gann began circulating petitions for their initiative only after the legislature's efforts to pass a tax-relief bill during its 1977 session collapsed in an atmosphere of acrimony and disarray. These efforts foundered on disagreements among liberal legislators, their conservative counterparts, and Governor Brown over the amount of tax relief and the extent to which it should be targeted to low- and moderate-income families. Uncertainty about the size of the state surplus made it difficult to agree on how much tax relief to provide. And with statewide elections approaching, how to apportion political credit for a tax cut became a bitterly contested issue. Specifically, Republican state legislators suspected Governor Brown of having allowed the surplus to accumulate in order to be able to provide a tax rebate at the time of his campaign for reelection. Their interest in thwarting the governor's political ambition made them reluctant to accept compromise proposals for tax relief that Brown would be willing to sign. On the Democratic side, meanwhile, the governor's long-standing aloofness from the legislature reduced his ability to force a consensus between the liberal and conservative members.

Finally, in early 1978, the specter of Proposition 13 elicited legislative action. After much squabbling, the Behr bill emerged. It proposed a property tax cut about half the size of the one Proposition 13 would require and created the opportunity for the state to tax residential and commercial properties at different rates. The constitutional changes required to implement this complex measure appeared on the June 1978 ballot as Proposition 8. It was bitterly attacked by Howard Jarvis as a "cruel hoax" that represented yet another attempt by "the politicians" to deny citizens a tax cut. Although a voter could vote for both Proposition 8 and 13 and thus attempt to guarantee himself some property tax relief, many citizens came to view these measures as antithetical. In the end, Proposition 8 was rejected by a margin of 53 percent to 47 percent: apparently numerous voters preferred no loaf at all to this particular half.

The Campaign

At the beginning of the campaign for Proposition 13, few, even in California, had heard of Howard Jarvis. A persistent crusader against high taxes, he had had a political career marked by consistent defeat. In 1962 Jarvis ran for the Republican nomination for the U.S. Senate and lost badly; in 1970 he failed to qualify for the November ballot a statewide initiative to cut property taxes; in 1972 he was defeated in an attempt to win a seat on the State Board of Equalization; and in 1977 he made no impression in the Los Angeles mayoral primary. Soon after the June 1978 election, however, Howard Jarvis was an international celebrity, the subject of cover stories in both *Time* and *Newsweek* that portrayed him as a folk hero, the general of a people's army that had successfully routed the well-equipped forces of the ruling elite. The soaring property taxes, double-digit inflation, and string of national failures that had bred mistrust of political leaders provided the new context in which Jarvis's familiar rhetoric elicited widespread and fervent agreement.

Despite a large natural base of support in disgruntled homeowners, the triumph of Proposition 13 was by no means preordained. Proposition 13 began as a grass-roots movement whose core was the United Organization of Taxpayers. Most of the members of this small organization were elderly; its chairman was Howard Jarvis. Using radio talk shows to solicit signatures for their initiative and to air their grievances to a large audience, the sponsors of Proposition 13 grafted their campaign onto local taxpayer and homeowner associations. As the campaign progressed, the leaders of these small groups found themselves called on to debate with much more experienced public officials and lobbyists for groups of public employees. By the end of the campaign, Californians for Proposition 13 had acquired the services of the Romagen Corporation, a professional campaign firm that employed sophisticated statewide mailings to collect money. Throughout, however, Howard Jarvis himself was the main resource of the tax rebels. Massed against him were: Governor Brown; Leo McCarthy, the Speaker of the State Assembly; the State Superintendent of Schools, as well as virtually every local school official; Ken Maddy, Pete Wilson, and George Deukmejian, Republican candidates for statewide office; large corporations such as the Bank of America, Crown Zellerbach, Standard Oil of California, and Southern California Gas; the AFL-CIO; and the California State Employees Association.

Lines of battle formed quickly. Supporters of Proposition 13 emphasized that they were promising a cut of almost two-thirds in property taxes. Because the new assessment procedures would be enshrined in the state constitution, the politicians, who, like mules, had to be hit with a club before they would pay attention, would be unable to circumvent the required reduction in taxes. In the face of this loss of revenue, government spending would also have to be decreased. And since landlords would realize substantial tax savings, it would be economically feasible for them to lower rents.

Those opposing Proposition 13 argued that a cut of almost $7 billion in the revenue of local governments would necessarily mean a "devastation" of local services. Local schools in particular would suffer. The state's surplus alone could not compensate for the lost property taxes, so if services were to be maintained, new taxes would be required. In this vein, Governor Brown cautioned against the assumption that the state would bail out local budgets and noted that any such diversion of funds would imperil the University of California and other state institutions.

Citing the predictions of the respected UCLA Business Forecasting Project, opponents of Proposition 13 warned of the loss of more than 250,000 jobs and a consequent slowdown in the state's economy. Highly publicized layoff notices to government employees accentuated the threat. The opponents of Proposition 13 charged that its main beneficiaries would be the large corporations that owned huge properties and the federal government, whose tax collections would rise as the deductions for property taxes paid by Californians declined. Under these circumstances, most state and local officials promoted the virtues of Proposition 8 and the Behr bill, which claimed to provide homeowners a tax cut of about 30 percent by allowing the introduction of a split roll, taxing homeowners and business at different rates. The supply of government services would thus be protected by excluding business from the application of the lower tax rate.

In rebuttal, Howard Jarvis mounted a vituperative attack on officialdom. They were "liars" and their arguments "a crock of manure." The state had a $6.5 billion surplus that would make up for the revenues lost through property tax relief. By eliminating massive waste, government could easily furnish the services people wanted for much less money. Lower taxes would stimulate, not retard, economic growth in California, thereby creating new jobs. Jarvis had little sympathy for the schoolteacher who might be unemployed after the passage of Proposition 13. There were teaching positions available in other states; why should workers in the public sector be given special protection against having to relocate? And "if a library here and there has to close Wednesday mornings from 9 to 11, life will go on. Who the hell goes to a library in the morning anyway?" What mattered was to cut taxes and teach the government a lesson.

At the beginning of the campaign, polls indicated majority support for Proposition 13. For example, a February 1978 California Poll reported that 51 percent of the public favored the Jarvis-Gann initiative, 32 percent opposed it, and 17 percent were undecided. With only minor variations, as table 2.1 shows, this pattern of preferences prevailed until mid-May. The same polls also suggested, however, that at least a portion of the pro-13 opinions were weakly held. California Polls conducted in February and late March followed up a question about the respondent's general attitude toward Proposition 13 by listing several of the arguments made in support and opposition and asking for reactions to these. The respondent was then asked how he would vote on Proposition 13 "if the election were held today." In both surveys, support for 13 declined substantially after its potential consequences (both good and bad) were enumerated.

In April, polls began to show a narrow margin in favor of Proposition 8, the establishment alternative, and this grew to an advantage of more than 20 percent after respondents had been read some of the pros and cons of each measure. Soon afterward, however, a climactic turn of events stopped the slippage in support for Proposition 13 and transformed a close election into a landslide victory for the populist insurgents.

On May 16 "city officials" in Los Angeles announced that the new assessments, to be released shortly, would show that the total assessed value of the property in the city had increased by 17.5 percent in just one year. Since only one-third of all property was reassessed each year, this meant that the average increase per reassessment would be more than 50 percent. Many homes had not been reassessed for three years in a period of rapid inflation; their owners faced the prospect of a tax bill double the previous year's. Also on May 16, Alexander Pope, the Los Angeles County Tax Assessor, announced that rather than waiting until July—well after election day—to learn how their property had been reassessed, voters could find out immediately by contacting his office. On May 17 the County Board of Supervisors went further, ordering Pope to mail the official reassessment notices to the county's 700,000 property owners by election day.

TABLE 2.1 Trends in pre-election voting intentions on Proposition 13 and Proposition 8.

	Proposition 13				Proposition 8			
	Pro	Con	Don't know	Margin	Pro	Con	Don't know	Margin
Feb. 11-23								
Initial vote intention[a]	34%	17%	48%	+ 17	–	–	–	–
Good/bad idea[b]	51	32	17	+ 19	–	–	–	–
Postargument vote[c]	46	39	15	+ 7	–	–	–	–
March 13-16[d]	39	31	30	+ 8	–	–	–	–
March 27-April 3								
Initial vote intention	29	28	44	+ 1	27%	22%	51%	+ 5
Good/bad idea	50	37	13	+ 13	56	28	17	+ 28
Postargument vote	44	41	15	+ 3	56	24	20	+ 32
April 24-27[e]	47	40	13	+ 7	49	29	22	+ 20
May 1-8[f]								
Initial vote intention	48	40	12	+ 8	43	36	22	+ 7
Good/bad idea	–	–	–	–	54	29	17	+ 25
Postargument vote	–	–	–	–	52	29	18	+ 23
May 22-27[e]	54	38	7	+ 16	46	41	14	+ 5
May 29-31[f]								
Initial vote intention	58	34	8	+ 24	40	46	14	– 6
Good/bad idea	–	–	–	–	57	28	15	+ 29
Postargument vote	–	–	–	–	46	42	12	+ 4
Election result	65	35	–	+ 30	47	53	–	– 6

Sources: California Polls (February 11-23, March 27-April 3, May 1-8, May 29-31); *Los Angeles Times* Polls (March 13-16, April 24-27, May 22-27).

a. Initial vote intention: This question was asked only of those respondents who had heard of the measure; those needing to hear more were classed as "don't know." The surveys of February 11 and March 27 asked whether respondents favored or opposed the measure, while in the two May studies the question was phrased in terms of intended vote.

b. Good/bad idea: Asked of all respondents, this question followed a simple descriptive statement about the measure. Respondents were asked how they felt about the "basic idea" of the measure.

c. Postargument vote: Asked of all respondents, this question followed others about the effects and purpose of the measure.

d. This question was posed in three different ways to a split sample. The responses reported are an aggregation of the three questions.

e. Asked of all respondents, this question was preceded by a brief description of the measure.

f. Sample confined to registered voters intending to vote.

These announcements created a firestorm of protest. The tax assessor's office was besieged by thousands of homeowners; the mass media graphically depicted the fear and anger of people anticipating tax bills they simply could not pay with their current incomes. Within a week, public pressure forced the Board of Supervisors to endorse unanimously a rollback of all assessments to 1977–78 levels. On May 24 Pope announced that he would cancel the 1978 reassessments for Los Angeles; the County Administrator admitted that such a freeze would force a rise in the tax *rate* if projected expenditures were to be met. This prospect mobilized homeowners who had been reassessed in the previous two years; they recognized that as the property tax *rate* increased, those whose assessments were most up to date would suffer most.

While tax assessors in other counties and the State Board of Equalization denounced the rollback as illegal and inequitable, Governor Brown, sensitive as ever to the tides of public opinion, called the Los Angeles Assessor "courageous." On May 26 he described the new assessments as "outrageous" and "unjust," and proposed a statewide freeze on reassessments. This plan was stillborn, however, and the governor was forced to abandon it on May 31. By that time the polls were heralding spectacular growth in support for Proposition 13, and the campaign for Proposition 8 collapsed. As table 2.1 shows, a *Los Angeles Times* poll conducted between May 22 and May 27 showed that the lead for Proposition 13 had grown by 9 percent, while the margin for Proposition 8 had slipped by 15 percent. The California Poll conducted between May 29 and May 31 showed 13 ahead by 24 percent; for the first time, more people were opposed to Proposition 8 than were for it. The dramatic surge in support for Proposition 13 was most pronounced in Los Angeles County. There, the aftermath of the announcement of the 1978 reassessments resulted in a growth of pro-13 sentiment from 43 percent in late April to 63 percent in late May; in the rest of the state a more modest rise of from 43 percent to 53 percent took place.

The furor in Los Angeles was a godsend for Howard Jarvis. The incident concentrated public attention on the specter of rising taxes, crowding out of the news the familiar warnings about the disruption of services that would result should Proposition 13 pass. The confused and contradictory responses of public officials, from Governor Brown on down, seemed to validate Jarvis's claim that "politicians" and "bureaucrats" were either unable or unwilling to provide adequate tax relief. The Los Angeles reassessments triggered an emotional response that altered the nature of the campaign. While those defending the public sector retreated into a discouraged silence, supporters of Proposition 13 became more ardent. The movement to cut property taxes acquired the flavor of an evangelical crusade: an aroused populace was on the march against government.

Fiscal Life after Proposition 13

The victory of Proposition 13 elevated fiscal conservatism to a status previously accorded such symbols of virtue as motherhood and the flag. Governor Brown made a dizzying reversal of position — pledging to implement the will of the people; appointing a blue-ribbon commission under the chairmanship of the much-admired former Legislative Analyst, A. Alan Post, to investigate the structure of California government and recommend reform; cutting the state budget; and adopting a hard line against pay raises for government employees. Brown's actions won the praise of the authors of Proposition 13 and are generally acknowledged to have secured his reelection that autumn. Other state and local government officials also scurried to embrace the new religion of "lean" government and to seek the blessing of its prophet, Howard Jarvis. Jarvis apparently played a crucial role in the defeat of at least five liberal Democratic State Assemblymen in the November election, which not only returned to office a governor who honored his pledge to be stingy but also strengthened conservative forces in the ensuing legislative debate over how to implement Proposition 13.

The first two years of fiscal life in California under Proposition 13 confounded critics on the central issue of the state's ability to survive a massive cut in taxes. Despite a reduction of almost $7 billion in property tax collections per year, local government operations remained relatively intact. Proposition 13 did reverse the continuing upward trend in the number of public-sector jobs, but although resignations and attrition reduced state and local government employment by 103,000, mostly in education, between May 1978 and May 1979, fewer than 2000 workers were laid off. Meanwhile, according to State Board of Equalization statistics, the typical homeowner received a cut of 52 percent in his property taxes during the first post-13 year, and taxes on commercial property dropped almost 60 percent. Property taxes in California fell in one year from a rate of 52 percent above to one 35 percent below the national average. According to Larry Kimbell and David Shulman of the UCLA Business Forecasting Project, this cut in property taxes strongly stimulated the state's economy. Kimbell and Shulman found that an assortment of California oil companies, airlines, industrial firms, utilities, and financial institutions outperformed a comparable set of firms elsewhere in the United States by 8.4 percent from May 1978 to May 1979.[14] Proposition 13 also provided small businesses with a chance for growth, investment, or higher profits. In sum, the tax cut promised by Howard Jarvis was delivered, while the doomsday predictions of public officials proved false.

To the chagrin of Jarvis and Gann, however, Proposition 13 failed to achieve the goal of reducing the level of government spending, at least in the short run. Allowing for the fact that property tax revenues provided 40 percent of all local revenues, the projected $7 billion shortfall implied a 23 percent reduction of expenditures. In fact, it has been estimated that in fiscal year 1978–79 local governments lacked only $857 million in the revenues required to maintain previous service levels, a deficiency of only 2.8 percent.[15] One reason for this relatively small gap is that higher assessments produced additional property tax revenue. In the year following the passage of Jarvis-Gann, assessed values grew by 13.8 percent,[16] partly because in 1978 the three-year reassessment cycle had not yet fully registered the effect of the upsurge in housing prices and partly because new construction and property transfers were exempted from Proposition 13's rollback requirements. In the context of a continuing boom in the real estate market, these factors produced an additional $405 million in 1978–79.[17]

But the main reason that Californians were able to enjoy reduced taxes without suffering painful cuts in services was the earlier accumulation of an enormous state surplus. In 1977–78, the state's tax collection was $14.85 billion, an increase of 40 percent over 1975–76. Since state expenditures grew by only 23 percent during the same two years, a large surplus was inevitable. The explosion in revenues without higher tax *rates* resulted from the strong economic recovery in California after the recession of 1974 as well as from inflation. The improvement in aggregate economic conditions boosted corporate profits and personal income; tax revenues from these sources and from taxes on sales made at rising prices grew correspondingly. And because the elasticity of the state income tax with respect to personal income in California is about 1.7, an inflation rate of 8 percent produces an additional 5 percent growth in real revenue for the state government.[18]

At the beginning of the fiscal year 1978–79, the surplus was estimated at $7.1 billion; had Proposition 13 been defeated, this would have reached $10.1 billion one year later. Interestingly, though, the size of the surplus, consistently underestimated by government officials, did not figure prominently in the election campaign. Newspaper references to this issue were scarce and typically buried in inside pages. Pollsters ignored the topic completely. And when information about the magnitude of the surplus finally did become available, in the last week before the vote, public attention had already been seized by the reassessments in Los Angeles.

After the victory of Proposition 13, some analysts argued that many people had voted for it because they were aware of the huge surplus and therefore confident that services would not have to be cut. But the evident lack of public information about the size or causes of the surplus makes this a dubious claim. We prefer to emphasize the upsurge in anger and fear in the wake of the reassessment gaffe.

In the event, the surplus was large enough to enable the state government to provide $4.4 billion in financial assistance to local governments in 1978–79. The bulk of this assistance went to support people-related services such as education, health, and welfare; after ten years, the pattern of financial responsibility Philip Watson had advocated became law. In the following year a long-range "bailout" bill was adopted and assistance to local governments rose to $4.85 billion.

In part because of Governor Brown's determination to freeze hiring and limit wage increases, the *growth* of state government expenditures has slowed significantly since the passage of Proposition 13, continuing a trend that began in 1975. But while the introduction of new programs has virtually ended, few existing programs at either the state or local level of government have been seriously altered. Despite the pervasive unpopularity of spending for welfare and public assistance, for example, no major changes in state policy have been enacted, and the 1979–80 state budget provided welfare recipients with a 15.1 percent increase in their monthly grants. For most local officials, the implementation of Proposition 13 initiated a search for ways to finance the status quo rather than a drive to eliminate programs.

One result has been the proliferation of fees for a wide range of public services. Libraries, swimming pools, zoos, parks, and museums, which had formerly been paid for entirely from property taxes, are now being partially financed by charges on those who use them. Many cities have increased their fees for business licenses, building permits, and garbage collection; in Inglewood, there is even a fee basis for fire protection. Although the total revenue collected by such user charges was estimated at less than $200 million in 1978–79, they are viewed by some as an illegitimate tax shift and have aroused substantial public antagonism.[19]

Proposition 13 has had several other unanticipated consequences. Discontent and militancy among public employees has grown. Because renters have failed to reap a significant portion of the property tax savings enjoyed by their landlords, a strong organized movement calling for rent control has developed and rent control measures have been passed in San Francisco, Santa Monica, Los Angeles, and Berkeley. Proposition 13 also has further accentuated the shift in the property tax burden from business to the single-family homeowner. William Oakland estimates that the homeowner's share of the property tax will rise from 43 percent in 1978–79 to 48.6 percent in 1981–82.[20] Owners of business property, as a class, have probably been the main beneficiaries of Proposition 13; if the state turns out to be unable to maintain its current program of tax relief for localities, the constituency for a split roll that allows business properties to be taxed at a higher rate than residences is likely to grow. The February 1979 California Poll reported that 46 percent of the respondents in a representative sample of California adults favored such a measure, 43 percent preferred the existing single-roll system, and 11 percent were undecided.

Proposition 4: The Gann Amendment

Following the passage of Proposition 13, its principal architects, Howard Jarvis and Paul Gann, who were reputedly no longer on speaking terms, selected different strategies for further limiting the fiscal powers of government. While Jarvis persisted in a direct assault on existing tax rates, Gann made his target government's ability to spend. Gann's new ballot initiative, which became Proposition 4 in the November 1979 special election, closely resembled Governor Reagan's earlier attempt to limit state spending, which the voters had rejected in 1973. Although he had drafted Proposition 4 before Proposition 13 became law, Gann justified this new measure as necessary to prevent the continued circumvention of the electorate's mandate to reduce government spending. Labeled the "Spirit of 13" initiative, Proposition 4 was designed to prevent state and local government expenditures, in real terms, from rising above 1978–79 levels. Specifically, beginning with the fiscal year 1980–81, Proposition 4 limited the growth in appropriations made by the state, counties, cities, school districts, and special districts to the percentage increases in population and the cost of living. To prevent the accumulation of large surpluses in the public treasury, it required that if a government entity receives revenue in excess of the amount it appropriates in that year, this excess must be returned to the taxpayers during the next two years. And to enhance the freedom of local officials to decide how to allocate expenditures within the limit prescribed for them, Proposition 4 required that the state reimburse local governments for programs it mandates.

Proposition 4 did not limit all appropriations of state and local government. The subset of appropriations "subject to limitation" excludes, among others, such significant items as debt service, which may be construed to include a portion of contributions to an entity's retirement system, refunds of taxes, and appropriations required to comply with court and federal government mandates. The appropriations limit also can be adjusted. This can occur (1) when voters approve a change, which can be in effect for no more than four years; (2) when a service is transferred from one government entity to another or to a private entity; and (3) when there is a shift in how a service is financed, as from taxes to user charges.

These loopholes in the application of the appropriations limit left public officials ample room to maneuver and implied that the passage of Proposition 4 would subject government to only a gentle form of discipline. For example, if the state's appropriations were under its limit and it had excess revenues, it could appropriate these in areas subject to limitation, or mandate local programs, and then provide for their reimbursement. Indeed, some critics, including Jarvis, who began by mocking the Spirit of 13 measure as a fraud and ultimately adopted a neutral stance, contended that because of the high rate of inflation, the initiative would result in higher levels of government spending than otherwise would be the case. According to this argument, if government is allowed to raise its expenditures by a certain amount it will do so, particularly when faced by employees demanding cost-of-living raises.

Although most voters were undoubtedly unaware of these nuances, the prevailing mood was very sympathetic to the idea of containing public expenditures. An August 1978 California Poll showed that 52 percent of the electorate favored a constitutional amendment to limit state-government spending; 34 percent were opposed and 13 percent had no opinion. Throughout the period preceding the special election on the Gann initiative, every published poll showed that people continued to approve of Proposition 13 by close to a two-to-one margin. There was less satisfaction, however, with the way it had been implemented. In the February 1979 California Poll, for example, 42 percent of respondents with a definite opinion believed that cuts in local-government spending after Proposition 13 had been insufficient, compared to 23 percent who felt that too much had been cut. Fully 82 percent complained that the reduction in local budgets had been made in the "wrong places," with both supporters and opponents of Proposition 13 unhappy that the top of the bureaucratic hierarchy had been spared. The state government was described as inefficient by 72 percent of those with an opinion, and 55 percent regarded city governments as inefficient.

In the context of a growing state surplus and the prevailing image of government as profligate, it is not surprising that Proposition 4 passed without serious opposition. With the lesson of Proposition 13 in mind, no politician dared to condemn the constitutional amendment to limit spending, although the knowledge that Proposition 4 would have no drastic consequences for the fiscal status quo in the short run must have made it easier for some to swallow. The ballot argument in favor of Proposition 4 was signed by both the Democratic Speaker of the Assembly and the Republican minority leader. Business organizations uniformly backed the initiative; the only organized opposition came from the public employees' unions. Proponents of the Spirit of 13 outspent its detractors by an estimated 126 to 1,[21] and after a desultory campaign that drew only 34 percent of the registered voters to the polls, it won by 3 to 1, gaining a majority in every county in the state, and 74 percent of the vote statewide.

Proposition 9: Jarvis II

When the state legislature responded to Proposition 13 by using the accumulated surplus to shore up public spending and employment, Howard Jarvis proposed a measure to slash state personal income taxes. Denying government the money to spend, he argued, was the only way to achieve a significant reduction in the size of the public sector. Jarvis II, as the initiative appearing on the June 1980 ballot as Proposition 9 came to be called, easily collected the required number of signatures. On this occasion, however, the campaign for a tax cut was run from the beginning by Butcher-Forde Consulting, a political consulting firm frequently employed by Republican candidates. Signatures were solicited entirely by direct mail; 5 million letters were sent to voters' homes; almost a million voters signed and returned a copy of the initiative; and over 250,000 contributed an average of $9.40 to provide the campaign with $2.5 million.[22]

Jarvis II proposed amending the state constitution to: (1) limit personal income tax *rates* to 50 percent of those in effect during 1978; (2) require that the income tax brackets be adjusted on an annual basis to reflect changes in the California Consumer Price Index or a successor index; and (3) exempt business inventories from property taxes. Since the legislature had already moved to liquidate a portion of the budget surplus by passing one-time tax cuts in

1978–79 and 1979–80, increasing the tax credit for renters, abolishing the business inventory tax, and providing full indexing of the personal income tax for 1980–82 and an adjustment for inflation in excess of 3 percent thereafter, the crucial feature of Jarvis II was the proposed reduction in the state income tax.

The debate over Proposition 9 centered on the amount of revenue the state would retain should it pass and the consequences of the lost revenue for the functioning of public institutions in California. Jarvis reiterated the main arguments he had made for Proposition 13. Taxes in California were much higher than required to provide needed services efficiently, and the state was continuing to amass a budget surplus. Moreover, the federal decontrol of oil prices would produce a large increase in royalties paid to the state and replenish the state's treasury as the surplus was drawn down to provide assistance to local governments.[23] Finally, Jarvis claimed that another tax cut would stimulate the economy, much as had occurred after the passage of Proposition 13, both creating more jobs in the private sector and mitigating the impact of lower tax rates on total revenues.

The Legislative Analyst estimated that the implementation of Proposition 9 would decrease revenues in the state general fund by $4.9 billion—almost 25 percent of total revenues—in fiscal 1980–81, by $4.2 billion in 1981–82, and by unknown but increasing amounts thereafter. Governor Brown responded by ordering state-government agencies to propose ways to cut their 1980–81 budgets by 30 percent. Opponents of Jarvis II pleaded that California simply could not absorb another major tax cut so soon after Proposition 13. They argued that the budget surplus would be practically liquidated by June 30, 1981, in any case, so that schools and local governments faced a financial squeeze even without Jarvis II. The passage of this measure, they held, would emasculate the long-range bailout plan in one rapid step and confront the entities providing public services with an immediate crisis.

Critics of the proposal also charged that it favored the rich; that the 10 percent of Californians who earn $40,000 or more a year would receive 55 percent of the dollar savings. Opponents also warned that in times of economic uncertainty it would be foolhardy to rigidify the state's fiscal structure by writing a specific set of tax rates into the constitution.

Jarvis's rebuttal was familiar. He denounced the politicians as "liars" who were "crying wolf" once more and who should be "tied down with a chain."[24] Official estimates of the loss in revenues resulting from Proposition 9 were overstated, in his view; he claimed the reduction in the first year would be $3.2 billion rather than $4.8 billion. And he claimed that his initiative altered the tax system in a progressive direction; for example, those earning less than $15,000 a year would receive a reduction of 70 percent in their state income tax bill, whereas those making more than $40,000 would save 54 percent.[25] It was true that the federal government would get another tax windfall, "but you can't solve all the problems with one goddamn constitutional amendment."[26]

The political alignments that formed during the campaign over Proposition 9 differed in several ways from the coalitions that had contested Proposition 13. Opposition from state legislators was slower to develop and confined almost exclusively to Democrats, who, mindful of the blow to official credibility caused by their unfulfilled predictions that Proposition 13 would be a disaster, were much more restrained in their criticisms. Republicans almost uniformly backed the measure.

Governor Brown broke a lengthy silence on Proposition 9 by announcing his opposition in a statewide television address on March 20, 1980. The governor's presentation avoided characterizing Jarvis II in the emotive terms he had employed to attack Proposition 13. Instead, he acknowledged the attractiveness of a tax cut but pointed out the risks to services for the sick, poor, and elderly, the damaging consequences of a potential downturn in the national economy, and the unfairness of a result that would disproportionately favor the affluent.

The strongest opposition to Jarvis II predictably came from public employees, particularly in education, and from local-government and university officials, who issued dire pronouncements of impending cuts in services and employment and warned that tuition fees and other user charges would become necessary if Proposition 9 passed. In the private sector, the California Federation of Labor opposed Jarvis once more. Business, which had been split over Proposition 13, resolutely stayed aloof. Conservative economist Milton Friedman did, however, defect from the ranks of the tax rebels, on the ground that specific tax rates should not become part of the state constitution.

The California Tax Revolt Survey conducted in late 1979 found that only 50 percent of the electorate had heard of Jarvis II. At that time, opinion was quite divided: 47 percent favored the measure, 42 percent opposed it, and 12 percent were undecided. A February 1980 California Poll reported a more positive public image: 54 percent approved of Proposition 9 and 34 percent were opposed. However, after respondents were asked about the possible impact of the proposed tax cut on services, other taxes, the responsiveness of government, and so on, the distribution of voting intentions shifted toward opposition. The second measurement of opinion found 46 percent in favor of Jarvis II and 42 percent against it. The sources of change in attitudes appeared to lie in beliefs about the size of the state surplus and the possibility of reduced services. For example, 40 percent of the respondents initially favorable to Jarvis II changed their opinion if they anticipated "serious" cuts in government programs.[27]

Between February and April, a significant portion of the electorate turned against Proposition 9. A mid-April California Poll found it trailing 43 percent to 48 percent for its opponents, and by mid-May it trailed among registered voters by 31 percent to 57 percent. The reasons for this impressive reversal, which presaged the defeat of Jarvis II, are beyond the scope of this chapter. Some tentative observations about the conduct of the campaign may, however, be suggestive.

The involvement and enthusiasm of large numbers of grass-roots citizens that had been so striking in the campaign for Proposition 13 were not evident two years later. The campaign on behalf of Proposition 9 was professionally run and enjoyed more support from elected officials. Yet it encountered financial difficulties in the last six weeks before the election, when the anti–Proposition 9 forces outspent its advocates by two to one.[28] Once again Howard Jarvis was the principal spokesman for the tax cut; this time, though, his abrasive style appeared to have lost much of its former appeal, even to his supporters. More generally, the public's image of Jarvis may have changed in the two years since Proposition 13. He had, after all, become famous. Many politicians courted him now, and those who opposed his new proposal studiously refrained from attacking him personally. In a curious twist, Jarvis had become something of an establishment figure, whose insults and vitriolic comments in debate made him appear a bully rather than an "alley fighter." By the end of the campaign, his advisers reportedly were urging him to be less combative and to "concentrate on the issues" instead.[29]

No single event during the campaign over Proposition 9 had the impact of the Los Angeles reassessments two years earlier. Indeed, it is our impression that the debate about Jarvis II was much less emotional than its predecessor and that the flow of information during the campaign favored the anti–Proposition 9 camp. For example, many observers contended that the Legislative Analyst's estimate of the amount of revenue Proposition 9 would cost was too high, that officials were crying wolf once more. Yet the higher official forecast remained the accepted figure in the campaign debate. With this and the much-publicized national recession in mind, it is not surprising that voters chose to minimize the risks of reduced services and new fees rather than to receive a relatively small tax saving. Only 39 percent voted for it.

Since the defeat of Proposition 9, voters in California have had additional opportunities to modify the level of their taxes by voting on state and local referenda. A special statewide tax on oil companies was rejected in 1980, as was a tax-simplicity initiative that would have shifted taxes from individuals to business.

At the local level, results have varied. In November 1980 California voters approved only fourteen of fifty-four local propositions to fund additional services. In April 1980 Berkeley, the state's bastion of liberalism and beyond, did impose a special tax on property that was earmarked for the city's libraries. On the other hand, despite rising fear of crime, Los Angeles voters rejected by a 58 percent to 42 percent margin a proposal to beef up police manpower at the expense of a maximum $58.85 per year increase in property taxes. The Spirit of 13 lives on: efforts to whittle away at its basic provisions have uniformly failed.

Outside California

The economic and political conditions that gave rise to the wave of protest against taxes and government spending in the 1970s obviously were not confined to California. The rapid growth in the size of state and local governments, the increased property tax burden, the impact of inflation on real disposable income and on the development of budget surpluses, and the spread of mistrust of government officials and institutions were nationwide phenomena. Efforts to limit the fiscal powers of government have taken two main forms in recent years: (1) proposals aimed at reducing existing levels of taxation, the Jarvis approach; and (2) measures designed to restrict the future growth of government spending, the approach of Gann's Proposition 4.

Although measures of both kinds were instituted outside California before the passage of Proposition 13, there is no disputing the unique and momentous impact of Proposition 13 in setting the course of the current tax revolt. The Jarvis-Gann initiative captured the attention of both the press and the general public. A CBS News Poll conducted three weeks after the vote on Proposition 13 found that 76 percent of the electorate living outside California had heard of it; of non-Californians with a definite opinion, 67 percent said they would vote for a similar proposition if given a chance. The National

Election Study conducted by the University of Michigan after the November election had similar results: 78 percent of those living outside California had heard of the measure; asked how they would vote "today," 66 percent of non-Californians in the sample who had a definite intention, compared to 71 percent of those from California, said they would support Proposition 13.

The passage of Proposition 13 rearranged the political agenda at all levels of government. Tax cuts and balancing the budget began to dominate public debate, while talk of a national urban policy and other costly innovations in social policy subsided. Proposition 13 created a heightened consciousness on the part of policymakers of the need to reduce individual tax burdens and make them more equitable, if only to forestall the imposition of more stringent restrictions on the fiscal powers of government by popular vote. It is no accident that Proposition 13 spurred consideration and implementation of indexing of income taxes, "truth-in-taxation" procedures, and property tax circuit breakers in many states.

At the national level, heightened concern about the political as well as the economic effects of inflation and high taxes not only renewed demands for tax cuts and statutory expenditure controls but also led some, including Governor Brown of California, to advocate an amendment to the U.S. Constitution requiring a balanced federal budget. And President Reagan quite simply made the main objectives of the tax revolt the centerpiece of his domestic program.

To recapitulate, similar measures aimed at limiting the fiscal powers of government have been presented to voters in California and in other states, with mixed results in both contexts. All states are subject to the influence of national economic and political trends, albeit to varying degrees. The next chapter will show in some detail that Californians' attitudes toward taxes, public services, and the efficiency of government closely resemble those held by people in other states. What, then, accounts for the fact that the tax revolt seems to have been more sustained, comprehensive, and organizationally developed in California than elsewhere?

In our view, the tax revolt in California was distinctive partly because the political context there is defined by the following historical and structural elements: a well-established tradition of using the initiative method to reform the tax system; the development of sophisticated techniques for collecting the signatures required to qualify such measures for the ballot; the weakness of the state's political party system, which facilitates the rise of political outsiders hostile to the establishment; and the relative invulnerability of the state's economy to a national recession. In the late 1970s, California's system of state and local taxation caused property taxes to soar at the same time that the state acquired an unprecedentedly large budget surplus. This combination of factors, which gave rise to Proposition 13 and permitted a smooth adjustment to its fiscal consequences, is unlikely to be matched in any other state. Certainly the adjustment to Proposition 2 1/2 in Massachusetts has been much more painful and disruptive. But if the nationwide economic and attitudinal forces that have increased public concern and anger over the tax burden persist, additional attempts to shift control over fiscal decisions from elected representatives to the voters are to be expected, both in California and in other states.

3

Opinions about Taxes and Spending

The high water mark of the California tax revolt came at the end of 1979. The tax rebels were still basking in the glow of Proposition 13. The Gann cap on state spending had just passed almost three to one in a special off-year election. Homeowners had just received their drastically reduced property tax bills. And the upcoming effort to cut the state income tax in half, Jarvis II, was leading by a small but steady margin in the polls. Within a few months, public support for Jarvis II would begin to deteriorate, and ultimately even the glow around Proposition 13 would begin to tarnish as the state began to run out of money. But in November 1979 the tax rebels were riding high.

Since our Tax Revolt Survey went into the field at the very crest of the revolt, we can analyze its support at its broadest and deepest point. In some sense, the most important question for our study is, "How could such radical anti-tax, anti-public-sector propositions draw so much support in such a liberal, seemingly well-administered, modern state?" So in the next few chapters we will mainly analyze its support at its zenith. At certain points we will look ahead a little, to contrast the public's reactions to these different ballot propositions with their different implications. But for the most part we will leave that story for Chapter 9. We begin by looking at the public's attitudes about taxes, spending, and government.

Taxes, No! Big Government, No! Services, Yes!

The main features of the political landscape during the germination of the tax revolt in California were an expanding public sector, rising taxes, rapid inflation that squeezed private incomes, and a national government whose popular standing had been eroded by a string of setbacks in domestic and foreign policy. Inflation was increasing at a rapid rate for seemingly incomprehensible reasons. The referenda were put to the voters in bewildering variety with dazzling frequency; the voters scarcely had time to catch their collective breath between trips to the polls. And each referendum presented ambiguous as well as technically complex choices. Usually they promised fairly clear consequences for the voter's own tax burden in return for the threat of uncertain consequences for the quality of government services in a wide variety of barely visible areas of life. It was hardly surprising, then, that the voters responded with a package of rather inconsistent general preferences about taxes and spending.

To make a long story short, substantial majorities of the California electorate wanted cutbacks in government spending and taxes, and expressed strong preferences for a smaller or less powerful government bureaucracy, while at the same time (and by equally strong majorities) requesting additional services in most areas of government responsibility. On the face of it, the public seemed to want something for nothing. This paradoxical mixture of attitudes prevailed throughout the period of the California tax revolt. And the same mentality is evident in the attitudes of Americans nationwide. Understanding it is one of the keys to understanding the tax revolt.

Hostility to Taxes

Resentment about taxes has been growing in recent years. According to Gallup, the proportion of the American public who felt they were paying an unfair amount of taxes rose from below 50 percent in the 1960s, those halcyon days antedating "stagflation," to a high of 72 percent in 1976. In 1978, 29 percent described themselves as "angry," and another 51 percent as "not satisfied," with the federal taxes they paid.[1]

Unhappiness about high taxes has also been pervasive in California. For example, in the Tax Revolt Survey 66 percent of the sample thought their combined federal, state, and local tax burden was either "somewhat" or "much" too high, and 53 percent felt this way about their state income tax bills. Table 3.1 shows that the dissatisfaction with state and local taxes was not diminished by the results of the tax revolt initiatives. Even after voting down the income tax reductions promised by Jarvis II, the public felt state and local taxes were too high.

TABLE 3.1 Perceptions of the tax burden in California.

Believe state and local taxes are:	July 1977		Feb. 1980		Sept. 1980	
Much too high	39%	} 70%	36%	} 71%	42%	} 78%
Somewhat too high	31		35		36	
About right	27		27		20	
Other/don't know	3		2		2	
N	1034		1027		1012	

Source: California Polls.

The unpopularity of a specific form of taxation is often thought to be related to its visibility and to the perception that it is rapidly increasing. This helps explain the unusual intensity of the Proposition 13 protest against property taxes in California. In a June 1977 California Poll, 62 percent of the sample answered an open-ended query about which of the taxes they paid were too high by naming the property tax. No other specific tax was mentioned by more than 20 percent of the sample. In a 1978 California Poll, 77 percent of the respondents reported that property taxes were taking a larger portion of their income in the last few years. Accordingly, 50 percent in California compared to 32 percent in the nation as a whole called the property tax the most unfair levy.

The implementation of Proposition 13 did partially assuage public anger about property taxes, indicating that attitudes toward the tax system are influenced by fiscal realities. The Tax Revolt Survey, conducted after homeowners had received their second post-13 bills, found that 65 percent now believed they were paying about the right amount and 29 percent felt they were paying more than they should (5 percent of California's homeowners altruistically thought their property taxes were too low). According to the California Poll, 62 percent of respondents cited the property tax as the most unfair state or local tax in 1977, but only 21 percent did so in 1980. The state income tax replaced the property tax on the most-hated list after Proposition 13, though it never received as much abuse. By February 1980, as the Jarvis II campaign began, 39 percent cited the state income tax as the most unfair, followed by the gasoline, sales, and property taxes.

However, this declining antagonism toward the property tax contained one potential time bomb. Those complaining about their property taxes were drawn disproportionately from those who had purchased their homes after July 1, 1975, and whose property tax, under the provisions of Jarvis-Gann, was approximately 1 percent of the purchase price of their home rather than the much lower 1 percent of its 1975–76 assessed value. As inflation drove housing prices higher and higher, the gap between these two values exploded. In late 1979, at the time of the Tax Revolt Survey, the average single-family home in Southern California was priced at $110,000; in July 1975 it had been only $44,000—an increase of 250 percent in four and a half years.[2] So, it makes sense that, of those who had bought since 1975, 42 percent thought they paid too much in property tax (22 percent "much too much"), whereas among earlier purchasers only 19 percent were so aggrieved. This suggests that as housing values rise and the proportion of all homeowners falling into the category of post-1975 buyers inevitably increases, discontent about property taxes will spread once again. Indeed, in the November 1980 election Californians rejected a constitutional amendment that would have relaxed the conditions under which local government could raise property taxes above the limit imposed by Proposition 13.

Smaller Government

The public castigates government as much for overspending as for overtaxing. In the Tax Revolt Survey, 62 percent of the respondents preferred a "smaller government providing fewer services," and only 28 percent a "larger government providing more services." This is a very standard finding, and typical of the American public generally. For example, a June 1978 Gallup Poll found that 84 percent felt "the federal government is spending too much money" and only 5 percent felt it was spending "too little."[3] And this charge of overspending appears to be part of a more general antigovernment feeling shared by many Americans. For example, in a January 1981 CBS/*New York Times* Poll 63 percent felt "the federal government creates more problems than it solves," and only 19 percent felt it solves more problems than it creates. And the 1978 Michigan election study found that people agreed by a three-to-one margin (of those with an opinion) that "the government in Washington is getting too powerful." In short, very strong majorities, in California and throughout the nation, felt "the government" was getting too big and too powerful and was spending too much money.

More Services

One might suppose that the majority who wanted smaller government also wanted government services to be cut back to a less lavish level. But no. While the dominant rhetoric inveighs against spending in general, government actually pays for *particular* services and bureaucracies that deliver them. And people want *more* services, if anything, rather than less. Throughout the period of the tax revolt there was strong public support for larger budgetary commitments in a wide range of domains. This was true both in California and throughout the United States, and it was true despite the equally widespread desire for less and smaller government.

The conventional approach to measuring public preferences for government services is to ask whether they favor an increase or a decrease in public expenditures, or the status quo, in a particular service area. Table 3.2 traces Californians' attitudes toward spending on selected problems from 1977 to 1980. The Percentage Difference Index (PDI) values reported indicate the extent of popular support for more spending in each specific policy domain by subtracting the proportion of respondents who want a cutback in spending from those advocating an increase.

The evidence is quite clear: the balance of opinion is favorable to continuing current levels of spending in almost every area. And among those who want a change, the general preference is for an *increase*, not a decrease, in spending. People overwhelmingly oppose cutbacks in the police and fire departments, education, public transportation, recreation facilities, and mental health. The one exception is that the majority consistently wants "welfare" spending cut.

Again, this California pattern reflects a more general national consensus, in this case for at least maintaining the status quo, or if anything, increasing government spending on most specific services. This can be seen clearly in the annual national General Social Survey conducted by the National Opinion Research Center (NORC). Respondents are regularly asked whether "we're spending too much money," "too little money," or "about the right amount" on each of eleven areas. In the seven surveys done between 1973 and 1980,

TABLE 3.2 Preferences for increases or decreases in government spending on specific services.

Services	July 1977	May 1978	Nov. 1979	Nov. 1979 (TRS)	Sept. 1980
Mental health	52%	32%	45%	*	46%
Police departments	51	20	52	45%	56
Fire departments	46	13	39	39	50
Prisons and corrections	17	8	20	*	30
Public schools	35	3	40	35	45
Public transportation	43	3	47	52	46
Parks and recreation	15	-5	12	17	18
Streets and highways	15	-7	13	*	12
Higher education	16	-3	19	21	23
Health care programs	15	-6	14	28	12
Environmental protection	19	-14	12	*	10
Public housing	7	-26	-6	*	13
Welfare	-37	-59	-40	-30	**
Mean	23	-3	20	26	30

Sources: California Polls, except for fourth column, which is from the Tax Revolt Survey.

Note: Entries are PDI values. PDI values are obtained by subtracting the percentage of respondents who want a cutback in spending in the are in question from those advocating an increase.

*The Tax Revolt Survey did not include questions about these programs.

**"Public assistance programs to the elderly and the disabled" had a PDI value of +63, while "public assistance programs for low-income families with dependent children" registered +4.

those responding "too little" outnumbered those responding "too much" in most service areas (indeed, by a two-to-one margin). And, as in California, even when budget increases were not preferred the status quo was usually the winner: only for welfare, space exploration, and foreign aid did a majority favor budget cuts. The same proved true in a January 1981 CBS/*New York Times* Poll: more respondents wanted to increase than decrease spending in six of eight budget areas, the exceptions being food stamps and unemployment compensation. Even in those cases the budget cutters were in the minority; most at least favored the status quo.

Within this general pattern of public support for maintaining spending, some services clearly are more favored than others. And the magnitude of support appears to reflect the symbolic meaning of these capsule descriptions of the service areas, in two respects. Table 3.2 suggests that programs whose benefits are available to everyone, at least in principle, such as police and fire and schools, are more widely favored than those with specialized clienteles, such as public housing and welfare. Universal access to such programs makes them expensive, of course, so we are left with the irony that the public supports expansion of the costliest governmental responsibilities, while simultaneously demanding reduced taxes.

And services whose clienteles are most widely thought to be racial minorities tend to be favored the least. Welfare, public housing, food stamps, and unemployment compensation are the obvious examples. The word "welfare" is such a negative symbol that its constituent programs receive a somewhat more favorable reception when they are presented separately. As table 3.2 shows, Californians are quite happy about supporting "the elderly and disabled," and support the status quo in spending on "public assistance programs for low income families with dependent children," to which a major portion of welfare funds is devoted. But they are less happy about the latter, presumably because of its image of black welfare mothers.

This preference for continued or increased spending held at virtually every time-point tested. It even held in the midst of the 1980 presidential campaign, which saw Ronald Reagan roll to a healthy victory in California over President Carter, presumably partly on promises to cut spending.

The one major exception was the poll taken on the eve of the vote on Proposition 13. Then the public was markedly less supportive of spending increases. Support for government spending was uniformly more negative in the May 1978 sample (one week before Proposition 13's victory) than in comparable polls done either earlier or later. In fact, at that time the public preferred cuts over increases in seven of thirteen areas, as can be seen in table 3.2. The mean PDI fell to -3 percent; a dramatic shift, since in all other polls it fluctuated narrowly between $+20$ percent and $+30$ percent. This shift in outlook could be attributed either to the heightened consciousness about the link between taxes and services as a result of an intense and widely publicized campaign, or to the influence of the frenzied anti-tax, anti-government mood that developed in late May. But even here those who wanted to maintain the status quo far outnumbered either expanders or cutters, who approximately offset each other.[4]

Thus it is not true that a majority favored less spending, even in May 1978.

Rather, even as the public prepared to vote a landslide for Proposition 13, the majority favored continuing spending at current levels. To be sure, in late May more people wanted cuts than wanted increases in most service areas. Nevertheless, the majority wanted to keep spending at least "the same," if not to increase it, in all but one of the thirteen spending areas listed in table 3.2.

And by the end of 1979 Californians' preferences for more spending were back to normal, pre–Proposition 13 levels. When the debate over Jarvis II began, the public demand for government services was at its usual level, rather than slackening. And as we will see later, in April 1980, when Proposition 9 began to slip in the polls, many voters believed there would have to be serious cutbacks in government services if the state's tax revenues were to be cut as severely as Proposition 9 promised to do.

Waste in Government

The third salient element in the public's attitudes about the tax revolt was the widespread belief that huge potential savings lay in the elimination of bureaucratic "waste." Californians held quite unfavorable opinions about the efficiency of government at all levels. For example, in May 1978, 43 percent considered state government "very inefficient," and another 31 percent "somewhat inefficient." In California Polls done at that time and again in February 1979, the overwhelming majority thought government at all levels was at least somewhat inefficient, and large minorities thought it was very inefficient. Relatively small minorities defended governmental performance in general.

The same mass belief in widespread waste in government could be seen when the public was asked how much the government could cut spending without reducing services. At all stages of the tax revolt, Californians overwhelmingly believed that it was possible to cut spending without reducing services, as table 3.3 shows. The only question was how much. As in other cases considered in this chapter, the high water mark of anti-government sentiment came on the eve of the vote for Proposition 13. At that time, a very large number of people, 38 percent, believed that the government could carry on at the same level of service even with a 40 percent cut in revenue. The median Californians at that time felt that about 25 percent of state and local government budgets could be cut without harming services.

As the tax revolt wore on, Californians continued to feel that cuts could be

TABLE 3.3 Californian's attitudes about waste in government.

Question	Would have to cut services	Could have same services	No opinion
May 1978 (N = 1317) With about _____ less money, could government provide the same level of services, or would it have to cut back?			
10% less	39%	54%	7%
20% less	43	49	8
30% less	47	43	10
40% less	50	38	12

How much could _____ government cut its spending without reducing services?	None	1%-20%	>20%	No opinion
May 1979 (N = 979)				
State government	16%	33%	38%	13%
Local government	18	38	34	11
Nov. 1979 (N = 1788)				
State government	17	51	21	10
Local government	30	45	15	10

	Would have to cut services	Could have same services	No opinion
Nov. 1979 (N = 1788) Do you think the public schools in your area could spend less without hurting the quality of education which they provide?	50%	41%	9%
Feb. 1980 (N = 1027) Would the state be able to provide the same level of government services with a 20 to 25% cut in its budget?	69	22	8
April 1980 (N = 1012) Would the state be able to provide the same level of government services with a 20 to 25% cut in its budget?	77	15	8

Sources: California Polls (May 1978, May 1979, February and April 1980); Tax Revolt Survey (November 1979).

made, but the perceived magnitude of waste in government dwindled. A year after the passage of Proposition 13, the median dropped to a little under 20 percent, as table 3.3 shows. By the time the Gann amendment passed in November 1979, the median Californian thought only 13 percent of the state budget (and 8 percent of local budgets) could be cut without harming services. By the time the Jarvis II campaign began to gather steam in February 1980, however, most were convinced that cuts of such magnitude would seriously reduce services. Overwhelming majorities felt that cuts of 20 percent to 25 percent would result in service cuts.

The high pay of government workers was perceived as a major source of wasteful spending. The Tax Revolt Survey found that 35 percent of the public believed that state and local government employees were paid more than they deserved compared to people in the private sector with similar jobs; 44 percent felt they were paid the right amount; and 12 percent thought they were paid too little.

In short, the belief that government was wasteful and inefficient at all levels was widely held in California. It dropped off considerably as the revolt progressed, but even as Jarvis II was losing, almost a quarter of the electorate still believed state and local governments could provide the same level of services with budgets reduced by at least 20 percent.

And this portrait of wastefulness, too, was shared by the national electorate. Nationally, according to the Michigan election studies, those believing the government "wastes a lot" of tax dollars rose from 47 percent in 1964 to 79 percent in 1978. A Gallup survey conducted in October 1978 makes this general opinion more specific: the median estimate for the amount of each tax dollar wasted was 48 cents for the federal government, 32 cents for state government, and 25 cents for local governments.

Belief in the profligacy of government would appear to be part of a decade of more generally declining public trust and confidence in the nation's political institutions and officials. Nationally, the proportion of those who felt you could trust the government to do what is right "all" or even "most" of the time fell from 76 percent in 1964 to 30 percent in 1978. Recent surveys show that majorities regularly express similar levels of disenchantment with government in California. The Tax Revolt Survey found that 57 percent of the state's citizens felt government could be trusted to do what is right "only some" of the time, with another 11 percent going even further and saying "almost never." And 64 percent believed the government was run for the benefit of special-interest groups rather than for the benefit of all. The December

1979 California Poll asked a series of questions specifically about the performance of the state government: 56 percent of the sample said they could trust the state government to do what is right "only some of the time," while 66 percent felt they were "not so well" represented by state government.

Thus the anti-government theme in Howard Jarvis's rhetoric fit comfortably with the prevailing mood. The extent of public cynicism about the ordinary processes of representative government is illustrated by responses to questions about the initiative method. A November 1979 California Poll found that by nearly a 4 to 1 margin, voting for propositions was considered a more effective method of influencing the government than voting for candidates. "The mule," in Jarvis's words, notices a "two-by-four." The tax revolt fed on the feeling that citizens had lost control.

Intensity of Public Concern

The electoral and budgetary fallout from Proposition 13 has been the main preoccupation of those in California government since its passage. And high taxes, overspending, and incompetent government have remained prominent issues for the general public. But how intensely did the public hold these concerns? The Tax Revolt Survey probed this by asking respondents to name the two main problems they thought were facing people in California these days. As was true nationally, inflation emphatically led the way throughout this period (mentioned by 46 percent in California), with energy a rather distant second (25 percent). As a set, the tax-revolt issues followed rather closely after that: high or unfair taxes were mentioned by 21 percent, government overspending by 8 percent, and untrustworthy public officials by 2 percent. Of course inflation is objectively implicated in these central issues of the tax revolt; it does funnel private money into the public treasury at a faster rate, for example. But it should be noted that concerns about inflation focus not on taxes but on the impact of rising prices.

So the public's attention was certainly caught by these concerns about taxes and services, but they were not the most central concerns, either personally or politically. This point is important, because it will later help us to understand both the rather limited impact of self-interest in the tax revolt and how quickly Californians backed away from radical cuts in taxes and spending when, in the form of Jarvis II, they threatened the status quo.

Something for Nothing

These are the major themes of the California public's (and indeed the national public's) attitudes during the height of the tax revolt: taxes are too high, government is too large and too wasteful—but the same or more should be spent on specific services. To be sure, at the moment of Proposition 13's triumph, perceptions of waste were especially high and desire for increased services was low. But by and large this package of attitudes characterized majority opinion in California throughout the tax-revolt era.

There is a clear paradox in this. How could the public feel so strongly that taxes are too high, and that government is too large and spending too much money—and at the same time want to maintain government services at current levels, or even increase spending? This sounds as if people simply have not faced up to having to pay the piper; the taxpayers seem to want something for nothing. Not only that, but they seem to be expressing some symbolic anti-government attitudes that the Founding Fathers would have found congenial: less government! But these symbolic concerns, too, seem compartmentalized from their desire for more services. These apparent contradictions are important analytic foci for us, and they remain central themes in the continuing national story of the tax revolt.

One starting point is the possibility that this paradox represents only an accident of aggregating data: perhaps although majorities on different items seem inconsistent, most individuals are not. But this turns out not to be true. Individuals show the same basic inconsistency as do aggregate majorities: most people feel taxes are too high and want smaller government in general, and yet want net increases in government spending for specific services. To show this, we developed a summary service-spending scale averaging preferences for increased or decreased spending in the eight service areas tested for in the Tax Revolt Survey (see table 3.2).[5] And as shown in table 3.4, most people wanted net increases in service spending no matter what their perceived tax burden or preferences about the overall size of government.[6] People who said they wanted larger government were reasonably consistent; irrespective of their felt tax burden, they overwhelmingly came down for increased spending in specific areas (with a mean PDI of +90 percent). But most of those who claimed to want smaller government still favored net increases in spending. Perhaps the most paradoxical cases are those who felt their taxes to be "much too high" *and* who wanted "smaller government" in general: even this group wanted increased spending, on balance, with a PDI value of +17 percent.[7]

TABLE 3.4 The basic inconsistency: attitudes toward spending on specific services as a function of preferred size of government and personal tax burden.

In general, prefer government:	Spending on all eight services		Spending on police and fire		Spending on welfare		Spending on other social services	
	Larger	Smaller	Larger	Smaller	Larger	Smaller	Larger	Smaller
Personal tax burden								
About right	+94%	+47%	+59%	+64%	+11	−51	+90	+50
Somewhat too high	+89	+47	+64	+58	−15	−57	+90	+51
Much too high	+86	+17	+59	+42	−19	−73	+84	+23
All	+90	+45	+61	+53	− 5	−62	+88	+40

Source: Tax Revolt Survey.

Note: Entries are PDI values: percentage wanting spending on the specific services indicated to be increased minus percentage wanting it to be decreased.

This pattern suggests to some observers a large-scale failure by the electorate to understand the inherent conflict between more expensive services and lower taxes. This suggests a failure in perception or reasoning that fits the view of many political behaviorists that "ordinary" citizens possess very limited political sophistication or awareness.[8]

But perhaps the apparent failure to acknowledge the tradeoff between spending and taxes is at least partially attributable to other, more sensible, factors. The widespread complaints about waste in government provide one possible explanation: perhaps government could reduce taxes without hurting services, by reducing waste. Alternatively, many individuals may have supported the tax revolt out of a strong opposition to a few selected governmental activities, such as welfare—an opposition that coexisted quite comfortably with an equally strong desire for increases in spending for other activities. In the remainder of this chapter we will try to assess the degree to which opinions and votes in the tax revolt were sensible, judged in terms of the public's general perceptions of governmental performance and budgetary realities, as well as their specific preferences for spending, services, and taxes.

One common resolution of the dilemma of how to cut taxes without cutting services is to "cut out waste." When Ronald Reagan, in the sole 1980 televised debate with Jimmy Carter, was asked how he expected to cut taxes, balance the federal budget, and increase defense spending, he replied that cutting out waste would be a major factor. Howard Jarvis made it very clear that he believed a lot of "fat" existed in state and local budgets, and that cutting out that fat would allow major tax cuts without completely dislocating government. Did the mass public resolve this inconsistency in the same way?

To be sure, the more waste people perceived, the more they wanted smaller government and cuts in spending on specific services. Table 3.5 classifies respondents according to how much they felt spending could be cut (in state and local government and in the public schools) without reducing services. The top row shows that net preferences for increased service spending declined among those perceiving a great deal of waste in government. The net PDI value was + 66 percent among those feeling there was little or no waste, as against + 30 percent among those feeling major cuts could be made.

TABLE 3.5 Perception of waste in government does not resolve the basic inconsistency.

	Amount of perceived waste in government			
	20% or more	Up to 20%	About 10%	Little or none
% wanting net increase in service spending (PDI)				
In the full sample	+ 30%	+ 44%	+ 55%	+ 66%
Among those who:				
Prefer smaller government	+ 15	+ 25	+ 37	+ 44
Prefer larger government	+ 88	+ 87	+ 89	+ 93
Own taxes much too high	+ 13	+ 18	+ 40	+ 58
Own taxes somewhat too high	+ 48	+ 65	+ 56	+ 62
Own taxes about right	+ 63	+ 57	+ 64	+ 71
% wanting smaller government in general				
In the full sample	79	70	67	53
Among those who feel that:				
Own taxes much too high	83	75	74	53
Own taxes somewhat too high	82	68	71	57
Own taxes about right	66	65	54	50

Source: Tax Revolt Survey.

Note: For explanation of the PDI values, see note to Table 3.2.

In other words, the belief that government was wasteful apparently cut the ranks of net spenders by 36 percent — a major effect. The seventh row of the table shows the same thing for preferred size of government: the more perceived waste, the more the respondent wanted smaller government (in this case by 26 percent).

But in fact perceived waste was not the solution to the smaller-government-with-more-services dilemma, as shown in rows two to six of table 3.5. People still wanted net increases in spending on specific services, no matter what level of waste they believed in, or whether they wanted smaller or larger government in the abstract, or claimed that their taxes were killing them. Even those who believed in huge amounts of waste — those who said 20 percent or more of government budgets could be painlessly cut — *and* wanted smaller government in general, tilted toward net *increases* in spending on specific services. The PDI was +15 percent even in this group, as shown in the second row. The fourth row provides yet another clear indication that this inconsistency cannot be explained adequately by perceived waste. Even those who should have been the most extreme Jarvisites — those who felt their own tax burden was much too high and who believed there were massive (20+ percent) amounts of waste — wanted net increases in service spending. The PDI was +13 percent in this group. But they were overwhelmingly for smaller government (83 percent), as shown in the eighth row of the table.

So it is true that perceptions of waste were associated with desires for spending cuts, smaller government, and feelings of paying excessive taxes. But the central paradox in Californians' thinking — wanting both smaller government and more spending on services — is not explained by perceived waste. The desire to have more for less is there even among those who are horrified by governmental inefficiency.

Perhaps the paradox can be explained by the modest level of political attention, and therefore sophistication, commonly found in the general public. Most surveys find the mass public's grasp of political information to be rather skimpy. The public's attitudes also generally show low levels of consistency and ideological thinking. It is therefore easy to conclude that a lack of political sophistication is widespread in the general public.

If this apparent attitudinal conflict is due to lack of political sophistication, then it should be most pronounced among the least sophisticated voters, and perhaps not present at all among the more sophisticated. To test for this, we redid the two lefthand columns of table 3.4 among those likely to be most sophisticated (the college educated and the 36 percent who said they followed news of California politics and government "very closely") and then again among the least sophisticated (those with no high school degree and those who followed the news "not too closely").

More sophisticated respondents were somewhat more consistent than were less sophisticated ones. But basically the same inconsistent pattern holds at all levels of sophistication: even among the most sophisticated, the desire for smaller government is not matched by any desire for net reductions in spending on specific services. Thus it seems that the inconsistency is not due to any marked lack of political sophistication.

Another possible explanation of this inconsistency is that people want to increase spending for the services they have a vested interest in, but cut everything else. Setting aside for the moment the extent to which spending preferences on specific services are founded in narrow self-interest (which we will take up in Chapter 7), we can examine the accuracy of this interpretation by looking at differential preferences among different services.

There is certainly more support for services that benefit everyone than for those that serve narrower clienteles. Almost everyone wants at least to maintain fully the universalistic safety services (police and fire departments). However, they are less enthusiastic about the social services, especially welfare, which serve only a minority.[9] It may be that most people do not think of the safety services as part of "big government," or really even of government at all. On the other hand, everyone knows who delivers welfare handouts: big, bloated, and inefficient government. So it might be that the majority in favor of "smaller government" is a coalition of two rather different groups. Some people may simply want to cut government in all its manifestations: as an abstract symbol, in its concrete services, and in its voracious appetite for taxes. A second group may identify "government" only with social services, and therefore want to cut them but maintain spending on safety services. Members of this second group might be especially likely to be political conservatives.

If this were the case, we would expect strong support for safety services throughout the public, irrespective of felt tax burden or fealty to the "small government" ideal. However, we would expect preferences for spending on social services to be reasonably congruent with these other two attitudes: those with high felt tax burdens, and those who want smaller government in the abstract, should want to cut social-service spending. And this tendency might be especially marked among conservatives, who have the strongest negative attitudes toward the "free lunch."

However, this distinction between safety and social services does not help to clear up the basic puzzle. There is no mystery about the spending preferences of those who feel their tax burden is "about right," or supporters of larger government, or liberals. All these groups overwhelmingly want increased spending on both safety and social services. This high level of support for both kinds of services holds even among mixed groups. For example, liberals who want smaller government, or who feel they pay much more in taxes than they should, want net spending increases for both safety and social services. The PDI values in these groups all exceed +40 percent.

But what about small-government enthusiasts, those who feel excessively burdened by taxes, and conservatives? Do they want to maintain safety services but cut social services, as this reasoning would suggest? True, they do like their safety. Both self-proclaimed conservatives who want smaller government and those who perceive they pay much more than they should in taxes are enthusiastic about increasing safety services (PDI values of +56 percent and +48 percent). But they do *not* want to cut social services much. The social-service PDI values for these same two types of conservatives were −2 percent and −1 percent, respectively. Even they were prepared to maintain the status quo on social services.

A more refined version of this hypothesis would treat "welfare" separately from the other social services. Table 3.4 shows that almost all groups wanted to cut "welfare." But what about the other social services, such as schools, parks, public health, higher education, and transportation? In some sense these represent the crucial turf over which the tax revolt ultimately will be fought and resolved. Does this basic inconsistency hold with respect to them, as well? Or do they too find overwhelming support even among tax rebels?

In fact, they enjoy almost as solid a consensus as do the safety services. This can be seen in table 3.4. To try to find a subgroup that wanted to cut social programs other than welfare, we again turned to the 27 percent of the sample that both wanted smaller government and felt they paid much more in taxes than they should. Table 3.4 already showed that even this group, as a whole, preferred some increase in spending on these social programs. But perhaps the politically conservative subset of this group (which amounted to 61 percent of it) would want cuts in these social programs, on the grounds of ideological opposition to them. Even these, however, wanted a net increase in these social programs by a small margin (PDI of +4 percent). Indeed, to find any subset of this group that favored spending cuts we had to turn to those who also favored cuts in police and fire departments. These finally yielded a slight margin in favor of cuts in nonwelfare social programs (PDI of −7 percent). But these bloodthirsty budget cutters are apparently only a microscopic fraction of the California electorate, for they represent only 4 percent of our sample. So it also proves to be very hard to find people who want to cut spending on social programs, aside from the highly stigmatized "welfare".

The puzzle, then, really turns on what people mean by "big government." Maybe people identify "big government" with "welfare," and since they are so antagonistic toward welfare, they may oppose big government as a symbol of welfare giveaways, while favoring the status quo for other social programs. Posed in this way, the analytic question focuses on the determinants of preferences for "smaller government." The most commonsensical model, perhaps, would suggest that the desire for smaller government is a joint function of how badly the voter's taxes hurt and how much he desires services—and that a major component of the latter is hostility toward "welfare." To test this model, we carried out multivariate analyses in which preferences about the size of government in the abstract were regressed on measures of the three subparts of specific service spending (safety, welfare, and the nonwelfare social programs), as well as on personal tax burden. This yielded a respectable though not overwhelming level of predictability ($R^2 = .19$). The analysis shows that how people feel about "big government" depends about equally on their attitudes about welfare and about the other social programs, but very little on their attitudes toward the safety services or taxes. The standardized regression coefficients for welfare and for the other social services were .23 and .27, whereas those for taxes and safety were .07 and .00. So, apparently, the meaning of "smaller government" is "fewer social programs," especially but not exclusively "less welfare."

Confronting the Tax-Service Tradeoff

Presumably people quite genuinely and naturally would prefer, in the best of all possible worlds, to have both lower taxes and maximum services. Yet, under most circumstances, such an outcome is impossible. The evidence suggests that Californians, and probably Americans in general, have not confronted the harsh reality that tax cuts, or "smaller government," will come only at the expense of cuts in specific services. That is, they seem to have compartmentalized these attitudes, so that they coexist without close examination of their fiscal relationships.

On the other hand, the voters are surely capable of making realistic choices between incompatible goods when they have to. If they are forced to make the real tradeoffs between continued services and lower taxes, they will probably do so. Their decisions on the three Jarvis-Gann propositions may have represented just such choices. But because each was a complex measure with considerable uncertainty about its consequences, they represent ambiguous tests of the voters' "true" preferences when confronted with hard and certain choices. What happens when they are forced to make such tradeoffs explicitly?

No matter when the tradeoff between services and taxes was put to Californians in survey questions, or how it was phrased, most opted for continued services rather than tax breaks, even when their electoral response seemed quite the opposite. The tradeoff was posed to them in three basic ways during the tax revolt period.

One version was the classic New Deal formulation: in order to have *more* services, would you be willing to pay *higher* taxes? Surprisingly enough, the overwhelming majority of Californians said they would accept higher taxes if necessary to protect or expand existing public services. As we have seen in table 3.2, the Tax Revolt Survey respondents wanted increased spending on most services they were asked about. In fact, almost all (95 percent) wanted increased spending in at least one service area. These were then asked if they would be willing to pay more taxes to support those increases. The vast majority were willing to pay more in taxes to pay for these service increases, while only 24 percent flatly stated they would forgo the increased services if it meant higher taxes.[10] Since Proposition 13 had made it highly unlikely that the state legislature would raise taxes in California, respondents were also asked how else to finance the particular increases in the services they themselves desired. Some respondents (21 percent) felt that cuts in other services should be made, others wanted cuts in waste (18 percent) or public employees' salaries (26 percent) and others (27 percent) had no real idea about what to do. But there was clearly no strong desire to cut government services.

The second version posed the tax-service tradeoff in terms parallel to those posed by the Reagan administration: in order to have lower taxes, would you give up existing levels of services? That is, it asked Californians explicitly to choose between tax reductions and maintaining *current* levels of government services. Surprisingly enough, they rejected such tax rebates overwhelmingly when they would come at the expense of service cuts. In our own Tax Revolt Survey, one-third of the respondents did not want spending cut in *any* of the eight service areas presented. Of the rest, half believed that money saved by service cuts should be spent on other services rather than returned directly to citizens by lowering taxes. Hence, overall, two-thirds of the sample wanted to maintain services rather than cut taxes. Only 32 percent wanted both to cut some services and to have the savings translated into tax cuts.

Similarly, early in the Proposition 13 campaign, the California Poll asked voters what government should do if the proposition passed; 52 percent preferred to raise other taxes, while only 27 percent wanted simply to cut back on public services. In another California Poll, shortly after Proposition 13 passed, they overwhelmingly (by 72 percent to 17 percent) approved of the transfer of the $5 billion state surplus back to schools and local government, to avoid service cuts. And only 2 percent disapproved of this "bailout" on the grounds that the state surplus should be rebated to the people. By early 1979, impatience with the state surplus was growing somewhat, but still a clear majority (57 percent to 43 percent) wanted it to be used to sustain local services rather than returned to the taxpayers as savings.[11]

The tax-service tradeoff was posed to Californians in a third way, less directly. The California Poll occasionally asked respondents their opinion of one of the tax-relief propositions, then presented some of the pro and con arguments (usually getting the respondent to evaluate their merits), and then asked for a final evaluation of the proposition. These arguments usually focused on possible service cuts. Hence the interview called the respondent's attention to the tradeoff between tax relief and maintenance of services, with a before-and-after measure of the respondent's electoral choice. Making the tradeoff salient reduced the margin for radical tax relief in every case. For example, a California Poll conducted in April 1978 found that 63 percent of respondents with a definite opinion favored "the basic idea" of the Jarvis-Gann initiative. After respondents were told that the measure might seriously impair local schools and fire services, this figure dropped to 54 percent. In 1978 and 1980 this approximate procedure was repeated on six occasions, and it reduced support for the tax revolt on each occasion, by an average of 17 percent of those with an opinion.[12] Hence the number advocating tax relief regularly diminished when the questions posed to citizens indicated that to obtain lower taxes they would have to sacrifice valued services.

This general preference for maintaining services, rather than receiving tax cuts, has held throughout the nation in recent years when such tradeoffs were posed to voters. For example, the Advisory Commission on Intergovernmental Relations, in five national surveys in the 1975 to 1980 period, asked respondents which they preferred, "Considering all government services on the one hand, and taxes on the other; decrease services and taxes, keep taxes and services where they are, or increase services and raise taxes." The first tax-cutting alternative never got more than 39 percent (or less than 30 percent). The status quo won a clear victory in each case, taking between 45 percent and 52 percent.[13]

As indicated earlier, inflation, not taxes, has been regarded as the main villain of the American economic piece in recent years. So on at least one occasion when Americans were asked to choose between "controlling inflation" and "cutting taxes," 90 percent opted for reducing inflation. When asked in early 1981 to choose between a balanced federal budget and a large tax cut, 70 percent wanted to balance the budget, and 62 percent preferred an increase in military spending to a tax cut. Nervous about the economic consequences of large tax cuts, only 24 percent wanted a "large" tax cut, and 52 percent a smaller one.[14] Americans in general, like Californians, usually did not opt for tax cuts when forced to confront the tax-service tradeoff; they too generally wanted to maintain the status quo in services.

These all are just hypothetical choices, and the respondents were aware that their responses would have little influence on government's actual policies. The three Jarvis-Gann propositions were another matter, however. As we have seen, Californians have some faith in the efficacy of their collective voice as expressed in proposition voting. Perhaps those votes represented decisions closer to "real" tradeoffs. We will return to this crucial issue in some detail in Chapter 9, when we consider the differences among the three propositions. They turn out to have posed very different tradeoff choices to the California voter. To anticipate that argument just briefly, Propositions 13 and 4 were not widely expected to result in major cuts in services, whereas Jarvis II was. And Proposition 13 was the only one perceived as likely to result in truly significant tax cuts, though Jarvis II did offer some, especially to high-income voters. So none of these votes really forced a clear hard choice between significant tax cuts and severe service cuts. But each did pose some significant tradeoff, as we will see later.[15]

Evidence from these tradeoff questions seems to suggest that, forced to choose, the public would opt for maintenance of services rather than for lower taxes. People's responses to these tradeoff items were moderately consistent with their other expressed attitudes about taxes and services. Those who perceived their tax burden as currently "about right" and who were most ready to raise taxes rather than cut services were most supportive of increased spending and wanted larger government in general. Similarly, people who considered their tax burdens much too great and who opted for the tradeoff solution of the Reagan administration — cut taxes and cut services — were least likely to want net increases in services, and most likely to want smaller government.

But even these apparently sensible responses to tradeoff questions do not clear up the basic dilemma that runs throughout our data. A clear majority of the people who should be most in favor of larger government — those whose tax burden is "about right" and who opt (in the tradeoff questions) for more services and higher taxes, or at least for maintaining services — still say they want smaller government in general. And contrariwise, those who should be most in favor of cutting specific services — those who feel "much too much" burdened by taxes, and who reject increases in spending rather than accepting higher taxes — still want net increases in services (with a PDI of + 31 percent). The only group to show a net desire to cut spending are those who feel much too much burdened by taxes and who explicitly opt for cutting both taxes and services. But even for these diehards, the net spending preference is barely on the "cut" side (a PDI of − 8 percent). And this is a relatively small group: only 15 percent of the sample.

It seems that these tradeoff decisions were made consistently in the direction of preferring the same or increased services at the expense of tax savings, even among those supposedly committed to smaller government and feeling highly burdened by taxes.[16] The tradeoff decisions themselves seem sensible, in the sense that both value priorities and felt tax burden have fairly clear main effects on them. At least when pushed, people seem not to be so unrealistic as to want something for nothing; they are willing to pay. Nevertheless, the basic conflict of wanting both more services and smaller government persists — even when we take into account responses to the tradeoff between taxes and services in its most direct form.[17]

Political Symbols: General and Specific

The majority's expressed desires for "smaller government" and "lower taxes" remain anomalous. They do not fit consistently with either service demands or the preferences expressed on the tradeoff items. Nor is "waste" seemingly part of any methodical calculus. The data raise the suspicion that all three — smaller government, lower taxes, and waste — are primarily symbolic epithets hurled against government, rather than part of a systematic evaluation of the role of the public sector. All three may be fairly distinct or compartmentalized attitudes toward different political symbols.

Suppose they are separate attitudes toward different symbols. A simple sociopsychological analysis would assume that each is a product of some longer-standing symbolic predispositions. Attitudes toward any given symbol ought to be some average of the predispositions that are relevant to it, because of strains toward affective consistency.[18] For example, the perceived magnitude of waste in the public schools ought to be an average of beliefs in governmental waste in general and general evaluations of the public schools.

Or responses to tax-service tradeoff questions ought to be an average of attitudes toward the particular tax in question and those toward the services in question. Hence the pre–Proposition 13 public should have been expected, for example, to support a slight increase in the sales tax (generally not much disliked) to fund increased police services (much desired), but strongly to oppose increases in the (hated) property tax to fund increased (despised) welfare payments. But it is important to remember in this analysis that if the input attitudes are moderately compartmentalized, we have to treat fairly specifically the actual symbol in question. "Smaller government" will elicit quite a different attitude than will "decreased spending for the public schools," for example. So in trying to understand the inconsistencies in the public's views, we need to be sensitive to the nuances of the symbols they were faced with, both in surveys and in election campaigns.

We need to ask what symbolic themes were most prominent in the tax revolt, and what the predispositional origins were of attitudes toward those symbols—as well as what happens when various symbolic goals are put in conflict in electoral campaigns or surveys. To do this, we need to develop some taxonomy for describing the universe of symbols involved. The anomaly is on the government-output side—the simultaneous desire for smaller government and more services—so let us focus on that side. We suggest that the public typically thinks about government outputs in a number of different ways, falling at different levels on a continuum that is general and abstract at one end, specific and concrete at the other. We also maintain that, within broad limits and at least in our era, the more specific and concrete the symbols describing the government output, the more favorable the public's responses to it.

The attitudes we have been talking about in this chapter seem to be responses to symbols at five discernibly different levels on this continuum:

1. The most general are preferences for "larger government" or "smaller government" in general, without specifying what particular services are involved. Our questions on larger or smaller government in general, and similar questions used in national surveys, tap in at this level.

2. Evaluations of "government services" in general, focusing more on the output side than on the entire apparatus of government, but still not specifying particular areas of output, form a slightly less general level. A good example is the question used in several Advisory Commission on Intergovernmental Relations surveys cited earlier, asking respondents simply to choose between increases or decreases in "all government services on the one hand, and taxes on the other."

3. Spending in particular service areas, such as "the public schools" or "the police," is more specific. We have represented numerous examples of such items in this chapter, both from California (see, for example, table 3.2) and from national surveys. But note that these too are rather general, omnibus symbols, each of which encompasses a wide variety of government activities in a wide area of community life.

4. Hence even more specific items would be required to test public support for specific programs, such as closing libraries on Tuesday mornings, refitting buses to accommodate the handicapped, or teaching arithmetic in elementary school. The public is usually not presented with such specific alternatives in either elections or surveys, probably because political decisionmakers, public opinion researchers, and the general public all agree that the mass public's input to budgetary decisions is most intelligently made at more general levels.

5. Finally, the most specific and concrete level of evaluation should focus upon a citizen's own particular experiences with government services, such as her receipt of social security benefits or her child's experience with his high school English teacher. The most detailed study of such experiences has been made by Daniel Katz and his colleagues, who asked respondents to describe and evaluate their specific experiences with government agencies in connection with such activities as finding a job, job training, and getting medical care.[19]

Generally Negative but Specifically Favorable

Virtually all the data at our disposal suggest that, at the present time, evaluations of government services are more positive when the symbols in which they are posed are more concrete and specific. This is certainly the case in our own data: attitudes toward spending in specific service areas (level 3) are certainly much more positive than attitudes about the size of government (level 1). We earlier cited national data (from the ACIR and NORC) that showed more positive attitudes toward current levels of government services when considered in the abstract (level 2) than toward more or larger government in general (level 1). And Katz and his colleagues found citizens feeling much more positive about their own actual concrete experiences with government (level 5) than about government bureaucracies in the abstract (levels 1 and 2).[20]

Similarly, tradeoff decisions are more likely to be resolved in favor of maintaining services rather than cutting taxes when services are described in more concrete terms. The tradeoff questions in the Tax Revolt Survey, for example, all traded off tax increases or rebates against the respondent's desire to increase or decrease spending on specific service areas (level 3). As we have seen, they all showed strong preferences for maintaining services. A California Poll item used in September 1980, on the other hand, counterposed a tax increase against service cuts in general (level 2), as follows: "If the state does face a budget deficit after this coming fiscal year, would you rather that it reduce the amount it spends even if it means cutting services, or would you favor a tax increase?" In this case the public mainly chose the anti-tax, anti-service side: 60 percent favored reduced spending, 30 percent a tax increase. It appears that people are more likely to come down in favor of services to the extent that their choices focus attention on specific government services rather than government spending in general.

Many researchers interpret such findings to mean that citizens actually evaluate government services very favorably, and that the demand for government services is strong and solidly based. They contend that evaluations of government at more general or abstract levels are made in a tide of distracting emotion, and may be quite negative for reasons of stereotype, conformity to some fad or temporary norm of rhetorical expression, ideology, or lack of information. But, the argument goes, when citizens evaluate the real nitty-gritty experiences they have with government, they are quite positive. Katz and his colleagues put this point of view forcefully: "It can be argued . . . that people actually organize their cognitions both at a pragmatic empirical level, and at a more general ideological level. Ideologically, they may be against large public bureaucracies; pragmatically, they are all for them."[21] In other words, according to this argument, the demand for a large and generous public sector is solidly rooted in genuine preferences, based on real and concrete experiences, no matter how much the public's anti-government rhetoric may belie it. We should believe people's experiences, not their rhetoric.[22]

This interpretation, which we believe is for the most part an accurate one at the present time, demands a couple of important caveats. First of all, the empirical relationship between service specificity and positive evaluation has some exceptions, which suggest that it could be dependent on some other factors. Second, we need to look further at the implicit assumption that evaluations of specific objects are more "real" than those of more abstract objects.

It has not always held true that more concrete objects are evaluated positively and more abstract ones negatively. For one thing, evaluations of government at the most abstract and general level have not always been so negative. In the late 1950s and early 1960s, for example, they were extremely favorable, no matter whether they focused on government in general or on various governmental institutions.[23] We have argued elsewhere that such evaluations are by their nature highly "ritualistic" or stereotypic, and that they are potentially quite labile, since their referents are ambiguous.[24] However, that instability contrasts with the quite stable support for current levels of spending in most specific service areas. As we have seen, this support has held during the tax revolt with its great public demand for tax cuts, and it also has been the stable result of surveys that put the tax-service tradeoff to the voters.

What is more, some population groups are not so favorable to government at a more specific level, and some programs are not so popular. Studies of ghetto residents, for example, found high levels of grievance about their treatment and the services received.[25] And along with the very favorable evaluations of experiences with service agencies, Katz and his colleagues also found quite negative evaluations of respondents' concrete interactions with "agencies of constraint," concerning matters such as traffic violations, police, or tax problems.[26] So any simple assumptions about evaluations of concrete experiences (our level 5) must be modified somewhat by information about the nature of the experience.

However, these exceptions do not appear to qualify our major point very much. Surveys of ghetto residents also always have found that they want more rather than less attention from government. Furthermore, the services that are at issue in the tax revolt's assault on the public sector are not those provided by "constraint agencies." Rather, they are those provided by social programs, especially in the areas of employment, health, education, and care of the aged, for which Katz and his colleagues report positive evaluations. So the debate does revolve around cutting services that, at the concrete level, the public generally experiences positively.

Finally, we have noted that at one level—the level of evaluating very specific programs—the mass public's evaluations of services have gone virtually unmeasured. It is possible that the specific-service-area symbols are more favorably evaluated than would be the specific programs they encompass, if the public knew in detail what the specific programs were. If that were true, more publicity about specific government programs might undermine the apparent support for government services. Social scientists will recall Senator William Proxmire's efforts to do just that to some federally funded scientific research with his Golden Fleece Award. How successful that effort was in discouraging public support for basic research, and what the effects would be of greater public information about very specific government programs, is hard to say. We are skeptical that it would have a major effect, mainly because of the difficulty of communicating such large amounts of detail to a relatively inattentive mass public. But it is a possibility.

Strength of Attitudes

A second question to be raised is whether citizens' concrete preferences or their general attitudes about government are stronger, and therefore more likely to prevail if one should be pitted against the other. If indeed concrete preferences tend to favor more government, and general attitudes less, their relative strength (if they do differ systematically) would have much to say about the ultimate outcome of the tax revolt.

One way to determine relative strength would be to press voters to decide between preferences expressed at different levels of generality. The tradeoff decisions described earlier attempt some such confrontation by forcing the respondent to choose which preference, for lower taxes or for maintaining services, is the stronger. And most people generally choose to maintain services. But in this form the tradeoff decision is between services and taxes both described at intermediate levels of generality, so it does not help resolve this question.

Another approach to the question is to ask *why* more concrete, or more general attitudes, might be the stronger. We can think of three obvious possibilities, although, as it turns out, they do not settle the matter either, because they imply conflicting answers to the question. First of all, attitudes toward more concrete experiences and programs should be more based in reality, and for that reason might be stronger than attitudes toward vague, amorphous, abstract concepts like "the government." For one thing, they might not be so vulnerable to attitude changes resulting from changes in meaning; a social security check is pretty much what it is, but "the government" can protect us from hunger and a Soviet invasion, or it can force us to fill out innumerable forms or deplete our savings account with its tax bill.[27] Additionally, attitudes based on direct experience should be more informed, and for that reason more difficult to change. Presumably people are better informed about whether the local schools need more funding than they are about whether the federal government is too large. And plainly a person would be more informed still about his or her own concrete experiences with government. But we are not convinced that contact with "reality" necessarily makes more specific attitudes the strongest. Most people probably have very little idea of how much money the local schools really do need. Many parents are not at all well-informed about the needs of their own child's school, much less those of their district as a whole. So we resist a simple assertion that attitudes about specific services are stronger because they are better informed about reality than those about government in general. Rather, they seem to us to be just as likely as are more global attitudes to be based in symbolic predispositions, rather than in direct contact with government.[28]

More specific attitudes might be more grounded in self-interest, and stronger for that reason. We will take up that question in detail in later chapters. Without trying to anticipate the complexities of the answer, its gist is that even quite specific attitudes tend to be grounded in self-interest in only a very narrow way, and usually only for a minority. As will be seen, preferences for larger or smaller government in general do not have a strong self-interest basis; they tend to be based more in symbolic predispositions. Even preferences for increased or decreased spending in specific service areas are not directly self-interested for more than a minority; for example, in our survey 81 percent wanted the same or increased spending on the public schools, though only 26 percent had children in such schools. Thus self-interest probably does not help us decide whether more specific attitudes are stronger than more abstract ones.

Then there is the opposite possibility, that more general and abstract attitudes are the stronger because they are more firmly based in broad political ideologies. Without denying for a moment the firm ideological basis of the general desire for smaller government, we think that this too is a deceptively simple guideline. Attitudes toward spending for specific services also are fairly strongly rooted in symbolic predispositions, as we will see in Chapter 8. For example, the old-fashioned American value of individualistic self-reliance, as embodied in the Protestant ethic, prizes thrift, the value of saving, and of taking care of oneself economically. All of these seem violated when people are "just given handouts," especially those "too lazy to work." In the surveys we have reviewed, this value surfaces in opposition to such specific services as "welfare," food stamps, and unemployment compensation. And presumably all these services can potentially attract quite different levels of public support depending on the particular symbols in which they are described.

Conclusions

Californians, like Americans in general, do seem to want "something for nothing" where government is concerned. They want smaller government and lower taxes, but they want to maintain or even expand services in most areas of state and local government responsibility. We tried to explain away this seeming inconsistency by invoking some other beliefs or conditions, but without success. The simultaneous desire for less government and lower taxes, on the one hand, and current service levels, on the other, held even among people who felt government operated with minimal waste and among the more sophisticated of California voters. Nor could it be explained by assuming that voters wanted to reduce the size of government by cutting out services they were unsympathetic to.

Hence we were left with the conclusion that the mass public had not really confronted the hard choices at the time of our survey, at the height of the tax revolt. Partly this was because they did not have to at that time, since the massive state surplus still disguised the growing gap between revenue and expenditure. As the consequences of tax reduction and spending limitations are made increasingly visible (a process that will probably continue in California for the foreseeable future), how will voters act when they have to make progressively harder choices between conflicting values and goals? The answer to this question remains up in the air at the moment. When respondents were forced to choose between reduced taxes and current services, most generally opted for maintaining current services. But there are too many uncertainties in the use of these relatively untried survey measures to be extremely confident that this preference will hold as the public is increasingly confronted with such choices in reality.

Part of the clue to the public's preferences lies in their understanding of public services. In analyzing this question, we feel it is helpful to assume that some underlying continuum of attitude objects about government outputs exists, that ranges from the most general and abstract to the most specific and concrete. In our time attitudes toward the most general also seem to be more negative (anti-government) than are the more concrete ones. Which attitudes are to be taken more seriously, because they are stronger and more "real" in some sense, is debatable. We have reason to be skeptical about the simplest and most obvious assumptions one could make, namely that preferences about specific services have some special strength because they are most based in reality or self-interest, or that generalized attitudes about government do because they are more embedded in extensive cognitive structures. Instead, the most parsimonious assumption is that aside from the level of individual concrete experiences with specific agencies, attitudes along this entire continuum have a symbolic quality and are heavily determined by symbolic predispositions.

Political rhetoric operates at each of the five levels of generality from time to time. Conservative Republican rhetoric generally has emphasized such highly general and abstract symbols as a "balanced budget," "smaller government," or "budget cuts." Certainly President Reagan's efforts to gather public support for his economic program in 1981 took this tack. He emphasized gross dollar amounts by which the entire federal budget would be cut, without being publicly specific about the particular service areas to be cut, or the particular programs.

Liberal Democrats, by contrast, have, at least since the New Deal, tended to talk about symbols at the level of specific service areas, invoking such relatively concrete symbols as "the public schools" or "the needy." As we have seen, the public seems to support budget cuts quite strongly when they are advocated in the abstract. And the Democrats in Congress were surprised, dismayed, and routed, during the early months of the Reagan administration's efforts to cut spending, when the debate was fought out at the most abstract level.

While surely the debate will always shift back and forth in level of generality, the serious attempt (both in California and in Washington) to make real budget cuts seems inevitably to focus attention on more specific levels. As in California, the federal budget cuts will ultimately result in actual cutbacks in services. No doubt there will be a lag at the federal level, as well, as programs are gradually phased out. The debate may then shift to what we have called specific service areas (level 3), for example, "too much is being spent on defense" or "the elderly are not being given enough," just as in California outcries have been heard about cutbacks in "the schools" or "the libraries." The debate could also focus on specific programs (level 4), such as interest-free loans to students, subsidies to the elderly poor for their home heating costs, or refitting buses for the handicapped. And it could be that the public generally values government aid to certain service areas, like care of students, the aged, and the handicapped, without any particular affection for the specific programs that are being cut. Indeed, some such programs might be widely viewed as frills, should the public be more fully alerted to them. So what will happen later on, when the public agenda is likely to focus more attention on specific, concrete cuts in programs, is an open question. But to the extent that the focus remains at such generalities as cutting government in the abstract, waste, and budget-balancing, many changes can be made in who gets the benefits and who pays the costs of government, without any very direct public scrutiny of the actual outcomes. And the game can be played out in the abstract, which seems at the present time to be conservative turf.

4

The Vote and the Tax Revolt Schema

The obvious inconsistency between the majority's desires for lower taxes and smaller government and at the same time for increased spending in specific areas held in California throughout the period of the tax revolt. Indeed it prevailed throughout the United States, as best we can tell, for the entire decade of the 1970s. The majority apparently does want something for nothing — or at least more for less. But is the public really as irrational as this suggests?

In this chapter we pursue this question in two ways. First, we have not yet considered Californians' votes on the three tax-reform propositions. These initiatives gave the ordinary citizen a rare chance to have a direct influence on government taxation and spending. Thus they may have elicited more genuine, and therefore more consistent, responses than our more hypothetical survey measures.

Our other attack on this problem begins with a distinction between two different criteria for consistency in public opinion. Up to now we have judged the public's consistency according to absolute standards of realism and logic. That is, are the outcomes desired on each separate item realistic and logically consistent when considered simultaneously? By this standard, the California public (and indeed the national public as well) seems to fall short, because most support seemingly incompatible goals.

But another possible standard of consistency — psychological coherence — may prevail even when logical consistency does not.[1] Individuals may be quite clear about what they want, and have well-informed, stable, and highly organized attitudes about the issues — even when the resulting package seems illogical to outside observers. Alternatively, individuals may be quite confused about the matters at issue, and have poorly informed, unstable, and disorganized attitudes, which also may lead to an illogical total set of aggregate preferences. Psychological consistency has been the subject of a great deal of research in the area of mass political behavior. This work assesses, among other things, the information base, level of abstraction or ideological conceptualization, affective consistency, and stability of an individual's opinions.[2] When a person's attitudes about some topic are well informed, ideologically based, affectively consistent, and stable, they can be characterized, in the language of social psychology, as "schematized." When they are not, the person may be described as "aschematic" with respect to this topic.

In this chapter, then, we look for consistency in the electorate's attitudes about the tax revolt, in two areas. One is their votes on the three tax-revolt initiatives. The other focuses on the five dimensions of attitudes about taxation and spending discussed at length in the previous chapter: preferred size of government, preferences about spending on specific services, perceived magnitude of waste in state and local government, perceived fairness of pay scales for government workers, and subjective tax burden. We attempt to assess consistency within and between these two areas. And we attempt to assess the possibility that the tax revolt elicited widespread schematic thinking about these issues in the mass public.

The Vote

As already indicated, three statewide votes were of central importance in the tax revolt: Proposition 13 and the Gann amendment, which won by better than two to one, and Jarvis II, which failed by a similar margin. It must be remembered that we are using survey data and not actual voting returns to assess the individual's behavior. This always raises a question of validity: how valid are our respondents' reports about their past votes and voting intentions? By and large, the final polls done before each of these elections were quite accurate in forecasting Californians' votes in the tax revolt. Table 2.1 showed that both the California Poll and the *Los Angeles Times* Poll clearly picked up the trend of the landslide switch from Proposition 8 to Proposition 13, though they did underestimate its final magnitude somewhat, probably because they were conducted between a week and two weeks prior to election day. Two weeks before election day, the advantage for Proposition 13 was 10 percent; one week ahead, 30 percent; and on election day, 36 percent. Similarly, when we analyze in more detail the differences among the three propositions (in Chapter 9), it will be seen that the final polls were quite accurate in forecasting those outcomes as well.[3]

The Tax Rebel Index

For analytic purposes we needed an ordinal scale of support for the tax revolt. Hence we constructed the tax rebel index, an additive index devised by assigning respondents a score of $+1$ for each of the three anti-tax propositions they supported at the time of the Tax Revolt Survey, a score of -1 for each proposition opposed, and a score of 0 for an undecided opinion or "don't know" response. By this index, 61 percent were on the pro-revolt side of neutral, and are described as "tax rebels" in the analysis that follows, while 33 percent were on the anti-revolt side of neutral.[4]

This summary index of support for the tax revolt will be our main dependent variable through most of the analysis. We justify this on two grounds. First, attitudes toward the three propositions were reasonably consistent with one another, as we will discuss in more detail later in this chapter. Second, attitudes toward the three propositions were related in much the same way to most of our explanatory variables. Consequently, so was the tax rebel index. This point is most simply made with respect to the attitudes on taxation and spending discussed in Chapter 3. Attitudes toward size of government, specific service spending, waste, overpayment of government workers, and the severity of one's tax burden all correlated positively with support for each proposition, and for the tax rebel composite index, in roughly the same order of magnitude. When separate regression equations are conducted on support for each proposition (using three-way breakdowns of support), very little difference shows up across the propositions. (This will be shown later in table 4.1.) The raw correlations and simple crosstabulations show the same thing. Of course some variables show quite dramatic differences across the propositions—especially those relating to the concrete differences in tax cuts they offered. We will emphasize those differences when they appear in our analysis—especially in Chapters 6 and 9. But for the most part we will use the composite tax rebel index.

Schematic Thinking

The concept of "schema" has not been widely applied to public opinion data. A schema, as we use the term, is a coherent set of attitudes toward the various attitude objects composing a limited area of political life. It is less comprehensive, taking in less political territory, than an "ideology," which may help to cognitively structure most of political life. And schema has more generality than a "symbolic predisposition," which refers to a long-standing evaluation of one particular symbol (or narrow set of very similar symbols).

The concept of schema mainly implies in rather general terms a series of consistency pressures, largely upon memory and other forms of cognitive organization.[5] However, the notion of schema has mainly been used in cognitive and social psychology, up to this point, and mostly in highly artificial, uninvolving laboratory situations. Hence it has usually described a coherent structure containing largely cognitive, nonevaluative beliefs. A schema for an Italian family restaurant might be a good example: posters of Capri, Portofino, and Mt. Vesuvius on the walls, tables with red-checked tablecloths, candles stuck in Chianti bottles. Inconsistencies would stand out (say, posters of Siberia or purple tablecloths), but more because they violate our a priori expectation than because we like them more or less than the other elements. That is, inconsistency is cognitive, rather than affective or evaluative.

However, when we are dealing with strongly held political preferences, inconsistency takes on a more affective flavor. Being a lifelong Republican who disliked Richard Nixon's involvement in Watergate created affective inconsistency, rather than simple cognitive inconsistency. We will return to this conceptual problem at the end of this chapter. But for now we want to note that we have added affective consistency to the description of a schema.[6]

Having a schema about a particular attitude object implies a tendency to think about, and evaluate, that object in terms of a specific set of dimensions, but without necessarily holding any specific set of positions on those dimensions. Applied to the tax revolt, this would imply consistent use of at least the five dimensions treated in Chapter 3: the size of government in general, specific service increases or cuts, perceptions of waste and overpaid government workers, and felt severity of tax burden. And attitudes toward the three Jarvis-Gann ballot measures ought to be consistent with these, as well.

The question of schemas should be distinguished from the question of whether or not specific factions exist; that is, from whether or not many people hold a particular set of consistent attitudes, matching some common a priori cluster. For example, Howard Jarvis held a specific package of beliefs. He believed in public frugality, wanted to cut government back, maybe at the expense of some conveniences, and believed that bureaucrats were paid excessively for some not very demanding work. So a separate question is how many people shared Jarvis's pattern of beliefs; that is, how large was the Jarvisite faction, defined in terms of the particular pattern of attitudes enunciated by its leaders?

Either schematic or aschematic thinking could potentially produce the aggregate-level inconsistency in attitudes toward taxation and spending documented in the last chapter. It is most obvious how such inconsistency could result from generally aschematic individual attitudes — unstable, inconsistent, poorly informed, and at low levels of abstraction. Such mass inconsistency often occurs on issues that are ambiguous, or on which the public has little information, or when the public's strongest predispositions are simply not relevant. A good example is the mass public's attitudes toward foreign policy, which are usually quite inconsistent at any given time, unstable over time, and highly vulnerable to momentary swings in elite postures.[7]

Even when the public's attitudes are highly schematized, its attitudes can look quite inconsistent at the aggregate level. This can happen when the underlying attitudinal dimension is strong and highly stable at the individual level, but different indicators of it tap into it at different thresholds. Here a useful example is racial intolerance in the United States. A wide variety of racial issues all draw from a strong underlying dimension of racial prejudice. They often yield very different aggregate preferences; for example, the white population opposes "busing for racial integration" by about a four-to-one margin, but prefers "desegregation" to "segregation" by about the same margin.[8] So whites' racial attitudes are highly schematized, by all the criteria we have cited, yet they yield seemingly inconsistent aggregate-level outcomes across different issues.

Similarly, in the aggregate the public can look quite inconsistent, even when individuals' attitudes match closely those of factional leaders. This can happen when the public is divided into two passionate and powerful opposed factions, each with stable, consistent, and well-informed attitudes, and a more moderate swing group with more mixed feelings. This group's swings over issues and over time give the aggregate distribution its inconsistent appearance. A good example is the partisan division in the American electorate over the past half-century. "Majority opinion" looks very inconsistent over time, since the Democrats sometimes win huge victories (61 percent in 1964), while the Republicans sometimes win equally overwhelmingly (61 percent in 1972). And it can even look very inconsistent at any given moment when presidential and congressional outcomes conflict; in 1972, the Democrats got 38 percent of the presidential vote and 52 percent of the congressional vote. But all that inconsistency at the aggregate level masks highly stable party identifications at the individual level. And it masks a highly stable aggregate division of underlying loyalties between the two major parties, as well.

The distinction between schematized attitudes and aschematic ones is no idle academic matter. As we have said, we are treating schematized attitudes as those which, on the issue(s) in question, tend to be (1) reasonably well informed, (2) affectively consistent and interdependent, (3) based in some broader, more abstract conceptualization, and (4) stable over time. Empirically these attributes are somewhat, though imperfectly, correlated, but aschematic attitudes generally do not have any of these characteristics.[9]

What political consequences does schematization have? Most obviously, it should trigger pressures toward affective, cognitive, and behavioral consistency with the attitudes in question. Hence the individual should become more resistant to influence, and more likely to deduce attitudes on new issues from pre-existing attitudes, to provide elaborate cognitive rationalizations for existing affective preferences, and to behave consistently with those attitudes.

If the tax revolt reflected predominantly schematized attitudes, then, we should find that the forces on each side tended to become more solidary, with defections harder to come by. Indeed, the tax revolt should be more likely to have a long political life, structured in approximately its current form. It might not be surprising to see it serve as the base for some partisan realignment. If it was not or did not become schematized, it may simply blow off into the wind, as do most issues that do not structure much of the public's thinking.

The next section is devoted to assessing the degree of schematization in the public's thinking about the tax revolt. A "tax revolt schema" would presumably include attitudes toward the various taxation and spending issues we dealt with in the last chapter, as well as attitudes toward the several Jarvis-Gann ballot propositions. Hence we will first test for the tendency to structure political choices along these dimensions. Then we will look for the presence, and assess the size, of particular factions in the California public, especially those matching the Jarvisite, Reaganite beliefs and those of more New Deal–oriented "public-sector defenders." Our ultimate concern will be with where the most political muscle is in the California public, in terms of the distribution of schematized attitudes across the political spectrum. In this connection we will pay particular attention to voting behavior, because these initiative measures allowed the public's voice to become law.

As we do this, our expectations should not be too exalted. Most research on mass publics finds relatively low levels of abstraction and coherence in their political attitudes. However, it is also true that consistency can be much higher within certain narrower areas, especially under conditions of strong information flow. For example, racial attitudes tend to be more organized than most, especially during periods of overt racial conflict, and partisan attitudes do also, especially during election campaigns.[10] So it is plausible that the highly publicized and much-discussed tax revolt developed out of, or generated, highly schematic thinking. And the political effects of highly schematized attitudes could be substantial, as we have already argued. So if a strong tax revolt schema exists, or existed, it could have powerful and enduring effects upon the mass public's political preferences in a wide variety of contexts. Candidates and policymakers would disregard it only at some peril to their own political futures.

The Tax Revolt Schema

We will begin by exploring the question of a tax revolt schema: To what extent did Californians structure their political thinking around the specific dimensions discussed earlier? In the absence of an established technology for assessing schematic thinking in public opinion data, we will try four different approaches: (1) levels of intercorrelation among the several dimensions of attitudes toward taxation and spending, (2) consistency among the votes on the three ballot propositions, (3) the association of the different attitudes toward taxation and spending with voting behavior on the tax-revolt propositions, and (4) a factor analysis of these individual attitudes.

Simple Affective Consistency

One technique for measuring affective consistency stems from the familiar notion of "constraint": simply the extent to which the various attitudes intercorrelate. The Pearson correlations among the five dimensions of attitudes toward taxation and spending range from .39 to .14, with a median of .22. This is about at the same level that Philip Converse reported for domestic-policy attitudes generally in the relatively apolitical 1950s, estimates which formed the basis for a generation of claims that affectively inconsistent thinking prevailed in the mass public.[11] So at first glance the tax revolt seems to follow the familiar model of mass public inconsistency, at the individual level as well as at the aggregate level described earlier.

Attitudes toward the three tax-revolt propositions were much more closely related to one another. We recorded these preferences, expressed as of the time of the Tax Revolt Survey, into pro, uncertain, and con. The gammas for opinions toward Proposition 13 with those toward the later propositions were .56 and .65, and for Gann and Jarvis II, .59. On the average, 62 percent fell on the diagonal, and 23 percent defected from pro to con or vice versa. As of the time of the Tax Revolt Survey, then, responses to the three propositions were quite highly correlated.[12]

More important, how consistent were these attitudes toward taxation and spending with the actual vote? Put another way, how predictable were the vote decisions from these proximal attitudes? First of all, all five of these attitudinal variables did independently contribute to support for the tax revolt. This is shown in table 4.1. This level of consistency is substantial though not overwhelming. The R^2 is 18.9 percent on the tax rebel index (that is, a multiple correlation of .44). These issues did form the main debating ground for the tax-revolt campaigns. If we had expected vote preferences to follow perfectly from these more general attitudes, we would be disappointed by this result. But if we compare this outcome with those from other studies of political opinion, this does represent a moderate level of consistency.

Anticipating some later results, it is useful to distinguish between *value priorities* — the extent to which the respondent wants government to do more or less — and *anti-government attitudes* — the extent to which the respondent perceives government to be inefficient and squandering money. Value priorities had a considerably stronger effect on vote preferences than did the anti-government themes, but all had significant effects. The pattern is quite similar across the several propositions, with a couple of fairly minor exceptions. Personal tax burden was a major issue principally with Jarvis II. But it must be remembered that since tax burden was measured in November 1979, it no longer reflected pre–Proposition 13 property-tax problems. As our later analyses will show, to no one's surprise, Proposition 13's appeal had a lot to do with tax reduction. And the anti-government theme had dropped out of attitudes toward Proposition 13 by eighteen months after its passage, leaving it almost an establishment reform by late 1979, rather than a wild-eyed populist attack on government. But otherwise the pattern is pretty much the same across the board.

In presenting the effects of these five proximate variables upon support for the tax revolt, we have assumed that they only have additive effects. Our initial expectations did include several interaction effects, such as that the impact of wanting additional services would depend on the individual's felt tax burden: wanting more services would have its maximum impact with a low personal tax burden. Or that if someone was strongly opposed to a large role

TABLE 4.1 Impact of attitudes about taxation and spending on the vote.

	Proposition 13 (recalled vote)	Proposition 13 (support)	Gann	Jarvis II	Tax rebel index
Value priorities					
Size of government	.12**	.17**	.12**	.04**	.15**
Service spending	.22**	.23**	.12**	.16**	.19**
Anti-government					
Waste	.04	-.01	.07*	.05*	.12**
Overpaid government workers	.12**	.04	.10**	.10**	.10**
Personal tax burden	.07*	.02	.07*	.18**	.11**
R^2	13.9%	12.2%	9.0%	11.8%	18.9%

Source: Tax Revolt Survey.

Note: Each column represents a single regression equation on the dependent variable shown as column head. The first dependent variable is dichotomous, while the next three are trichotomous, with undecided respondents in the middle. Entries are the standardized regression coefficients. N is 1513 in last column.

*p < .05.
**p < .001.

of the public sector in the society, it might not matter very much whether it was perceived to be efficient or paid fairly. Or that individuals who believed in the possibility of large cuts in spending without any impact on services might simply not see additional taxes as necessary—no matter how willing they said they would be to pay higher taxes *if* they were necessary.

But none of these complex interaction hypotheses were sustained in our data. As a result, we have come to believe that each of these tax- or spending-related measures captures an at least partially independent aspect of the public's decisionmaking with respect to the California tax-revolt propositions, and all five seem to have played a visible role for all citizens—no matter how homogeneous or sharply defined the citizens' attitudes were on the other factors involved.

Similar but modest main effects also emerged from the tradeoff items. Those who were unwilling to pay more taxes to support increased services, or who wanted tax rebates from spending cuts, were each 18 percent more supportive of the tax revolt than were those who came down on the public-sector side of these tradeoff choices (in analyses not shown here).

How is this consistency to be intepreted? Did the voters respond to these decisions with some sensible calculations, given the pattern of their beliefs on taxation and spending? Or does it appear that they responded in a more affective manner to the political symbols presented in these campaigns? The predominance of main effects, rather than interactions, suggests an interpretation of the vote as a rather reflexive response to the relevant affectively loaded symbols, such as "taxes," "big government," "waste," "police," "welfare," and so on. Much evidence suggests that such affects are combined with relatively simple additive or averaging processing principles.[13] So at this stage of the analysis we lean toward this more primitive process in the absence of evidence for more complex, more calculated combining of these various attitudes. We will return at the end of this chapter to this contrast in the possible interpretations of schematic thinking about the tax revolt.

Factor Structure

The tax revolt schema, if it was widespread, should have resulted in more than just a pattern of individual relationships. It would be a very clear packaging of attitudes toward government. Political decisionmakers generally believe that the size of government, spending, waste, and taxes are all functionally related to one another; if one changes, so must the others. Beliefs about one of these topics should imply specific beliefs about most of the others. So if the public is engaging in schematic thinking, we should find evidence of systematic variations in agreement across those several dimensions. Can we find evidence that the public treated the several issues raised by the tax revolt as a total package, and then accepted it, rejected it, or bought about half of it, more or less as a package? That is, did people tend to evaluate incoming information in terms of a common pre-existing network of underlying dimensions of attitudes, even if they did not all share exactly the same position?

To test for this version of schematic thinking, we conducted factor analyses of the five attitudes used in previous analyses (see table 4.1), plus the tax rebel index. Factor analysis is a procedure that extracts the main underlying dimensions from intercorrelations among some given set of individual variables, such as these six. The first stage, a principal components analysis, searches for the degree of clustering among all items. If a common underlying dimension—degree of agreement or disagreement with the tax revolt schema as a whole—underlay the public's attitudes, a principal components factor analysis should show almost all the variance concentrated in a single first factor, on which all these variables should load positively and heavily. If people were responding to them in a more differentiated fashion, as separate dimensions rather than as several facets of a common theme, the variance ought to be more dispersed among several factors, and the variables might load in different ways on any given factor.

A single tax revolt schema comes through loud and clear. As shown in the first column of table 4.2, all six dimensions load heavily on the first factor, and it explains the most variance. This finding justifies our talking about the tax revolt schema as a unified structure of attitudes. Voters varied considerably in their preferences on these dimensions, but they tended to respond to them as a set rather than completely independently.

Did this schema exist primarily among the well-educated, as earlier research by Converse and others would lead us to believe? Not really. The first factor in the principal components analysis explains 93 percent of the variance for the college graduates, and 81 percent for those with no college.

TABLE 4.2 The tax revolt schema: factor analysis.

Factors	Principal Components		Varimax Rotation		
	1	2	1	2	3
Value priorities					
Size of government	**.53**	-.24	**.53**	.11	.24
Service spending	**.69**	-.18	**.61**	.39	.09
Anti-government					
Waste	**.57**	.19	.26	**.51**	.21
Overpaid government workers	**.36**	.20	.11	**.35**	.18
Personal tax burden	**.37**	.15	.14	.24	**.33**
Tax rebel index	**.53**	.03	**.34**	**.26**	**.34**
Eigenvalue	1.63	0.19			
% of variance	85.4	9.8			

Source: Tax Revolt Survey.

Note: Entries are factor loadings.

However, the tax rebel index loads much more highly on the first factor for the college graduates (.71) than for those with no college (.46), indicating that the better-educated respondents embedded their voting preferences more deeply in their general attitudes about taxation and spending than did the less educated. So among the more highly educated there is evidence of somewhat tighter structure and stronger impact of the tax revolt schema upon voting behavior. But schematic thinking about the tax revolt issues seems to have prevailed fairly broadly throughout the California public.[14]

This overall tax revolt schema seems to be composed of two somewhat separate but related versions, one emphasizing value priorities (size of government, increased government spending), and the other, anti-government attitudes (beliefs in high levels of waste and overpaid government workers). This contrast emerges in a fairly weak second factor in the principal components analysis, as shown in the second column of table 4.2. But the varimax rotation of these correlations makes it much more clearly. A varimax rotation is designed to produce as many independent (or "orthogonal") dimensions as possible within this set of intercorrelations. So in this situation where all variables seem to be fairly clear indicators of the same underlying dimension, a varimax rotation will try to force them apart, and emphasize whatever divergences from this unidimensional pattern underlie it. In this case, the varimax rotation emphasizes the independence of the value-priorities dimension from the anti-government dimension (compare the third and fourth columns in table 4.2). That is, preferences about *how much* the public sector should do are to some extent independent of *how well* it does it, in terms of perceived waste and overpayment. And, finally, the varimax rotation also turns up a third separate factor that focuses on personal tax burden.[15] The tax rebel index loaded on all three of these factors, indicating again that the tax revolt drew support from all three sets of dimensions.

The main story, though, is that people tended to evaluate all those elements from the perspective of a general tax revolt schema, as is shown in the principal components analysis. And this gives evidence of reasonably schematized attitudes in the California public. But it is noteworthy that the varimax rotation finds people responding somewhat independently to the three underlying elements of the tax revolt — spending, waste, and taxation — and responding in common to the tax rebel index. That is, attitudes toward the vehicles for the protest — the three ballot propositions — provided the primary "glue" that held together some rather more disparate reactions to government's value priorities, performance, and levels of taxation.

Factions

A second question concerns the extent to which the tax revolt pitted two large and homogeneous factions against each other. This can be tested both in terms of attitudes on taxation and spending, as discussed in Chapter 3, and in terms of votes on the three ballot propositions.

Taxation and Spending: The Pure Types

As we looked for pure factional types on the taxation and spending items, our general strategy was to set up a series of a priori definitions of the Jarvisite and public-sector-defender types, varying from quite restricted to quite relaxed, and then to determine how many respondents fit each of these types. The data are presented in table 4.3, with each column representing a different definition of a "pure type," ranging from the purest Jarvisites at the left, through more mixed definitions, to the purest public-sector defenders at the right.

We defined the purest Jarvisite type as believing in smaller government, wanting net spending cuts on specific services, believing in high levels of government waste, feeling that public-sector workers were paid too much, and feeling that one's own taxes were much too high. As shown in the first column of table 4.3, only 3 percent of the sample met these criteria for being a pure tax rebel (of the 80 percent with complete data on all five dimensions). At the other extreme, only 2 percent were pure defenders of the public sector—wanting larger government and more spending, and believing in little waste, that public employees were paid fairly, and that their own taxes were reasonable. Interestingly enough, much larger numbers of people had *none* of the beliefs defining the pure Jarvisites and public-sector defenders: 17 percent and 11 percent, respectively. This simply emphasizes the relative rarity of these stereotypical types.

We also tested the impact of relaxing the definitional criteria for the two polar types to include individuals with more moderate positions on the component variables. But even with these loosened definitions, relatively few pure types emerged from either faction. For example, we classified as "moderate" tax rebels or public-sector defenders those who met the strict criteria on two dimensions and more relaxed ones on the other three dimensions. But, as shown in the second and sixth columns of the table, this yielded only 8 per-

TABLE 4.3 Frequencies of factional types on taxation and spending issues.

	Extreme tax rebels	Moderate tax rebels	Minimal tax rebels	Inconsistents	Minimal public-sector defenders	Moderate public-sector defenders	Extreme public-sector defenders
Frequencies							
Pure types	3%	8%	19%	28%	19%	8%	2%
One wrong	7	15	27	50	32	22	12
Two wrong	14	22	28	21	26	28	21
Three or four wrong	59	47	27	1	23	35	54
None in common	17	8	—	—	—	6	11
Total	100	100	101	100	100	99	100
Criteria							
Value priorities							
Size of government	smaller	smaller	smaller	smaller	same or larger	same or larger	same or larger
Service spending	cut	net increase of just one	cut welfare at least	increase	same or increase	same or increase	increase
Anti-government							
Waste	almost 20%	at least 10%	at least 10%	[any]	less than 10%	less than 10%	none at all in 2 or 3 areas
Overpaid government workers	too much	too much	[any]	[any]	about right or too little	about right or too little	about right or too little
Personal tax burden	much too much	much or somewhat too much	much or somewhat too much	much or somewhat too much	[any]	about right	about right

Source: Tax Revolt Survey.

Note: Respondents with missing data are omitted from table. These include those missing on at least three of the eight service-spending items, or on at least one of the other dimensions. This constituted 20 percent of the respondents except in column 3, which had 19 percent missing.

cent in either camp. Finally, to turn up "minimal" members of each camp, we let any response at all to one dimension meet the criterion, relaxed three, and kept only one strict definition (on "easy" items: smaller government for the tax rebels, and government workers paid "about right" for the public-sector defenders). As shown in the third and fifth columns, even these most minimal definitions yielded only 19 percent in each camp, which gives some indication of how far away most Californians were from sharing the exact package of attitudes that political leaders enunciated. And it should be remembered that all these estimates ignore the 20 percent of our sample with missing data.

Were that group to be taken into account, only 15 percent of the entire sample would meet even these minimalist criteria on each side.

Our greatest success in finding pure types, ironically enough, came with those who purely embodied the basic *in*consistency described in the last chapter: feeling taxes were too high, wanting smaller government, and wanting net *increases* in spending for specific services. There were 28 percent who thought that way, as shown in the fourth column. The bald truth is that the overwhelming majority of citizens had mixed sentiments about the issues that defined the public debate over the tax revolt. A very large number of California citizens had pro-tax-revolt opinions on some dimensions and anti-tax-revolt opinions on others.

This has several important implications. One is that the stereotypical image of California public opinion at the time of the tax revolt, embodied in the person of Howard Jarvis, was something of a myth. Relatively few people agreed with him in every detail. Another is that the large variety of mixed patterns of attitudes facilitated a flexible, and indeed volatile, response from public opinion as the focal point of the tax revolt moved from issue to issue. And a third is that most people were moderates, on balance, and preferred a blend of outcomes rather than some ideologically pure extreme.

The Vote: The Pure Types

In developing this portrait of ambivalence, inconsistency, and moderation we have not yet considered Californians' votes on the three tax-reform initiatives. Since such votes do influence the way government actually operates, they could conceivably elicit more consistent and sensible responses from the electorate than do the more hypothetical choices offered by attitude questions in a survey. So, the degree of consistency of people's votes on the three propositions is a clue to the existence and relative size of cohesive blocs of opinion favorable and antagonistic to the tax revolt.

We constructed a typology of voters on the basis of their preferences on the three ballot propositions.[16] Table 4.4 shows the patterns of choices among those respondents, classified according to three increasingly permissive standards of voting participation and opinionation. As will prove true throughout our analysis, support for the tax revolt was more intense and steady than opposition sentiment. The numerical superiority of the "consistent rebels" among the active and informed segments of the population is striking: among the voters they outnumbered the so-called public-sector defenders by three to

TABLE 4.4 Typology of opinions on the tax revolt propositions.

Type	Criteria			Frequency		
	Proposi-tion 13 (vote)	Gann amendment (opinion)	Jarvis II (opinion)	Voters only	Opinion-ated only	Full sample
Consistent rebels	yes	yes	yes	45%	47%	36%
Moderate rebels						
Early converts	no	yes	yes	3	5	2
Enough is enough	yes	yes	no	11	15	9
Opponents						
Not going out on a limb	no	yes	no	10	13	13
Disillusioned	yes	no	no	11	4	6
Public-sector defenders	no	no	no	15	12	12
Other						
Mixed	Various other patterns			4	4	4
No opinion	At least two nonresponses			–	–	18
Total				99	100	100
N				487	1033	1668

Bracketed groupings in Frequency columns: Consistent rebels + Moderate rebels = 59% (Voters only), 67% (Opinionated only), 47% (Full sample). Opponents = 36 (Voters only), 29 (Opinionated only), 31 (Full sample).

Source: Tax Revolt Survey.

Note: "Voters only" includes only those who said they had voted on Propositions 13 and 4. "Opinionated only" includes only those who expressed definite opinions on all three propositions. The full sample includes all respondents, and assigns those with only one nonresponse to the most appropriate row.

one—45 percent to 15 percent.[17] And adding in the more ambivalent respondents on each side reinforces the impression of rebel strength; the margin becomes 59 percent to 36 percent.

The distribution of opinion becomes somewhat less favorable to the tax revolt as one moves from the most active and informed section of the electorate to the entire public. Including all those who had opinions on all three propositions, whether or not they voted in the two elections that had already been held, still shows the consistent rebels to dominate by more than three to one. But when we expand the portion of the sample under consideration to include respondents who held opinions on only two of the three initiatives, in the final column of the table, the consistent rebels decline to only 36 percent of the total, and the total number of rebels exceeds the number of opponents by only about a three-to-two margin.

The large number of consistent rebels among the voters, then, contrasts quite strongly with the small number of pure Jarvisites as defined by their more general attitudes toward taxation and spending (see table 4.3), and a considerably smaller number of consistent rebels in the population as a whole. This yields two important conclusions. The seemingly overwhelming support given the tax revolt, at least in its early stages, was somewhat exaggerated by virtue of its supporters' greater tendency to turn out and vote. And support for the tax revolt as indexed by preferences on the ballot propositions much overestimates support for the more concrete policies it embodied. In reality, the adult population as a whole had much more mixed attitudes than was reflected by the narrower subgroup of steady voters' support for the tax revolt initiatives.

Initiative to the Tax Rebels

Through most of the tax revolt, the tax rebels were on the offensive and the public-sector defenders on the defensive. As with any initiative campaign in California, the original impetus for the revolt had come from the rebels, who had collected a large number of signatures on petitions to put their propositions on the ballot. The advantage remained with the rebels through most of the Proposition 13 campaign, and in the late stages they collected more money, enjoyed a huge surge of support, and gained the ascendancy in political debate. There also followed an apparent groundswell of support for conservative, tax-revolt-like policies across the nation. This helped sweep Ronald Reagan into the White House and left liberal Democrats apparently floundering, without ideas for regaining mass popularity.

This imbalance in political thrust is a theme that recurs throughout our data. It manifests itself in several ways that are relevant to this chapter. First of all, the tax rebels felt more intensely about the cost of government than did supporters of the public sector: 32 percent of those supporting all three antitax issues named high taxes as the main problem facing Californians and an additional 12 percent complained about the size of government. Among those rejecting Propositions 13, 4, and 9, the comparable proportions were only 10 percent and 4 percent respectively. The imbalance also manifests itself in more schematic thinking on the part of the tax rebels than among public-sector defenders. After all, if tax reductions and the limitation of the public sector are ideas whose time has come, it makes sense that their enthusiasts should show more organized, structured thinking than the embattled defenders of old, outdated solutions, who have supposedly lost confidence in their own guiding precepts. To test this, we simply compared the top (tax rebels) and bottom (public-sector defenders) quartiles on our tax rebel scale in terms of constraint and tightness of factor structure. The tax rebels did, in fact, think more schematically. The mean interitem correlation among this group was almost twice as high, and the mean factor loading was considerably higher as well (.47 versus .36).[18]

The pro–Proposition 13 forces turned out to vote more than did its opponents. In August 1978 the California Poll found that 67 percent of those who claimed to have voted favored Proposition 13, compared to 60 percent of nonvoters. At the time of the Tax Revolt Survey, those who had voted supported it by 73 percent (of those with opinions) whereas only 60 percent of the nonvoters did. But this same advantage for the rebels did not hold very markedly for either of the other two initiatives. The Tax Revolt Survey found that 68 percent of those who claimed to have voted supported the Gann initiative, compared to 72 percent of the nonvoters. People who had voted on both Proposition 13 and Gann did support Jarvis II by 6 percent more than nonvoters. But in May 1980, just before the balloting, 31 percent of registered voters expressed an intention to support Jarvis II, compared to 29 percent of the unregistered. Thus on these last two the actual vote was broadly representative of public opinion at the time of the vote. And though Proposition 13 was strongly advantaged by greater turnout among its supporters, it had a clear majority even among nonvoters. So turnout differences did advantage the rebels, but given that the margin of victory in all three contests was so decisive, the results would have been the same had every eligible citizen voted.

The tax revolt generated a high level of citizen participation, even by the standards of the most visible and hotly contested partisan elections. As table 4.5 shows, 69 percent had discussed the revolt with friends, and 30 percent had signed a petition concerning taxes and spending in the previous two years.[19] The four items in table 4.5 not concerned with voting were added to form a "tax activism" scale; on it, 32 percent reported no activity at all, and 42 percent discussion only, while 27 percent engaged in discussion plus some other activity.

Again, tax rebels display a higher level of activation: 45 percent of this group compared to 28 percent of the public-sector defenders had done more

TABLE 4.5 Participation in the tax revolt.

	Total sample	Tax rebel index				
		Strong pro-revolt	Moderate pro-revolt	Neutral	Moderate anti-revolt	Strong anti-revolt
Voted on both 13 and 4	32%	44%	28%	12%	23%	46%
Talked to friend	69	79	66	54	66	80
Active beyond talking to friend	28	28	18	10	24	44
Signed petition	30	46	27	12	18	20
Wrote letter	14	16	13	7	13	21
Gave money	13	22	10	6	5	14
N	1634	489	507	169	346	123

Source: Tax Revolt Survey.

Note: The entry is the percentage active in the tax revolt in the manner specified, in the full sample (column 1) and at each level of the tax rebel index (columns 2-6).

than merely discussing the initiatives with a friend. This difference in involvement is largely a function of the greater use of petitions by the advocates of cutting taxes. In fact, table 4.5 shows that the few anti-revolt extremists were slightly *more* likely than the strong tax rebels to vote on both Propositions 13 and 4. In general, though, the strength of the movement to contain the fiscal powers of government in California has rested on the larger number of voters sympathetic to its goals willing to give active and steady support.[20]

Conclusions

How affectively consistent were the California voter's attitudes about the tax revolt? We have approached this question from three points of view: how schematized the public's attitudes were (both about the underlying issues of taxation and spending and about the three ballot propositions); how many voters shared the particular clusters of attitudes held by the leadership elites on both sides; and whether the attitudinal and behavioral thrust was more powerful on the pro-revolt side than among its opponents.

We did find evidence for a reasonably widespread tax revolt schema. A factor analysis yielded a common first factor, binding together support for the tax-revolt ballot propositions, reduced service spending, opposition to big government and to high taxes, and beliefs in high levels of waste and excessively high pay scales in government. Further analysis revealed some differentiation between value priorities (essentially the size and level of responsibility of the public sector), perceived government performance (waste and overpaid public-sector workers), and tax burden. Support for the three Jarvis-Gann ballot propositions was the strongest glue holding all these elements together. But the main finding was of a single tax revolt schema bound together by common affects toward all its elements.

Many political observers had concluded that large numbers of Californians — perhaps a majority — shared the main beliefs enunciated by Howard Jarvis toward taxation and spending — about taxes and spending being too high, government too large and inefficient, and so on. Upon careful examination, though, only a rather small minority held this particular configuration of beliefs, even when it was defined quite loosely. Nor did many pure public-sector defenders exist. In contrast, large numbers of respondents held a pure version of the basic inconsistency elaborated in the last chapter — wanting lower taxes, less government, more services. In general, the clearest finding was that most Californians held mixed beliefs on these dimensions. Consequently, most were, on balance, moderates with respect to the constituent elements of the tax revolt schema.

Can the votes on the three ballot propositions legitimately be interpreted as tests of the voters' confrontations with the hard choices of taxes versus services? Only in a limited way, from the evidence presented in this chapter. The voters seemed to have responded in a rather reflexive way to the affective symbols of the tax revolt. All elements — waste, smaller government, cutting services, overpaid bureaucrats, excessive taxation — contributed in a simple manner (linear, noninteractive) to electoral support for the tax revolt. There was little evidence of widespread complex reasoning about the interrelationships among these ingredients of the revolt. *Affective* consistency, rather than some more cognitive economic calculus, bound these several beliefs together. That is, voters tended to have consistent affective responses to the visible symbols of the tax revolt: "taxes," "waste," "bureaucrats," "government," "spending," and the ballot propositions. This is not to say that supporters and opponents lined up in two neatly divided camps. But their attitudes toward any given symbol of the tax revolt were reasonably predictable from their other attitudes toward the revolt.

Three additional points should be made about the psychological processes implied by this analysis. First of all, the various elements of the tax revolt set quite different thresholds. It was "easy" to be for smaller government, to believe in a lot of waste, and vote for the Gann amendment; it was "hard" to be for cutting specific services or to vote for Jarvis II. As a consequence, even a moderately high level of affective consistency resulted in quite a mélange of configurations of belief, considering all the elements of the revolt.

A second point concerns the process by which these various elements were combined. Two contrasting possibilities suggest themselves. If highly cognitive, logical, quasifinancial calculations were being made by very many people, these attributes would interact with each other rather than being related according to simple main effects. For example, the effects of service-spending preferences on voting behavior ought partly to depend, logically, on felt tax burden; they should have a stronger effect when one's tax burden is felt to be reasonable, because then resistance to taxes is not itself such a strong factor. On the other hand, if the dominant mode of response to the tax revolt consisted of simple affective responses to its various symbols, we would expect a simpler combinatorial principle. An averaging model would seem most likely. By this principle, the response to two or more symbols in combination is predictable from the average of the valences placed upon each separately. A respondent who feels extremely burdened by taxes, but wants more services, should be about neutral on the tax rebel scale, because the two attitudes are offsetting. But a respondent who hates both taxes and service spending should be a strong rebel, since both symbols separately attract pro-revolt valences. Hence this process by which affects are simply averaged would predict that all these attitudes would relate to each other via main effects rather than interactions.[21]

And in fact that is exactly what the data show. We found that these attitudes relate to one another via simple main effects rather than through interactions. This was clear in the interrelationships of the several attitudes toward taxation and spending shown in the preceding chapter (see tables 3.4 and 3.5), and in the relationships of these attitudes to the vote (see table 4.1).

A third point has to do with our treatment of a schema as a cluster of affectively consistent attitudes, rather than as something more cognitive. We should make explicit this departure from current usage in social psychology. To us it seems justified if the schema notion is to be applied to cognitive contents that have strong emotional feeling attached to them. The psychological processes invoked by the notion of a schema should be similar, but as responses to affective inconsistency as well as to disconfirmed expectations and other cognitive inconsistencies.

The relatively high degree of consistency and factionalization that characterized the public's attitudes toward the tax-revolt propositions was not so evident in more general attitudes toward taxation and spending. The tax revolt was, in this respect, quite similar to other protest movements. It is often true that support for a movement is much more consistent and coherent than are attitudes toward its constituent goals. This was true, for example, of the followers of Father Charles Coughlin and Senator Joseph McCarthy on the right, and of the supposedly antiwar followers of Senator Eugene McCarthy on the left. And at a milder level it has also been true of the followings of many presidential candidates. Support for the candidate frequently is stronger, more stable, and more consistent than support for the candidate's policy program.[22]

Similarly, it is likely that the conservative mood of the United States today, manifested in the landslide electoral victory of Ronald Reagan, is not as strongly based in conservative thinking on the many more general issues underlying its policy choices. Support for President Reagan himself, and for the most abstract and vague goals his administration espouses (such as "getting government off the back of the people"), probably do not reflect comparably strong support for the more detailed cuts being made in the federal budget.

We have found no evidence of any new majority in California that shares Howard Jarvis's beliefs in detail—no suggestion that large numbers of people are swinging to conservative, anti-public-sector beliefs. Such a trend would make good media copy, but the copy would be wrong. Instead, inconsistencies and idiosyncratic mixes of beliefs leave most Californians, on balance, somewhere in the middle. Their attitudes mostly tend to cancel out. They are mostly moderates on matters of taxation and spending.

But—and a very important "but" it is—such idiosyncratic mixes of attitudes also produce a high level of malleability in the California electorate. The public agenda changes rapidly, sometimes because of larger economic or political forces (such as the disappearance of the state surplus) and sometimes because of faddism and short attention spans in the media (such as the disappearance of Howard Jarvis as a folk hero). Such agenda shifts can quickly bring new symbols to front and center and alter the coalitions supporting and opposed to any given policy. If the property tax, for example, gets a lot of publicity, attitudes toward it will influence other political choices.

This implies that a majority coalition can form in response to new information because it can pick up a wide variety of supporters. But it also makes majority opinion highly volatile. We will consider this in much more detail in Chapter 9, in contrasting the landslides for and against Propositions 13 and 9. For now, the point is that the absence of pure types, and the presence of many mixed types, promotes just such wild swings in majority opinion. John Mueller made an analogous point in his excellent study of Californians' voting on ballot propositions: "passage or defeat of any given proposition is due to the combined efforts of a body of voters who are quite unlike in their voting on other ballot measures."[23]

Nevertheless, as we have noted at several junctures, the tax rebels seemed politically stronger than the opposition. Not only were they more numerous, they were also more consistent in their vote preferences, more schematized in their attitudes, more concerned about problems of taxation and spending, more likely to turn out to vote, and somewhat more active in the tax-revolt campaigns. It would be premature for us to try to explain this imbalance, but it is worth mentioning the main possibilities. It could simply be that the tax rebels were of more favored social backgrounds, and hence displayed the higher levels of politicization characteristic of such persons. The next chapter will address that question. Or it could be part of some longer historical cycle, by which initiative and energy seem to swing rather regularly from right to left and back again.[24]

Whatever the reason, their superior political strength no doubt contributed to the general overestimation of the number of pure Jarvisites. In somewhat the same way that the Goldwater campaign overestimated the number of pure conservatives in 1964, the tax rebels, being more politicized and more vocal, were more visible to political observers than were their opponents.[25]

5

The Social Base

Why did Californians vote as they did on the three tax-revolt propositions? Why did they develop the attitudes and perceptions about taxes, spending, and government that presumably determined how they would vote? And what led them to campaign for the propositions? We begin our attempt to answer these questions by describing the social composition of the tax revolt — that is, by asking which social groups supported it most and which opposed it most.

Support for the Tax Revolt

A number of plausible hypotheses have been suggested about the social characteristics that might have led people to favor or oppose the tax revolt. Each of these ideas can be reviewed, and its predictions tested, in terms of the standard demographic variables used in political surveys. Our general strategy will be to look at the relationship of each demographic variable to Californians' support for the three propositions at the key points in the development of the tax revolt, using the following sources of data: (1) the last California Poll before the success of Proposition 13 (late May 1978); (2) the first post–Proposition 13 California Poll (August 1978); (3) a sampling of Californians as part of the 1978 University of Michigan election study (CPS/NES; November 1978); (4) our own Tax Revolt Survey (November 1979); (5) and (6) the final two California Polls just before the demise of Jarvis II (April and May 1980); and (7) the tax rebel scale from our own survey, as a summary measure of support for the tax revolt as a whole.

Class Conflict

Most obviously, given the state government's emphasis on services to disadvantaged citizens, the tax revolt might reflect some form of class conflict. Any
proposition that so clearly benefits the propertied or high-income classes
should be expected to draw disproportionate support from them, and opposition from less-privileged groups. We can identify two alternative versions of
this frequently mentioned possibility. Simple *class conflict* based on direct
economic self-interest is the more familiar and plausible. According to this
straightforward hypothesis, more affluent Californians would benefit most
from tax reductions, and would be little affected by cuts in public services,
which they are not very dependent on. The poor, by contrast, pay little in
property or income taxes and would be more likely to be the direct victims of
service cuts. Hence, these two groups should diverge on proposals to cut
taxes, with middle-income groups taking an intermediate position.

The notion of a *middle mass* is a qualification or complication of the simple class-conflict hypothesis. In this view, the most affluent, upper-status people are especially public-regarding, and therefore join with the low-status
direct recipients of services in opposing tax reductions. As a result, the tax
revolt is primarily supported by the remaining "middle mass," which feels
overburdened by rising taxes and resentful of the free ride lower-status people seem to be getting, such as people on welfare who could work, or the beneficiaries of affirmative action. Group differences of this sort presumably represent a blend of economic self-interest and symbolic politics: the affluent upper class should respond symbolically rather than selfishly by supporting the
idea of good government instead of seeking to reduce their own tax burdens;
lower classes should respond selfishly, by seeking to perpetuate the governmental programs that benefit them directly; and the middle class should respond both selfishly and symbolically, wanting their taxes reduced and wanting more traditional values (such as thrift and hard work) to guide government policies toward the poor and minorities.

To test these two versions of the class-conflict hypothesis, we used the standard three measures of class or status: income, education, and occupation
(though occupation is not available in our own Tax Revolt Survey). And indeed, the data showed that high-income Californians were generally much
more supportive of the tax revolt. Table 5.1 shows this relationship for the entire period under consideration. Income is linearly related to support for the
tax revolt; the intermediate groups fall in order between the extreme ones. Income differences are strongest for Proposition 13 just before that election, and

TABLE 5.1 Social class and race correlates of support for the tax revolt.

Characteristics	Proposition 13				Gann	Jarvis II			Tax rebel index	% in sample
	May 1978	Aug. 1978	Nov. 1978	Nov. 1979	Nov. 1979	Nov. 1979	April 1980	May 1980		
Income										
<$10,000	52%	62%	79%	57%	76%	50%	39%	26%	52%	26%
$11-20,000	59	61	65	64	80	51	46	37	61	30
$21-30,000	67	66	85	72	81	52	47	39	63	22
>$30,000	69	67	74	79	80	55	55	41	69	22
Difference	+17	+ 5	- 5	+22	+ 4	+ 5	+16	+15	+17	
Education										
Less than high school	74	64	68	64	76	59	59	44	58	16
High school	68	72	86	68	83	54	45	40	60	34
Some college	64	66	66	66	82	55	47	36	65	26
College grad	69	60	69	75	77	44	54	36	62	16
Beyond college	45	53		72	69	36	39	27	58	8
Difference	-29	-11	+ 1	+ 8	- 7	-23	-20	-17	0	
Race										
White	66	68	na	71	81	55	49	39	64	80
Hispanic	60	54	na	59	80	47	54	36	53	13
Black	18	40	na	41	59	40	30	20	39	6
Difference	+48	+28		+30	+22	+15	+19	+19	+25	

Sources: California Polls; CPS 1978 election study; Tax Revolt Survey.

Note: Entries are percentages of those with a definite opinion supporting specified proposition, except in the case of the tax rebel index, where the entries are the percentages who favored more of the three propositions than they opposed.

then again eighteen months later, and strongest for Jarvis II just before its defeat. They are weakest for Proposition 13 after its victory, and for the Gann amendment. But income maintains a reasonably strong and consistent effect, as summarized in the column reporting our tax rebel index.

Education seems at first glance to have had rather inconsistent effects, none very compatible with a class-conflict theory. In six of the polls shown in the table, it had a negative effect on support (more education was associated with *less* support for the tax revolt); in only two cases did it have a positive effect, and even then the effect was weak.

But income and education are sufficiently highly correlated ($r = .41$ in our survey) that their effects need to be considered simultaneously. And doing so simplifies the picture considerably. Regressions were run at each time-point on each tax measure shown in table 5.1, with both education and income as predictors. As it turns out, education contributed to opposition to the tax revolt, and income to support for it. Working in opposite directions, they suppress each other's effect. When both are included in regression equations, both effects are clarified, so that in all cases income had a positive and significant effect, and education had a negative effect (though it was not significant in the last two Proposition 13 surveys). However, these are mainly rather small effects. For income the median beta was .15, and for education, $-.07$; the median R^2 was 2.1 percent. So these effects are rather consistent in direction, but weak. And in any case their contrasting directions argue against a simple class-conflict explanation.

Education had its strongest negative effects just before the voting on the most radical propositions—Proposition 13 and Jarvis II. We might speculate that the highly educated were somewhat nervous about these rather radical plans, with their largely unforeseeable consequences. Indeed, those with advanced degrees were by far the most opposed of all. For example, in May 1978 only 45 percent of those who had gone beyond college supported Proposition 13, and in April 1980 only 39 percent supported Jarvis II, both far below the majority support given these propositions even by college graduates (69 percent and 54 percent respectively).

But after election day passed and business went on pretty much as usual, perhaps they relaxed. Indeed, when we looked at changes over time in support for Proposition 13 (crosstabulating education and income together, because of their correlation), the highly educated were the ones who changed most over time. In the Tax Revolt Survey, when recalled vote was compared with current opinion toward Proposition 13, support increased among those with college degrees at all six income levels, by from 6 percent to 17 percent. At only one other combination of education and income did support for Proposition 13 increase over this time span. The same picture emerges from comparing the last pre-election California Poll with our survey eighteen months later; those with college degrees increased support for Proposition 13 at all four income levels (though in this case support increased in about half the other combinations of education and income as well).[2]

What about the middle-mass theory? The main effects of income were invariably linear, increasing monotonically, throughout the income range, so there were none of the obvious curvilinear patterns predicted by the middle-mass notion. Table 5.1 shows that the same was true for education, though the pattern is a little muddier. Nor did looking at income and education jointly improve the case for this theory. In all the surveys we considered, the middle mass—defined as high school graduates or those with some college with income from \$11,000 to \$25,000 per year—showed patterns virtually identical to those for the sample as a whole.[3] Occupation did show some evidence of the middle-mass effect, however. In the two California Polls for which occupational measures were available (May and August 1978), support for Proposition 13 was by far the strongest among middle-status occupations: sales and skilled workers. It was weakest among the professional-technical class, and then again at the bottom of the social ladder (operatives, service workers, and laborers). Managerial and clerical workers fell in between.

In short, higher-income people were more likely to support the tax revolt, but people with higher education were more likely to be opposed to it. This does not square with a simple notion of class conflict. Such findings are, however, consistent with a blend of two other interpretations: that higher income produced support for the revolt because of self-interest, and that higher educational and occupational status promoted symbolic opposition to it because of some public-regarding sympathy for governmental activity in general. We will return later to more pointed tests of these interpretations. In any case we found only weak evidence of any special enthusiasm for the revolt among the middle mass.

Racial Conflict

After Proposition 13 passed, some liberals charged that support for the measure was simply another form of disguised racism—that it represented the desire of affluent whites to cut social programs and monies available to the poor, but especially to blacks. It is true that whites were much more likely to support the tax revolt than blacks, as shown in table 5.1. The racial difference varies in size over time, but is always substantial. Indeed, during the period of our study, blacks were the *only* social group in which a majority consistently opposed the tax-revolt propositions. Although white voters varied significantly in their response to the tax revolt, blacks were staunch opponents; as a group, they supported only the Gann amendment. It might be noted that California's large Hispanic population was only slightly less supportive of the tax revolt than Anglos were. This is a fairly standard finding in California, where Hispanics usually exhibit political attitudes somewhere between those of white and black citizens, but closer to whites.

Generational Conflict

For several reasons, it seems reasonable to expect older people to have been more supportive of the tax revolt. Their self-interest was potentially more at stake, since they were more likely to be homeowners and less dependent on such government services as the public schools. Furthermore, older people are more often Republican and conservative. In fact, however, the middle-aged (50–64) were the most supportive of the tax revolt, with opponents most numerous among the young, as shown in table 5.2. Intermediate age-groups showed intermediate levels of support. Additionally, support dropped off a little among those of retirement age. Such age differences are quite marked in almost all of our surveys, and this curvilinear pattern is fairly consistent throughout the period.

TABLE 5.2 Other demographic correlates of support for the tax revolt.

Characteristics	Proposition 13				Gann	Jarvis II			Tax rebel index	% in sample
	May 1978	Aug. 1978	Nov. 1978	Nov. 1979	Nov. 1979	Nov. 1979	April 1980	May 1980		
Age										
18-24	49%	50%	66%	53%	76%	43%	48%	31%	49%	14%
25-34	56	59	70	62	81	48	41	38	56	28
35-49	62	64	79	74	79	54	45	37	66	25
50-64	71	73	74	78	83	61	56	43	68	19
65+	69	78	93	70	77	59	53	36	63	14
Difference	+20	+28	+27	+17	+ 1	+16	+ 5	+ 5	+14	
Region										
Bay Area	64	63	na	61	75	45	40	35	53	24
Other Northern California	59	58	na	66	81	49	48	32	60	22
Other Southern California	58	64	na	70	79	58	50	40	62	17
LA-Orange Counties	66	68	na	73	82	58	52	39	66	38
Difference	+ 2	+ 5	na	+12	+ 7	+13	+12	+ 4	+13	
Sex										
Male	66	67	80	71	79	56	52	40	65	46
Female	59	63	68	63	80	50	40	33	57	54
Difference	+ 7	+ 4	+12	+ 8	÷ 1	+ 6	+12	+ 7	+ 8	

Note: See table 5.1 for sources and description of entries.

Region

The state of California is geographically quite variegated, ranging from the rocky coast of the north to the beaches of the south, from high Sierras to desert wastelands, from the fertile agricultural valleys in the center of the state to the large metropolitan areas around San Francisco Bay and Los Angeles. The major political cleavage, which has been evident since the creation of the state, divides Northern from Southern California. Usually these regions are defined as being separated by the Tehachapi Mountains, which run across the state in an east-west direction just below Bakersfield, at the southern end of the San Joaquin Valley, reaching the coast in the vicinity of Santa Barbara. Sometimes the conflict revolves around practical issues on which the two regions' interests diverge, such as water supply. And sometimes it shows up on moral issues, such as prohibition, pornography, or fair housing.[4] In general, Southern California has been somewhat more conservative than Northern California, though almost as strongly Democratic. So it is a reasonable supposition that the more conservative political culture in the southern part of the state would yield more support for the tax revolt there.

And this expectation is generally supported by the data: the tax revolt received consistently greater support in Southern California. The Bay Area was the region most opposed to the tax revolt, consistent with its generally liberal history. However, the strongest support for the tax revolt, unlike that for past conservative causes, was located in the Los Angeles metropolitan area, rather than in the outlying, less urbanized reaches of Southern California. This contrast is shown in table 5.2. As we will see in later chapters, this regional difference holds up quite strongly when all other important causes of tax-revolt support are held constant simultaneously. Thus, any argument that greater support for the tax revolt in the south should be attributed to that region's distinctive political culture must be complex enough to explain why that culture's impact cannot be explained with standard attitudinal measures. Instead, we will focus on the role of political events in Los Angeles—specifically, the great property reassessment gaffes of May 1978—in influencing the way voters in that metropolitan area perceived the tax revolt. And we will explore the possibility that the unique aspects of Southern California's support for the tax revolt had their major impact on the youngest group of voters—that is, that political culture most strongly affected those with least political experience.

Sex Differences

Men consistently showed more support for the tax revolt than did women, as shown at the bottom of table 5.2. As will be seen in the next chapter, the two sexes do differ in their potential self-interests in the revolt. Men feel more burdened by taxes, and have higher incomes, more education, and higher employment rates. Women benefit more from government services, since they more often rely on government assistance, more often have responsibility for children in the public schools, and are more worried about their financial situations. But these factors do not wholly account for the special attraction of the tax revolt for men. For example, men are more likely to support tax-revolt propositions among homeowners and renters alike, and even after income, public-sector employment, service dependency, and parenthood are all controlled. So other explanations for these sex differences must be explored.

Confounds and Interactions

We have identified significantly greater support for the tax revolt among those who were high-income, less educated, middle-occupational-status, middle-aged, white, male, and/or living in Southern California. These findings do not by themselves resolve the basic question of the relative contributions of self-interest and symbolic predispositions, because people in these social categories tend (with some exceptions) both to have the most to gain selfishly from tax reductions and to be most conservative politically in general. But before we move on to that analytic conundrum, a necessary next step is to determine how robust these demographic differences are. Do they need to be substantially qualified because of confounds or interactions among the demographic factors?

The question of confounds can be resolved by use of multiple regression. As it turns out, each of these effects holds up on the tax rebel scale even with all demographics considered. This is shown in table 5.3. For example, the apparent effect of race remains just as strong with income controlled; blacks were 32 percent and 24 percent more opposed to Proposition 13 than whites in the two lowest income levels ($0–5000, and $5–10,000).[5] Only the effect of education is significantly altered; as mentioned before, it is suppressed by its correlation with income. Consequently, in the multiple regression equation it is shown to have a reliable negative relationship with support for the revolt.

TABLE 5.3 Summary regression analyses: effects of demographic factors.

Demographic factors	Support for tax revolt					Issue public		Tax revolt schema				Participation	
	Tax rebel index	Proposition 13 (recalled vote)	Proposition 13 (support)	Gann amendment	Jarvis II	Issue salience	Opinionation	Size of government	Service spending	Waste	Overpaid government workers	Vote frequency	Tax activism
Income (high)	.12**	.12	.15**	.05	.05	.06	.06	.14**	.17**	.03	.04	.13**	.17**
Education (high)	-.08*	-.23**	-.03	-.09*	-.13**	-.06*	.11**	.06*	.04	-.01	-.03	.24**	.21**
Race (white)	.12**	.07*	.09**	.09*	.09**	.05	.06*	.21**	.16**	.12**	.06*	.07*	.11**
Age to 65 (old)	.14**	.13**	.15**	.03	.10**	.11**	.03*	.15*	.11**	-.08*	-.01	.34**	.11**
Elderly (old)	.03	.05	.04	-.03	.02	-.01	-.03	.04	.07*	-.09*	.02	.28*	.03
Region (L.A.)	.11**	.07*	.10**	.05	.10**	-.03	.03	-.01	-.03	-.03	.01	-.04	-.01
Sex (male)	.07*	.08*	.08*	-.01	.07*	.05	.08*	.06*	.05*	-.01	.02	-.02	.08**
R²	.077	.087	.084	.018	.047	.027	.047	.135	.101	.027	.007	.290	.156

Source: Tax Revolt Survey.

Note: Each column describes a separate regression analysis on the variable in the column heading. Entries are betas. A positive entry indicates an association between the demographic characteristic cited and pro-revolt attitudes and behavior.

*p < .05.
**p < .001.

Nor in most cases did these demographic factors interact with each other. Interactions were tested for by rerunning this basic regression among respondents above and below the median on each of the other demographic variables. Income and education had a slightly stronger effect among the young than among the old, and education among residents of Los Angeles County, but otherwise income, education, age, and race did not interact with other variables.

Two sets of interesting interactions did appear. Among women, those whose life circumstances most fit the traditional female sex role supported the tax revolt most. Put another way, the most traditionally feminine women, those who were older, low-income, poorly educated, renters, and housewives, most resembled men in support for the tax revolt. In contrast, men and women differed most among the young, high-income, highly educated, homeowners, and employed fulltime. This set of interactions could stem from the greater independence of younger, better-educated, employed, and so on women, who do not conform as much to norms set by men. Or it could stem from more specifically liberal, pro-public-sector political attitudes in this more "modern" group of women, who may in many ways not share the more traditional and conservative attitudes of more old-fashioned women. We will take up this question in more detail in Chapter 10.

A second set of interactions concerns region. The north-south split shows up most vividly among the least politicized social groups: women, the young, and those with lower incomes and the least education. For example, 67 percent of the young people (18–24) in the Los Angeles metropolitan area supported the tax revolt, whereas only 26 percent of the young in the Bay Area did, a difference of 41 percent. This difference did not exceed 13 percent in any other age-group. People in these less politicized groups tend to have relatively weak political predispositions, and therefore should be particularly vulnerable to pressures to conform. We will later look at how different age-groups responded to the different political events occurring across the state in the tax revolt.

Changes in the Social Base?

We have described the massive support for Proposition 13 which developed quickly in the middle of the campaign, the overwhelming support for the Gann amendment, and the resounding defeat of Jarvis II, even though it too promised a healthy return to the taxpayer and was sponsored by much the same group of backers that won so convincingly on the other occasions. Were some social groups particularly responsible for that change? Put another way, did some social groups fall off the tax-revolt bandwagon more resoundingly than others?

The answer to this question seems to be clearly negative. Generally speaking, Jarvis II seems to have lost support (from the majorities for Propositions 13 and 4) across the board, rather than in easily identified social groups. Comparing the final pre–Proposition 13 California Poll (May 1978) with the final pre–Jarvis II equivalent (May 1980), tables 5.1 and 5.2 show large defections from the Proposition 13 majority in every social group. The only real exception was blacks, few of whom supported either proposition (18 percent and 20 percent).

This constancy of demographic differences does conceal one major change, namely the change in the base of support for Proposition 13 during the months after it passed. Highly educated people became much more enthusiastic about it following its passage and early implementation, as shown in table 5.1. Meanwhile, it lost some support among less-educated people. Taking income into consideration further elaborates this finding, since low-income people also moved against it and high-income people toward it. As we have already suggested, the well-educated may have initially been skeptical of such a radical tax cut, and then relaxed when it turned out not to have disastrous consequences (mainly because of the state surplus). Or perhaps self-interest-based class conflict emerged when everyone concerned began to realize that it especially benefited the wealthier and propertied classes. In any case, the consolidated support for Proposition 13 was evidently not transferable to Jarvis II, about which the well-educated resumed their skeptical posture, as shown in table 5.1.

Finally, it should be noted that, taken together, these six demographic factors (excluding occupation, which is not available in our survey) do not have an overwhelmingly strong impact on support for the revolt. The R^2 is only 7.7 percent, and the betas range from .07 to .14. Any effort to explain the tax revolt in terms of conflicts between social groups encounters the very formidable obstacle that these groups simply did not differ enormously.

The Tax Revolt Issue Public

Was the issue public for the tax revolt concentrated in any particular demographic location? We have several ways of approaching this question, and they yield somewhat different answers. First of all, attention to the tax revolt, like support for it, was only modestly related to social factors. Since tax-related issues were major sources of controversy for over two years, it is not surprising that at least minimal levels of attention were present in all social groups. For example, citing taxation and spending as the most important issue facing California (issue salience) and having definite opinions on the three propositions (opinionation) were not especially related to any demographic factors ($R^2 = 2.7$ and 4.7 percent, respectively, as shown in table 5.3). And the 41 percent of the public who talked to their friends about the tax revolt (but took no other action besides voting) were distributed evenly through all social groups.

A second criterion for being in the tax revolt issue public is holding the appropriate supporting attitudes on other issues relevant to the revolt. Hence we need to test for demographic effects upon the more proximal attitudinal variables introduced in the last chapter: attitudes toward the size of government, government spending, and perceptions of waste and overpaid bureaucrats. Additionally, if demographic variables affected these proximal attitudes in the same manner as they influenced support for the tax revolt, it becomes plausible that they served as the paths by which group conflict was expressed. To test this, we conducted regressions of the demographic factors upon these attitudes toward government.

In brief, support for specific spending cuts and smaller government in general have roughly the same demographic correlates as does the tax rebel index, underlining again their intimate involvement in the tax revolt. (This is shown in table 5.3.) Indeed the demographic effects were even stronger in the cases of these attitudes, yielding R^2's of 10.1 percent and 13.5 percent, respectively. Higher-income, white, older men all were more supportive of small government and of less spending in specific service areas. Such findings enhance the likelihood that wanting small government, even at some very general level, was a crucial determinant of the tax revolt.

Demographic differences in these proximal attitudes diverged from those on "tax rebel" in three main areas. First, and most important, questions of waste and overpaid government workers did not show the same pattern. Indeed, demographic variables did not contribute much at all to understanding variations in these two dimensions ($R^2 = 2.7$ percent and 0.7 percent, respectively). This provides further evidence for the argument made in Chapter 4, namely that value priorities about the size and responsibilities of government were more central determinants of support for the tax revolt than were these two anti-government themes.

Second, social class had a more straightforward effect on spending priorities than on support for the tax propositions. On "tax rebel," it will be recalled, the components of social class had opposite effects: income positive and education negative. Here they both made positive contributions, though education was weaker. The well-educated wanted smaller government and cuts in services, rather than being especially public-regarding as the middle-mass theory would suggest.[6] This characteristic was masked at certain times by their pre-election skepticism about the most radical tax-cutting proposals, but their basic desire for less government emerged in their increased support for Proposition 13 after it had been safely and sanely implemented. Hence class polarization is revealed in a simpler and more direct manner in these underlying attitudes than in support for the tax revolt itself: better-off Californians wanted less government, and the disadvantaged wanted more.

A third deviation is that region had no effects on any of these attitudes. This lack of regional differences is only the first of what will prove to be quite a long list, leaving the special support of Angelenos for the tax revolt propositions as a rather isolated phenomenon, rather than a part of a broader conservative political culture.

A final criterion for being in an issue public is thinking schematically about the issues at hand. We will consider this more thoroughly in later chapters. For now it is enough to note that the expected emerges: better-educated citizens thought more schematically about the tax revolt than did others. The mean correlation (Pearson) among the four proximal attitudes just discussed was .29 for college graduates and .22 for those with no college background. The tax rebel index correlated .38, and .23, with these four dimensions, on the average, in the two groups. Hence as we saw in Chapter 4, the college educated think more schematically in general, but especially so in their ability to relate these more general issues of taxation and spending to their attitudes about the tax revolt.

Activism in the Tax Revolt

Active participation in the tax revolt was much more strongly determined by demographic factors than were subjective orientations toward it. And the most intense forms of participation were strongly concentrated in the social groups traditionally most active in conventional politics. In general, older, white, higher-income, better-educated males were more likely to be active in campaigns over the tax-revolt propositions. We had two indices of such activism. One was voting turnout, reflecting voting participation in the Proposition 13 and 4 elections. The other was a tax activism index, which simply added the four forms of participation other than voting, as shown at the top of table 4.5. Voting turnout and tax activism were strongly determined by social factors, especially by education. The results were largely parallel for the two indices, though income had the greater effect on activism and age had a much stronger effect on the number of votes cast than on more active forms of participation.

These group differences in activism seem to resemble those which are normal for any type of American political campaign, rather than being especially unique to the tax revolt.[7] Social class (both income and education) generally quite strongly predicts voting frequency and overall indices of political participation. Participation usually has a strong positive relationship to age, though it does tend to retreat somewhat among those over 65, largely because the elderly tend to be of lower social class, because of their generally lower income and educational levels.[8] And whites generally tend to be more active than blacks, though racial differences also diminish when social class is considered. And finally, in the tax revolt as in other political participation, these demographic factors have cumulative effects, so that the impact of social disadvantage in one respect is compounded when accompanied by other inhibiting factors (for example, in very young, poorly educated women, or very old, low-income blacks).

The groups that had the highest turnout, then, were also the most enthusiastic supporters of the tax-revolt propositions. Indeed, the social groups that typically have low rates of voting—the poor, blacks, the less-educated, and those who rent rather than own their homes—also tend to be relatively heavy consumers of government services who could realize only minor dollar savings from a tax cut. This raises the obvious question of whether the outcomes of the three initiatives would have been substantially altered by a higher rate of participation. Perhaps the tax revolt succeeded as well as it did only because of a low and demographically biased turnout.

Certainly the turnout did fall short of perfection. When Proposition 13 won, 69 percent of those registered to vote went to the polls. Turnout fell precipitously to only 34 percent at the special off-year election in which Proposition 4 won, but then rose to 61 percent at the June 1980 primary election when Jarvis II was rejected. And turnout was related to support for the revolt, as we have already seen in table 4.5.

But the margin of victory in all three contests was so decisive (65 percent, 74 percent, and 61 percent on the winning sides) that the outcomes would have been the same had every eligible citizen voted. And in fact the similarity in the outlook of active and apathetic members of the public is striking, as shown in Chapter 4. Thus, each result was quite representative of public opinion at the time of the vote; the tax revolt was not merely an artifact of the most-favored social groups' greater propensity to go to the polls.[9]

Conclusions

It is fair to say, as a first crack, that the tax revolt was centered among white, high-to-middle-income, middle-aged men, residing in Southern California. This statement can be qualified in a number of ways, but it is a clear starting point. The attitudes that mediated these group differences seem to focus on value priorities about balancing the public and private sectors. Attitudes about the best size of government yield essentially the same demographic pattern as support for the tax revolt. The same is not so true for anti-government attitudes about waste and overpaid public employees. This suggests that the demographic differences have more to do with some basic left–right ideological differences than with cynical, alienated attacks on governmental institutions.

Although the group differences reviewed in this chapter are both statistically and politically significant, it is important not to exaggerate their strength. Demographic factors explained relatively little of the variation in support for the tax revolt (the proportion of variance they accounted for did not exceed 8 percent), and they were only modestly successful in accounting for the development of an issue public for the tax revolt.

The major social groups did differ in the extent of their participation in tax-revolt campaigns. In particular, middle-aged, high-income, highly educated white men were the most active. In most cases, these same groups were also those most likely to support the tax revolt; they also are traditionally the most politically active groups in American society. This similarity represented an important advantage to the pro-Jarvis side in each of the tax-revolt campaigns.

Finally, differences among social groups do not explain the different outcomes of the votes on the three tax-revolt propositions, for the effects of demographic variables remained relatively constant over time. So our analysis must turn to more proximate variables, starting with economic self-interest and symbolic predispositions, and then returning to the various attitudes and perceptions toward government spending and taxation.

6

The Pro-Revolt Interests

Any major political change is likely to alter the private lives of individual citizens, and the tax revolt was no exception. The promise of reduced taxes and the threats of reduced government services and of laid-off government workers all meant some Californians might be helped and others hurt. These promises and threats might well be expected to determine voters' reactions to the tax revolt. Hence the next two chapters examine the role of self-interest as a determinant of support of or opposition to the tax revolt.

We define self-interest in terms of the direct personal impact of the tax revolt on the material circumstances of the person's private life and those of family members. That is, to what extent would tax and spending limitations affect the respondent's personal life? This leads us to focus particularly on taxes, direct financial benefits from government, free or low-cost government services such as the public schools, and government employment. We also look at aspects of voters' personal economic situations that might indirectly influence the effect of the tax revolt on their lives, such as employment difficulties and anxieties, slipping personal finances, or inflation's impact. But we exclude from the self-interest rubric any nonmaterial interests the person might have, such as pride in the excellence of the university system, or pleasure in seeing bureaucrats squirm at the sound of Howard Jarvis's raspy voice.

Self-interest can be indexed in objective terms: for example, with homeownership status. Proposition 13 reduced the property tax bills of homeowners, but renters generally received little benefit. Or it can be indexed more subjectively: for example, with perceptions of one's tax burdens. Some Californians believed their state income tax was excessively high, and others did not. Some indices of self-interest are retrospective: for example, some respondents had been unemployed or laid off and might have been concerned about reduced government benefits. Others are prospective: some employed respondents were worried about losing their jobs in the future, while others were not.

The logic of the trade-off between taxes and services immediately suggests three main classes of self-interested people: *taxpayers* who pay for government services, *government employees* who pass them on, and *service recipients* who are their beneficiaries. It would make sense to expect the tax revolt to pit taxpayers against service recipients. To this simple picture we add a fourth potential interested constituency, people with deteriorating personal financial situations, especially as a result of *inflation*. This group might have had two rather different stakes in the tax revolt. As we have seen, inflation had driven taxes up quite dramatically. While people generally could not do much about the escalating cost of living elsewhere in their economic lives, the tax revolt did offer them a direct mechanism for at least reducing their taxes. Second, such people may have felt diffuse anxieties about inflation and a deteriorating economy, and these feelings may have motivated much of the support for the tax revolt. We refer to this second group as suffering from *economic malaise*.

Examining the tax revolt in terms of self-interest promises unusual analytic opportunities. Most psychological and rational choice theories treat self-interest motivationally: it should motivate the formation of self-serving attitudes toward public policy. As indicated earlier, past research directly assessing the political effects of self-interest in the mass public has obtained disappointingly weak results. However, voters' private interests are not usually so tangibly affected by electoral outcomes as they promised to be in the tax revolt, nor have most previous studies collected such rich data about voters' material stakes in their political choices.

But self-interest is also thought to bear important consequences for cognitive activity. Hence it should affect more than support and opposition; it should direct attention, motivate information-gathering and formation of bolstering beliefs and attitudes, spur cognitive activity, and ultimately promote more organized cognitive structures. Converse has described people who are attentive, informed, and thoughtful and have highly organized and consistent cognitions about a particular political or social issue as being in its "issue public."[1] And while some previous research has indicated that self-interest does not play much of a role in generating issue publics (at least on some issues)[2] the tax revolt here too may have provided unusually fertile soil for the effects of self-interest.

If self-interest helped to create an issue public for the tax revolt, it should have directed attention to the tax revolt, making voters perceive taxation and spending as important problems facing California. That is, self-interest should be a prime determinant of *issue salience*; the voter's private agenda should determine what is on the public agenda. And it should have generated greater *opinionation* on the three tax-revolt propositions. In this vein, self-interest ought also to have helped to generate the appropriate *supporting attitudes* toward the various aspects of the tax revolt schema. It should have generated more *schematized thinking* about taxation and spending as political issues, and in that way have promoted more organized, constrained, consistent thinking. Finally, self-interest should also motivate self-serving political *behavior*; that is, it should contribute both to voter turnout and to other forms of participation in the tax revolt.

Our general strategy in this chapter and the next is to begin with a quick first-cut assessment of the role of self-interest in generating support or opposition toward the tax revolt, in creating an issue public around the tax issue, in promoting self-serving attitudes toward taxation and government spending, and in promoting active participation in the tax-reform movement. In all these analyses we will try to identify the unique effects of direct self-interest apart from those which simply reflect demographic location, which in our analysis is treated as a grosser prior classification. Then we will go back and explore in more detail the most promising and potent effects of self-interest on the tax revolt. We will present this more textured account in two parts: focusing in this chapter on the interests that should have supported the revolt (taxpayers and the inflation-distressed) and in the next chapter on those which should have opposed it (public employees and service recipients). At the end we will return to the basic question in all these cases: the size and political effectiveness of the selfish interests on each side.

Overall Effects of Self-Interest

Self-interest quite clearly had extensive effects on Californians' response to the tax revolt, but these effects varied substantially across both interest groups and dependent variables. Regression analyses of self-interest upon support for the tax rebellion, inclusion in its issue public, support for the various elements of the tax revolt schema, and participation in the revolt are all shown in table 6.1. We will describe the self-interest indicators in more detail later. Briefly, "taxpayers" were identified by homeownership and perceived

TABLE 6.1 Summary regression analysis: effects of self-interest.

	Attention			Tax revolt schema				Participation	
	Tax rebel index	Issue salience	Opinion-ation	Size of government	Service spending	Waste	Overpaid government workers	Vote frequency	Tax activism
Pro-Revolt Interests									
Taxpayers									
Homeownership	.17**	.07*	.07*	.15**	.17**	.06*	.03	.24**	.15**
Subjective tax burden	.20**	.18**	.06*	.15**	.18**	.21**	.14**	.03	.12**
Economic malaise									
Declining finances	.02	−.03	.02	.03	.04	.03	.01	.07*	.02
Inflation impact	.03	.01	.02	−.01	−.03	.01	.01	.03	.03
Anti-Revolt Interests									
Public employees	.18**	.02	.03	.02	.01	.06*	.20**	.14**	.08**
Service recipients									
Gov't assistance	.01	.04	−.01	.04	.07*	.04	.02	.05	.06*
Employment status	.05*	.02	−.07*	.04	.02	.04	.01	.03	.08*
Work problems	.06*	−.06*	.06*	.06*	.06*	.02	.05	.12**	.05*
Child in public school	.02	−.01	−.02	.01	.01	.04	.04	.04	.00
R²	.113	.045	.020	.067	.079	.068	.065	.075	.067

Source: Tax Revolt Survey.

Note: Entries are betas. A positive entry indicates position is associated with the specified self-interest in the hypothesized direction. That means pro-revolt interests should be associated with support for the revolt, and for the tax revolt schema, while anti-revolt interests should be associated with opposition to both. All forms of self-interest should be associated with attention to the tax revolt and more participation.

*p < .01.

**p < .001.

personal tax burden; economic malaise was identified by a perceived decline in personal finances over the prior year and feeling badly hurt by inflation; public employee status, by working for state or local government; and recipients of government services, by receiving direct financial aid from various specific government programs, being unemployed or having a variety of other employment problems in the family, or having a child attending a public school or university.

Self-interest clearly did have some influence on support for the tax revolt. The several self-interest indicators together accounted for 11.3 percent of the variance in the tax rebel index (a multiple correlation of .34), which is substantial. However, it generally had less impact in forming an issue public or on participation, as table 6.1 shows. We saw in Chapter 4 that attitudes toward the tax revolt tended to be more consistent than those toward taxation and spending in general, and here it appears that self-interest shows the same pattern: more impact on attitudes toward the tax-cutting propositions than on those about government in general. In Chapter 8 we will see that the latter orientations tend to be much more strongly controlled by longer-standing symbolic predispositions. And self-interest has little effect on participation, either. As we saw in the last chapter, activism too is controlled by longer-term forces, mostly by the respondent's social background and current social location.

But self-interest has some strong and interesting effects. The *taxpayers*, as defined here, consisted of homeowners and those who felt especially burdened by taxes. As can be seen in table 6.1, both these variables had consistent and moderately strong effects upon almost all dependent variables concerned with the tax revolt: support for it, inclusion in its issue public, support for the various elements of the tax revolt schema, and participation. Unsurprisingly, the "taxpayer rebellion" was quite plainly strongly motivated by grievances about taxes.

By contrast, those suffering generalized *economic malaise* did not have distinctive responses to the tax revolt. For this group only one of eighteen relationships was statistically significant, and only half were in the expected direction (as would have been expected by chance). Nevertheless, we should not jump to the conclusion that economic malaise is utterly irrelevant to the tax revolt, since it is likely to have interacted with income, homeownership, and other indices of financial insecurity or vulnerability to taxes.

Public employees showed the expected fairly strong self-interested opposition to the tax propositions, but the only other attitudinal evidence of their self-interest was limited to the policy attitude most specifically relevant to their own pocketbooks—pay levels for public employees. Additionally, they showed unusually high levels of participation in the revolt, both in terms of voting turnout on Propositions 13 and 4 and in terms of other forms of activism. Because public employees are generally better educated and more affluent than the population at large, and because social class is such an important determinant of political participation, demographic controls will be especially important in interpreting this finding.

Several different categories of *service recipients* were included in the analysis: those receiving direct financial assistance from government, those with a recent history of employment problems, those worried about losing their jobs in the future, and parents of children in the public schools. But these groups showed only the slightest evidence of self-interested pro-public-sector attitudes. And the data in table 6.1 suggest that service recipients, if anything, were somewhat *less* active participants than those not so dependent on government services. Again demographic controls are needed, to determine whether this is merely a matter of their generally lower status, or whether it is specific to their dependence on government in particular. But this apparent lack of self-interestedness among the recipients of government services will deserve close scrutiny, since it is potentially one of our most important findings.

When demographic variables are included in the equations, only two real changes occur in the findings, both concerning participation in the tax revolt. The positive effects of homeownership on both frequency of voting and tax activism become nonsignificant, and so do the negative effects of being a service recipient. Hence the greater participation by pro-revolt interest groups seems largely to be due to their more favored demographic status, not their self-interest per se. However, the other findings are not affected very much: the strong opposition to the tax revolt among public employees holds up attitudinally and behaviorally, as does the strong attitudinal support for the revolt by taxpayers.[3]

Overall, then, self-interest seems to have motivated the large group of tax-burdened voters to strong support for, and active participation in, the tax revolt. It also motivated the much smaller group of public employees to active opposition. But recipients of government services seem not to have been mobilized in their own self-interest either attitudinally or behaviorally. All these findings need more detailed and specific examination. In the rest of this chapter we begin by looking in more detail at the pro-revolt interest groups.

"The Taxpayers"

Almost everybody pays taxes. But some pay more than others, and some feel hurt by taxes more than others. Hence some people regard themselves as part of "the taxpayers," and these would seem to have been prime candidates for self-interested politics in the tax revolt. In earlier chapters we described the large and rapid increase in property- and income-tax burdens borne by California taxpayers during the 1970s. Both Propositions 13 and 9 provided clear and virtually certain payoffs to taxpayers. Voters could calculate in advance the dollar difference to their own tax bills of these propositions' success or failure. Many political issues attempt to deal with painful social realities, but on few do the voters' responses have such tangible and immediate consequence for their pocketbooks. So if ever self-interest were to dominate voters' opinions, this should have been a prime time.

Property Taxpayers

A potentially huge interest group consisted of property taxpayers, as Howard Jarvis emphasized in 1978. California Polls in this period typically found that between 60 percent and 65 percent of respondents owned their own residences, and so paid property taxes. In the Tax Revolt Survey, 61 percent were homeowners. Such figures are comparable to those for the nation as a whole.

Where California was unusual prior to Proposition 13 was in the rapid inflation of the property tax, and it was experienced as extremely onerous. Early in the campaign for Proposition 13, in the spring of 1978, the California Poll found the property tax far outdistancing its nearest fellow villain, the federal income tax (by 51 percent to 21 percent), as the specific tax Californians felt was too high. As we have already indicated, the extreme inflation in the California housing market, and its relatively prompt and honest reassessment procedures, made the property tax much more painful in California than in the rest of the nation. So Americans in general were not as angry about the property tax as Californians were: for example, in a national survey in early 1978, 32 percent found it the least fair tax, compared to 30 percent who considered the federal income tax the most unfair.[4]

Proposition 13 promised to alleviate the pain of property taxes in three ways. First of all, it promised to reduce the tax rate from an average of around 2.6 percent to about 1 percent of assessed value. Second, it severely limited future increases in assessments despite rapidly escalating property values. The best survey data (an August 1978 California Poll) indicated that the median homeowner thought his or her property taxes would have risen in the following year by $233 had Proposition 13 not passed. The exact frequencies are shown in table 6.2. And for most homeowners, Proposition 13 promised yet a third tax break. For houses bought before July 1, 1975, assessments would be rolled back to their assessed value as of that date. This applied to 61 percent of the homeowners in our sample. Houses bought after that date would be assessed at purchase price.

The immediate cut in the tax rate would, all by itself, bring a major cash benefit to most homeowners, and it was one that was well publicized before the election. Many estimates were floating around. For example, the *Los Angeles Times*, ten days before the election, presented a simple box score comparing Proposition 13 with the legislature's alternative, Proposition 8, on the front page of its Sunday Metropolitan section. It estimated that property taxes would be cut 57 percent, or $765 per year, on a typical $60,000 home. In San Francisco, where inflation had not hit quite so hard, a pre-election newspaper estimate was that the average local homeowner would save $562. The official estimates made by government officials were comparable. The Assembly Revenue and Taxation Committee estimated that the average homeowner in California, owning a home valued at $52,000 in 1978, would realize an immediate tax cut of $870. And the State Board of Equalization estimated that the immediate cut would reduce property taxes by 52 percent.[5]

These estimates did not take into account the other two aspects of Proposition 13's benefits to the homeowners, which affected assessed value, probably because it was so hard to predict inflationary increases in real estate values. And they did not take into account what was perhaps its major attraction, stopping the inflation-created escalation in property taxes. This was especially important in the Los Angeles metropolitan area. When all three of these benefits are put together, the next property tax bill on the *average* residence in Southern California, arriving in November 1978, would have been over $2300 without Proposition 13. With Proposition 13 (and assuming the house had been owned at least three years), the tab would have been less than $450. This savings, of nearly $2000 per year, could fairly be described as the order of magnitude of the typical benefit in the seven-county Southern California area that gave Proposition 13 its strongest support.[6]

Given such high stakes, self-interest not surprisingly had a substantial effect on the attitudes and behavior of homeowners. Table 6.3 shows that at every stage, from pre-election to a year and a half later, homeowners supported Proposition 13 substantially more than did renters.

TABLE 6.2 Prospective dollar savings and support for Proposition 13 and Jarvis II.

Proposition 13 (as of Aug. 1978)

	% of sample	Recalled vote	Support
Expected no increase in property taxes			
Renters	36%	55%	46%
Owners	4	48	52
Expected increase in property taxes			
Don't know amount	14	63	63
Up to $200	11	64	67
$200-399	15	78	77
$400-599	5	75	80
$600-799	3	76	86
$800-999	2	100	96
$1000+	8	82	84
Total	98		
Total effect on vote		+27	+38

Jarvis II (1980)

	% of Sample		Support as of	
	Feb.	April	Feb.	April
Expected no income tax savings	8%	11%	40%	37%
Didn't know whether to expect savings or not	34	25	62	45
Expected savings				
Up to $50	5	7	42	38
$51-200	16	18	55	46
$201-500	14	17	66	48
$501-750	9	9	76	57
$751-1000	3	3	76	50
$1000+	10	10	69	65
Total	99	100		
Total effect on vote	+29	+28		

Source: California Polls.

Note: Some totals fall short of 100 percent due to rounding error. Base for vote or support is all those with a definite vote or opinion.

Support for it was closely related to the magnitude of the savings, too. Table 6.2 shows that support for Proposition 13 went up steadily, and strongly, as the expected savings increased. Support approached 90 percent for those who had expected their taxes to increase by over $600, whereas it only broke even among those expecting no tax increase. And support for it a year and a half after it passed was closely associated with perceptions that it had reduced the respondent's taxes. In the Tax Revolt Survey, 40 percent felt it had decreased their overall tax burden, while 14 percent said it had increased it. At that point it was supported by 84 percent and 46 percent of these two groups respectively.

At the same time we might mention one limitation on this role of self-interest. People who had bought their homes before July 1975 would have their assessments rolled back three years, in a period of wildly inflating real estate inflation, so they ultimately would have considerably lower taxes than those who had bought later. And by the time of our survey, homeowners had received two post–Proposition 13 annual property tax bills, so they should have

TABLE 6.3 Homeownership and support for the tax revolt.

	Early buyers (pre 7/1/75)	Late buyers (post 7/1/75)	All owners	Renters	Difference (owners minus renters)
Proposition 13					
May 1978[a]	—	—	69%	46%	+ 23%
June 1978					
(vote recall)[a]	—	—	71	55	+ 16
(vote recall)[b]	76	79	77	58	+ 19
Aug. 1978[a]	—	—	73	46	+ 27
Nov. 1978[c]	—	—	80	63	+ 17
Nov. 1979[b]	76	77	76	56	+ 20
Gann amendment					
Nov. 1979[b]	80	86	82	75	+ 7
Jarvis II					
Nov. 1979[b]	58	58	58	45	+ 13
April 1980[a]	—	—	52	40	+ 12
May 1980[a]	—	—	40	33	+ 7
Tax rebel index[b]	66	69	67	52	+ 15

Sources: a. California Poll. b. Tax Revolt Survey. c. American National Election Study.

Note: Entries are percentages of those with a definite opinion supporting specified proposition, except in the case of the tax rebel index, where the entries are the percentages who favored more of the three propositions than they opposed.

become at least partially aware of its consequences for their property tax burdens. Yet the "early" and "late" buyers did not differ in support for it, despite the very different benefits they would reap from it, as shown in table 6.3. Of course this was not the most highly publicized clause in a very complex ballot measure. And the effects of this difference would not be felt nearly as profoundly then as they would some years later, as housing prices continued to escalate.[7]

Proposition 13 did not promise anything explicitly to renters. Howard Jarvis claimed to have persuaded some landlords with large holdings to promise to pass on lower tax bills in reduced rents if Proposition 13 passed. But this claim apparently ran into a lot of cynicism about landlords' reducing rents for any reason. Proposition 13 was generally perceived as not likely to benefit renters. In an August 1978 California Poll, only 13 percent of the homeowners, and 7 percent of the renters, expected landlords to pass their savings on to tenants.

The homeowners' greater support for Proposition 13 was not just an artifact of their higher income levels. Controlling income has almost no effect at all on the size of the owner-renter difference in support for Proposition 13 in the last pre-election California Poll, or in recalled vote as obtained later in the Tax Revolt Survey.[8] So we will treat the owner-renter distinction as a relatively simple and pure index of self-interest in the rest of this chapter.

At one level, such self-interest effects are uncomplicated. Presumably almost everybody would prefer to pay less in taxes, everything else being equal. But the rhetoric of the Proposition 13 campaign, and of its opponents, complicated matters. They presented quite different images of the kind of people most passionately in favor of Proposition 13.

Supporters emphasized the vulnerability of many homeowners, or would-be homeowners, to threatening levels of property taxes. The argument was that many homeowners feared losing their homes, or at least being unable to cover their property tax bills, because of the dramatic inflation in property taxes, and that would-be homeowners feared that they might never be able to afford to buy. Voting to cut property taxes, and to limit their future growth, was a way to stave off personal disaster. Presumably this issue had a particularly powerful emotional effect because owning one's own home is such a central part of the American Dream.

Another school of thought saw Proposition 13 as a greedy "revolt of the haves." According to this view, its strongest supporters were personally quite affluent, profiting enormously from escalating property values, not personally dependent upon government services, and hence more than willing to have services cut back. Whether consciously or unconsciously, "the haves" voted for Proposition 13 because of the very large windfall tax savings they could get at little or no personal cost.

Property tax vulnerability. One of Howard Jarvis's major arguments for the fairness of Proposition 13 was that certain classes of homeowners were being taxed excessively given their incomes. Homeowners with limited or fixed incomes were particularly squeezed since they had limited resources with which to cover rapidly increasing property taxes. To pursue this notion of vulnerability, we tried to identify special groups of homeowners that would be most squeezed between inflating property taxes and limited income. Prime among them would be low-income homeowners, particularly women, the elderly, and those badly hurt by inflation; homeowners trying to get by on government assistance; women who owned homes and did not work; and medium-income homeowners badly hurt by inflation. As can be seen in table 6.4, such groups recalled voting somewhat more for Proposition 13 than did the sample as a whole, by about 8 percent on the average. However, they were not unusually supportive of Proposition 13 or the tax revolt in general at any other times in this era. So these data only partially validate Jarvis's claims.

Moreover, the most pro-13 of these vulnerable groups were quite small in number. For example, low-income homeowners aged 50 and over numbered about 9 percent of the sample; low-income homeowners badly hurt by inflation represented about 3 percent of the sample. These hardship cases provided ideal symbols that Jarvis used effectively to sway more disinterested voters, but they were not themselves the backbone of his movement.

A second vulnerable class consisted of renters who wanted someday to become homeowners but who were rapidly being priced out of the market, partly because of the burdens that would be placed on their incomes by property taxes. Presumably many high-income renters, especially those either young or feeling pinched by inflation, would normally have moved toward buying a home. Medium-income renters might also have been considering it. But as table 6.4 shows, such renters were actually *less* enthusiastic about Proposition 13 and the tax revolt than the rest of the sample. And here too there were actually very few cases: for example, only 6 percent of the full sample rented and earned over $25,000 per year. Nor did renters feel markedly more pinched by inflation than did owners, even in the post–Proposition 13 period of our survey (68 percent of renters and 61 percent of homeowners felt "hurt" by inflation). So there is not much evidence of special support for Proposition 13 from renters' self-interested desire to leave the door open to future homeownership.

TABLE 6.4 Property tax vulnerability and support for the tax revolt.

	Proposition 13				
	Vote intention (May 1978)	Recalled vote (Nov. 1979)	Later support (Nov. 1979)	Tax rebel scale	% in sample
Support in full sample	63%	71%	68%	61%	
High-vulnerability homeowners					
Low income (0-$15,000)	+ 3%	+ 7%	− 1%	0	15%
Badly hurt by inflation	na	+ 17	− 6	+ 2	3
Women	− 4	+ 4	− 4	− 1	10
Middle-aged or old (50 +)	+ 5	+ 13	+ 4	+ 6	9
On government assistance (2 +)	na	+ 12	+ 2	+ 5	8
Housewives (not looking for work)	na	+ 10	+ 11	+ 8	14
Medium income ($16-25,000)	− 1	+ 4	0	+ 9	18
Badly hurt by inflation	na	− 5	+ 3	+ 8	2
High-vulnerability renters					
Medium income	− 11	− 8	− 8	− 7	10
Young (18-34), high income ($26,000 +)	− 9	− 40	− 10	− 7	3
High income, badly hurt by inflation	na	*	*	*	1
Low-vulnerability homeowners					
High income ($26,000 +)	+ 11	+ 5	+ 12	+ 8	23
Men	+ 9	+ 10	+ 16	+ 14	13
Not hurt by inflation	na	+ 5	+ 15	+ 9	6
Employed full time	na	+ 4	+ 11	+ 8	33
Men	na	+ 9	+ 16	+ 15	21
No government assistance	na	+ 4	+ 11	+ 8	35

Sources: All data are from the Tax Revolt Survey except vote intention, which is from California Poll 7806.

Note: Entries in the first four columns are the percentages by which each category exceeded, or fell short of, the full-sample level of support shown in the top row.

*Too few cases to obtain reliable estimates.

Revolt of the haves. The evidence suggests that Proposition 13 drew its support more from fairly affluent people attracted to a large cash bonus than from these vulnerable groups. This can be shown in several ways. First and most simply, the bottom of table 6.4 shows that low-vulnerability homeowners — high-income, fully employed, not dependent on government assistance—supported the tax revolt fairly consistently. Their home values were rapidly escalating, and their incomes were ample, yet they strongly supported a shift of the state's tax burden to other, less affluent sectors of the population. Moreover, these low-vulnerability groups supporting the tax revolt were larger in number than the high-vulnerability groups. Hence they contributed many more supporters to Proposition 13. High-income homeowning men, who strongly supported Proposition 13, numbered about 13 percent of the sample. Fulltime-employed homeowning men, another group of supporters, numbered 21 percent of the sample. Second, those escalating property taxes were the consequence of equally swiftly escalating property values, which suddenly and effortlessly increased the financial worth of most homeowners. Not surprisingly, then, support for Proposition 13 was greatest among high-income homeowners feeling least hurt by inflation.

There can be no question that homeowners felt seriously aggrieved by the property tax before Proposition 13. And Proposition 13 provided a very large windfall cash savings to the homeowner, as well as choking off out-of-control inflationary increases. Our data document a specifically instrumental, self-interested, property-tax-saving basis for voting for Proposition 13. Some tax-vulnerable groups did respond to Proposition 13 in a self-protective way, but the major support came from a much larger, more secure, affluent group, already profiting considerably from inflation, successfully shifting the tax load to others. To be sure, even some high-income Californians would have suffered temporary cash-flow problems when facing the sudden increases in property taxes guaranteed by the long intervals between reassessments. And the big increases in their property values could not necessarily be turned immediately to profit, since one's home is not the most liquid of assets. But the regular assessment cycle did allow many homeowners, and not a few speculators, to plan ahead. And in the long run the combination of inflated property values and minimal property taxes after Proposition 13 did place holders of California real property in a greatly advantaged position. And this windfall benefited a great many Californians.

The legacy of Proposition 13. By and large Proposition 13 defused the property tax as a political issue based on self-interest in California, at least for the moment. As we have indicated, perceptions of its unfairness fell precipitously, from 62 percent in 1977 to 20 percent in 1980. In our survey, only 29 percent felt they were paying more than they should in property taxes (as opposed to 67 percent who felt that way about taxes in general). Perhaps most impressive, only 6 percent of the entire sample felt both that Proposition 13 had reduced their taxes and that they still paid more in property taxes than they should.

Nor was this remaining property-tax burden especially politically consequential. It was not associated with greater support for Proposition 13, even among the "early buyers" whom it most advantaged. It was not closely related to anti-tax feelings in general: in the Tax Revolt Survey, perceived property-tax burden correlated only .14 with perceived overall tax burden. It was associated with somewhat more support for Jarvis II, but the relatively small numbers of people still dissatisfied with their property taxes gave this relatively little political impact.[9]

But the homeowners' fondness for Proposition 13 did spread to support for the tax revolt in general. Even after Proposition 13 passed, homeowners remained loyal to the tax revolt, even though the later propositions promised no special direct selfish return to them. Table 6.3 shows this continued homeowner support for the tax revolt, though at a lower pitch of enthusiasm than their support for Proposition 13. And this loyalty that homeowners transferred to later stages of the tax revolt was due to the direct tax-reducing advantages of Proposition 13, not merely to their higher income or some other factor. Of the 40 percent who said their overall tax burden had been reduced by Proposition 13, 75 percent were "tax rebels" on our tax rebel index (as opposed to 54 percent and 43 percent of these who felt their taxes had not been affected, or had gone up, respectively). And homeownership contributed to support for Jarvis II, even with income taken into account.[10] The homeowners were grateful, and did not forget their benefactors.

On the other side, few landlords did in fact pass on their tax savings to their tenants. Instead, rents continued to escalate with inflation. This helped perpetuate opposition to the tax revolt among renters, and fueled the rent-control movement throughout California.

Less affluent Californians evidently perceived this class bias of the tax revolt, because they increasingly fell away from it. This tendency created increasing class polarization as the tax revolt wore on. Table 5.1 showed that income differences over Proposition 13 increased considerably in the year and a half following its passage, largely no doubt because the highest-income homeowners got the largest immediate reductions in their tax bills, whereas the less affluent profited less. This direct benefit contributed to support for the later aspects of the tax revolt, as we have already seen. Rather than being satisfied with some tax relief, the affluent wanted more. Because so many Californians benefited from it, Proposition 13 has to date been perceived more often as legislation for the people, not for the rich, regardless of the realities. But Jarvis II did tend to be identified as "class legislation" more often as its campaign wound to a close, and this image contributed to its defeat.

Finally, Proposition 13's provision that reassessed property to market value when it was sold guaranteed some generational cleavage down the line. In our sample 77 percent of the homeowners who were past their mid-thirties had purchased before July 1975, and hence had pre-inflationary assessments. Only 34 percent of the younger homeowners were in this favored position. As more and more of the younger generation become homeowners, their assessments will be more and more out of line with those of their elders. The conflict this generates should be mitigated by the fact that none will be assessed much above purchase price, and so their assessments will be in line with their expectations at the time of purchase. But this remains a potential source of perceived inequity and hence social conflict.

State Income Tax

In the aftermath of Proposition 13, Howard Jarvis turned his attention to the state income tax. Almost everyone in California had to pay some: when the Tax Revolt Survey asked respondents if they paid any state income tax or not, only 4 percent said they did not. It was also the object of some grievance; as we saw in Chapter 3, after Proposition 13 it replaced the property tax as the state or local tax thought least fair. In our survey, 22 percent felt they paid "much more" than they should and 28 percent "somewhat more." And just as the property tax had been at the heart of personal tax grievances before Proposition 13, the income tax had become so after Proposition 13. Respondents' feeling of overall tax burden was correlated .50 with feeling burdened by the state income tax, but only .14 with feeling burdened by the property tax, as already noted.

Nevertheless, the state income tax was a less promising lever upon the mass public's self-interest than the property tax had been. Largely paid by withholding, it was less visible. It had inflated, but in small increments rather than large chunks, since inflation had been less dramatic in overall income than in real estate. And the absolute amounts of money involved were simply not as large. For example, the median income in our sample was a little over $18,000. For the 1980 tax year, this would have obligated a typical married couple to a little over $250 in taxes. Consequently Jarvis II did not promise a large, immediate payoff. It sounded initially as if it would, for it promised a 50 percent cut, but most Californians did not expect it to return much to them. California Polls in February and April 1980 asked respondents how much they thought Jarvis II would return to them, and on both occasions only a minority expected more than $100 annually. As shown in table 6.2, even if we ignore those in the "don't know" category, the median estimates were $265 and $211 in the two surveys.

And it should be remembered that these tax cuts would have been implemented largely by reducing the withholding tax, which would have added only about $5 to the average weekly paycheck.

Despite this relatively meager financial payoff, support for Jarvis II was strongly influenced by self-interest, just as with Proposition 13. In the Tax Revolt Survey, people who felt they paid "much more" state income tax than they should supported Jarvis II much more strongly than did those who felt their personal tax burdens were "about right," as shown in table 6.5. The same pattern showed up in the February 1980 pre-election California Poll: 92 percent of those who felt their state and local taxes were "much too high" supported Jarvis II, compared to 32 percent of those who felt their taxes were "about right." Thus feeling excessively burdened by state and local taxes strongly increased support for Jarvis II.

Furthermore, the larger the expected dollar saving from Jarvis II, the greater the support. In two California Polls done relatively early in the Jarvis II campaign (before its popularity level took its final fatal plunge), about 40 percent supported it even though they expected no personal savings, while almost 70 percent did among voters who expected to save at least $1000 (see table 6.2).[11]

So Californians seem to have responded just as self-interestedly to Jarvis II as to Proposition 13. The major difference was the much smaller return promised by Jarvis II. A conservative way of estimating how voters perceived the difference is to add the immediate cut of $765 promised the average homeowner by Proposition 13 (as published in the *Los Angeles Times* just before the election) to the median increase in property taxes of $233 homeowners apparently expected had Proposition 13 not passed (shown in table 6.2). This yields a very crude, but minimum, estimate that the average homeowner expected an immediate saving of about $1000 from Proposition 13. Respondents who expected a return that large from Jarvis II overwhelmingly supported it, by 69 percent and 65 percent in the two relevant surveys (table 6.2). But to get a $1000 saving from Jarvis II, a family of four would have had to earn about $40,000 in 1980 — and only 11 percent of our sample reported household income that high. The implication is that a major cause of the difference in popularity of the two propositions was simply the size of the monetary return to the voter.[12]

The Taxpayers as an Issue Public

What creates an "issue public" on a controversy such as the tax revolt? In Chapter 4 we found that the issue public for the tax revolt was most sharply

TABLE 6.5 Felt burden of state income tax and support for the tax revolt.

	State income tax burden				
	Pay much more than should	Pay some-what more than should	Pay about right amount	Pay less than should or none	Effect
% of sample	21%	28%	40%	7%	
Support for tax revolt in full sample					
Proposition 13					
(vote recall)	81	77	62		+ 19
Proposition 13					
(current support	77	74	60		+ 17
Gann amendment	85	84	74		+ 11
Jarvis II	78	57	37		+ 41
Tax rebels	77	66	50		+ 27
Support for Jarvis II by income level					
$26,000 +	75	54	34		+ 41
$16,000-25,000	84	60	39		+ 45
< $15,000	75	55	37		+ 38
Income effect	0	− 1	− 3		

Source: Tax Revolt Survey.

defined with respect to the three ballot propositions. Enough cognitive organ-ization existed among other related attitudes to justify describing the whole cluster as a tax revolt schema, but they were rather loosely connected except for their common relationships to support for the tax revolt ballot proposi-tions. But what controls the level of political attention, opinionation, adop-tion of supportive attitudes, and schematic thinking that would justify talk-ing about a real issue public? As we have indicated, social psychologists have argued theoretically that selfish motives ought to spur such cognitive activity. This theoretical notion has not been empirically applied very much to real po-litical controversies, however. So our next question is whether or not the tax-payers' vested interest in cutting their own tax burdens did convert them into a real issue public.

Self-interest among the taxpayers was associated with greater issue salience and opinionation: people who thought they paid "much too much" in taxes were 20 percent more likely to mention taxation or spending spontaneously as a major California problem than were those who felt they paid about the right amount. Homeowners were also significantly more likely to believe that tax reform was the most important issue, as shown in table 6.1, and both these indices of taxpayer self-interest contributed significantly to opinionation, but these three effects were of small magnitude (less than 10 percent).

Self-interest also affected taxpayers' attitudes about other elements of the tax revolt schema: value priorities about government spending, perceptions of waste, and public-sector salaries. Those feeling particularly burdened by taxes showed unusually high levels of agreement with all aspects of the tax revolt schema. Homeowners usually shared this value priority of wanting smaller government and less service spending, but joined less strongly in the more anti-government themes of perceiving especially high levels of waste in government or overpayment of government workers.

This apparently self-interested thinking about each of these separate matters does not necessarily indicate schematic thinking. All these separate elements may not have been drawn together into any tight cognitive structure about the tax revolt as a whole. We used several tests to examine whether the taxpayers' self-interest promoted more schematic thinking. First, we reasoned that self-interested people, compared to disinterested people, would show higher constraint among the four components of the tax revolt schema (excluding tax burden and the tax rebel index). We treated as self-interested the homeowners and those paying "much more" taxes than they felt they should. The disinterested were the remainder of the sample in each case. Here self-interest failed to produce any more schematic thinking. The mean correlation among these dimensions was .21 in each of the two self-interested groups, and .19 and .18 in the two disinterested groups. Second, we reasoned that self-interested people should show a more powerful single factor running through these several components of the tax revolt schema. But the single tax-revolt-schema factor runs through the attitudes of self-interested and disinterested parties alike, with scarcely any variation. The median factor loading was .49 for the self-interested, and .47 for the less interested, with eigenvalues of 1.95 and 1.90, versus 1.82 and 1.84. The same divergence between value priorities and anti-government attitudes noted earlier held for both, with anti-government attitudes loading less heavily in all groups.

Another indicator of schematic thinking would be if the cognitive effects of self-interest (such as homeowners' desire for smaller government) were the reason for its impact on support for the tax rebellion. The appropriate test is to determine whether the self-interested taxpayers' positions on the tax revolt are fully accounted for by the ostensible cognitive linkage. Hence we conducted two regression analyses on the tax rebel index: one that included the various self-interest indices shown in table 6.1, and a second that added to these the four attitudinal elements of the tax revolt schema. This showed that these other elements of the tax revolt schema accounted for only about a third of the effects of perceived tax burden and hence that the taxpayers' support for the tax revolt was *not* strongly bolstered by supporting cognitive rationalizations – or at least not by these particular ones.[13]

So there is little evidence here that self-interest itself motivated the formation of elaborate political schemas that determined voting behavior in the tax revolt. Insofar as self-interest had any effect, it was upon the most concretely self-serving policy preferences; it did not form a foundation for a larger ideological structure.

The taxpayers were generally more highly mobilized than other respondents: they voted at a higher rate and were more active in various ways (as shown in table 6.1). But this too was mainly due to the taxpayers' favored demographic characteristics rather than to self-interest. Taxpayers were more educated, affluent, and middle-aged than other respondents, and these characteristics are generally strongly associated with political involvement and participation (as seen in the last chapter). When the demographics are included in the equation, all the self-interest effects on vote frequency and tax activism become quite weak, though they are still mainly statistically significant.[14]

Taxes as a Political Symbol

So far we have treated these measures of taxpayers' self-interest as indicators of their financial impact on the individual voter. But this makes two assumptions that may not be fully justified. It assumes that the stakes are financial rather than something else, and that they are specific to the tax in question rather than reflecting attitudes about taxes in general.

Another possible interpretation of these measures is that they express more general attitudes about "taxes" as a political symbol. When someone is asked whether he pays too much in state income taxes, his response may reflect a symbolic attitude about taxes in general rather than the size of the financial bind his most recent state income tax bill put him in. Even concrete dollar estimates may express very general symbolic attitudes. When someone says he expects that his annual property taxes would have risen $1000 had Proposition 13 not passed, he may be expressing his cynicism about taxes, tax assessors, politicians, and government in general, rather than some carefully calculated estimate of the probable fluctuations in his tax bill.

Our data indicate that both interpretations contain some truth. On the one hand, there is considerable evidence that voters respond quite differently to questions about different taxes, and in that sense their responses are specific to the tax in question. We have seen here, as well as in Chapter 3, how Californians reviled the property tax before Proposition 13; afterward, their anti-tax feeling was spread more evenly across the several types of state and local taxes. Furthermore, if all these attitudes about different taxes merely reflected a common underlying anti-tax feeling, they should all be highly correlated. But as we have already seen, the three questions on subjective burden of taxes (property tax, state income tax, and overall tax burden) correlated together only .27 on the average. Nor does interrelating these three items reveal any large group that blindly feels all taxes are too high. For example, only 19 percent felt they paid "much more" than they should of taxes in general and the state income tax, while 22 percent felt both were "about right."

The specificity of the resentments against particular taxes can also be seen in the fact that income has little residual effect upon support for the tax revolt with indices of taxpayer self-interest considered. For example, income no longer significantly affects the tax rebel index when included in a regression equation with homeownership and subjective tax burden — but they both retain strong effects (the three betas are .04, .16, and .20). Similarly, the felt burden of the state income tax was moderately associated with income ($r = .28$), but fully accounted for all effects of income upon support for Jarvis II, as shown in table 6.5. In other words, higher income levels generally produce higher income tax obligations, but whatever greater pain is produced by that seems fully explained by the state-income-tax-burden variable. So it seems appropriate to interpret these feelings of tax burden as reflecting in some large part the specific felt personal burden of each separate tax, and therefore as having the potential to direct voting behavior against the offending tax.

Nevertheless, some of these measures of taxpayer burden are highly subjective. Subjective feelings about one's own taxes, for example, contrast with homeownership and expected dollar return from anti-tax propositions, which come closer to being objective indicators of tax burden, tied to concrete facts. Such subjective grievances should be convenient vehicles for expressing broader symbolic grievances against government as well as a fairly focused resentment of the personal impact of the specific tax. And this more symbolic anti-tax feeling does surface at several points in our data. For one thing, even though these specific felt tax burdens related most closely to action against the offending tax, they did also relate to support for all aspects of the tax revolt. As table 6.3 showed, homeowners were unusually supportive of the Gann amendment and Jarvis II, which had no bearing on the property tax. And table 6.5 shows that feeling burdened by the state income tax was associated with support for Propositions 13 and 4, neither of which bore directly on the income tax. During the Proposition 13 campaign, its support was related almost as closely to grievances about "state taxes" as to grievances about "county and city taxes," even though no property tax revenues went to the state.[15] And in the Tax Revolt Survey, the generalized personal tax burden and the specific burden of the state income tax contributed equally strongly to support for Jarvis II when both were considered simultaneously (the "much" burdened differed from the "about right" group, on the average, by 24 percent and 27 percent for each of the two dimensions, respectively, with the other controlled). So there is some clear evidence of a "spread of affect" from resentment of one tax to support for the cutting of another tax.

Other evidence for the symbolic nature of anti-tax feeling comes from the fact that the more subjective measure of taxpayer self-interest, perceived tax burden, had much more far-ranging cognitive effects than did the objective measure, homeownership. Table 6.1 shows the greater impact of the former on issue salience and the more anti-government aspects of the tax revolt schema. And when demographic factors are included in those equations, about half the homeownership effect disappears in each case, while the subjective-tax-burden effects are completely unchanged. So the anti-tax grievances captured by the tax revolt were not all logically calculated dollars-and-cents returns.[16]

Inflation and Economic Malaise

The taxpayers had perhaps the simplest and most tangible self-interest in the tax revolt, since it was their money that was being spent by government. But individual voters were also personally affected by changing economic conditions in the late 1970s — by inflation, and, as the decade drew to a close, by worsening economic conditions generally. Many observers felt there was rising economic discontent or "malaise" in the electorate, which played a role in generating the tax revolt.

Two distinctions must be made before analyzing economic discontents.

One concerns time perspective, that is, whether voters look backward or forward. A "retrospective voting" model views people as wanting to change government and its policies when economic conditions have hurt them in the recent past. This notion has been used to explain variations in congressional or presidential voting; when economic conditions turn sour, incumbents suffer at the polls. It is a specific instance of a simple psychological principle: negative affect accrues to stimuli associated with pain or hardship.[17] The forward-looking view is advocated by rational decisionmaking models. According to such models, the voter calculates the future costs and benefits of a particular set of alternatives, and within certain limits chooses the maximizing (or satisficing) alternative.[18] In an inflationary period such rational choices may be biased toward risk aversion. The individual will take definite action now that will avoid the uncertain risks of the future, even if it entails some short-term costs.

The second distinction is between discontents about specific, concrete economic problems and about problems that are more diffuse and pervasive. Unemployment, for example, tends to be a specific problem with a specific solution; the unemployed person has no job, and presumably would be happier with one. But inflation is a mixed case. In some respects it has quite specific and localized effects in an individual's life — one's income may be readjusted regularly for inflation, or taxation may take ever larger proportions of one's income through a progressive, nonindexed income tax. And not all of the tangible effects of inflation are bad. Indeed, some people profit greatly from inflation, as California homeowners did in terms of their homes' values.

Inflation also has intangible effects, since it is a pervasive kind of economic problem. No simple solution exists for inflation. It has confusing effects, benefiting some people and harming others, even benefiting one individual in some respects and harming him in others. It pervades the voter's entire life, creating uncertainty and anxiety without any clear focus. These intangible effects of inflation seem to be more generally experienced as unpleasant. A few high-rolling speculators may thrill at the sudden changes in the financial rules of the game, and view inflationary pressures as offering new opportunities. But the most common reaction of mass publics is quite negative. They do not like to live in an uncertain and anxiety-provoking world.

The main political effects of economic discontents that have been empirically investigated are those upon partisan voting behavior and presidential popularity. Much of the early research was conducted at the aggregate level, relating falling national economic indicators to slipping fortunes of the president's congressional supporters and his own popularity. Inflation rates, how-

ever, have not proven to be among the more powerful predictors of these political effects (though the value of such tests is limited by the fact that inflationary periods have been so rare and so special in other respects, so that they
are severely confounded with other variables). Tests of this retrospective voting hypothesis at the individual level have turned up less impressive results.
The political effects of perceived changes in one's own financial well-being
over the past year, personal financial expectations for the next year, and personal impact of inflation have so far proven to be rather weak and occasional
at best.[19]

In the tax-revolt context, some of the effects of these variables ought to be
quite straightforward. Inflation in the housing market shot property taxes up,
as we have seen. And inflation escalated the state income tax by pushing taxpayers into higher brackets. One might expect these effects of inflation to produce rather direct self-interested support for the tax revolt. In part such
effects should have been captured in the analyses of tax burden presented
earlier in this chapter. But the burden of taxes may have been especially painful for those also feeling squeezed by inflation, so that additional component
needs to be treated here.

Inflation may also contribute to a "malaise." Taxpayers can be angry about
their most recent income tax or property tax bill, and feel that it is undermin-
ing their financial well-being or risking their economic futures. Alternatively,
bad economic conditions can, in a more diffuse manner, produce anti-
government protests and outbursts, or even a generalized malaise, that might
not have any very direct and obvious instrumental value. It is this more
diffuse feeling that we are concerned with here.

Quite plainly many people profit from inflation. Most obviously, property
owners in many parts of California rode the inflationary spiral to huge capital
gains. Workers whose union contracts included cost-of-living escalators did
much better than did most nonunionized workers or people on fixed incomes.
And so on. Nevertheless, Californians were upset by and angry at inflation.
In our survey (as in many others done both in California and throughout the
nation in the late 1970s), inflation was overwhelmingly cited as "the most important problem facing people these days." By 1978 it was far and away the
most-mentioned national problem.

And people felt inflation was a problem for them personally, not just in the
abstract. In our survey, most felt their family's standard of living had been
hurt by inflation in the past few years — 14 percent "badly" and 48 percent
"somewhat" hurt. Only 3 percent said they had been "helped." Similarly, in
California Polls done in November 1979 and May 1980, 45 percent expected

their incomes to increase less in the coming year than the amount of inflation, while only 1 percent in November 1979 and 11 percent in May 1980 expected them to increase more than the rate of inflation. Not surprisingly, then, 56 percent and 48 percent felt inflation was a "very serious" problem to them personally, whereas only 12 percent and 17 percent felt it was "not too" or "not at all" serious.

And few were optimistic that it could be kept under control. From 1974 to 1980 the California Poll asked seven times how confident people were that inflation could be kept within reasonable bounds. "Not too confident" or "not at all confident" responses were given by between 60 percent and 70 percent of the sample every time. So throughout this period inflation was a very real, seemingly relentless, and very personal, threat.

The California economy as a whole was perceived as strong in this period, at least throughout the Proposition 13 campaign. In early 1978, as the campaign got going, 42 percent thought the California economy as a whole was in good times, and 26 percent in bad times. They felt just as positive about their own personal financial prospects. In January 1978, Californians overwhelmingly thought they were better off than they had been a year earlier (by 17 percent) and that they would be better off still a year hence (by 20 percent). Indeed, according to the California Poll, such perceptions were the most upbeat since the 1960s.

In 1979, however, the economy started to sag, and the voters perceived the growing problem. In our survey 55 percent expected the California economy to get worse, and only 17 percent to get better, over the next year. Almost identical figures held in a California Poll conducted on the eve of the Jarvis II election. And people began to express the same gloom about their personal prospects. From mid-1979 until the defeat of Jarvis II, all polls showed more Californians feeling they were worse off than better off financially compared to a year earlier, with the margin varying from 11 percent in May 1979 and May 1980 to less than 1 percent in our November 1979 survey.[20]

How should these discontents have influenced the tax revolt? The simplest hypothesis is the retrospective voting model already presented, which predicts that those with slipping finances and those feeling especially hurt by inflation would be especially drawn to the tax revolt. The risk aversion hypothesis holds that those expecting a falling economy, personal financial problems, and out-of-control inflation would be tax rebels. A more complex mixture of these hypotheses focuses on "stagflation": Robert Kuttner, for example, emphasizes the one-two punch of inflation-created tax inequities (particularly in the tax levied on homes) and more generalized economic distress created by a slowing economy. Hence he argues that those both badly hurt by inflation *and* financially discontented in general should have been most lured to the tax revolt.[21] A final variant suggests that inflationary times may simply inspire more selfishness, shortsightedness, and greed. In an uncertain world, where one's money might not be worth anything in the future, one might as well take all one can right now. That is, short-term self-interest might produce stronger effects among those especially worried about the economy or inflation.

Retrospective Voting

Much evidence was available to test the simplest version of the retrospective voting hypothesis. The Tax Revolt Survey and the November 1979 and May 1980 California Polls of past economic problems, included several measures, identifying those who felt "financially worse off" than a year earlier, who (with their families) had been "badly hurt" by inflation, who mentioned inflation as one of the two most important problems facing Californians, who felt inflation was a "very serious" problem to them personally, or who felt their family income had not kept up with inflation over the previous twelve months.

As plausible as the retrospective voting hypothesis is, it receives no support whatever in these data. Those who felt "worse off" financially in general differed from those who felt "better off" by no more than 2 percent in being tax rebels in our survey, or in supporting Jarvis II in the two California Polls. Nor did the inflation-impact items show any stronger results. In four of the five cases (using the tax rebel index in our survey, and support for Jarvis II in the two California Polls), those feeling most affected by inflation differed from others by no more than 3 percent one way or the other. The only exception is in the November 1979 California Poll: those feeling inflation was "very serious" were 10 percent more likely to support Jarvis II than the rest of the sample. But in our survey, done at the same time with a considerably larger sample, the analogous difference was only 2 percent. So we conclude that neither sagging personal finances nor the personal impact of inflation increased support for the tax revolt in any simple sense.[22] There is little support here for a simple version of the economic-malaise version of the retrospective voting model, or indeed for any role at all of generalized personal economic discontent.

Risk Aversion

If inflation or other economic dislocations make people risk averse, they should hesitate to take dangerous chances with their own finances, and may act politically to freeze their current financial situation in place. In the present context, this should have led to strong pressure for tax limitations among people who were pessimistic about their own (or the state's) economic future, especially among those worried about continuing inflation.

The available data provide several measures of personal expectations. As indicated already, the November 1979 and May 1980 California Polls identified those who felt they would be "worse off financially" a year hence, who expected to be able to save less money than they had in the previous year, who were "not at all confident" inflation could be kept within reasonable bounds in the future, who expected that in the coming year their family income would increase less than the amount of inflation, who felt the California economy in general would get worse in the next twelve months, and who felt California was economically in bad times now.

Again the differences are very small. In only two cases did those who were anxious about inflation or economic conditions differ by more than 6 percent from those who were more sanguine about their own, and the state's, future. Those who in November 1979 felt they would save less in the coming year were 10 percent more in favor of Jarvis II (but the analogous difference in May 1980 was just 4 percent). And, in a reversal, pessimists about the California economy were 14 percent *less* likely to be tax rebels. It is most prudent to conclude that this diffuse form of risk aversion hypothesis was not borne out by the data.

Stagflation

The stagflation variant on the risk aversion hypothesis suggested that the unique conjunction of inflation and a slipping economy was responsible for the strength of the anti-tax sentiment. On the face of it, this hypothesis seems inconsistent with the electoral outcomes, because the highly successful Proposition 13 campaign was waged in boom times and with great optimism about the economic future, as we have seen, whereas the unsuccessful Jarvis II campaign was waged amidst growing fears of recession. But this aggregate-level inconsistency does not necessarily mean the hypothesis could not hold at the individual level.

Again voters could have been primarily concerned with the recent past or with the future. To test the pure retrospective version first, we looked at the respondents who felt *both* that their finances had been slipping *and* (in the Tax Revolt Survey) that they had been "badly hurt" by inflation or (in the

California Polls) that it was a "very serious" personal problem. However, in our survey, the *lowest* proportion of tax rebels fell into this cell. In the two California Polls, these cells fell within 4 percent of the support for Jarvis II in the samples as wholes. Thus the stagflation version of the retrospective voting hypothesis has little merit either.

Kuttner focused more particularly on a slightly different mixture of past financial difficulties and anxiety about future inflationary trends. His idea was that the most threatened would be people who felt that they were doing more poorly all the time and that the economy was out of control, and that these people would want to cut costs immediately wherever possible. To test this, we looked at people who felt most seriously personally affected by inflation, and who also believed the California economy was getting worse. In the Tax Revolt Survey, pessimists who had been "badly hurt" by inflation constituted only 10 percent of the sample. And this group gave the *least* support to the tax revolt of any combination of personal impact of inflation and economic pessimism or optimism. Even more risk aversion might be expected from those who had not *yet* been badly hurt by inflation but who expected the economy to go sour, but these were not very supportive of the tax revolt either. The two California Polls included three different measures of inflation's impact (it was a "very serious" problem for respondents personally, they felt their own income had not kept up with inflation, or they felt their income would not be likely to keep up with inflation in the near future). The personal impact of inflation had almost exactly the same effect among optimists and pessimists about the California economy, in each of four comparisons. Indeed, if anything, in every case the strongest support for the tax revolt came from respondents who had been affected by inflation but who were optimistic, not pessimistic, about the economy. But none of the effects of inflation were large enough to be statistically reliable.

Inflation-Induced Selfishness

If inflationary pressures increased selfishness, inflation's impact should have interacted with self-interest: people would want to change government when they had been hurt personally *and* when the change might profit them. Hence we might expect that homeowners suffering from inflation would have been the greatest boosters of Proposition 13, because their anxieties could have been soothed with large tax rebates. Again the data show no effect: the homeowner-renter difference in support for Proposition 13 was 24 percent among those badly hurt by inflation, and 19 percent among those unaffected.

Those with high incomes who had been hit hard by inflation might have been especially attracted to Jarvis II, because of the tax savings it offered them. Another possible version of this hypothesis is that middle-income people who felt most squeezed by inflation would join the tax revolt more, because their income levels would not absorb inflationary increases in taxes. Both hypotheses could be tested quite thoroughly in the data available to us. All told, we had six inflation-impact items in the Tax Revolt Survey and in the California Polls done during the Jarvis II campaign. Inflation was generally felt to be most painful by the poor. But the data give little consistent support for any hypothesis: the differences are in mixed directions and generally rather small. On the average, over these six comparisons, more severe impact of inflation increased support for Jarvis II by about 4 percent among the high- and middle-income groups, and by 1 percent among the low-income group. We can find no scrap of evidence for any impact of inflation in its diffuse, generalized form on the tax revolt.[23]

Issue Publics and Participation

Since economic malaise had no discernible impact upon support for the tax revolt, it is not surprising that it did not help to generate an issue public for the tax revolt, or greater participation in it. Table 6.1 shows that neither declining finances nor inflation's impact had any influence at all on issue salience, opinionation, or the four attitudes about government in the tax revolt schema. Because of this overwhelmingly null pattern, we did not test further for malaise-inspired schematic thinking. Declining finances was associated with some increase in voting turnout, but it utterly washes out with demographics controlled (the beta falls to .03).

To summarize: inflation's impact, financial distress, and pessimism about the economy had little effect on support for the tax revolt. Those most harmed by inflation tended to be the poor and minorities, and they were not enthusiastic about the tax revolt. Nor did such economic malaise exacerbate self-interest; it was associated with less short-term political selfishness as often as with more. And these dimensions did not contribute to the formation of a tax-revolt issue public or to heightened participation in the revolt.

Conclusions

We will defer our general conclusions about the role of self-interest until after we consider the anti-revolt interests in the next chapter. But a few comments are in order here. We considered the consequences of tax burdens, inflation, and a generally declining economy, on the assumption that all would contribute to an economically self-aggrandizing (or at least threat-minimizing) response to the tax revolt. The clearest self-interested responses came from those with large property tax, and/or income tax burdens. Support for the tax revolt, not surprisingly, was strongly associated with all indicators of tax burden.

Contrary to what we expected, we did not find that the strongest support for the revolt came from people whose tax burdens had made them most economically vulnerable, such as elderly homeowners or those on low incomes feeling most squeezed by inflation. Rather, the characterization "a revolt of the haves" comes closer. Middle-aged, white, fully employed, affluent male homeowners were the greatest enthusiasts for it. And the large cash saving provided by Proposition 13 attracted much more support than the small one promised by Jarvis II. It would exceed our data to fix a price on a Californian's vote, but the average homeowner had a stake in Proposition 13, over the first year alone, of more than $1000, and in Jarvis II of more like $200. If Jarvis II had promised a return comparable to that of Proposition 13, it too might well have passed.

This specific dollar-value kind of self-interest did not, by itself, do much to motivate the development of an issue public for the tax revolt. Taxpayers who stood to gain from the revolt did pay more attention to the revolt, and did have more pro-revolt attitudes on the several elements of the tax revolt schema than did others. But self-interest provided no coherent self-serving schema for the taxpayers. The cognitive effects of self-interest were rather limited. And indeed, our somewhat fragmentary evidence suggests that even these cognitive effects were induced by the symbolic, rather than the self-interested, aspects of taxation. That is, it was not the dollars, but the symbols associated with taxes that created some modest schematic thinking.

But these were very concrete and specific dollars-and-cents versions of self-interest: How many dollars will I save or lose if the tax structure changes? Other economic discontents were rampant in the populace, ones with a much more diffuse and generalized character. Inflation seemed out of control, and the economy was lagging, at least toward the end of the revolt period. We posed a number of hypotheses about the possible effects of such generalized economic malaise. But none of them panned out.

Our tentative assessment of self-interest as a factor on the pro-revolt side is that it operated quite specifically and narrowly. Specific dollar returns contributed to support for the revolt, whereas diffuse and generalized economic discontents did not. The cognitive effects of self-interest did not extend far beyond the specific ballot measures that would return the most dollars to the voter. And self-interest seemed to motivate little more political activism than would have been expected from the generally advantaged social status of the taxpayers. To be sure, self-interest had a much stronger effect upon pro-revolt political preferences than has been the case in other political settings we have studied. Yet it failed to produce three other political effects in the California mass public that might have expected from it: it did not produce broadly rationalizing attitudes toward government in general, or self-interested activism, or strong anti-government sentiments.

7

The Anti-Revolt Interests

The tax revolt proposed to cut taxes, and thereby to reduce the scope of government. One would expect that the beneficiaries of government would resist such cuts, on a self-interested basis if on no other. At the start of the last chapter we reported that the recipients of specialized government services seemingly did not mobilize, either cognitively or behaviorally, to resist the tax revolt. Public employees, by contrast, appeared to respond in a very self-protective manner. They defended their own roles in government quite staunchly, even if they did not defend the status quo of government operation in most other respects. Now let us look more closely at these two groups and their quite different responses.

Service Recipients

Tax reductions or spending limitations would sooner or later inevitably cut services, and so would have a negative impact on the recipients of services. Assessing this impact is difficult, though, because of the vast number of services provided by state and local governments. It would not be practical to identify the recipients of all of them. Moreover, some services have much narrower and more specialized clienteles than others. For example, almost all Californians use the public roads and depend on local police and fire departments for protection. But only a minority are on welfare or have children in the public schools. We chose, therefore, to concentrate on areas of public services that (1) were vitally important to the recipients and (2) had specialized rather than universal clienteles. We theorized that these clusters of service recipients would be the most likely to feel threatened by the tax revolt and to engage in organized opposition to it. That is, if any recipients of public services would respond in a self-interested way, we thought these would. We looked at three different groups of service recipients: those benefiting from public education, those who received direct financial benefits from state or local government, and those who were unemployed or whose families had had difficulty maintaining full employment.

The largest of these groups consists of the parents of children in public school. Our surveys estimated the number of such parents at around 26 percent of the adult population.[1] The public schools received most of their support from the property tax, and then, after Proposition 13, from state taxes, to which the income tax was a major contributor. So the public schools stood to be disadvantaged quite seriously by reductions in these taxes. Indeed, throughout the tax revolt period, Californians consistently believed that the services provided by the public schools were the most likely to suffer cuts. Two months after Proposition 13 passed, 34 percent said they had expected it to have unfavorable effects on their own neighborhood schools (and 9 percent, favorable effects). Early in the Jarvis II campaign, 32 percent said it was "very likely," and 25 percent "somewhat likely," that Jarvis II would lower the quality of public schools. Later that summer, two California Polls asked respondents if they had "seen, heard, or experienced yourself" reduction in government services because of Proposition 13, and the public schools were mentioned spontaneously far more than any other service area, by 31 percent of the full sample in each case.[2]

Furthermore, public opinion consistently held that school cutbacks were the least desired outcome of the tax revolt. The most common reason for supporting the state bailout of local governments after Proposition 13 was to prevent school cutbacks; 31 percent gave that reason (the next most common, 22 percent, was that the state surplus was unnecessary anyway). And five polls from August 1978 through September 1980 asked if post–Proposition 13 cuts had been in the right or wrong places, and if wrong, where. In the feverish summer of 1978, before the schools reopened, the most common "wrong place" cited was "at the bottom" — meaning that low-level employees, rather than fat-cat bureaucrats, were being cut — but in all the later polls schools were cited most often, gradually rising from 17 percent to 32 percent of the full sample.[3]

Another potential interest group consists of those with a direct stake in California's renowned system of public higher education. The University of California was especially active in the campaign against Jarvis II. Its president, David Saxon, was particularly outspoken in forecasting dire consequences for the university. A California Poll in February 1980 assessed the attitudes of three groups of people who might have some personal stake in public higher education, because either they themselves or someone in their immediate family was (1) a graduate of the University of California (13 percent of the sample), (2) currently enrolled in an institution of public higher education (one of the branches of the university, or of the state college system, or of the community college system; 29 percent of the sample), and/or (3) had graduated from one of these institutions (36 percent of the sample).

A third patently self-interested group of people received direct financial benefits from state or local government, in the form of unemployment compensation, pensions, public assistance such as AFDC, or medical aid. Such direct-aid programs were the targets the public most wanted the budget cutters to attack, as we saw in Chapter 3. So they might well have been expected to be among the most vulnerable government programs if state and local taxes were to be cut radically (though in fact it was not easy to cut them much; for example, welfare was funded by the state, not by the property tax, and therefore immune from Proposition 13, and much publicly financed medical care is funded by federal taxes). To measure the respondent's dependence on services, a "government assistance" scale indexed the number of these programs providing aid to the respondent and his or her immediate family. By this standard, the truly dependent were rather small in number: only 17 percent depended on two or more of these benefits.[4]

Unemployment, or the threat of unemployment, provided a fourth potential source of self-interest. Since the New Deal, government assistance has provided an economic cushion for those who are permanently or temporarily unemployed. Cuts in the public sector might jeopardize that cushion. Moreover, it was widely predicted, during the campaign for Proposition 13, that its passage would trigger a recession in the state economy. So people who were already having problems maintaining employment might well have expected the tax revolt to create further problems for them.[5] Again, a rather small group is involved: 5 percent of the work-force sample were unemployed and looking for work, or laid off, and another 10 percent were employed but worried about losing their jobs. This constituted an "employment status" scale. When we expand the time frame and take the immediate family into consideration, the frequency of employment problems is greater. A total of 38 percent had (themselves or someone in the immediate family) had at least one of the following serious work problems during "the last couple of years":

unemployment, layoff, losing a job, reduced work hours, or a cut in pay. We used the number of such problems as a "work problems" scale.

The intersection of those receiving direct financial benefits and those troubled about employment illustrates both the existence of a needy, marginally self-sufficient subgroup and the fact that it is a small political constituency. Only 9 percent were *both* getting any of these forms of public assistance *and* either unemployed or worried about losing a job. Similarly, only 10 percent both had one or more family work problems and were either unemployed or worried about it, and 21 percent were on some form of government assistance and had had one or more family work problems in the previous two years.

The characteristics of the service recipients will come as no surprise. They were relatively poor and less well-educated than the rest of the population. Old people (65 +) were much more likely to receive direct financial assistance from the government than anyone else, while young people (especially 18–24) experienced a disproportionate share of the unemployment and other work problems. Racial minorities were slightly more likely to fall into these categories, but here the differences were not large. Parents of children in public school were distinguished demographically principally by their age: 93 percent were in the 25–49 age-group. They were not especially atypical in race or sex, or in social class as indexed by income and education.

In contrast with the responses of taxpayers and public employees, self-interest played almost no role in the service recipients' attitudes toward the tax revolt. But the response of parents of schoolchildren is somewhat different from that of people with more global financial dependency on government. Let us consider these in turn.

In the overall regression analysis of the tax rebel index, the parents of children in the public schools were not significantly more opposed to the tax revolt than anyone else (see table 6.1). The same holds when we look at cross-tabulations of support for each individual proposition; parents of public school children differ from nonparents by only 1 percent or 2 percent.[6] And demographic controls do not alter any of this. These data reveal no protest from the schools' major constituents. This is a most important fact, given the major impact Proposition 13 had on the public schools. And it is especially noteworthy since this impact was so widely perceived by the public.

Nor is it evident that those with a personal stake in public higher education showed any very great opposition to Jarvis II. Neither graduates of the University of California nor alumni of the state's public higher education institutions in general showed significantly more opposition to it than did the rest of the citizenry. Those who either were enrolled or had a family member enrolled in public higher education did, though the effect was unimpressive (gamma = .13).[7]

Those who were most economically dependent on government also showed only weak opposition to the revolt, as shown in table 6.1. The government assistance scale did not relate significantly to the tax rebel index. The employment status and work problems scales did, though quite weakly, and with demographic controls, the latter finding becomes nonsignificant. Because these last three service-recipient scales are so skewed, such regression analyses could underestimate their true effects. Hence we tested their relationships to the tax rebel index with crosstabular analyses. For the most part, the same picture of weak effects emerges. Those on government assistance programs were only 2 percent less likely to be tax rebels than were the unassisted; those with any personal or family work problems were 3 percent less likely to be than were the untroubled; and again employment status yields a little more: those worried about losing a job, or unemployed, were 13 percent less likely than the unworried employed to be rebels.

When we look at the small minority that was most distressed, there is a slight upturn in opposition. This is detectable in the 5 percent of the sample that received aid from at least three of the four assistance areas, the 5 percent that were unemployed or laid off, and the 10 percent that had at least three family work problems. These extreme groups had somewhat more defenders of the public sector than did the less dependent majority, but again the differences were for the most part not very great, averaging a little over 10 percent.[8]

In short, being the parent of a child in the public schools had no effect at all. Being in the most economically depressed 5 percent of the population, whether in terms of being dependent on direct financial aid from the government or in terms of current unemployment, did lead to somewhat greater opposition to the revolt. But any other indicator of dependency on government services simply had no effect. This is quite a striking absence of opposition to the revolt among those it presumably would harm the most. We will explore the possible reasons for this passivity below; for now it is enough to note that it gave the tax rebels quite an important political advantage.

Narrow Self-Interest

The service recipients' self-interest generated self-serving attitudes only in the narrowest sense: it did not help to generate an issue public opposed to the tax revolt. Most important, their self-interest did not promote broader rationalizations boosting the role of the public sector. Hence when the tax revolt came on the scene, service recipients did not have the necessary generalized beliefs about the value of the public sector—what we have described as the components of the tax revolt schema—to guide them to strong opposition to it.

The lack of cognitive activation generated by their self-interest is shown in table 6.1 in two ways. First of all, self-interest generated no increase in attention to taxation and spending issues. It was associated with *less* salience of these issues, if anything (though the one negative relationship washes out with demographics controlled). And it had no clear effect on opinionation regarding the three propositions (unemployment decreasing it slightly, and family work problems slightly increasing it, with only a weak effect for the latter—a beta of .05—surviving demographic controls).

Second, self-interest produced no very general pro-government or pro-public-sector attitudes. Only three of the twelve associations of service recipience with the components of the tax revolt schema were statistically significant, but even these were quite weak and none survived controls for demographic variables. Self-interest simply did not lead those who were dependent on government to adopt generalized pro-public-sector attitudes. To take a couple of extreme examples, majorities of those dependent on at least three government programs, and of those with at least four family work problems, wanted smaller rather than larger government in general.

Exactly parallel tests cannot be made upon those with some self-interest in public higher education, since they were identified only in a California Poll that did not contain any of the elements of our tax revolt schema. But those respondents were asked how much of the state income tax cuts proposed by Jarvis II could be covered by the state surplus, and how much services would have to be cut if it passed. Both questions measured broader support for the public sector to some degree. Again self-interest had little effect; only one of the six relationships between the three indicators of self-interest in higher education and these two questions was statistically significant.

Even if the service recipients did not particularly defend the public sector in general, they might have been expected to show some special defense of the programs that benefited them most directly. To test this, we looked first at the public schools. The schools had historically taken a very large share of the property tax revenues. And some writers saw the success of Proposition 13 as partly reflecting a waning of support for the schools, especially among affluent whites.[9] With a dropping birthrate, and "white flight" from court-ordered school integration, fewer homeowners may have wanted to pay property taxes for other people's children. Moreover, as we have seen, by far the biggest complaint about post–Proposition 13 budget cuts was that they victimized the schools too much.

Parents of public school children were not especially protective of big government, or its efficiency, or public employees' pay scales, as shown in table 6.1. But they did at least show some selfish special support for spending on the public schools, compared to nonparents, in several polls through the tax-revolt period, as shown in table 7.1. The difference is not enormous, averaging about 15 percent, but it is quite consistent. Moreover, homeowners (who

TABLE 7.1 Self-interest and spending preferences regarding the public schools.

Net % favoring increased spending on public schools (PDI)	June 1977	May 1978	Aug. 1978	Nov. 1979	
Parents	+43%	na	+23%	+56%	+46%
Nonparents	+32	na	+10	+36	+31
Difference	+11	na	+13	+20	+15
Owners	+30	– 6	+ 6	+37	+28
Renters	+48	+27	+30	+48	+49
Difference	–18	–33	–24	–11	–21
Childless owners	+24	na	– 2	+31	+22
All respondents	+36	+ 3	+14	+40	+34
% with children					
Owners	44	na	39	31	31
Renters	18	na	29	20	21
All respondents	35	na	34	27	26

Sources: California Polls (June 1977, May 1978, Aug. 1978, Nov. 1979); Tax Revolt Survey (Nov. 1979).

Note: Entries are PDI values: percentage wanting increased spending on public schools minus percentage wanting decreased spending. The wording of the spending item varied somewhat. In June 1977 respondents were asked whether the amount of "tax money" spent should be increased, held at the current level, or cut back. The August 1978 California Poll and the Tax Revolt Survey asked whether the current level of "expenditures" or "money spent" should be cut back, held the same, or increased. In the June 1978 and November 1979 California Polls the question was: "Some areas of public spending . . . might be affected by lower tax limits, . . . you think the amount of tax money for each one should be increased, held the same, or cut back."

paid most of the school bills through property taxes) were less supportive of school spending than were renters by fairly large margins — especially right around the feverish climax of the Proposition 13 campaign. And childless homeowners were by far the least supportive of the schools (though, interestingly enough, even they felt school spending should be increased, on balance, except during the relatively unusual summer of 1978). Moreover, in our survey the parents were somewhat (11 percent) more likely than nonparents to think the schools could not significantly cut their costs. There is a fairly clear pattern of self-interest here, at least in terms of a defense of the most personally relevant services.

When we look at other groups of service recipients, we do not invariably find that their budgetary priorities are equally self-interested. Some are; as table 7.2 shows, people whose families drew funds from Medicare or Medicaid were much more supportive than others of more spending on public health. People currently or recently on public assistance or unemployment

TABLE 7.2 Self-interest and preferences for spending on specific services.

	Type of Self-interest				
Spending on:	On Medicaid or Medicare	Public school parents	On unemployment compensation	On public assistance	On government pension
Public schools	+ 38%	+ 15%	+ 12%	+ 18%	− 8%
Higher education	+ 26	+ 2	+ 12	+ 12	+ 4
Parks and recreation	+ 16	0	+ 11	+ 10	− 1
Welfare	− 24	− 5	+ 11	+ 39	0
Public health	+ 38	− 8	+ 11	+ 27	0
Public transportation	+ 55	− 11	+ 3	+ 1	− 6
% self-interested	31	26	17	12	8

Source: Tax Revolt Survey.

Note: Entries are the difference between interested and disinterested groups (for example, public school parents minus nonparents) in the PDI value for spending on the service area specified (for example, percentage wanting an increase minus percentage wanting a decrease in spending on public schools). The larger the positive value, the larger the tendency for the interested group to want more spending, relative to the disinterested group.

compensation supported spending on welfare and public health much more than did others.[10] But there are examples of the failure of self-interest here, as well. Those on government pensions show no special enthusiasm for social programs. When California Poll respondents were asked whether the university should be given more or less money, those with self-interest in public higher education averaged only 3 percent higher in the spending PDI than did disinterested respondents (the largest difference being only 6 percent). Indeed, graduates of public colleges and universities in general were no friends at all of the University of California: their spending PDI was 2 percent lower than that of nongraduates.

And in any case, table 7.2 adds to our impression of the cognitive narrowness of this self-interest. Once we move beyond the specific program from which the respondent benefits, the service recipients' greater enthusiasm for public-sector spending rapidly dissipates. The median entry is just below +4 percent. This means that service recipients show, overall, just barely more support than do nonrecipients for spending on services other than the ones benefiting themselves. Government programs in general get no beneficial spread of affect from those who benefit from one. And self-interested support for spending drops off surprisingly quickly as the individual's interest becomes less direct. Parents of schoolchildren show no special support for either higher education or parks and recreation, even though their families might be more likely than others to benefit from them. Welfare recipients do not constitute a supportive constituency for public transportation. Pensioners do not give special support to any of these public services, even though presumably many of them take advantage of government-supported welfare, public health, and public transportation programs. Similarly, in data not shown here, neither the young nor the old, nor those on low incomes, give any special support to public transportation, even though they presumably are its heaviest users (the analogous values range from −1 percent to −7 percent). Similarly, those with a stake in higher education extended no special protection to the public elementary and secondary schools against possible budget cuts threatened by Jarvis II: none of our three groups with a presumed stake in public higher education were significantly more opposed than anyone else to cutting spending on the schools (the difference averaging under 4 percent).

In short, preferences for spending in specific service areas do *not* have any very general basis in self-interest. Rather, respondents usually (but not invariably) give special support to spending on the specific service they benefit from, but this dependence on government does not inspire them to any special support for social services in general, or even for expanded programs in areas that seem closely related to those they already benefit from. Since service recipience showed no sign of generating an issue public opposed to the tax revolt, we did not pursue further the question of schematic thinking among those dependent on government.[11]

Finally, as already indicated, the service recipients were not behaviorally activated any more than they were cognitively organized. Table 6.1 shows that if anything they were *less* active than those not dependent on government. Of the eight relationships between service recipiency and vote frequency or tax activism, three are significantly negative, and one is positive. Any significantly *lower* level of activity by assistance-dependents is mainly due to their disadvantaged social location (poorer, less-educated, and so on). Including the demographics removes all their significant deficiencies in voting and activist participation. But it leaves unchanged the fact that self-interest does not promote any special activism in these groups.

Why does self-interest seem to have such weak energizing effects on the recipients of government services? The service recipients tend to come from population groups that are usually the least politicized—especially the poor, minorities, and the very young and very old. But as we have seen, this fact has not suppressed true underlying self-interest effects. When demographic factors are taken into consideration, the picture does not change.

Presumably a general precondition for self-interest effects would be some causal attributions linking political events to one's own welfare.[12] A key one would be a perception that the tax revolt would have a negative impact on one's own personal receipt of government services. And such a perception does not seem to have been widespread, either in the population as a whole or in the special groups of service recipients we have identified. Many thought that services would be cut, at least before the Gann amendment and Jarvis II elections. In the full Tax Revolt Survey sample, 52 percent thought the Gann amendment would cut the overall level of government services. But our four groups of service recipients did not think it much more likely than did anyone else: parents, 55 percent; those on three or more government assistance programs, 63 percent; and those with three or more work problems, 56 percent. Similarly, our three indices of self-interest in public higher education did not relate strongly at all to the fear that Jarvis II would lower the quality of the university, that tuition would have to be instituted, or even that a drop in quality would be a very serious matter if it did occur. The largest self-interest effect in these nine comparisons was 8 percent, and the average was 4 percent.

Secondly, service recipients were not much more likely than anyone else to believe their own services had been especially harmed by the changes that occurred in the first year and a half after the passage of Proposition 13. Only a relatively small minority of the California population perceived any impact of Proposition 13 on the government services they or their family received. In the Tax Revolt Survey, and in three California Polls done from August 1978 through February 1980, relatively few (between 16 percent and 27 percent) said their own services had suffered. Persons in our three groups of service recipients were, on the average, only 3 percent more likely than the sample as a whole to feel that government services for their own family had changed for the worse.

Finally, when real cuts did occur in the specific services they benefited from, service recipients were no more aggrieved than anyone else. This, again, is clearest in the case of the public schools. In August 1978, after Proposition 13 had canceled summer schools across the state and threatened other radical cuts in the fall, parents were only 9 percent more likely than nonparents to say that Proposition 13 had had a bad effect on education. Parents were only 2 percent more likely than nonparents to cite the schools for why they supported the post-13 state bailout of local government, and 7 percent more likely to cite them for why post-13 cuts had been made in the wrong places (though a California Poll conducted just after the Gann amendment passed did find the gap widening somewhat on the latter item, to 14 percent). In short, parents showed a striking tendency *not* to bias their perceptions of the tax revolt with self-serving rationalizations.

None of this suggests any great and unique outcry among service recipients about government cuts, even in their own services. Obviously the state surplus cushioned much of the tax revolt's impact, which it no longer will do. But for whatever reason, the service recipients' response to the tax revolt was quite quiescent. It was only very narrowly self-interested, to the extent that it was self-interested at all. So it is quite possible that even with the appropriate attributions, service recipients would not have responded in a very self-interested manner.

Public Employees

The purveyors of public services constituted another major interest group: 9 percent of our sample were employed by state or local government, and 16 percent more had some public employee in the family.[13] Unlike service recipients, public employees were strong opponents of the tax revolt. The difference was systematic and showed up on every poll on which it was assessed, as shown in table 7.3. Most public employees were opposed to Proposition 13, and they were overwhelmingly opposed to Jarvis II. In fact, the drop from their mild opposition to Proposition 13 to their overwhelming opposition to Jarvis II is quite startling in its solidarity. Eventually much of the rest of the public joined them, but public employees got out of the blocks fast.

TABLE 7.3 Public employees and the tax revolt.

	Public employees themselves	Public employees' families	Others	Difference
Support for the tax revolt				
Proposition 13				
May 1978	40%	—	56%	− 16%
Aug. 1978	44	50	68	− 24
Recalled vote	45	66	77	− 32
Nov. 1979	55	63	71	− 16
Feb. 1980	47	57	69	− 22
Gann amendment				
Aug. 1978	44	54	57	− 13
Nov. 1979	59	79	83	− 24
Jarvis II				
Nov. 1979	26	48	57	− 31
Feb. 1980	35	57	66	− 31
April 1980	21	41	53	− 32
May 1980	22	23	42	− 20
Tax rebel index	41	55	65	− 24
Participation				
Voted on both Propositions 13 and 4	51	30	30	+ 21
Talked to friends about revolt	90	72	66	+ 24
Other active participation	34	29	26	+ 8

Sources: Los Angeles Times Poll (May 1978); California Polls (Aug. 1978, Feb. 1980, April 1980, May 1980); Tax Revolt Survey (recalled vote, Nov. 1979).

Public employees were also unusually vigorous and effective in this opposition. They were more likely to vote: 51 percent voted on both Propositions 13 and 4, as opposed to 30 percent in the rest of the public. They were more likely to participate actively in these campaigns in other ways: 90 percent talked about the revolt with their friends (contrasted with 66 percent of the others), and 34 percent engaged in some direct action (26 percent of the others). These differences are also reflected in the regression analyses in table 6.1.

Table 7.3 also shows that the families of public employees tended to fall somewhere in between in opposition to the tax revolt, but closer to the rest of the population. The same is true of attitudes relevant to the tax revolt. So in further analyses we will concentrate primarily on those who actually worked for government, rather than on their families.

Public employees tend to be rather advantaged socially and economically relative to the rest of the population. They are, on the average, considerably better educated than the rest of the California population (73 percent have some college, compared to 47 percent of those who are not public employees and have none in their immediate family), considerably younger (74 percent are between 25 and 49, while only 50 percent of the others are), and earn comfortable though not lavish incomes (73 percent earn at least $15,000 per year, compared to 58 percent of the others). But this demographic advantage was *not* responsible for either their extraordinary level of opposition to the tax revolt or their extraordinary level of activity in these campaigns. None of the public-employee effects on the tax rebel, vote frequency, or tax activism scales is materially diminished with all the demographic variables included in the equations.[14] Hence the public employees' unique role in the opposition to the tax revolt stemmed apparently from self-interest rather than from social advantage.

This finding is of considerable interest. Public employees across the United States generally show unusually high voting turnout. Raymond Wolfinger and Steven Rosenstone's analysis of this phenomenon locates it especially among working-class government employees, and especially in states with highly developed political machines; presumably it is a strongly induced (if not forced) vote by patronage employees anxious about their jobs. But they find little evidence of any especially high turnout by public employees in "reform" states like California that have relatively few patronage jobs, and almost none among the white-collar workers that dominate in California's governments.[15] So this extraordinary level of participation seems to have been elicited especially by the tax revolt.

Narrow Self-Interest

The public employees also prove, however, to have been a narrowly focused issue public. They were no higher in issue salience or opinionation than anyone else, as shown in table 6.1. Since they were especially opposed to the tax revolt, however, it was important to explore in detail the extent to which this opposition was founded in much broader, more organized, schematic attitudes defending the public sector in its many manifestations. Our strategy was to compare public employees with other citizens on as many questions measuring support for the public sector as we could, in the California Poll shortly after Proposition 13, in the Tax Revolt Survey, and in two California Polls during the Jarvis II campaign. Table 7.4 provides a representative sample of these results. Our basic goal throughout this discussion is to clarify exactly where public employees differ in a self-serving manner from other Californians, and where they do not, to establish the cognitive boundaries of their self-interest.

Public employees responded to questions concerning their own employment and wages in an unsurprisingly strong self-interested way. For example, they were much more likely than the public as a whole to feel their own pay levels were appropriate. Like most of the service recipients, then, they show self-interested attitudes at the most concrete level.

The early stages of the tax revolt did not appear to threaten them very much. As we have already indicated, they and their organizations did not put on a do-or-die campaign against either Proposition 13 or the Gann amendment; table 7.4 shows that they were not particularly concerned about either of these propositions. This apparently benign reaction seems appropriate to the times, since the state surplus protected the public sector from serious cuts until well after Jarvis II went down to defeat. And the Gann amendment attempted to choke off the expansion of the public sector, but did not attempt to reduce it. Perhaps the "crying wolf" quality of the establishment political leaders' rhetoric before the vote on Proposition 13, the many layoff notices that were in fact mailed out, and then the comparatively small number of actual post-13 layoffs had lulled them into thinking they were in little jeopardy. Still, public employees turned at least wary about this time; they were unusually likely to have heard of the fairly low-profile Gann amendment (93 percent had, against 79 percent of the rest of the sample).

When Jarvis II was at hand, however, public employees saw it as a distinct and direct threat. A great many perceived it as likely to put public employees out of work, and considered that effect very serious. They thought it would

TABLE 7.4 The narrowness of public employees' self-interest.

| | Public Employee in Family | | | |
	Self	Family member	None	Difference
Own pocketbook				
Government workers are not overpaid[b]	85%	66%	58%	+ 27%*
Gann amendment no personal threat				
Government spending cut too much since				
Proposition 13[c]	32	21	22	+ 10
Would Gann cut public employment[b]?	65	64	61	+ 4
Would Gann limit public-sector pay[b]?	70	64	62	+ 8
Jarvis II a threat				
Would produce very serious service cuts[d]	50	41	30	+ 20*
State surplus would cover little of revenue shortfall[d]	51	50	36	+ 15*
Very likely to cut public employment[c]	44	36	29	+ 15*
This is a very serious effect[c]	51	38	24	+ 27*
No general support of public sector				
Democratic[b]	45	46	48	− 3
Liberal[b]	40	40	37	+ 3
Government can cut at most 10%[b]	24	27	25	− 1
Want larger government in general[b]	32	28	30	+ 2
Want increase in service spending[a]	37	31	37	0
Want increase in service spending[b]	77	70	72	+ 5
Support state bailout[a]	80	71	71	+ 9
Losing local control over schools to the state is				
very bad[a]	31	37	31	0
Jarvis II not likely to improve economy[c]	50	50	40	+ 10
Jarvis II not likely to slow inflation[c]	68	62	61	+ 7
Except for education				
Schools can cut no more than 10%[a]	50	49	42	+ 8
Proposition 13 had bad effect on education[a]	50	51	34	+ 16*
Jarvis II very likely to hurt school quality[c]	52	43	32	+ 20*
This is a very serious effect[c]	56	63	53	+ 3
Jarvis II will restrict access of poor to college[c]	45	33	24	+ 21*
Should not impose tuition at public universities[d]	68	75	61	+ 7

Sources: a. California Poll 7807. b. Tax Revolt Survey. c. California Poll 8001. d. California Poll 8002.

*p < .05.

produce drastic budget cuts, and that the remaining state surplus was insufficient to cover the shortfall. Again, they were quite accurate in this forecast; even without Jarvis II, the surplus began to run dry, and its depletion began to force real cuts in services.

Nevertheless, public employees' self-interest was quite narrow and did not extend to any general defense of the public sector. Table 7.4 gives numerous examples, and others could be given. They were simply *not* more in favor of the public sector on any elements of the tax revolt that did not affect their own particular interests directly. They were not more Democratic or liberal in general than others. Their value priorities were not especially for lavish public services or larger government. They were not especially defensive about government waste; they were no more skeptical than anyone else about extravagant claims of massive waste in government. They were not unusually supportive of the state bailout that allowed local governments and schools to engage in something resembling business as usual after Proposition 13. Nor were they especially concerned about local government's plea that Proposition 13 would take all control away from local government and turn it over to the state. They were no more likely than anyone else to see Jarvis II as producing a host of evil consequences, other than the ones impinging directly on their own livelihoods. Table 7.4 shows the results for the effects of Jarvis II on the economy and inflation, and equally nonsignificant differences existed on questions about whether Jarvis II would make government more efficient, make public officials pay more attention to the people, and raise other taxes to make up for the revenue shortfall (in data not shown here).

Hence among the many questions asked of public employees in these surveys, hardly any show them in any unusually strong defense of the public sector in general. We see little evidence that public employees, as a group, approached the tax revolt with any especially broad schematic thinking about the role of the public sector. Nor was their attention to the tax revolt especially enhanced by their self-interest. They found the taxation-spending issue no more important than others did, and they were not significantly more opinionated on the ballot propositions. Their own self-interest seems not to have inspired them to any especially rich and complex cognitive activity. And their families show even less.

The one exception to this seems to be in the area of education — but even in this case, their responses seem pallid and not terribly intense. As table 7.4 shows, public employees were especially concerned about the effects of Proposition 13 and Jarvis II on the quality of the public schools, and they were much more concerned than others about Jarvis II's impact on the quality of education at the University of California, and about its limiting access to the universities by disadvantaged students. At the same time, table 7.4 shows that public employees were not especially emotionally concerned with such matters; they did not consider these effects to be any more serious than anyone else did.

So public employees' unique role in the governmental system apparently did not spur them to any exceptional defense of the public sector. They were outspoken defenders of their own jobs and wage levels, but aside from that, their attitudes were very similar to those outside the public sector.[16]

By several standards, public employees showed no more schematic thinking about the tax revolt than did other respondents. First of all, in the Tax Revolt Survey, the level of constraint among the several elements of the tax revolt schema was almost identical in the two groups; the average intercorrelation was .24 for public employees and .27 for the others (whether or not the tax rebel index is included as one of the elements). The first factor of a principal components factor analysis extracted very similar levels of variance: 72 percent and 83 percent, respectively.

Finally, the elements of the tax revolt schema had little to do with public employees' opposition to the revolt. Including all four variables in the equation reduces the impact of public employee status on the tax rebel index only slightly (the b-weight drops from .55 to .48). So their opposition was not carried by a web of associated attitudes.

The one place we do find some evidence of special schematic thinking among the public employees again emphasizes how limited it is to their own welfare. Two items assessing the possible effects of the Gann amendment focused on the possibilities that it might lead to a decrease in the number of state and local employees, or slow their wage increases. As shown in table 7.4, public employees were only slightly more fearful than others that it would have such an effect. But such effects were somewhat more potent for them; these items correlated .24 and .25 with the tax rebel index for public employees, and .05 and .00 for others. And they were somewhat more correlated with the two anti-government themes in the tax revolt schema, averaging $r = .14$ and .04, respectively.[17]

Hence self-interest worked in a vary narrow manner for this group also, though more effectively than among the service recipients. Their unusually high levels of opposition to and activity in the tax revolt must be treated as fairly narrowly self-protective. Broader attitudes about the public sector did not have much to do with it. Contrary to the fears expressed by observers such as Daniel Moynihan, then, public employees do not appear to have highly schematized political attitudes, and so do not represent a very organized interest group, at least not in the electoral context. They are not by themselves a large group—less than 10 percent of the population in California. Adding in their family members gives them more imposing numbers, perhaps up to 25 percent. But as narrow as the public employees' own political definition of their self-interest was, their families' were narrower still—they showed very little evidence of special support for the public sector.

Conclusions

It is time to take stock of what we have learned about the role of self-interest in the tax revolt, on the sides of both the rebels and the public-sector defenders. First of all, the contest was quite uneven, at least insofar as self-interest contributed to it. Self-interest advantaged the tax rebels more than the opposition in several ways. The self-interested constituencies on the pro-revolt side were numerically much larger than were the constituencies whose self-interest should have led them to opposition: most Californians own their own homes and pay income taxes; relatively few are public employees or heavily and directly dependent on government assistance. Secondly, "the taxpayers" were from demographic circumstances that normally promote high and effective levels of political action, and especially high voting rates—white, upper-status, middle-aged, fully employed men. The service recipients, by contrast, were predominantly from groups that are generally less politically effective—the elderly or the very young, minorities, poorly educated, marginally employed, and women.

Self-interest also promoted somewhat more organized and robust cognitive structures among "the taxpayers" than among anti-revolt elements. Even the public employees did not rationalize their self-interest with any great defense of the value priorities or efficient performance of the public sector. In this sense, the taxpayers' self-interested onslaught upon the public sector, root and branch, assumption and operation, was not countered by an equally self-interested defense of the whole enterprise. To the extent that self-interest promoted a defense against the tax rebels, it did so only in the very narrow sense of defending one's own small chunk of turf. Some groups with a personal stake in defeating the tax revolt did convert their own specific problems into some self-serving political attitude or other. However, none generalized this into a more full-blown view of taxation and the public sector that would allow for a stronger response to the tax proposals. So it would seem that the cognitive prerequisites for effective political action were met most clearly by the taxpayers. Service recipients responded as a series of unconnected single-issue constituencies, which ill prepared them to defend themselves against a full-scale attack on government as a whole. In this sense the failure of the public sector lay both in poor persuasion and in poor political mobilization.

Part of our interest in the tax revolt lay in its promise as a rich area in which to study the political effects of self-interest in the mass public. Previous studies had yielded disappointing results, but frequently on issues or in campaigns where the self-interest component was bound to be rather sparse. Such was not the case here. What was the basis of the unusually extensive self-interest effects in the tax revolt?

The key element seems to have been the very large, tangible, easily computed, cash rebate, within the voter's easy control, offered by Proposition 13. And those who were promised the biggest savings — the most affluent homeowners — were most enthusiastic about it. More usually the mass of voters is offered vaguer, less immediate, more multi-dimensional choices, or choices with relatively minor payoffs, and the decisions with hard concrete or major consequences are left to government officials. So, for instance, in the present case, global retrospective judgments about personal economic hardships, or more prospective fears about potential future economic problems, played at most a minor role. Apparently anxiety about confiscatory property taxation among homeowners with limited incomes, or anxiety about the future of the economy more generally, did not play any major role either. We suggest, therefore, that the keys to these self-interested choices in the mass public were: (1) clear consequences, (2) a tangible and sizable cash reward, and (3) direct control over the outcome. All are unusual political circumstances, alone or together.

One theme that recurs throughout much of these data is the specificity of the origins of self-interest effects. Hence self-interest appears to influence only those attitudes most immediately, tangibly, and specifically relevant to the specific interest variable in question. Homeownership and the felt burden of the state income tax, not income itself, promoted support for Proposition 13 and Jarvis II, respectively. Indeed people differentiated fairly precisely the burdens of their different taxes; relatively few felt personally burdened by taxes in general in an undifferentiated manner. Public employees were concerned only with their own salary levels, parents only with the schools, and service recipients only with the specific services they depended on. Even public employees' families did not share very much in their anti-revolt feelings.

A second theme is the narrow cognitive underpinnings of self-interest. Our expectation had been that people would rationalize their own self-interest in rather broad ideological terms. But we found very little surrounding cognitive support for self-interested policy preferences. Self-interest had little effect on issue salience or opinionation and did not promote more schematic thinking. There was no evidence that it fostered any special set of attitudes undergirding or rationalizing selfish votes on the tax propositions.

The taxpayers (homeowners and those feeling especially burdened by their taxes) represented some modest exception to this, in that they did see taxation and spending as especially salient policy problems, and did have especially anti-government attitudes in general. But even they showed little evidence of especially high levels of information or cognitive organization. Neither homeownership nor perceived tax burden influenced level of opinionation or schematic thinking very much. And "early buyers" did not show greater support for Proposition 13 than "late buyers," even though its subtleties gave the early buyers a significant tax break. So self-interest had surprisingly weak effects on cognition about the tax revolt, in general.

The general implication of these findings is that self-interest has very limited effects on the *scope* of attitudes toward government, even in a political climate with high levels of information and attention. How is this to be interpreted? It should be remembered that the apogee of the tax revolt came with a massive cut in property taxes, which probably saved the average homeowner over $1000 per year. We have seen that the great enthusiasts for the tax revolt were those who could profit most from it, not those most vulnerable to the ravages of inflation and other sources of economic distress.

As we have indicated, the mid-to-late 1970s were a period of rapid increases in the value of residential property, far outstripping the general inflation rate. A great many Californians participated in what were essentially windfall increases in their own financial worth, often of quite astonishing magnitudes. Most were probably well aware of, and often actively boastful about, these rises in their wealth. Yet these affluent Californians showed a curious blindness to the role of inflation in this increase. In the midst of so many small fortunes accumulated through effort no more complex than mowing the front lawn, only 3 percent of all the homeowners in our sample said they had actually been "helped" by inflation. Similarly, of those earning over $40,000 per year, only 3 percent felt helped by inflation. But in reality, *most* respondents in either group must, on balance, have been helped.

Why were they so blind to the inflationary roots of their wealth? A substantial literature in social psychology has documented a common bias in casual explanations for the good and bad things that happen to people: they tend to perceive themselves as causally responsible for good things, and to blame external causes for the evils that befall them. Hence people tend to attribute the good things that happen to them to their own skill, hard work, and so on, and the bad things to bad luck, bad economic conditions, unsympathetic friends and associates, and so on.[18] Let us suppose that affluent Californians widely shared this attributional error, and concluded they had "earned," with their own sweat and toil and their own sagacity, the large inflation-induced increase in the value of their property. It is easy to see why they would be resentful at the government's taking away their "hard-earned" money.

Thus we concur with Kuttner in part:[19] characterizing the tax revolt as a "revolt of the haves" seems fair enough, even limiting ourselves to the mass public and ignoring the general tax shift from business to homeowners. But the role of a general economic malaise does not come through in our data; rather, the operation of self-interest seems to be a simpler and more straightforward preference for reduced taxes, especially among the affluent.

8

Symbolic Predispositions

Among the generalized political predispositions potentially relevant to the tax revolt, party identification and liberal versus conservative ideologies were perhaps the most obvious. Since the days of the New Deal, liberal Democrats have differed from conservative Republicans most centrally on the value priorities at the heart of the tax revolt: expansion or contraction of the role of the public sector, and the level of public taxation. In California, Edmund G. "Pat" Brown, governor from 1959 to 1967, presided over a period of greatly expanded public services in the classic liberal Democratic mode. His successor, the dedicated conservative Republican Ronald Reagan, governor from 1967 through 1975, attempted (though not always successfully or even very wholeheartedly) to roll back government, set spending limits, eliminate waste, and cut taxes. Much research has shown that policy attitudes and voting choices are powerfully influenced by these two partisan predispositions.[1] So we should expect both party identification and liberalism-conservatism to have contributed to attitudes about the tax revolt.

Some liberal political commentators believe the tax revolt was motivated not so much by philosophical conservatism as by racism. Since the social programs most vociferously attacked by the tax rebels, such as welfare and public housing, have the image of catering to the poor and minorities, it was tempting to interpret these attacks as motivated by racism. But the campaigns were plainly not fought on overtly racist grounds, so it is important to be explicit about how we will use the term in this context.

Before the 1960s, political divisions over race generally focused on the legal barriers to racial equality, in such arenas as public accommodations, schools, and private housing. When formal segregation became illegal, reactions to racial issues were more often governed by what we have called "symbolic racism." This blends simple anti-black affect with the traditional American moral values originally based in civil Protestantism. A typical manifestation of this predisposition is opposition to affirmative action or busing of white children for racial integration, on the grounds that such preferential treatment for blacks gives them benefits that have not been "earned" through hard work. Cutting government could well be perceived as striking a blow against such racial policies. So symbolic racism too may have contributed to support for the tax revolt.[2]

Racial issues had been at the forefront of Californians' political attention, off and on, for almost twenty years. The great successes of the civil rights movement in the South during the early 1960s were followed quickly, in California, by Proposition 14 in 1964, which by a two-to-one landslide vote repealed the state's fair housing legislation, and then a year later by the massive destruction wreaked in the heart of Los Angeles by the Watts Riots. In the mid-1970s court decisions mandated school desegregation in Los Angeles, San Francisco, San Diego, and other major cities. The result was bitter controversy, white flight, and open racial antagonism in school board elections and deliberations. So race was a major item on the political agenda in California, particularly in its large metropolitan areas, in the years preceding the tax revolt.[3]

Another class of relevant predispositions concerns generalized feelings about government itself. These attitudes can be distinguished according to their objects.[4] Attitudes toward the regime, labeled variously as "diffuse system support," "cynicism," "trust in government," or "alienation," are conceptually distinct from those toward more specific objects, such as incumbent officeholders and specific institutions. The tax rebels' rhetoric included assaults on government as a whole, on its mode of operation, and on its remoteness from the people. The main carriers of opposition to the tax revolt were incumbent officials in state government, local government, and the public schools. We therefore explore the impact of anti-government attitudes of both kinds on support for the tax revolt.

It must be noted that much research has shown these several symbolic predispositions to be empirically interrelated, though they are conceptually distinct. Evaluations of incumbents' performance are influenced by partisanship, and political cynicism often is most prevalent in the party that is not in power. Conservative Republicans tend to be more skeptical about government in general, and less supportive of civil rights, than are liberal Democrats. So we will begin by treating all these predispositions separately, but in the final analysis we will deal with their interdependence explicitly.

The symbolic politics hypothesis proposes that these predispositions are evoked in the public by symbols in the ongoing flow of political information that resemble, cognitively, the predisposition itself. Without the appearance of such symbols, the general predispositions would probably not be triggered or engaged and consequently would have little political influence. The tax revolt campaigns presented to the public a variety of symbols that "fit" these predispositions. Conservative symbols — of cutbacks in government services, of layoffs of public employees, and of confiscatory levels of taxation — abounded. By implication, though not often explicitly, much of the damage would be done to services especially valuable to the poor and minorities; indeed, the most sought-after victim was "welfare" spending, which popular stereotypes often associate primarily with blacks. Especially during the Proposition 13 campaign, politicians divided along partisan lines, with many Republicans supporting, and most Democrats (like Governor Brown and Assembly Speaker McCarthy) opposed. And anti-government themes, or even themes of rebellion against government (a "second Boston Tea Party"), abounded. So the campaigns luxuriated in symbols that would evoke these predispositions, and it is likely that the predispositions guided voters' attitudes on matters of government spending, waste, and public-sector pay, as well as on the tax propositions themselves.

Symbolic predispositions may help develop issue publics. The social-psychological literature on schemas has generally treated them in purely cognitive terms to be sure, but much other evidence emphasizes the powerful role of affective commitments in generating supportive cognitive structures. People do change their cognitions extensively to rationalize changes in their affective preferences, and such political predispositions as party identification strongly influence other political beliefs. In Chapters 6 and 7 we saw that self-interest generated mainly rather narrow issue publics, and did not increase schematic thinking. But symbolic predispositions have the advantage of a much longer history of cognitive content and cognitive activity. For example, party identifiers and ideologues have spent years deliberating their partisan choices, and trying to explain them to others in cognitively respectable form. And the long history of racial conflict in this country has had the same effect on racial attitudes. So symbolic predispositions might well be more powerful than self-interest in generating broader and more organized political thinking.

We have already presented in Chapter 4 evidence of some schematic thinking in the California mass public, tying support for the tax revolt to a whole package of attitudes about taxation and spending. But Howard Jarvis's view of government embodied an even broader schema. The beliefs we have described as the tax revolt schema were for Jarvis tied into a more comprehensive ideology centering around his Republican conservatism and general political cynicism. But how far into the mass public did such broader schematic thinking go? The mass public is frequently suspected of thinking politically in a relatively nonideological, "morselized" manner. But if voters' schemas about the tax revolt are based in long-standing generalized political commitments, the chances for continuing conflict over these issues are much greater. So a final focus of this chapter will be on the role of symbolic predispositions in promoting schematic thinking in the tax revolt. Here we will be especially alert to the possibility suggested by our data in Chapter 4 (see table 4.2) of two more specific schemas in the tax-revolt area, one mainly concerned with value priorities, which might be linked to longer-standing partisan predispositions and symbolic racism, and another mainly concerned with government performance, which might be linked to general political cynicism.

Party Identification, Ideology, and Symbolic Racism

In our survey, Democrats outnumbered Republicans by 45 percent to 21 percent, and 33 percent said they were "Independent" (using the standard seven-point Michigan measure of party identification). At the same time, conservatives outnumbered liberals by 56 percent to 38 percent, with only 6 percent declining to express a preference (using a five-point liberal-conservative item). Considering both dimensions at once yields three groups of about equal size: conservative Republicans (23 percent), conservative Democrats (27 percent), and liberal Democrats (29 percent).[5]

Support for the Tax Revolt

Both political ideology and party identification powerfully influenced support for the tax revolt at all its phases. In the surveys we have been relying on most heavily, Republicans supported the three tax-revolt propositions 18 percent more than Democrats did, on the average, and conservatives supported them by 19 percent more than liberals did. These differences held quite constant across surveys and the different propositions; the largest fluctuations were some reduced effect regarding the Gann amendment (both down, to 13 and 14 percent), and party polarization up somewhat toward the end of the Jarvis II campaign (to 24 percent), but even these deviations were small, and otherwise the effects were quite constant.[6]

Moreover, these two dimensions had significant independent effects. This is shown in the regression analysis summarized in the first column of table 8.1. And they had additive rather than interactive effects. Most important, separating out the large group of conservative Democrats adds little further information; for example, in the Tax Revolt Survey, 75 percent of the conservative Republicans were tax rebels, as against 61 percent of the conservative Democrats and 49 percent of the liberal Democrats. We initially thought the conservative Democrats would be a somewhat unusual breed, but in virtually all our analyses they fell about halfway between the other two groups, so we have used the ideology and party identification variables rather than some typology combining the two.

Symbolic racism, somewhat to our surprise, turns out to have had just as important an impact on support for the tax revolt as these more conventional and familiar predispositions. In Chapter 5 we saw that whites supported the

TABLE 8.1 Effects of symbolic predispositions on the tax rebel index.

Regression equation	1	2	3	4	5	6	7
Symbolic predispositions							
Political ideology	.19**	.14**	.14**	.10**			.09**
Party identification	.14**	.10**	.10**	.05			.06*
Symbolic racism		.24**	.23**	.17**			.15**
Political cynicism					.06*	.01	0
Incumbent disapproval					.10**	.05*	−.04
Race (black dummy)			−.06*	−.03			
Tax revolt schema							
Size of government				.14**			.13**
Service spending				.19**			.15**
Waste						.23**	.12**
Overpaid government workers						.14**	.09**
R^2	7.3%	12.6%	13.0%	19.2%	1.8%	10.2%	21.5%

Source: Tax Revolt Survey.

Note: Each column is a separate regression equation. All entries are betas. The race variable compares blacks with all other respondents.

*p < .05.
**p < .001.

tax revolt much more than blacks did. Indeed blacks were the only popula
tion group that steadfastly opposed the tax revolt at all junctures. This racial
difference has at least two possible explanations in terms of our model. To the
extent that blacks tend disproportionately to consume government services,
and whites to pay the taxes for them, this racial difference might simply
reflect self-interest. Tax-burdened whites want to pay less, while service-recipient blacks resist the inevitable service cutbacks. In fact, however, adding
our self-interest variables to the demographics in a regression equation
predicting to the tax rebel index does not diminish the effects of race, as it
should if self-interest was responsible for the racial difference. This will be
discussed further in Chapter 10.

Alternatively, the contrasting responses of blacks and whites to the tax revolt might reflect longer-standing symbolic predispositions about the proper
role of government, especially regarding race policy. To test this we generated a symbolic racism scale. As indicated above, we have conceptualized
symbolic racism as the conjunction of two separate underlying dimensions: a
specifically anti-black attitude, and conservative value priorities, which stress
individual effort and responsibility rather than government activism. Our
scale therefore used two items that measured opposition to special government aid for blacks: support for an anti-busing proposition that appeared on
the November 1979 ballot along with the Gann amendment (28 percent voted
for it, and another 46 percent favored it but did not vote), and a question ask
ing whether or not the government should make a special effort to help blacks
and other racial minorities (35 percent felt it should not, 15 percent
"strongly").[7]

Symbolic racism did make a powerful additional contribution to support
for the tax rebellion. At the zero-order level, it correlated .30 with the tax
rebel index. In cross-tabular analyses, those above and below the midpoint
on symbolic racism differed in support for the tax revolt just as much as
liberal Democrats differed from conservative Republicans.

For present purposes, however, the crucial question is whether this represents specifically anti-black feeling on the part of whites, or just another expression of conservative value priorities. We conceive of symbolic racism as
having a strong component of nonracial conservatism, which could have
been its main input into the tax rebellion. We tested this possibility in a number of ways. Table 8.1 displays a series of regression analyses in which other
variables are successively added to the equation, to determine whether or not
they could account for the effects of our symbolic racism scale without invoking specifically racial attitudes. But all seemed to leave intact the finding

that specifically racial attitudes were central determinants of support for the tax revolt. First of all, the effect of symbolic racism is diminished only slightly by including party identification and ideology in the predictive equation, as shown in table 8.1 (column 2). Its effect on the tax rebel index drops only from .30 to .24. Indeed symbolic racism has a unique effect almost as strong as that of the other two partisan predispositions combined; symbolic racism increases the R^2 by 5.3 percent above and beyond the 7.3 percent contributed by the two other predispositions. Nor is this simply due to the presence in the sample of the obviously more pro-black black respondents. When race is controlled by being included in the equation (table 8.1, column 3), symbolic racism has just as strong an effect as before (its beta falls only from .24 to .23). In fact, including *all* the demographics reduces the effect of symbolic racism very little.[8]

Is there some other interpretation of this effect that would militate against a conclusion that specifically *racial* attitudes were involved? For example, does our symbolic racism index merely reflect more general preferences for smaller, less intrusive government, with no unique racial focus? Controlling for attitudes toward the public sector more generally is required to extract the unique impact of racial antagonism. Hence we added the two value-priority proximal variables (size of government and service spending) to this analysis. Table 8.1, column 4 shows that some fraction of the symbolic racism effect (as well as of party identification and ideology) is due to such manifestly nonracial value priorities. But uniquely *racial* attitudes retain a powerful effect; the beta falls only to .17. The influence of symbolic racism on support for the tax rebellion among whites in California is still greater than that of either of the more usual partisan predispositions, party identification and liberal-conservative ideology.

This effect of symbolic racism completely overshadows the effects of race itself, which virtually disappear when both symbolic racism and more general value priorities are considered (see column 4 of table 8.1).[9] In other words, the most important impact of the racial issue on attitudes toward the tax revolt lay in the symbolic racism it evoked, not just in the polarization of blacks from whites.

A potentially serious analytic problem is that these symbolic predispositions are not independent of self-interest. Self-interest might conceivably create them (for example, property owners might be conservative because of their concern with property rights or the tax-burdened might become racist out of resentment over the fate of their tax dollars), or, conversely, partisan predispositions might influence self-interest (or at least subjective self-interest; for example, conservative Republicans might be especially inclined to feel their tax burden was excessive when liberal Democrats controlled the state and federal governments). But in fact such possibilities occurred only to a minor degree. When we ran regressions predicting from self-interest indicators to these three predispositions, very few of the relationships were statistically significant; those which were, were almost invariably small (betas of less than .10); and even those generally washed out with demographic variables controlled. Four of the twenty-one possible relationships remained significant with demographics included in the equations, and only one of those four showed signs of any real strength (tax burden retained a beta of .14 on symbolic racism).[10] So self-interest had little relationship with these symbolic predispositions, and therefore not surprisingly had little indirect influence through them on support for the tax revolt.

Issue Publics and Schematic Thinking

These symbolic predispositions did strongly contribute to the development of issue publics focused on the tax revolt, in contrast to the weak roles demographic and self-interest factors played in this respect, as discussed in the previous three chapters. They were strongly implicated in almost all the attitudinal aspects of the tax revolt. The appropriate regression analyses are shown in table 8.2. Conservative Republicans were much more likely than liberal Democrats to express anti-public-sector value priorities. For example, 85 percent of the conservative Republicans wanted smaller government in general, while only 55 percent of the liberal Democrats did. And they were much less likely to support government: the percentage difference index (PDI) on the specific-service-spending scale was +18 and +78 percent for the two groups, respectively. Conservative Republicans were also more likely to express anti-government attitudes concerning waste and overpaid government employees, though these differences were not as great as those on value priorities. For example, conservative Republicans were only 12 percent more likely than liberal Democrats to consider government workers overpaid.

Here too symbolic racism had a surprisingly strong effect. It influenced all these attitudes more strongly than either ideology or party identification considered separately, and almost as strongly as both put together. For example, those above and below the midpoint on the symbolic racism scale differed by 27 percent in preferred size of government and by 34 percent in the PDI for spending on specific services. Table 8.2 summarizes the substantial effects of

TABLE 8.2 Summary regression analyses: Effects of symbolic predispositions.

	Attention				Tax revolt schema			Participation	
	Tax rebel index	Issue salience	Opinionation	Size of government	Service spending	Waste	Overpaid government workers	Vote frequency	Tax activism
Ideology	.14**	.10**	0	.07*	.18*	.11**	.10**	.02	.01
Party identification	.10**	.02	.04	.14**	.13**	.02	0	-.01	.10**
Symbolic racism	.24**	.10**	.01	.17**	.20**	.16**	.10**	.20**	.07*
Cynicism	.06*	.07*	.05*	.12**	.12**	.17*	.13**	.03	.09**
Incumbent disapproval	.01	.06*	.11**	.10**	.12**	.11*	.03	.18**	.16**
R^2	13.1%	4.3%	2.1%	13.1%	20.1%	12.0%	5.2%	9.5%	7.3%

Source: Tax Revolt Survey.

Note: Entries are betas. Each column is a separate regression equation. A positive entry indicates that the symbolic predisposition is associated with the dependent variable in the hypothesized direction; for example, conservatism or cynicism with support for the tax revolt and the tax revolt schema, more attention to the tax revolt, and greater participation.

*p < .05.

**p < .01.

symbolic racism on all four of these components of the tax revolt. And it shows, as well, that the effects of symbolic racism are independent of those of ideology and party identification. Although all are correlated, the anti-black feelings reflected in symbolic racism have major effects above and beyond their association with these other predispositions.

The far-reaching attitudinal effects of these predispositions stand in vivid contrast to the narrow cognitive effects of self-interest discovered in the last two chapters. This contrast can be made most directly in the one area in which self-interest did seem to have some cognitive effects – on spending preferences for particular services. It will be remembered from the last chapter that service recipiency led to support for increased spending on the specific program yielding direct benefits to the person, but it did not lead to any special support for the public sector in general. Symbolic predispositions, by contrast, strongly influence support for the public sector irrespective of the level of generality in which government services are described, whether highly general or rather specific.

As might be expected, then, symbolic predispositions influence spending preferences on services across a broad area, whereas self-interest tends to have only spotty and narrowly specific effects. This is shown in table 8.3. The top of the table shows the powerful effects of symbolic predispositions on spending preferences, regardless of whether we consider specific services such as the schools or welfare, pool all the specific services, or ask about "larger government" in the abstract. All three symbolic predispositions make significant contributions to each one of the value priorities shown. In contrast, fewer than half the self-interest terms are significant, and none is very strong (only one exceeding a beta of .10).[11] And self-interest again has its strongest effects upon policy preferences most narrowly related to the interest in question, as we contended in the last chapter. Significant service-recipience effects still occur most often regarding the services from which the individual receives direct benefits. Preferences about school spending are most dependent on whether or not the person is a parent; about welfare spending, on being on public assistance, worrying about losing one's job, or receiving medical support; and about public health, on receiving financial aid for health problems.

The pooled effects of all variables in each category are shown at the bottom of the table. They show that the total variance accounted for by the symbolic predispositions averages around 12 percent on these measures, while self-interest contributes less than one-third of that. A similar but somewhat more demanding comparison would ask how much each category of variables adds

TABLE 8.3 Joint effects of symbolic predispositions and self-interest on service spending preferences and preferred size of government.

	Spending on:				
	Public schools	Welfare	Public health	All services	Size of government
Symbolic predispositions					
Ideology	.16**	.11**	.15**	.19**	.07*
Party identification	.09**	.09**	.17**	.13**	.16**
Symbolic racism	.16**	.26**	.14**	.22**	.19**
Self-interest					
Parent of school child	.09*	−.02	−.04	−.02	−.04
Government assistance scale	(.02)	(.14)**	(.07)*	(.09)**	(.06)*
On public assistance	.02	.07*	.04	.05	.08*
On medicare/medicaid	.01	.12*	.06*	.09**	.02
On unemployment compensation	0	.01	0	−.01	.01
Composite employment scale	(.07)*	(.05)*	(.05)*	(.05)*	(.08)*
Work worry	.03	.08*	.05*	.04	.08**
Work problems	.06*	0	.03	.05	.01
Variance accounted for (R²)					
Symbolic predispositions only	9.6%	12.9%	11.9%	16.2%	9.9%
Self-interest only	2.5	5.4	2.6	3.6	3.6
Both combined	11.1	16.5	13.3	18.1	12.0

Source: Tax Revolt Survey.

Note: Each column is a separate regression equation. Entries are betas. The variance estimates use the individual items rather than the two composite scales regarding government assistance and employment; the beta-weights for regressions using the latter are presented in parentheses for comparative purposes.

*p < .05.
**p < .001.

to the other in variance accounted for, and in that sense asks how much variance each category uniquely accounts for. From the figures given at the bottom of table 8.3 it is easy to compute that symbolic predispositions here contribute, on the average, 10.7 percent to R² above and beyond that contributed by self-interest, whereas self-interest contributes only 2.1 percent beyond that contributed by the predispositions. So these findings reinforce our general theme, that symbolic predispositions contribute much more to schematic thinking than does self-interest. They certainly had much to do with the development of an issue public for the tax revolt. And beyond that, these findings suggest some strong role for these affective predispositions in developing schematic thinking.

To what extent did symbolic predispositions in fact promote more structured thinking about the tax revolt? This can be tested by determining whether or not self-professed political ideologues show stronger structure than nonideologues. We compared strong ideologues ("strong" liberals and "strong" conservatives) with other respondents with respect to the five basic elements of the tax revolt schema discussed in Chapter 4, along with the tax rebel index. The strong ideologues display considerably more structure by several standards. The level of constraint among the individual items is higher (the mean correlations are .34 for strong ideologues and .22 for other respondents), their loadings on the first factor of a principal components factor analysis are higher (averaging .60 and .48 in the two groups respectively), but this factor accounts for only slightly more variance in the interim correlations (79 percent versus 76 percent). Moreover, support for the three ballot propositions was a much more integral part of the tax revolt schema for the strong ideologues than for the weak ideologues. The difference in factor loadings between strong and weak ideologues was greater for the tax rebel index than for any other item (.72 versus .50). This means that ideology helped provide the attitudinal "glue" that allowed voters to come to decisions about the tax revolt propositions consistent with their other attitudes about government. In short, strong political ideology in general helped people develop more schematic thinking about the tax revolt.[12]

Mistrust of Government

A consistent theme in the campaigns to limit the fiscal powers of government in California was the claim that public officials were selfish and wasteful, eager to promote expensive programs for special interests while ignoring the cost to the average taxpayer. In advocating Proposition 13, Howard Jarvis called upon the electorate to "send government a message," to bring the politicians and bureaucrats to heel. Regardless of whether or not they had a tangible personal stake in the reordering of taxing and spending policies, voters were provided an opportunity to engage in a powerful symbolic protest against government. How important was such protest in creating support for the revolt? And did such protest spring from stable and long-standing antigovernment attitudes, or was it a more specific response to the recent performance of California government?

The familiar analytical distinction between attitudes toward incumbent officeholders and attitudes toward the political regime—its institutions, underlying values, and operative norms—is hard to implement operationally because these orientations tend to be empirically correlated. Evaluations of incumbents tend to be a function of both established partisan attitudes and appraisals of their current performance. And while affects toward political institutions are thought by contrast to be established in early political socialization, there is substantial evidence that these beliefs about the trustworthiness and responsiveness of government are also responsive to contemporary events.[13]

In the Tax Revolt Survey we attempted to assess anti-government attitudes at three distinct levels of this incumbent-performance-oriented to regime-oriented dimension. We measured support for incumbent officeholders by asking respondents whether they approved of how Governor Brown and the state legislature were "doing the job." In each case 43 percent approved, while 49 percent and 39 percent, respectively, disapproved.[14] We combined these into an incumbent disapproval index. However, this anti-incumbent sentiment bore only a modest bivariate relationship to support of the tax revolt; 67 percent of the disapprovers, and 55 percent of the approvers, were tax rebels.

Next we constructed a political cynicism index. Two items were drawn from the standard five-item trust-of-government scale used in the University of Michigan National Election Studies. One asked people whether they could "trust in government in general to do what is right"; 68 percent said they could do so "only some" or "almost none" of the time. On the second item, 64 percent said they felt government was "mainly run for special interests" rather than "for the benefit of all the people." As has been frequently remarked, during recent years most Californians, like most other Americans, have expressed a jaundiced view of government; 54 percent expressed such cynical feelings, or worse, on both items.[15] Politically cynical respondents were somewhat more likely to be tax rebels than the minority expressing trust in government; 65 percent of those above the median in cynicism, as opposed to 56 percent of those below the median, were tax rebels.

Finally, the most regime-oriented item was asked of those who said they could trust government "only some" or "none" of the time: did they feel they lacked trust in government because of the particular individuals now in office or because "something is basically wrong with the way government is organized"? By this standard, 35 percent of the total sample felt that the system itself was flawed. This distinction between those disaffected from the regime and those who simply blame current officeholders yielded only a 2 percent difference in support for the tax revolt.

However, even these modest effects overstate the potency of mistrust of government. Disapproval of incumbents in Sacramento was, not surprisingly, related to more general feelings of political cynicism ($r = .30$). Hence when both measures are entered into a regression equation to predict the tax rebel index, they have somewhat reduced effects. Indeed, together they account for less than 2 percent of the variance in support for the tax revolt (table 8.1, column 5). Plainly mistrust of government had much less impact than the three predispositions more concerned with value priorities — ideology, party identification, and symbolic racism. And when all five predispositions are placed in the same equation, the disparity is glaring. Cynicism and incumbent disapproval have scarcely any residual effect at all, while the others retain strong effects (table 8.2, column 1). Put more forcefully, the two dimensions of mistrust in government uniquely account for less than 1 percent of the variance in support for the tax revolt, while ideology, party identification, and symbolic racism together add over 11 percent.[16]

The small significant effect of mistrust that does remain comes from political cynicism. So while we must be cautious in assigning causal influence among these entangled, mutually reinforcing attitudes, it does appear that generalized and symbolic disenchantment with government, rather than either a focused hostility against particular incumbent officials or rejection of American institutions at a more systemic level, contributed to support for the tax revolt.

Mistrust of government had much more impressive impact in helping to generate an issue public for the tax revolt. Both cynicism and incumbent disapproval contributed to attention to the revolt, in terms of issue salience and opinionation. And both had quite consistent effects upon the several components of the tax revolt schema — preferring smaller government and less spending, and perceiving greater amounts of waste and excessive payment to public employees. All this is shown in table 8.2. There is also some evidence that they contributed to schematic thinking about government, as well. The two antigovernment themes in the tax revolt schema (waste and overpaid government workers) almost completely account for the effects of cynicism and incumbent disapproval upon the tax revolt index (table 8.1, compare columns 5 and 6). This cynical, derogatory thinking about government performance had a widespread effect upon the public's thinking about the issues raised by the tax revolt, even if it had only a modest direct effect upon support for it.[17]

Origins of Political Cynicism

Do the origins of cynicism fit our original model, whereby early political socialization generates long-standing predispositions? Or are they products of more current realities, such as personal economic problems (especially in an inflationary era), unfavorable first-hand experiences with government, or unfavorable appraisals of the government's value priorities, its performance, or specific incumbents?

One source of cynicism plainly is evaluations from afar of government policy. Elsewhere Citrin has shown that mistrust of government in general results in great part from dissatisfaction with the outcomes of ongoing public policies and negative evaluations of the incumbent administration. Political cynicism at any given time is expressed by opponents of government from both sides of the spectrum; some are dissatisfied because they want government to do more and some because they want it to do less. And the current incumbent, rather than his party or longer-standing ideological commitments, tends to be held responsible for social and political ills. Consistent with this view, in our data cynicism is much more closely related to incumbent disapproval ($r = .30$) than to underlying party identification ($r = .01$), ideological outlook ($r = .06$), or symbolic racism ($r = .09$). And including these last three dimensions in the equation predicting the tax rebel index does not erase the modest effect of cynicism, as shown in table 8.2 (column 1).[18]

Second, political cynicism was related to a variety of subjective economic complaints. Cynical respondents were more likely to say their tax burden was too high, more likely to be pessimistic about the California economy, and more likely to say that they had been suffering financially, both in general and from inflation. These were not large differences; the most cynical half of the sample differed from the others by no more than 13 percent on any of these items, though they did complain more in each case. This still does not identify the roots of cynicism very precisely, however, since the origins of gloomy economic feelings in turn are hard to pin down.

On the evidence available, we must ascribe a major portion of this cynicism to a generalized malaise or unhappy mood rather than to a direct response to the objective circumstances of one's life or a direct evaluation of personal experiences with government. Demographic differences between cynical and trusting respondents were inconsequential. It seems not to be a function of objective personal strain, because it was scarcely correlated at all with such self-interest indicators as homeownership, public employee status, employment difficulties, parenthood, or service dependency. Nor does it seem to be based in any very concrete, simple, direct way upon evaluations of personal experiences with government. We have cited earlier the finding that personal experiences with bureaucratic offices are generally evaluated favorably. The actual participants in even such widely reviled government policies as the

Vietnam war and busing for school integration were not nearly negative enough to account for such high aggregate levels of political cynicism.[19]

Moreover, we do not believe that the role of generalized cynicism in the tax revolt was a function of focused negative judgments of specific current incumbents, for two reasons. First, although incumbent disapproval is correlated with cynicism, the effects of incumbent performance on the tax rebel index are accounted for by cynicism, rather than the other way around. Second, there is considerable evidence that evaluations of specific politicians, including incumbents, tend on the average to be quite positive, while evaluations of stereotyped, aggregated groups of them (such as "politicians" or "bureaucrats") tend to be much more negative.[20] Indeed, our respondents generally expressed much more negative feelings on the political cynicism in dex than they did in evaluating either the governor or the legislature. As with government spending, then, abstract and generalized forms of anti-government sentiment were considerably more negative than were more specific and concrete forms. Hence to the extent that this generalized cynicism is a reac tion against current incumbents and their policies, it does not seem to reflect a very direct or concrete process of evaluation.

Participation

The symbolic predispositions did make some modest contribution to participation in the tax revolt. Their simple effects are shown in table 8.2; together they contributed something under 10 percent of the variance in vote frequency and tax activism. Again the direction of these effects helped the rebel side. Republicans, and those opposed to aid for minorities, were more active in the revolt. Similarly, much publicity has been given to the claim that "alienation" has caused declining conventional political participation, especially lower turnout rates. In our data, cynicism and disapproval of incumbents contributed to voting frequency and to other forms of tax activism.

But much of this is a product of the more favored demographic location of the rebels rather than of their distinctive predispositions, just as was the case with self-interest. As indicated earlier, social location (principally being older, of higher income, and better educated) was the main predictor of both voting frequency and activism. The demographic locations of these partisan predispositions are similar: conservative Republicans and those high in sym bolic racism tended disproportionately to be older, white, high-income, and living outside the state's major metropolitan areas. Hence here too the primary determinants of participation turn out to be demographic. When the demographic variables are entered into these equations, the effects of symbolic predispositions are sharply reduced. The unique variance contributed by the demographics to these two indices of participation is 23 percent and 11 percent, respectively, whereas the unique variance contributed by the several symbolic predispositions is only 3 percent in each case.[21] The remaining effects of symbolic predispositions mainly concern mistrust of government: disapproval of incumbents remains significantly associated with both vote frequency and tax activism, and cynicism, with the latter (the betas are .09, .11, and .07). Mistrust of government played an important role in activating the tax revolt, then, even though its role in generating support for it was secondary.[22]

So the original conclusion stands: tax-related political activity was determined mainly by more favored social locations, irrespective of partisan preference. But cynical and distrusting Californians were more active even taking that into consideration. The location of the tax revolt in the more affluent *and* more cynical segments of California society meant greater mobilization for both reasons. This reinforces one of our themes: the weakness of the opposition to the tax revolt in activating its followers. Not only did the anti-government forces have the advantage of coming from the more highly politicized strata of society, but their hostility to the incumbents fueled still more vigorous political action.

Schematic Thinking Revisited

Schematic thinking is a central ingredient in "symbolic politics." Whether or not people think schematically in a particular domain can determine how broad a range of symbols will trigger their symbolic predispositions. The predispositions of a person who is aschematic, or whose schema is very narrowly based, probably will be evoked only by symbols that are relevant to the predisposition in a very literal sense. For example, an aschematic person who is against "welfare" probably would be mobilized to support cuts in welfare programs only if they were defined as "welfare," and not if they were defined as "aid to the disabled."

As we have seen, symbolic predispositions have far-ranging cognitive effects in the tax revolt, quite unlike demographic factors and self-interest. Throughout this chapter, we have seen how symbolic predispositions have helped to organize attitudes about the separate elements of the tax revolt schema, and to relate them to voters' decisions on the ballot propositions. Self-interest had little such effect. Anti-tax feelings did have some substantial cognitive effects, but even that appears to be because they are more symbolic grievances than tangibly self-interested ones.

A Broader Schematic Context for the Tax Revolt?

Our discussions of symbolic predispositions and schematic thinking to this point leave us with two major unanswered questions, however. One is the extent to which the tax revolt schema was embedded in a larger and more enduring schema organized by symbolic predispositions that transcend the revolt itself. To the extent that it was, the issues and conflicts raised by the tax revolt are more likely to be with us for a long time. Were the voters' schemas about the tax revolt embedded in still larger, more general political schemas

TABLE 8.4 The value priority and malaise schemas: Factor analyses.

	Principal Components		Varimax Rotation	
	Factor 1	Factor 2	Factor 1 (Value priorities)	Factor 2 (Malaise)
Value priorities				
Ideology/party identification	**.47**	.27	**.50**	− .11
Symbolic racism	**.49**	.18	**.49**	.06
Size of government/service spending	**.65**	.08	**.58**	.23
Tax rebel index	.53	.25	**.61**	.15
Government performance				
Incumbent disapproval	.47	− .26	.19	**.27**
Waste/overpaid government workers	.43	− **.05**	.34	**.26**
Malaise				
Cynicism	.39	− **.50**	.05	**.57**
Personal economic complaints	.23	− **.27**	.07	**.39**
Eigenvalue	1.78	0.56		
% of variance	69%	22%		

Source: Tax Revolt Survey.

Note: Entries are factor loadings from factor analyses. In this analysis some variables used previously are combined into overall scales, including the variable indicated. Personal economic complaints include own tax burden, declining finances, and inflation's impact (see Chapter 6).

organized by long-standing symbolic predispositions? Howard Jarvis's schema about taxation, spending, and incumbent officeholders certainly went far beyond the tax revolt itself. To be sure, he felt government wasted a great deal of money, that bureaucrats were overpaid and underworked, and that government was too large — and consequently, that taxes were too high and should be cut. But he treated this as a part of a larger political schema centering around cynicism and conservative Republicanism.

To what extent was the California mass public's thinking schematized along these lines? To test for this, we conducted factor analyses that included both the elements of the tax revolt schema and the symbolic predispositions. To simplify the presentation, we collapsed into single scales those separate variables which our analysis to date has shown to be correlated and to have similar effects: ideology and party identification; size of government and service spending; waste and overpaid government workers; and personal economic complaints about taxes, declining finances, and inflation.

The results are shown in table 8.4. The tax revolt schema does indeed appear to have been tied cognitively into the more general political schemas involving these symbolic predispositions. The first factor of a principal components factor analysis, shown in column 1 of table 8.4, shows the conservative, anti-minorities, small-government, cynical tax rebels lined up against the liberal, trusting, public-sector supporters. It accounts for 69 percent of the variance, and has an eigenvalue of 1.78. All elements of the tax revolt schema load on the first factor, but the strongest by far is the size of government/service spending variable. This reinforces the earlier finding that the tax revolt was connected to symbolic predispositions mainly through the link between the partisan predispositions (party identification, ideology, symbolic racism) and value priorities. General anti-government attitudes (cynicism and incumbent disapproval) did not tie in as closely to the tax revolt schema, and indeed form a somewhat autonomous second factor.[23]

A varimax rotation of these data clarifies the existence of these two separate schemas, one centering on value priorities and the other on malaise, each with its unique elements from the original tax revolt schema well as its particular symbolic predispositions. The results are shown in table 8.4. The first factor (column 3) picks up the value priorities schema, centering on ideology and partisanship, symbolic racism, and attitudes toward service spending and size of government. The second factor (column 4), a malaise factor, centers on cynicism, criticism of government performance, and personal economic complaints. These data make it quite clear that the elements of the tax revolt schema, and therefore presumably that schema itself, were in fact embedded quite solidly in more general symbolic predispositions.

Support for the tax revolt was right in the heart of the value priorities schema, with a factor loading of .61. The prime connection appears to be the question of whether government should provide more or less service, which had the strongest loading on the value priorities-schema. However, support for the tax revolt was only weakly implicated in the malaise schema, with a factor loading of only .15. The malaise schema, then, seems to be peripheral to support for the tax revolt. It could be, of course, that this relatively low-profile impact was due to the quiet period in which our survey was taken. By November 1979, many of the passions raised by the Proposition 13 campaign had calmed (see Chapter 2). The malaise schema might have been much more powerful in those earlier frenzied months. We make that argument in the next chapter. But its implication is that a central role played by malaise was the exception rather than the rule in the tax revolt era.

The appearance of personal economic complaints in the malaise schema, and its lack of relationship to support for the tax revolt, is further evidence of one of the major themes of our research—the narrowness of the impact of voters' personal problems upon their stances toward the tax revolt. These personal complaints, except about taxes, did not have any direct effects on support for the tax rebellion, as shown in Chapter 6. Still, these subjective complaints about one's own life might have interactive effects with blaming government that would produce more tax rebels. That is, anti-government symbolic predispositions might become more potent when energized by a sense of personal grievance and malaise. To test this interactive hypothesis, we reran a series of regressions on the tax rebel index separately for people high in personal economic complaints (as defined in table 8.4) and for people low in them. However, the predictive strength of the symbolic predispositions and demographic variables was very similar in the two groups, and the R^2 was about the same. So, consistent with our original theorizing, "symbolic politics" seems irrelevant to personal threat, rather than stimulated by it, at least in the tax revolt context.[24]

Ambivalence in the Value Priorities Schema?

At several points in this chapter the tax revolt has proven to be more closely linked to a value priorities schema than to one centering on malaise. But there is a problem with assuming that a widespread general value priorities schema exists in a very simple form. That is the major anomaly in voters' thinking about government which we discussed in Chapters 3 and 4: the apparent inconsistency between wanting smaller government and wanting increased spending on government services. On the one hand, as we indicated earlier, public opinion polls have over the past few years shown overwhelming evidence of majority support for cutting government back, reducing spending, balancing budgets — whenever these goals are phrased in the abstract. On the other hand, those favoring increased spending in a specific service area have considerably outnumbered those favoring reduced spending almost invariably throughout the last decade. We have ample reason to believe that both convictions regularly attain majorities both in California and in the nation as a whole. This contrast has largely resisted analysis.

Everett Ladd and Seymour Martin Lipset, writing on the United States in the 1980s, feel that this reflects two competing feelings in the public: "What we have is a strange mix of attraction-rejection, a genuine ambivalence with regard to the state." They expect the public "to play Hamlet" throughout the 1980s.[25] Our own earlier analysis, in Chapter 4, found that this paradox could not be accounted for by perceptions of governmental waste; nor was it a product of either unusual political naiveté or widespread opposition to some highly visible social services serving specialized constituencies. This mixed or ambivalent view also persisted after the voter was confronted cognitively with the hard tradeoffs between taxes and services. But we have not yet gone beyond simply stating the sturdiness of this pattern of beliefs, so this issue demands further attention in the context of thinking about Americans' broader values.

The notion of ambivalence suggests that mixed emotions toward the public sector exist within individual voters, not just that the electorate as whole contains some who attack and some who defend it. How would this come about? Earlier we argued that one dimension underlay both attitudes, and that the different symbols associated with them elicited pro-government attitudes at different thresholds. It is hard to be in favor of "larger government" but easy to support more money for the police department.

But another possibility is that two or more schemas about government commonly coexist within individuals. Ladd and Lipset argue that this ambivalence reflects the conflict between Americans' traditional values of individualism and egalitarianism. These could constitute two schemas. Another possibility is that "smaller government" indeed evokes individualistic values, but that the question of spending on specific services evokes a different set of attitudes based more narrowly on those specific services; for example, support for the university, or for public health clinics, treated rather autonomously. No matter what the supposed content of each horn of the ambivalence, though, the idea is the same. Two separate schemas would be involved, and either might be elicited at any given time *in the same individual*, depending on what symbols were most salient to that person—and these symbols might vary quite widely, according to public events, political and economic changes, the informal public agenda, or even the specific content of interview items.

Our data do not suggest, however, that such multiple schemas underlie these two anomalous sets of attitudes—toward size of government in the abstract, and toward concrete services. Rather, only one schema is involved. These attitudes appear to reflect a common underlying dimension of support for or opposition to the public sector. They simply hit that dimension at different thresholds. There are several indications of this. The two indices are reasonably highly correlated. The abstract size-of-government item correlated .39 with our specific-service-spending scale. Considering the gross imbalance in their marginals, and the fact that the size-of-government item is trichotomous, this is substantial. More pertinent to the question of multiple schemas, they invariably showed up on the same factor in any factor analysis we conducted.[26] We also tested whether they might have different antecedents or consequences, by creating three groups of approximately equal size: (1) consistent New Dealers, who wanted larger government in the abstract and more concrete services (32 percent); (2) inconsistents, who wanted smaller government in the abstract but more concrete services (32 percent); and (3) consistent public-sector opponents, who wanted smaller government in the abstract and fewer concrete services (36 percent). In point of fact, however, the "inconsistents" were almost exactly halfway between the other two groups on virtually every demographic and attitudinal dimension we have thus far discussed. So instead of reflecting two sometimes inconsistent schemas, these two attitudes seem to reflect one common powerful underlying value-priority dimension.

We argued earlier (Chapter 3) that the crucial determinant of support for the public sector is the symbolic content of the way in which it is presented. Every symbol hits this underlying value-priority dimension at a different threshold. There are two sources of variation: symbols differ in the average threshold they strike in the public as a whole, and individual voters differ in the thresholds struck by any given symbol. The underlying dimension has a great deal to do with the Protestant Ethic that has so dominated American culture. In general, waste, laziness, debt, reckless spending, and giveaways are negative symbols, whereas efficiency, honesty, pay-as-you-go, self-sufficiency, and thrift are positive ones. To some extent these are virtually universal American values, a part of the American culture. So they help to shape political symbols that become closely associated with them. "Public assistance programs to the elderly and the disabled" and "public assistance programs for low-income families with dependent children" receive vastly more support than "welfare" (see table 3.2). "Eliminating free school lunches for children of families who can afford to pay" and cutting food stamps and "shortening the time people can receive such benefits [as unemployment compensation]" receive much more support than "cutting federal aid to primary and secondary education" or cutting "Medicaid."[27] Attitudes toward all these value priorities seem to reflect, then, a common underlying schema. And they are tied to familiar and more general symbolic predispositions.

Conclusions

The dominant symbolic predispositions in the tax revolt reflected long-standing partisan divisions about the proper role of the public sector. Both Republican party identification and general political conservatism contributed substantially to support for the tax revolt. Republicans are a minority in California, as in the rest of the nation, but the large pool of conservative Democrats and Independents provided additional fertile territory for the tax revolt forces.

Fully as powerful, if not more so, was symbolic racism. The blunt truth is that race remains a central issue in American domestic policy today, as it has been virtually throughout American history. It plays a powerful role in the public's decisions even on issues with no manifest racial content and in campaigns with relatively little explicit reference to race, as in the case of the tax revolt. Large numbers of whites remain fundamentally opposed to special government efforts to aid blacks, and that opposition was a central determinant of white support for the tax revolt.

A third contributor, though less important, was mistrust of government in general. The only form of this that showed a significant contribution was generalized feelings of cynicism about government, without any very specific referents. Neither radical desires for fundamental changes in the structure and system of California government, nor, at the other extreme, disapproval of the performance of specific incumbents of the moment, played as strong a role as this less focused cynicism. Although even cynicism had a rather weak effect in this sense, its pervasiveness gave it a more important role. Because it was so widespread, it held even among supposed supporters of the public sector; for example, 54 percent of those expressing a desire for *more* services said they mistrusted government. This helps to account for the rather defensive and unenthusiastic quality of opposition to Proposition 13: the pro-government coalition had important misgivings about the performance of the officials and programs it was defending.

The symbolic politics model assumed these symbolic predispositions were largely the residue of political socialization (principally in early life). The origins of mistrust of government are not so clear. In our study it was associated with personal economic complaints of various sorts; thus it may reflect a more current and volatile mood, the boundaries of whose referents are still unclear. One set of voters may be unhappy because too much is being spent on welfare, another set because too little attention is being paid to this problem; in Arthur Miller's terms, there are cynics of the left and of the right.[28] Complaints about "government" also frequently reflect generalized unhappiness with the state of the nation — when most of the news is bad, public authorities are likely to be criticized, whether fairly or not. In addition, the American political culture is traditionally suspicious of authority. Ours has never been a deferential society. The popular stereotype of "politicians" and "bureaucracy" has always been negative in America, but with the decline of public trust in government over the past fifteen years, contemptuous references toward the political realm have become increasingly legitimate. In this sense, feelings of political disaffection resemble an ocean or a reservoir into which many tributaries of discontent flow. Thus, different people may adopt the same attitude toward government, but for quite different reasons. The ideological antipathy toward "big government" among conservatives is just one facet of the prevailing mood. The variety and diffuseness of anti-political sentiments, we believe, created a climate of opinion in California that was favorable to the tax revolt's objectives, even though political cynicism did not greatly distinguish those who voted for the relevant ballot measures from those who voted against them. But what matters for present purposes is that goodwill toward government is eroded from all directions.

The symbolic politics model also assumed that these predispositions influenced response to the tax revolt via a series of associated specific, proximal values about government priorities and judgments about government performance. Indeed they were associated with rather different proximal attitudes. Party identification, ideology, and symbolic racism were most closely associated with value priorities about the scope of the public sector's role — about *what* government should be doing. Republicans, conservatives, and those unsympathetic to government help for blacks tended to favor smaller government in general and less spending on specific services. Cynicism, by contrast, was more closely associated with disrespect for government performance — disapproval of *how* government was doing its job, how efficiently and how thriftily. These proximal attitudes explained some but not all of the impact of symbolic predispositions on support for the tax revolt. The predispositions themselves had substantial residual impact, presumably because of the direct association of their symbols with those of the tax revolt, without the more complex intervening rationales implied in these proximal attitudes.[29]

An important further question for this chapter was the extent to which support for the tax revolt was linked to broader schemas about politics and government. To some extent the tax revolt schema was embedded in larger schemas about politics in general, as the earlier individual relationships might have led us to expect. The tax revolt schema — preferences for a smaller public sector, perceptions of waste, overpayment of public employees, excessive tax burdens — was tied to conservative Republicanism, symbolic racism, cynicism, and disapproval of incumbents' performance. So there was a general schematization of the public's thinking at the time of the tax revolt.

When we attempted to force out the independent but more limited schemas, however, the links to broader political schemas revealed two distinctive patterns: the value priorities schema and the malaise schema. The first linked the long-standing partisan predispositions — party identification, ideology, and symbolic racism — to value priorities about government activism. The second tied cynicism, disapproval of incumbents, and general economic complaints to more specific criticisms of government performance. Support for the tax revolt itself was tied much more closely to the former than to the latter. That is, the central issue in the tax revolt was how much government should be doing, not so much whether it was doing it well or badly. The argument was over the scope of government responsibility, not the competence of its performance or some general malaise.

What can we therefore say about the public's value priorities? The public is not really ambivalent about the size of the public sector so much as it is divided along a single underlying continuum. There are many symbols of different points along this continuum, ranging from "smaller government" or "balanced budget" or "cut welfare" at the negative end to "maintain good schools" and "help to support the elderly and disabled" at the positive end. Different symbols seem to set different thresholds along this continuum, so they elicit variable amounts of support for an active public sector.

It is clear that the Jarvis-Gann campaign evoked (or created) all of these schemas — the partisan and malaise schemas that brought in broader political attitudes as well as a schema focused specifically on the tax revolt. So, presumably, did the Reagan presidential campaign. Why the tax rebels were so successful with Propositions 13 and 4, and in the fall of 1980, and so patently unsuccessful with Jarvis II, cannot be settled from the data in this chapter. This question demands a consideration of the important differences among the campaigns.

9

Proposition 13: The Peculiar Election

The zenith of the California tax revolt was the overwhelming victory of Proposition 13 on June 6, 1978. The next week Howard Jarvis, "crusty" now, not "crazy," was on the cover of *Time*, and soon after he was conducted on a triumphal tour of Washington by California's liberal Democratic Senator Alan Cranston. Jarvis was now the messianic leader of a movement of the "people" that had taken the first step toward wresting control over their lives — or at least their taxes — from government. Erstwhile critics scurried to join the ranks of Jarvis's army, though no one matched the dizzying speed with which Governor Brown reversed positions. For more than a year the tax rebels held sway, passing the Gann amendment to limit the growth of state spending with hardly a murmur of opposition.

But nothing is forever, particularly in California's showbiz environment. The people once more surprised the establishment, rejecting Proposition 9 (Jarvis II or "Jaws II"). In a brief two-year span Howard Jarvis moved from the obscurity of the political bit player to the limelight of stardom and then to the sidelines with declining ratings. He left the stage after the defeat of Proposition 9 muttering a somewhat inexact comparison with what he called the "Jap" attack on Pearl Harbor — "they" had won the battle but "we" would win the war.

Until now we have treated the tax revolt in California as a unitary phenomenon. The strength of the correlations among attitudes toward the three ballot measures in California and the similarity in the determinants of these attitudes are justification for this analytic strategy. Yet the sharp contrast between the outcomes of Propositions 13 and 9 and the uneven results of anti-tax referenda in other states require careful attention. Why did the pendulum swing so far and so fast in California? Was the shift caused mainly by differences in the specific provisions of 13 and 9, by changes in the political or economic climate, or by the specialized circumstances of each electoral campaign? And what does this imply for the future of the tax revolt in California? Has the appetite of the popular beast been sated, or does it lurk quietly waiting for another bite out of the public sector, as President Reagan's sweeping legislative victories in his first few months might imply?

Our answer begins by emphasizing the peculiarity of Proposition 13. Its victory, we should recall, was discontinuous with the recent history of anti-tax initiatives in California. From the early 1950s until 1978, Californians had consistently defeated efforts to reduce the size of the public sector even when this meant giving up the promise of savings in taxes. From November 1968 through June 1980, nine tax-limitation measures appeared on the California ballot. Six failed. The two winners other than Proposition 13 were relatively mild and noncontroversial. Proposition 13, the most radical of all such efforts, stands out as the real exception. How can we understand its unusual success?

Proposition 13

Although this may seem surprising in retrospect, Proposition 13 was not a certain winner. Many observers expected it to follow the usual pattern in California: an early lead when the public was poorly informed, followed by the mobilization of opposition by the establishment and a close race in the polls, and finally, a last-minute surge against the populist initiative. And as we have seen in Chapter 2, Proposition 13 did in fact assume an early lead before the legislature proposed Proposition 8 as an alternative. But by April its support had stabilized and seemed to be slipping, while Proposition 8 was gaining. This would seem to have indicated a clear victory for the continuation of a well-funded, high-quality public sector. The electorate consistently expressed a preference for the moderate alternative over a period of two months in the middle of the campaign.[1]

But even in this period, Proposition 13 had enjoyed more support than would be expected from the past history of such ballot measures. Why? Some explanations are easy to rule out on the basis of our previous analyses. There has been a long-standing constituency ideologically committed to cuts in the public sector. But the conservative Republican portion of the electorate was not large enough to provide more than strong minority support for Proposition 13. We have uncovered no evidence that this faction was growing much in California during the late 1970s. And more specifically, there is also no evidence of a drop in support for the activities of the public sector during that same period, and the most recent polls continue to reflect this consensus for maintaining high current spending levels on government services. Nevertheless, it is true that this support dropped to the lowest level recorded in the late 1970s just before the vote on Jarvis-Gann. A temporary increase in anti-public sector feeling thus was associated with the victory of Proposition 13. But this factor cannot explain the enduring solid approval of the proposition, since the demand for maintaining or increasing public services soon returned to previous levels (see table 3.2). It is the temporary nature of that decline in demand that requires explanation.

We have already rejected the idea that awareness of the huge state surplus accounts for the high level of initial support for Proposition 13 and for its electoral margin. In theory, voters could have realized that a large cut in property taxes would not result in the disruption of valued services. But, as we noted in Chapter 2, little news about the surplus was disseminated, no polls reported on reactions to it, and there is simply no compelling evidence that many voters were aware of its existence or magnitude.[2]

Rather, the main reason for Proposition 13's early popularity was the promise of a big tax break. As we have seen, the rise in the property tax had been severe and dramatically vivid for many homeowners. And Proposition 13 both promised a very large immediate cash payoff and blocked further horrifying increases. None of the previous tax-cutting propositions had ever offered such a dramatic dollars and cents reward.

Still, these factors alone do not adequately explain the phenomenon of Proposition 13. As Chapter 2 showed, the period between May 8 and May 22 of 1978 saw an explosive reversal in the fortunes of the two rival propositions (see table 2.1). In the first week of May, the governor's and legislature's alternative, Proposition 8, had a larger margin of approval. By the last week of May, the picture had totally reversed, and the position of Proposition 8 was getting worse by the day. Proposition 13 won going away. What happened in this intervening few weeks to create such a dramatic turnaround?

We should note first that the largest shift in attitude occurred in Los Angeles County. As shown in table 9.1, during mid-May support for Proposition 13 jumped 12 percent in Los Angeles County but by only 2 percent elsewhere in the state. So let us review what was happening in Los Angeles in that period.

TABLE 9.1 Regional differences in support for Proposition 13 during 1978.

	Level of support		Owner-renter difference	
Polling date	Los Angeles County	Rest of the state	Los Angeles County	Rest of the state
Feb. 11-23	67%	59%	+18%	+11%
Feb. 17-20	57	43	+13	+10
March 27-April 3	55	49	+20	+31
April 24-28	58	52	+26	+18
May 1-8	56	53	+32	+19
May 22-27	68	55	+15	+9
May 28-30	68	60	+24	+23
Election-June 6	67	64	—	—

Sources: California Polls (Feb. 11-23, Feb. 17-20, March 27-April 3, May 1-8, May 28-30); *Los Angeles Times* Polls (April 24-28, May 22-27). Entries on the left are the percentage supporting Proposition 13 of those with a definite opinion. Entries on the right are the percentage of owners supporting it minus the percentage of renters supporting it, again of those with a definite opinion.

May 1978 began with a deluge of horrifying budgetary predictions from public officials. The Los Angeles County Administrator said it would "devastate" county services, and layoff notices were sent to 37,000 employees. The May 8 front-page headline in the *Los Angeles Times* read, "Will be broke by July if Jarvis passes, County says." The mayor of the city of Los Angeles requested new budgets from all departments reflecting 30 percent budget cuts. UCLA business forecasters predicted a 10 percent unemployment rate. And the city superintendent of schools called it a "blue-print for disaster" and said it would close the district down for the summer.

This wave of doomsday forecasts may have been successful in April and early May in retarding the growth of support for Proposition 13. But the publicity given the coming disaster to services came to an abrupt halt in mid-May when the massive increases in property reassessments were leaked to the press. Many homeowners would plainly be stunned to discover that their homes assessed at double or triple previous value, reflecting the rapidly inflating housing prices of the previous three years. This was particularly true for the more affluent sections of the county near the coast, where the most vocal of Los Angeles's citizens dwell. All this was front-page news.

As we saw in Chapter 2, the "politicians" bungled this frightening fact of life about as badly as was possible. The county tax assessor, Alexander Pope, announced that homeowners could go to one of his offices, or telephone one, and learn the worst for themselves. Frightened and angry homeowners then physically inundated the assessor's office, and his phones rang off their hooks; the County Board of Supervisors then ordered Mr. Pope to mail all reassessments to the county's 700,000 property owners before election day. They next promptly reversed themselves, and unanimously voted to roll back all assessments to the 1977–78 levels. This set off another giant angry reaction from the other two-thirds of the homeowners who had not been reassessed, who quickly perceived that *their* taxes would have to go up to accommodate a necessarily increased tax rate. At this juncture Governor Brown made his pitch to freeze reassessments all across the state, allowing, he said, judgments about taxes to be made in "an atmosphere of calm and rationality." But this impulsively offered plan was equally quickly withdrawn, as the governor soon saw it had little legislative support.

This reassessment-and-freeze sequence dominated the news about the Proposition 13 campaign for about two weeks from the original leak on May 15 to Brown's back-pedaling on May 31. Almost all other coverage of Proposition 13 was swept from the front pages and television news. Disastrous official predictions about the effects of Proposition 13 on services got short shrift, and the state surplus received little attention. It was a tale of reckless government, conflict between panicky officials trying to save their political skins, and indecisive jumping back and forth among widely varying radical alternatives. Public officials appeared bumbling and inconsistent, unable to act firmly to ameliorate large and abrupt increases in the property taxes owed by many ordinary families. The news now reported spectacular rises in support for Proposition 13, especially in Los Angeles County. The Jarvis forces were gleeful, reveling in the upsurge of angry homeowners and the new blow to voters' confidence in government.

Many taxpayers felt they had to take matters into their own hands; public officials were not going to help them. Certainly this was a political issue in which the self-interest stakes were high. And at the same time nothing could have better fit Howard Jarvis's schema for contemptible government. Here were bumbling politicians only out to save their own skins, with seemingly complete indifference to the consequences for ordinary people. So this great leap forward for the tax revolt could have been propelled by the heightened salience of self-interest, and by the higher stakes. Or the bumbling might well have converted Proposition 13 into a highly symbolic anti-government protest.

In fact, self-interest explains the jump in support less well. As table 9.1 shows, the owner-renter difference in Los Angeles actually *diminished* steadily during the period following the reassessment publicity.[3] Nor is it likely that this jump came from more general economic tensions displaced from some other source, such as anxiety about inflation or about the economy. In 1978 the California economy was, and was perceived to be, in excellent shape. And as we saw in Chapter 6, economic malaise was not related to support for the tax revolt in any of the several surveys in which such measures are available.

The Malaise Schema

The inept response of public officials to the threat to the voters' economic futures exactly matched the "malaise" schema of government that Howard Jarvis was selling—and we argue that this fit of external symbols with preexisting schemas induced mass opinion change. As a general matter, we might hypothesize that new strong affects will appear in public opinion mainly when the shifts in the public agenda make salient symbols that evoke strong symbolic predispositions. This should be particularly likely when these new symbols are organized in the same schematic manner as voters' predispositions. The symbols associated with Proposition 13 changed in the last month of the campaign, and it acquired new "meanings" that attracted more and different adherents.

The emotions it evoked were so intense that the popular response can be described as a "craze" or a "hostile outburst." The literature on collective behavior documents many instances in which mass publics have become quite emotional, when contagious attitudes have led a mass to one extreme or another. Labels for these phenomena vary principally according to the emotion predominant in the crowd. A "panic" describes mass anxiety, a "craze" mass greed, and a "hostile outburst" mass anger.[4] In all these instances reason is overcome by emotion, and the crowd's dominant emotionality overcomes each individual's separate identity.

What symbols were already on the agenda by mid-May, and what new ones did the reassessment mess add? *Escalating property taxes* were at the forefront of the public's attention even before the reassessment gaffe. Exactly half of the prospective "yes on 13" voters in the California Poll conducted during the first week of May explained their choice as based on a desire to lower property taxes. The consistent difference between owners and renters in attitudes toward Proposition 13 also shows the salience of the property tax (see table 9.1). The publicity surrounding the massive reassessments no doubt re-emphasized property taxes, but this issue was already prominent. Conservative value priorities, in terms of *reduced government spending*, were also highly salient. This can be seen in the high frequency with which "government over-spending" (28 percent) and "send a message to cut spending" (20 percent) were given as reasons for supporting Proposition 13 in the same early May poll. This too had been a theme early in the campaign.

But the key to the events of mid-May is that the symbols of the malaise schema were pushed up to the top of the public agenda. The image of *insensitive, out-for-themselves politicians* came to the fore. The reassessment mess certainly conformed to the schema Howard Jarvis had constructed about politicians and bureaucrats as remote, self-serving, and unaware of the problems "the people" actually face. Even when they know, they don't care, worrying only about covering their own electoral hindquarters, not about "serving the people."

Americans generally have much more negative affects toward such stereotypical, generalized attitude objects as "politicians" and "bureaucrats" than toward specific individuals in public life, such as Mayor Bradley, Supervisor Hahn, Governor Brown, or the specific individuals they encounter in government offices.[5] Presumably the reassessment mess put "politicians" and "bureaucrats," rather than these specific individuals, front and center, because all of them — tax assessors, county supervisors, mayors, legislators, the governor — behaved in roughly the same way. It therefore was more likely to evoke the long-standing negative affects most people had toward the collective objects than their more positive affects toward specific elected officials.

The symbols of *big government, waste,* and *incompetence* also came to the fore. As we saw in Chapter 3, most Americans do stereotype government performance, in the abstract, as inefficient (more so than the private sector), wasteful, and staffed by incompetents. The reassessment mess made incompetent performance the salient issue and pushed value priorities into the background.

Since Californians' attitudes on such malaise dimensions were much more anti-public-sector than were their attitudes on the value priorities dimensions, Howard Jarvis's cause was well served by the events that made an issue of the performance of government rather than having the debate revolve solely around the supply of services.

The result of the surge in anti-government sentiment was that Californians' usual support for spending on specific services declined concomitantly with the collapse of the opposition to Proposition 13, as we saw in Chapter 3. In the California Poll conducted a week before Election Day, cuts in services were preferred to increases in most service areas, whereas in all polls before and after that period, the public had favored an increase to a decrease in spending on just about everything but welfare.[6] For example, the percentage difference index (PDI) on the composite service spending scale in the July 1977 California Poll was +52 percent, and in the Tax Revolt Survey in November 1979, using the same services, +53 percent. But in Late May 1978, a week before the election, it was −14 percent! Perceptions of the magnitude of government waste were highest just before Proposition 13 passed. At that point the public was about evenly divided on whether or not government could absorb a 25 percent budget cut without cutting services; by April 1980, the public thought this would not be possible, by a five-to-one margin (see table 3.3).

We interpret the surge of support for Proposition 13, and these unusually anti-government sentiments, then, as reflecting the heightened salience of the malaise schema, mixed with a widespread mood that was highly emotional, angry, and vengeful. But these attitude changes that surfaced just before that election might be explained by the alternative hypothesis that on this occasion the voters, for once, really faced up to the hard tradeoff between taxes and services. Wanting a major tax cut, they decided to forgo some services in order to get it. In other words, at that point their service preferences might have been more tightly connected to their tax-cutting preferences than was the case at other times during the tax revolt, when sample surveys posed only hypothetical choices. If so, their attitudes toward spending on specific services should have been closely related to support for Proposition 13 in the last California Poll before the election, at which time, by this view, voters were making a realistic tradeoff. But they may not have been so closely linked in the Tax Revolt Survey conducted eighteen months later, when the voters had gone back to their "something-for-nothing" mentality, with the level of support for specific services resuming its normal high levels. Contrary to this line of reasoning, however, there was no evidence of such greater consistency at the time of the original vote. The statistical association (gamma) between the service-spending scale and support for Proposition 13 was .57 one week before the election, and .55 in November 1979.

Also, if the election over Proposition 13 had really imposed such hard rational tradeoff choices on the electorate, we should have found that better-educated people in particular related their service preferences to their votes, because as a group they tend to be better-informed and are more likely to engage in schematic thinking. Certainly the college-educated reflected the surge of anti-government feeling as much as anyone else: the PDI values for service spending were, for college graduates, −24 percent in May 1978 and

+ 39 percent in November 1979, compared to − 9 percent and + 59 percent for those never attending college. The shift was almost exactly the same in the two groups. But in the crucial period just before the Proposition 13 vote, the college-educated did not tie their vote intentions to these service-spending preferences more tightly than did the less-educated. Indeed the service-spending scale was *less* related to Proposition 13 voting intentions among college graduates than among other respondents (gammas of .48 and .69 for the two groups, respectively).[7] So it appears that the increased support for service cuts at the time of the Proposition 13 vote was due more to a broadly based temporary surge in anti-government feeling than to raised consciousness of the painful tradeoffs that must be made to receive a large tax cut.

This surge was not stronger among homeowners than anyone else, even though they were the apparent victims of the politicians' bungling. The politicians' mistakes lowered the government's standing throughout the entire public. Their incompetence was most flagrant, and therefore most costly, in Los Angeles, where an especially strong pro-revolt climate of opinion developed. And as usually happens, the enduring effects of such a climate of opinion are greatest on the segments of the population that were previously least political — the young, the least educated, and political Independents. In the Tax Revolt Survey, the regional difference in support for the revolt (the greater number of tax rebels in the Los Angeles metropolitan area than in the Bay Area) was 41 percent among those aged 18–24, 19 percent among those aged 25–34, and only 8 percent among those 35 and over. It was 22 percent among those with no college, and 5 percent among those who had attended college. And it was 20 percent among Independents, and 9 percent among party identifiers. Like other examples of crowd psychology, this surge component of the tax revolt spread fastest among those without firm political predispositions.[8]

Accommodation

The post election accommodation to the provisions of Proposition 13 came quickly. The state legislature and the governor, of course, had moved immediately after election day to woo back the voters on two fronts. The governor endorsed Proposition 13 and promised faithfully to implement the tax cut. But the state's leaders also developed the bailout plan to shore up the public sector. The massive state surplus was used to replace lost property taxes and to fund most pre-existing levels of services without increasing other levies.

The bailout bill strongly contradicted the radical reorientation of government that Howard Jarvis had interpreted as "the message" of Proposition 13. It provided for business as usual rather than for massive cutbacks of government. Not surprisingly, the public had much the same inconsistent reaction we have seen throughout this book. On the one hand, they strongly approved of the bailout, apparently expressing their more usual pro-public-sector value priorities. In the August 1978 California Poll, 75 percent approved of the bailout, and only 19 percent disapproved. Very few disapproved of the bailout on the grounds that it reflected insufficient cutting of government spending (about 10 percent) or that the surplus should be rebated to the taxpayers (about 2 percent).

On the other hand, the remnants of the anti-government surge continued to influence strongly the public's thinking. Hence the public was not completely happy about the way things had worked out. Several California Polls over the next eighteen months showed that about 60 percent regularly said cuts had been made in the "wrong places," and only about 15 percent said they were in the "right places." Almost 75 percent in May 1978 had wanted to cut "city and country administration," by far the strongest support for a concrete cut. In August, the biggest complaint (expressed by 46 percent) was that cuts were taking place "at the bottom" rather than at the top of the government. Bureaucratic heads that were meant to roll had once more escaped the public guillotine. When asked to explain why school costs kept going up, respondents blamed too many administrators, excessively high administrative salaries, administrators who were not doing any work, and lazy and exploitative service recipients who could "con" government out of money.

But as the passage of Proposition 13 receded into the past, the content of Californians' complaints shifted. Presumably the malaise schema—on which Californians were predominantly anti-government—was evoked less and less often, while the value priorities schema—on which they were more moderate—reasserted its previous dominance. The general consensus remained that cuts were made in the "wrong" places, but the nature of what was perceived as wrong changed markedly as the surge receded, and changed from anti-government malaise to pro-government value priorities. The complaint that cuts were taking place at the bottom rather than at the top diminished with time—in a California Poll done in February 1979 only 27 percent mentioned it, and in November 1979 and February 1980, only 20 percent did. Instead, complaints about cuts in specific services began to mount. In August 1978, only 34 percent cited cuts in schools and teachers, while by September 1980, 53 percent did. Growing numbers also complained about cuts in other services, such as police and fire.

Even with this apparent sabotage of Howard Jarvis's dream of actually cutting government, approval of Proposition 13 remained very steady, ranging only between 58 percent and 63 percent in California Polls conducted from August 1978 through September 1980. The dynamics of this support changed and indeed converted the meaning of Proposition 13 into something much more consonant with the long-term ethos of California support for the public sector. But this succeeded in consolidating substantial long-term majority support for Proposition 13. Subsequent efforts to tinker with it have consistently been rejected.

The Jarvis campaign, then, had argued that taxes and state spending were too high, that spending should be cut and tax monies returned to the taxpayers. The Proposition 13 campaign put together a successful coalition of property taxpayers, political conservatives, and a vengeful last-minute surge of anti-government sentiment. And it did successfully reduce public tensions about the property tax. But Jarvis had misread public sentiment about actually cutting back what government provided. When it came to reducing services and benefits, the majority opted for the status quo rather than for radical cuts. Because of the surplus, Californians could have something for nothing – at least temporarily. This helped generate stable, long-term, majority support for Proposition 13, and made it the great exception among California's tax limitation propositions.

The Gann Amendment

We have described the electorate as plunging ahead with Proposition 13 almost heedless of its consequences for government, in a semi-vindictive spirit. Then as time wore on, the public became more concerned about its possibly destructive effects upon the social web in California. The Gann amendment was a transitional point in this story, partly because of the continuing great popularity of Proposition 13 and the reluctance of public officials to get burned politically once again. But in addition Gann was generally perceived by both government officials and the public as very unlikely to have disastrous effects.

And our evidence indicates that voters did not especially view the Gann amendment as an instrument for making changes they desired in California

government. If this had been so, we would expect to find that any given perceived effect of Gann should have mattered most in the voting decisions of
those who most valued (or opposed) that possible effect. Specifically, its tax-
cutting potential should have most affected voters who felt most burdened by
taxes, and its service-cutting potential should have most affected voters who
wanted some change in service levels.[9] But as table 9.2 shows, voters' expectations about the effects of the Gann amendment did not influence their support
for it differentially among those who favored or opposed that particular
effect. The impact of expected tax reductions did not depend on tax burden,
nor did the impact of expected service cuts depend on desire for service cuts.
Rather, voters tended to support the Gann amendment to the extent that they
expected taxes to be cut, expected services to be maintained, felt burdened by
taxes, or wanted lower services; that is, all these variables had simple main
effects rather than the expected interactions. Nor did voters' tradeoff decisions (see Chapter 3) interact with these expected effects of Gann, in data not
presented here. So the voters did not generally treat the Gann amendment as
a measure that would have a profound effect upon end-states they felt most
strongly about.

TABLE 9.2 Support for Gann amendment as a function of tax burden, spending preferences, and expectations about its effects.

	Expects Gann amendment will:		
	Lower taxes	Not lower taxes	Difference
Tax burden			
Much too much	87%	74%	+ 13%
Somewhat too much	88	76	+ 12
About right	74	57	+ 17
All respondents	84	70	+ 14
	Not cut services	Cut services	Difference
Service spending scale: prefers to			
Decrease spending	94%	86%	+ 8%
Hold the line	82	79	+ 3
Increase spending	76	67	+ 9
All respondents	81	71	+ 10

Source: Tax Revolt Survey.

Note: Entry is percentage supporting Gann amendment of those with a definite opinion.

Jarvis II

Jarvis II promised another seemingly radical tax cut, but went down to a convincing defeat. The campaign for it was not as emotional as the fight over Proposition 13. But beyond that, what can we say about the voters' apparent reversal of preference? The first important fact is that by and large the same variables predicted support for Jarvis II and Proposition 13. We approached this comparison in three different ways. The bivariate relationships for each of the separate categories of major demographics, self-interest, symbolic predisposition, and proximal-attitude variables have been presented in earlier chapters. And their effects upon Proposition 13 vote intention (or recalled vote) were very similar to those upon Jarvis II vote intention. The only real difference was that homeownership was a good bit more powerful on Proposition 13 whereas felt state income tax burden was more potent on Jarvis II. Otherwise there was little difference.[10]

A second strategy was to include all the distal predictor variables in regression equations on support for the three ballot propositions at as many time points as possible. Hence these analyses used our usual set of demographic variables; the two most powerful objective self-interest variables, homeownership and public employee status; and two of the most powerful symbolic predispositions, ideology and party identification. These were available in three polls each on Proposition 13 vote intention (or recalled vote), on later support for it, and on the Gann amendment; and five on Jarvis II. The two predictor variables that we have found to be important that were not available outside our own survey, subjective tax burden and symbolic racism, were not included.[11]

These analyses show strikingly parallel results for all four categories of dependent variables, despite some inevitable differences in measurement and procedure across the surveys. Because of this parallel, the scope of the analyses, and redundancy with earlier analyses, it is perhaps enough to discuss the data in summary fashion here rather than presenting them in detail. Ideology, party identification, and public employee status had the expected effects in every case, and homeownership in all but one. And these were reasonably strong effects, statistically significant in about three-quarters of the cases. The demographic variables had highly consistent effects but generally not strong ones. White, higher-income, older, male, Los Angeles metropolitan area residents—and those with less education—showed most support for the tax reform propositions, in at least eleven of the fourteen regressions for each variable. However, only in the cases of education and sex were the effects strong enough to be statistically significant more than half the time.

A third strategy was to do a series of regressions based on more proximal variables; specifically, the symbolic predispositions, self-interest, service spending, and perceived waste. These were available in five surveys on Proposition 13, three on Gann, and two on Jarvis II.[12] In all these cases both the latter variables had significant effects. So the most obvious generalization from these analyses is that the same predictors regularly had much the same effects, on all three propositions.[13]

So regardless of whether voters' preferences were assessed at election time, much earlier, or much later, approximately the same structure of attitudes and life circumstances predicted support for the tax revolt — despite the very different outcomes of the three elections. We ask once more, then, why were the outcomes so different?

Direct tax savings were a major factor in the appeal of both Propositions 13 and 9. Indeed, for these two propositions the same dollar amount in anticipated savings resulted in the same boost in support. But Proposition 13 promised more people more savings. At the end, Jarvis II was winning a majority only among those promised at least $500, which amounted to less than a quarter of the citizenry. Besides offering a smaller cash reward, Jarvis II offered it in a less enticing form. The property tax is usually collected in the most painful way possible — as a lump-sum payment. The state income tax, by contrast, is mainly paid through withholding. Many people do not have to pay anything on April 15 but get refunds instead. And any lump-sum payment at tax time is dwarfed by one's federal income tax bill.

Another factor is that public employees were more effectively mobilized in opposition to Jarvis II than they had been against Proposition 13. This is harder to document with the survey data available to us. But table 7.3 shows that as a voting bloc, public employees were much more strongly opposed to Jarvis II, even six months before the election, than they had been to either of the other propositions. Public employee organizations were considerably more active in pumping out publicity and anti-Jarvis propaganda. So public sector workers became a much more formidable obstacle to the tax revolt, perhaps a harbinger of more such conflicts to come in the future.

The other major difference is that the voters expected Jarvis II to result in real service cuts, whereas few had expected them to follow from Proposition 13 or the Gann amendment, or had experienced those propositions as actually cutting services. On the eve of the Proposition 13 vote, as we have seen, a majority of voters felt that state and local governments could provide the same services with a 20 percent reduction in tax revenue. And in four surveys done from August 1978 through February 1980, up to the point when the Jarvis II campaign was getting underway, relatively few reported that their families had experienced a decline in services as a result of Proposition 13.[14] So Proposition 13 was initially experienced by most as a cost-free tax reduction. Nor was the Gann amendment widely perceived as likely to threaten services: as already indicated, less than half the public thought it would reduce services.

But in California Polls in both February and April 1980, most of those with an opinion felt the state surplus could cover at most "some" of the revenue shortfall expected from Jarvis II. Less than 15 percent felt it would cover "all" the shortfall. Not surprisingly, then, most Californians felt "serious" service cuts would have to be made if Jarvis II passed. This is shown in table 9.3. And this time there was no malaise-induced desire for reduced services; the voters by and large did not want services cut. These expectations led to overwhelming opposition to Jarvis II. And as the campaign wore on, this became a bigger and bigger obstacle, for two reasons. The seriousness of the expected cuts in services became more obvious, and the strength of their impact on vote preference increased as well. This too is shown in table 9.3.

In short, the California electorate perceived a very changed situation in 1980. Tax cuts would probably cause service losses. And the tax revolt therefore suffered massive defections among those opposed to service cuts. Analyses of the Tax Revolt Survey show a large-scale shift from support of Proposition 13 to opposition to Jarvis II in the largest group of people in the electorate: those who wanted to maintain or increase services, on balance, and who when presented the tax-service tradeoff were willing to pay more taxes to support the services they really wanted. In this group, 23 percent defected, whereas only 4 percent of the Proposition 13 opponents were recruited to the cause.

Analysis of the somewhat later February 1980 California polls shows a similarly rampant rate of defection from the tax revolt among those who anticipated that the state surplus would cover only "some" of the revenue lost to an income-tax cut, or even "moderately serious" cuts in government services. In these groups well over 20 percent defected from their earlier support of Proposition 13 to opposing Jarvis II, while the tax revolt gained only about 5 percent new recruits. Only those confident that the surplus would "cover most" of the shortfall, or that no serious cuts would have to be made, remained even close to loyal to the revolt: in this group defectors barely outnumbered the recruits.

This reasoning returns us to the question of how the public handles the

TABLE 9.3 Anticipated effects of Jarvis II.

	Frequency		Support for Jarvis II	
	Feb. 1980	April 1980	Feb. 1980	April 1980
Has the state government any surplus money available to offset a 20 to 25 percent cut in revenues? If so, how much will it cover?				
Has no surplus	23%	25%	53%	24%
Has a surplus, enough to cover				
A little	6	5	61	23
Some	16	18	69	51
Most	21	19	70	67
All	14	10	73	79
No opinion; don't know	21	21		
Total	101%	98		
Effect on the vote			+ 20	+ 55
With a 20 to 25 percent cut in state budget, would the state supply same level of services, or have to cut? If cut, how seriously?				
Would have to cut				
Very serious	21%	30%	38%	15%
Somewhat serious	26	28	67	39
Not too serious	19	17	86	80
Could provide same level of services	22	15	84	84
No opinion; depends	13	10		
Total	100	100		
Effect on the vote			+ 46	+ 69

Source: California Polls 8001 and 8002.

Note: Entries in the lefthand columns are the percentages expecting each effect indicated. Entries in the righthand columns are the percentages supporting Jarvis II given each effect shown.

tradeoff between taxes and services. In Chapter 3 we concluded that, at least when such tradeoffs were put to the electorate in the abstract, sentiment tended to favor maintenance of the status quo in services, even at the expense of forgoing tax cuts. Proposition 13 offered many Californians a very large cash savings with minimal cuts in services, which was quite a different matter. Not surprisingly, most bought it. And Jarvis II offered a relatively meager tax cut but threatened massive service cuts. Californians overwhelmingly rejected this package.

By this reasoning, the California public was confronted at least in part with a tradeoff between the direct tax savings Jarvis II would provide to them, on the one hand, and the probable diminution of government services they estimated. This choice has been discussed recently as one between "sociotropic" and "egocentric" bases for voting behavior. That is, did people choose on the basis of what they think is best for the community, or on the basis of what they think is best for themselves in some immediate sense?[15] To estimate the California public's resolution of this dilemma, we looked at support for Jarvis II as a function of these two variables simultaneously: how much of the revenue shortfall they thought the state surplus would cover, and the cash savings they estimated they would get from cutting the state income tax. In both the February and April California Polls, the threatened revenue shortfall proved considerably more important than personal gain (betas of .29 and .14 in February, and .39 and .14 in April, respectively). When the two variables are cross-tabulated, so that they are both controlled, those that believed the surplus would cover "most" or "all" of the shortfall supported Jarvis II by 46 percent more, on the average, than did those who believed it would cover "little" or "none." Personal tax savings were less important; those expecting a savings of over $500 supported Jarvis II by only 14 percent more than did those expecting to save $50 or less annually. "Sociotropic" thinking dominated the public's choice about Jarvis II.

Finally, the explosion of emotion surrounding Proposition 13 beginning in May 1978 through its tapering-off sometime in 1979 expressed a stridently anti-government mood in the electorate, like a sudden storm overtaking it in late May and early June of 1978. The rise and fall of this surge of emotion is evident in many places in the polls of the 1978 to 1980 period, as we have seen. By the time Jarvis II came to the electorate, it seems to have declined to a low ebb. But why did it decline? The actions of Governor Brown and the legislature clearly helped. Brown symbolically acknowledged the anti-government grievances, both by endorsing Proposition 13 and later by advocating a constitutional amendment to force a federal balanced budget. And the realities of high property taxes were addressed by their reduction, with few cuts in services. There may also be some cathartic value to the mass expression of anger inherent in such a surge, that makes it unlikely to last long. Perhaps the body politic, like individual persons, cannot long sustain such a high level of emotional intensity, so all such upsurges of feeling "run their course." Moreover, to the extent that attention to the tax revolt depended on the interest of the media, it was bound to fade. Such popular excitements have a life course that craves novelty, and they may be easily satiated.[16]

Conclusions

Proposition 13 had two unique elements that converted a basically minority, ideologically conservative appeal into a smashing victory: a large, bird-in-the-hand cash benefit for a large segment of the California public; and an anti-government emotional surge induced by ineffective and even deceptive behavior by public officials at a crucial moment in the campaign. The Los Angeles reassessments, bureaucratic bungling, and Brown's surrender transformed the Proposition 13 campaign from a specific grievance against the rising property tax to a broader symbolic protest against government. This fusion gave Proposition 13 both its majority and the intensity of its support. The process spread the enthusiasm for Proposition 13 as if by contagion from those most directly affected — Los Angeles homeowners — to the rest of the state and to renters. The events of mid-May enlarged the agenda and created a climate of emotionality that made Jarvis's crude attacks on politicians seem legitimate, indeed gratifying. In the last weeks of the campaign Proposition 13 took on the quality of a messianic movement in which fear and anger overrode an enduring commitment to the provision of government services. The drastic nature of the proposition became an asset, not a liability.

With Jarvis II, then, there was a return to the cautious orientation in favor of the status quo. Government was still perceived as wasteful, but this was no longer a symbol at the forefront of public consciousness. Politicians and bureaucrats lay low, and did little other than try to portray some effort to cut. Ironically, the measure expected to win lost, even though it did not face dire predictions of lack of money (indeed the surplus was much more in evidence as a topic of discussion than it had been before Proposition 13) and even though the major institutions (political ones and some economic ones like the Bank of America) refused to come out against it. Without the earlier combination of an intense economic grievance, widespread opportunities for financial gain, and a symbolic protest, the tax rebels lost.

10

Putting the Pieces Together

Until now we have presented our many findings in a piecemeal fashion. It is time to take stock, to summarize the main themes of our analysis, in terms of both the psychological processes uncovered and their political consequences. We began by hypothesizing a three-step flow of causality in generating support for and participation in the tax revolt. Social background and current social location were assumed to generate variations in self-interest and symbolic predispositions; these in turn promoted certain attitudes toward government, taxation, and spending; and these were the proximate causes of the nature of involvement in the tax revolt.

A Summary Model

One conventional way of testing such a complex model is to present some overall causal analysis.[1] And such a model is the starting point for this summary chapter. This hypothesized causal chain implies that when considered in isolation each class of predictor will have a significant influence on support for the tax revolt, but also that in many instances this apparent causal influence will be diminished or eliminated when other factors "closer" in the chain are included in the predictive multiple regression equations. Thus the ensuing analysis makes a distinction between the *direct* effect of a hypothesized cause of the tax revolt, which refers to the relationship between an independent variable and the dependent variable after all other more proximate predictors have been controlled, and its *total* effect, which includes that portion of its influence which is funneled through intermediate points in the causal sequence and which is measured by the regression coefficient in an equation that does not include the more proximal variables.

It should be noted at the outset that the causal sequence hypothesized involves a series of assumptions—for example, that political cynicism of a diffuse kind temporally precedes the perception of government workers as wasteful rather than resulting from this specific opinion. Obviously, it would be more realistic to assume some degree of reciprocal influence, but the statistical procedures we employ require that we stipulate nonrecursivity (or one-way causality), and we are confident that the predominant direction of influence is reflected in our model.

This overall model, summarizing our findings on support for the tax revolt, is presented in both figure 10.1 and table 10.1. The figure highlights the most important empirical findings to emerge from this analysis. The table draws together the multiple analytic threads into one complex model of support for the tax revolt, using all the predictors we have employed, and presents the exact statistics for this model.[2]

A first general conclusion is that each general category of cause retained some statistically significant influence on support for the tax revolt. This can be seen in the left-hand column of table 10.1. This underscores our argument that the movement to limit taxes and government spending drew its strength from an ability to attract followers on the basis of diverse factors. A variety of demographic conditions, self-interest, and symbolic predispositions were involved. But when we look beyond this superficial conclusion, the details of the findings are more interesting, and sometimes puzzling. Before turning to these puzzles, though, let us reiterate the main themes in our results. We have identified these themes with the same numbers in figure 10.1 as in the text so that they can be easily compared.

1. Being male, less educated, and/or a resident of the Los Angeles metropolitan area directly affected support for the revolt. We have earlier presented interpretations of these effects, but have no explicit empirical test of these interpretations.

2. High income and age (at least up to retirement age) contributed to support, primarily because they were in turn associated with homeownership and higher perceived tax burdens.

3. White and/or older voters were also more racist, conservative, and Republican, and more pro-revolt due to these symbolic predispositions.

4. Self-interest among "the taxpayers" also contributed directly to support, independent of their demographic characteristics.

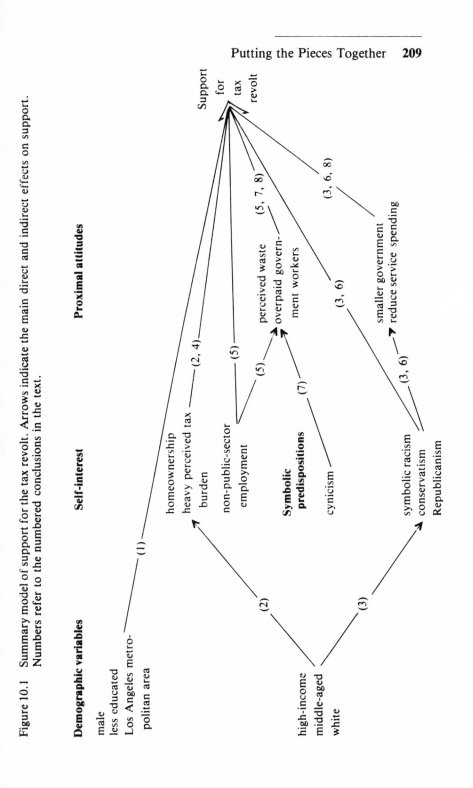

Figure 10.1 Summary model of support for the tax revolt. Arrows indicate the main direct and indirect effects on support. Numbers refer to the numbered conclusions in the text.

TABLE 10.1 An overall model of support for the tax revolt.

	Total effect	Direct effect
Demographic variables		
Age	.11	0
Race	− .14	− .05
Sex	.07	.06
Education	− .04	− .05
Income	.16	0
Region	.10	.11
Symbolic predispositions		
Party identification	.15	.03
Ideology	.21	.10
Symbolic racism	.21	.11
Political cynicism	.08	.01
Self-interest		
Homeownership	.13	.12
Personal finances	.02	0
Tax burden	.19	.14
Government employee	− .16	− .12
Work problems	.01	0
Children in public school	0	0
Government assistance	− .01	0
Proximal attitudes		
Size of government	.16	.12
Service spending	.11	.10
Waste	.14	.10
Overpaid government workers	.08	.08

Source: Tax Revolt Survey.

Note: Entries are standardized coefficients. In general, coefficients exceeding .05 are statistically significant ($p < .05$). The dependent variable is the tax rebel index.

5. Public employees tended to be more opposed to the revolt than other respondents, mainly just because of this role, but also mediated to some mild extent by their self-serving views about public-sector waste and pay levels.

6. The symbolic predispositions most concerned with value priorities—symbolic racism, ideology, and party identification— made a strong direct contribution themselves, and also did so indirectly by influencing

preferred government spending level (which as we have seen was manifested in preferences about both size of government and spending on specific services).

7. Political cynicism had no direct effect, but did contribute to perceived waste and preferring smaller government, and in that manner indirectly influenced support for the revolt.

8. Finally, all four proximal attitudes — size of government, service spending, waste, and overpaid government workers — had substantial direct effects.

All told, our predictor variables accounted for 27.5 percent of the variance in the tax rebel index; that is, the multiple correlation was .52. This same model largely held for all three tax-revolt propositions. Its power in accounting for voters' preferences varied considerably across them, but the relative contribution of each individual variable proved quite similar.

Some of the null relationships that turned up in this model are as interesting as those that came through strongly. The opposition of the highly educated to the tax revolt was not due to any special public-regarding spirit; on the contrary, they generally preferred substantially *less* spending on public services than other people did. Women were more dependent on public services than men — more likely to receive direct financial aid from government and to have children in the public schools. But their greater opposition to the revolt was not due to this dependence, or to any greater ideological liberalism. Recipients of government services did not especially oppose the revolt, even considering their demographic characteristics. On the other hand, the public employees' opposition to the revolt did not derive from any hot-tub liberalism associated with their relatively favored social location — it derived specifically from self-interest. Symbolic predispositions influenced support for the revolt not because of self-interest but, presumably, because of longer-standing values. And the effects of symbolic racism were due to specifically racial attitudes, not such ostensibly race-neutral factors as more general ideological or spending preferences.

The same kind of summary model could be constructed for the prediction of vote frequency and tax activism, but as indicated in earlier chapters, these stories are much simpler. Vote frequency is very powerfully predicted by the demographic variables; the R^2 for them alone is 29.1 percent, and adding all the other variables shown in table 10.1 increases this only to 35.3 percent. A similar but less dramatic pattern held for tax activism; the demographics alone accounted for 15.6 percent of its variance, while all the other variables increased this only to 21.3 percent. Hence, we have consistently found that participation in the tax revolt, in terms of both voting turnout and activist behaviors, was controlled more by social location than by our self-interest or attitudinal variables.[3] However, being a "tax rebel" did make a significant additional contribution to tax activism (beta = .11, p < .001). The political initiative was on the rebels' side.

Specific Themes

Self-Interest

Self-interest played a significant role in determining attitudes toward the tax revolt. The direct dollar savings promised by Jarvis's proposals to cut the property tax and the state income tax attracted significant numbers of supporters. On the other side, the threat posed to public employees' jobs and wages generated opposition among them. As a set, the self-interest variables contributed 8.4 percent of the variance explained in the tax rebel index above and beyond the 7.8 percent already accounted for by the demographic variables. Moreover, self-interest influenced people's preferences and priorities about spending, though to a considerably more limited extent.

Self-interest worked in a quite specific and cognitively narrow manner. Perceptions that one was heavily burdened by one kind of tax, or anticipated savings from reducing that burden, did not generalize much to support for cuts in other types of taxes. Property tax relief was strongly backed by homeowners, but income level made little additional difference; similarly, income levels strongly influenced support for income tax relief, but homeownership made little additional difference. A direct and tangible cash break seemed to be necessary for self-interest to have some impact. Economic threats or discontents that were not directly and tangibly related either to government services or to possible tax cuts had little effect. We plumbed exhaustively for some possible role of anxieties about inflation, but found none. Sagging personal finances also had no clear effect; and people dependent on government services did not especially oppose the tax revolt.

The cognitive narrowness of self-interest is also illustrated by its failure to produce more schematic thinking, ideologizing, or broader belief systems. Its effects could be seen only on attitudes most directly and tangibly related to the welfare of the interested person. For example, self-interest did foster preferences for increased spending on services of direct personal benefit, but not the desire for a larger public sector in general. Among public employees self-interest inspired defense of their own pay levels, but not any broader ideological defense of the public sector in general, in terms of efficiency or value. Nor did self-interest dramatically increase the perception that taxation and spending were a critical public problem, or opinionation about the tax revolt.

These findings suggest once more that self-interest plays a narrow and encapsulated role in the American mass public's political attitudes. However, self-interest seemed to be more important in the tax revolt than we have found it to be in studies of other issues. One reason, presumably, is that large, direct, and visible cash benefits were at stake, whereas usually the public is asked to express preferences on issues or candidacies whose direct relevance to their own finances is much more modest or indirect. Also, we have probably assessed in more depth than usual the wide variety of voters' specific self-interests, and their preferences about taxes and spending.

Too, a broader definition of self-interest could conceivably capture more of the motivation for these attitudes. In this book, we define self-interest in a direct, short-term, material way: has this government policy paid off for me recently, or is it likely to in the near future? But the individual might regard with self-interested eyes something that might benefit him at some time in the distant future. For example, a working individual might currently have little need for social security but expect that in retirement she will. Some services may elicit this longer-term self-interest more than others: for example, pensions and public health measures, which are especially important to the elderly, or police and fire protection, which deal with improbable contingencies, more than schools or higher education, which generally directly serve only children and thereby their parents. But for the present context, the cognitive narrowness and specificity of self-interest are impressive.

One surprising finding was that self-interest seemed to operate in a benefit-maximizing rather than a cost-minimizing manner, contrary to what might have been expected from some basic psychological research.[4] Greed, at least as much as fear, was at work in the tax revolt. Persons who were most vulnerable to the possible loss of vital government services, or of their homes, or of the possibility of ever owning a home, or whose solvency was being most radically eroded by inflation, did not respond to the tax revolt in an especially self-interested way. Well-fixed Californians, however, did—especially those with high incomes, fully employed, whose home values were benefiting from inflation, and those who stood to gain many hundreds of dollars in windfall cash profit from lowering taxes.

Symbolic Politics

Long-standing symbolic predispositions played a straightforward role in the tax revolt. General political conservatism and Republican party identification boosted support for the tax revolt, each by quite a considerable margin. But the most influential of these attitudes, surprisingly, was symbolic racism, even though almost no explicit discussion of race took place during the tax revolt. As we have indicated, symbolic racism had for many years been a powerful latent issue in California politics, periodically rising to the surface in controversies about fair housing, ghetto riots, black militancy, affirmative action, and busing. Some scholars and many blacks had seen racism in the midst of a great many political issues that had little manifest racial content. The tax revolt appears to have been another one of them.

These predispositions influenced the revolt both directly and indirectly. People opposed to government support for minorities, and conservative Republicans, jumped on the tax revolt bandwagon irrespective of whatever else they believed. In this direct sense, their positions represented a fairly pure case of "symbolic politics." But the influence of racial attitudes and conservatism was also partly mediated by the conventional value priorities about government activity associated with these predispositions, with the more anti-black and conservative Republican respondents wanting smaller government and less government spending. The clearest predictors of such predispositions were generational standing and urban residence; self-interest as described above played no role in generating them.

Unlike self-interest, symbolic predispositions contributed strongly to the development of issue publics concerned with these value priorities. This contrast was perhaps seen most clearly in analyzing preferences for spending on particular services. All three symbolic predispositions had an overriding effect, no matter what service area was at issue. But self-interest tended to contribute support only for spending in areas where people had some very concrete stake, and generally weakly even in those cases; it tended to add very little to the variance explained.

Another set of predispositions contributed to what we called the "malaise schema" but had little direct impact on individuals' support for the tax revolt. The most central of these was generalized cynicism about government. But a wide variety of other complaints were implicated as well, including charges of massive waste and inefficiency in government, disapproval of current incumbents' performance, and generalized complaints about one's own personal economic situation. And on most of them, the public as a whole expressed high levels of antagonism toward the government and the status quo. The malaise schema, and its constituent dimensions, did not help very much to distinguish the revolt's supporters from opponents. But this antagonism meant that the California public did not trust government enough to be very sympathetic to the public-sector defenders.

Political symbols helped trigger support or opposition to the revolt in a number of other ways. Part of the antagonism toward taxes was purely symbolic, in that it had little to do with the voter's own tax obligation. Homeownership was partly symbolic; the feeling that "a man's home is his castle" recruited support for the revolt above and beyond the tangible stakes of homeownership in terms of property tax reduction.

"The tax revolt" also took on some symbolic life of its own, quite aside from its links to other symbolic predispositions, fueling its own social movement all by itself. That is, it became a significant symbolic protest for many Californians. Indeed in some ways it became a more potent unifying symbol than were the various constituent ideas about taxation and spending that it developed out of. This role of the tax revolt as a symbolic protest in its own right can be seen in a number of ways in our data. Factions in the tax revolt unified more solidly around support or opposition to the tax revolt propositions than they did around the underlying issues of taxation and spending, as we saw in Chapter 4. Attitudes toward the propositions were more consistent with each other than were these so-called proximal attitudes. And the "glue" that held the latter together in a tax revolt schema was the voter's attitude toward the revolt itself rather than toward some more intangible underlying dimension.

The tax revolt raised a number of questions about the process of symbolic politics that could not be settled with the data we have available. Two in particular call for additional research. First, public support for government programs depends to a great degree upon the particular symbols with which they are described. It is tempting to go further and assert that more concrete descriptions of government services lead to more positive reactions. While that assertion fits available data from the current era reasonably well, it is plainly an oversimplification and depends upon some quite arguable assumptions about the wisdom and social responsiveness of those who plan and determine public policy. Nevertheless, we feel some analytic leverage can be achieved by assuming that the specificity or generality of such diverse symbols does influence the public's approval or disapproval of them.

Second, it seems clear that the tax revolt, like many other political controversies, was in the last analysis a clash over control of the public agenda. If the particular symbols in which government programs are described depend upon who controls the public agenda, and if they in turn determine public reactions, the agenda-control process itself is very important. To the extent that analyzing this process involves studying elites, such an analysis is beyond our purview. But the public is not wholly passive in this respect. The very same symbols that today seem so alive and appealing will tomorrow seem out of date and stale. The day will surely come when Californians will ask why they were mad as hell and be unable to remember very well. And the reason will not be only that the television cameras no longer go on when Howard Jarvis speaks; the public will have had some influence over the change of agenda. This elite-mass interaction over agenda control seems to us to be poorly understood.

The Tax-Service Tradeoffs

Did the votes on Propositions 13, 4, and 9 express realistic tradeoff decisions about Californians' natural desire for certain government services and their equally natural desire for lower taxes? The tradeoffs offered to the voters by these three propositions varied considerably, and presumably the similar propositions offered in other cities and states and cities across the country vary in at least as many ways as well. And the particular terms of these tradeoffs had much to do with these election outcomes. We have seen that the voters generally did not view Proposition 13 as a major service-cutting venture, or at least they did not in the first two years after it passed, when the state surplus protected the status quo in the supply of state and local services. Yet it provided a large tax savings. So it offered no real cuts in services in return for a large tax savings; not a hard choice for many homeowners. The Gann amendment also seemingly threatened no very severe service cuts, but it offered little in the way of tax savings either. It seemed simply some guarantee of stability in the size of the public sector without any major short-term changes. Jarvis II, by contrast, offered a generally modest tax savings combined with the threat of major dislocations in the supply of public services. So, in a sense, the public never was presented with the very hard choice: a major return in private monies in exchange for major cuts in the public sector. Presumably now that the state surplus is gone, and the state begins to run a deficit, such choices will be forced on the public at last.

There was much evidence of an affectively consistent dimension underlying these various attitudes toward taxation and spending. Preferences for decreased spending on specific services and for smaller government, perceptions of waste and overpaid bureaucrats and an excessive personal tax burden, and tax-service tradeoff decisions for reduced taxes and reduced services all tended to be associated with one another. Moreover, they all related in predictable ways to support for the tax revolt in general, and to support for Proposition 13 and Jarvis II specifically. Defectors—supporters of Proposition 13 who opposed Jarvis II—held the attitudes one might expect: they wanted service increases, were willing to pay for them with additional taxes, and believed that Jarvis II would threaten services. These relationships with voting behavior were not the spurious results of some other relationship; they genuinely reflected a consistency in affective responses to these specific symbols.

These reactions more often revealed the additive effects of simple affective preferences than the interaction effects that logical reasoning would have predicted. For example, the Gann amendment might have been especially attractive to those who both felt very burdened by taxes and expected the initiative to lower taxes, or it might have been especially unpopular among those who expected it to cut services but wanted services increased. But as we have seen over and over, such interactions, no matter how "reasonable" in theory, did not appear in fact. There was little evidence that voters reasoned very carefully from their basic preferences about taxation and spending and the effects they forecast of these tax-reform measures, to a vote decision. Nor did the rationalizations for self-interest, however logically "appropriate," always direct people to the equally appropriate vote decision. For example, it was not primarily the public employees' self-protectiveness toward their own wages that led them to oppose the tax revolt, nor did parents' preferences about school spending affect their votes on Proposition 13 any more strongly than nonparents' preferences affected theirs. Throughout our data the voters seem to respond to symbols in an affectively consistent but not necessarily logical or reasoned way.

Moreover, throughout most of the tax revolt period the electorate wanted "smaller government" but also the same or increased spending on specific services. This was affectively consistent, in the sense that both variables reflected a common underlying dimension: how much, or how little, should government do? But this combination quite clearly involves a logical tension, and there were no other beliefs that we could add into that particular equation that would render that combination more sensible. We thought that perhaps voters believed services could be maintained, and government shrunk, as well, if only waste were eliminated. Or perhaps the inconsistency held primarily among unsophisticated voters, who might not realize the two goals were incompatible; or that voters equated "big government" with some especially unpopular services (such as welfare), and wanted to cut those but maintain others thought to be more essential (such as police and fire protection). Or perhaps voters were indulging a wish-fulfilling mood when responding to surveys, and only confront the hard tradeoffs between taxes and services when faced with them explicitly at the ballot box. But none of these escape routes succeeded in explaining away this basic anomaly: it prevailed even among people believing in small amounts of waste, the most sophisticated voters, and both liberals and conservatives. When the "hard tradeoffs" were put to the voters explicitly in the survey, most opted for maintaining or increasing services, even if it meant raising taxes or forgoing tax rebates that might follow service-cutting. Cognitively the two sets of preferences seemed compartmentalized, though affectively they reflected the same general sentiments. The dominant, and quite stable, preference throughout the tax revolt period, then, was at least to maintain current levels of government services.

Issue Publics and Schematic Thinking

Another major focus of our study was on the determinants of issue publics concerning the tax revolt issues, and of schematic thinking about them. A central question about any protest concerns its issue public. To what extent do people pay attention to the issues it raises, think of them as major items on the public agenda, and come to see all of them as bearing upon one another?

The tax revolt issues presumably would be more likely to spark continued conflict in the future if people had highly organized patterns of belief about them than if they merely reflected the momentary confluence of isolated beliefs.

We defined the tax revolt issue public in terms of four characteristics: perceived importance of issues of taxation and spending, degree of opinionation about the revolt, holding the appropriate attitudes on the ancillary issues concerning taxing and spending, and schematic thinking about the revolt.

Self-interest played quite a minor role in developing an issue public for the tax revolt. "The taxpayers" did show higher issue salience, greater opinionation, and more consistent attitudes on the related issues of taxation and spending, relative to the less tax-burdened. But they showed no greater schematic thinking. Nor did the other self-interested groups — those with high levels of economic malaise, the service recipients, and the public employees

—show much if any evidence of high levels of attention to the revolt or schematic thinking about it. Symbolic predispositions, in contrast, seemed considerably to influence the development of an issue public around the tax revolt questions. From this we concluded that the affects embedded in symbolic predispositions help strongly to focus attention and organize thinking, whereas self-interest plays a much more cognitively encapsulated role in the individual's political thinking.

The clearest example of mass schematic thinking we uncovered was the "tax revolt schema" itself, comprising attitudes toward spending priorities, taxation, waste, public-sector pay levels, and the tax revolt ballot measures. Attitudes reflecting decisions on tax-service tradeoffs were rather consistent with the tax revolt schema. More refined analyses revealed two more specific schemas—a "value priorities" schema, which related the question of how *much* government should do to such symbolic predispositions as ideology, party identification, and symbolic racism; and a "malaise" schema, which related questions of government performance, how *well* government does it, to more general political cynicism and personal economic complaints. The value priorities schema turned out to be much more centrally related to attitudes toward the tax revolt itself.

One extremely important caveat to this finding of a coherent tax revolt schema is that very few respondents took consistently extreme positions on all dimensions, so very few (only 3 percent) were "true believers" in the tax revolt (or whole-hearted defenders of the public sector, either). The tax revolt schema therefore represented a tendency to think about all these dimensions in a related way, *not* a tendency to adopt positions at one extreme or the other on all of them as a package. Most Californians had mixed, or at least moderate, attitudes toward the tax revolt schema. But nearly half of the voters at the time of our survey supported all three propositions, indicating that much of the electoral support for the tax revolt was coming from people who did not support in detail the conservative ideology and complaints about government articulated by Howard Jarvis and his allies. Jarvis's wrath against "big government" as a symbol was widely shared, but his zeal for actually cutting back its activities was not. Yet the shared hostility was sufficient to produce the "frenzy" after the reassessment gaffe that ultimately would lock radical change in fiscal authority into the state constitution.

In sum, the California public was movable in the anti-government direction. But it was not so hostile to the public sector that the tax revolt (or the support for Reagan in 1980) should be interpreted as a broad mandate for hacking away the main structures of government that have accumulated over the years. The tax revolt is not in and of itself evidence of a dramatic turn to the right or a reversion to conservatism on the part of the American public.

"The Revolt of the Haves"

In presenting the major social divisions over the tax revolt, we concluded that its most enthusiastic supporters were white, middle-aged, higher-income men, especially those from Southern California. Opposition was more likely to come from blacks, the young, those with lower incomes, women, and residents of the Bay Area. Such group differences might possibly be explained either by self-interest or by symbolic predispositions, since the supporters came from groups that both were most likely to profit from the tax revolt personally and tended to be at the conservative end of the spectrum on all the symbolic predispositions. Enduring political conflicts are frequently organized around such social divisions, so it is important to understand why they arose in the tax revolt. Including the self-interest variables almost completely eliminates the effect of income, and halves the effect of age. Principally, the greater tax burden felt by the well-to-do and middle-aged was responsible for their greater support for the tax revolt; that is, to a considerable degree their support reflected the effects of self-interest. This bolsters one of our main themes, that support for the tax revolt, particularly after the passage of Proposition 13, represented a "revolt of the haves."[5]

A qualification on this finding is that persons at higher educational levels were somewhat nervous about the tax revolt (once the greater support induced by their higher income is set aside). Hence in our analyses education had its most potent effect on vote for Proposition 13, and its least effect on attitudes regarding the same proposition eighteen months later when it was being implemented without radical dislocations in the public sector.[6] The general tendency was for higher-status people to support the tax revolt, so this initial nervousness of the better-educated stands as something of an exception.

Racial differences in support for the tax revolt are explained almost entirely by symbolic racism, and by value priorities, as shown in table 8.1. Hence although whites, a relatively more advantaged group, supported the tax revolt more strongly than blacks, this difference appears to be based in group conflict and prejudice more than in pure self-aggrandizement.

The same picture emerges when we look at behavioral involvement in the tax revolt. We indicated earlier that voting turnout and other forms of active effort were most heavily dictated by demographic factors, and specifically by social advantage: middle-aged, higher-income, better-educated white men voted and participated most. Including all other variables in these equations does not change matters much at all.[7]

The rather balanced portrait of public opinion drawn here was obscured by the strategic political advantages of the tax rebels vis-à-vis the public-sector defenders. Most important, the pro-revolt forces tended to come from politically favored demographic situations. Affluent, middle-aged, white men register, vote, and participate in politics more than other segments of the population. The rebels themselves were more active even aside from this. They thought more schematically; they were happy to attack high taxes and both the priorities and performance of big government, whereas the public-sector defenders were much discomfited by having to defend it all. The rebels were more loyal to their cause across the several elections. Disapproval of incumbent performance was particularly likely to motivate turnout and political action. And the rebels were more active in the tax revolt than the public-sector defenders, even taking all other factors into consideration. And those who actually turned out to vote were more favorable to Proposition 13, and to cutting spending, than were those who stayed home.

Moreover, self-interest was a considerably more potent weapon for the rebels than for their harried opponents. The big tax savings offered by Proposition 13 (and to some by Jarvis II) mobilized the most politicized and vocal segments of the electorate to support the revolt. Selfish support for the public sector came mainly from the relatively small set of public employees. Apparently the recipients of government services did not perceive a direct personal threat. However, the limited savings promised by Jarvis II proved, in the end, to be a weak source of support for that reform.

Protest and the Male Animal

We noted a persistent tendency for men to support the tax revolt more than women. Was this a matter of self-interest? Men are better educated, have higher incomes, and are more likely to be working full time. Hence they are less dependent on the public sector: they use less government assistance and are less likely to have a child in public school. But greater male support for the tax revolt holds just as strongly among those most dependent on the public sector — among low-income, unemployed, program-dependent, public-school-parent respondents. Other self-interest explanations also fail — men are *more* likely to be public employees, feel slightly *less* burdened by taxes, and indeed are *less* likely to be homeowners. Did their greater support arise from longer-standing symbolic predispositions? No. Women and men do not differ appreciably in partisanship, cynicism, or disapproval of incumbents.

The women who opposed the tax revolt most were young, high-income, highly educated, homeowners, and full-time employees. It should be noted that such women were also strongly opposed to Ronald Reagan in his presidential campaign, and indeed that the parties polarize today on women's issues about as much as they do anything else. As might be expected, then, part of the political difference between the sexes is explained by value priorities. Women support government services more than do men, and this partially explains the difference in support for the tax revolt, since controlling for them halves the sex difference.

In addition, men like aggressive, angry, belligerent, "macho" politics more than women do in general. They are more favorable to riots, police repression, war, bulldog candidates like George Wallace and Sam Yorty, punitive responses to deviation, and so on. So a frontier spirit of rebellion against the government, a cause whose posture was overtly hostile in style, should have a relatively greater appeal to men than to women. Howard Jarvis's belligerence, his stance of defiance of the political establishment, was a call to arms and not to mushy compromise. Consistent with this view, the difference between the sexes was strongest during the frenzied period around the vote on Proposition 13 (as indicated on the vote-recall in the Tax Revolt Survey), and nonexistent regarding the mild-mannered Gann amendment.

The Surge Phenomenon

Some of these analyses have emphasized the "reasonableness" of the public's response to these issues, in that the public was partly responding to some economic and political realities. Taxes had been rising, as had government spending. Government had gotten so large that no doubt it did conceal considerable inefficiency, incompetence, and perhaps numerous programs that would be unpopular if given enough publicity. So the rise of political opposition to these trends is at least a comprehensible, and probably at some level a sensible, public response to them.

We also have emphasized, however, a surge of recklessness, a period of nearly blind emotion, surrounding the passage of Proposition 13, when anger at government seemed to dominate the public's thinking. The usual explanations for the voters' choices still held sway, but this added hostility proved a potent weapon for the tax revolt. At that point, the tide of anti-government emotions eroded stable attitudes about what government should do. The public's desire for maintaining the status quo of services plummeted, their perceptions of governmental inefficiency rose considerably, and their anger focused on the "bureaucrats" who were seen as cutting out teachers and essentials in the schools rather than useless administrators and other forms of waste. This was the one instance in which the anomalous desire for smaller government and more services eroded and a more logically consistent pattern of beliefs was relatively common.

There is evidence that this frenzy helped create a more enduring and influential pro-revolt climate of opinion in Los Angeles County. The greater support for the tax revolt there than in the Bay Area was quite stable. This could not be explained by the social or political composition of the two areas, so we take it to derive from the more serious inflation in the housing market in Southern California and the hapless way "the politicians" handled local reassessments in 1978. Other data suggest that these factors combined to form a strong pro-revolt climate of opinion in the Los Angeles area. And as is typical with climate-of-opinion effects, it proved most influential on the opinions of the least politicized segments of the population. Hence the region difference was huge among the young, Independents, and the least educated, but scarcely visible at all among those normally more politicized.

The Unexplained

Every social-scientific effort to explain a complex social event ultimately winds up with too much unexplained. This is true in our study, in two senses. First, and perhaps least surprisingly, we fall short of explaining all the variance in our key dependent variables. With all predictors included, the maximum multiple correlation on the tax rebel index was .52. To be sure, we use a linear additive model, and measures of quite finite reliability, which limit us to some unknown extent. Still it is a forceful reminder that much remains to be accounted for.

The same is true of the proximal attitudes. Although they presumably reflected the main content of the tax revolt debates, and therefore the main reasons why voters might support it or oppose it, they collectively only produced a multiple correlation of .43 on "tax rebel." They clearly did not pick up all the nuances of each individual's thinking.

As is usually the case, our model was more successful in accounting for attitudes on the two higher-visibility propositions, Proposition 13 and Jarvis II, and among voters, than on the lower-visibility Gann amendment or among the public as a whole. Analyses including the demographic variables, home-ownership and public employee status, and ideology and party identification yielded an average R^2 of 19 percent in two surveys of Proposition 13 voters; 14 percent in the three postelection surveys of Proposition 13 support; 6 percent in three surveys on the Gann amendment; and 12 percent in five surveys on Jarvis II (but rising from 9 percent to 14 percent as the campaign wore on).[8]

We also are not fully satisfied with our explanation for the abrupt changes that occurred in public opinion in May 1978. To be sure, the sharp turnaround in the fortunes of Propositions 13 and 8, especially in Los Angeles County, coincident with the bungling of the property reassessments, fits the notion of a "hostile outburst," "panic," or "craze." And the unusually low levels of desire for specific services, and the strong anti-government attitudes, evident at the same time also fit that portrait. We speculate that these expressed opinions abruptly changed because of a shift in the subjective agendas of voters. But our evidence for this and for the claim that these responses were linked in people's minds to the mistakes of "politicians" and "bureaucrats" is indirect. These emotional and impulsive surges are frequent among democratic voters, particularly in America where mass upheavals are only loosely contained by fragmented political party organizations. But their internal dynamics deserve much closer attention, for these surges can have potent and enduring political consequences.

11
Comparisons and Implications

The tax revolt in California was not an isolated event. This is hardly surprising, for other states and nations also experienced many of the political, cultural, and economic changes that provided the background for the protests in California. The decline of public confidence in government's ability to solve pressing problems manifested itself throughout America and in most European countries.[1] So too did concern about the erosion of traditional values and communal institutions. And in the late 1970s, complaints that the reach of state activity had gone too far gained in political strength. In the economic realm, the impact of the world recession, to which California, in fact, was relatively immune, stretched governmental resources, while inflation boosted both income taxes and property taxes for most people.

The expansion of the welfare state in most Western countries thoughout the 1950s and 1960s was smoothed by the sustained economic growth that simultaneously furnished governments with more revenues at the same tax rates and raised the individual wage-earner's take-home pay.[2] In the 1970s, however, the costs of public policy rose at a much more rapid rate than the growth of the private economy. Whatever fiscal dividend the government enjoyed now came from inflation's pushing people into higher tax brackets rather than from real economic progress. Public spending increased steadily in all Western countries from 1970 to 1977, but real disposable income fell in at least one year in each of them.[3] In the absence of a shift in public tastes away from private consumption to government services, this reallocation of collective resources prepared the ground for diverse forms of resistance to taxes.

The rebellious response to the squeeze of rising taxes on stagnant income has taken several forms. An essentially private mode of the tax revolt is simply to evade or avoid taxes—either by cheating or by participating in an "underground" economy in which transactions are demonetized exchanges of personal services or conducted in cash at a reduced rate. Several scholars have argued that this kind of tax rebellion has been growing in recent years.[4] One collective mode of protest is the "populist insurgency" along the lines of Proposition 13, when resentment at the grass roots mobilizes for electoral action. Another is the "institutionalized austerity" of conservative administrations, such as Margaret Thatcher's or Ronald Reagan's, which convert mass protests against high taxes into official policy and broaden the objectives of the tax revolt to encompass an ideologically based reordering of governmental activities. An exhaustive survey of protests against taxes outside California is beyond the scope of this study, but a brief selective review of major developments on the American scene illustrates clearly that Proposition 13 was an aspect of a broader political phenomenon.

Other American States

The passage of Proposition 13 stimulated a rash of similar initiatives in other states. Throughout most of the country taxes and government spending had been rising, so it is easy to understand the onset of the anti-government contagion. But it is hard to generalize about the results of these ballot measures.[5] As noted in Chapter 2, the tax rebels succeeded in some states where the tax burden and government spending were relatively high—California in 1978 and 1979, Massachusetts in 1980—but there were losses in such states too, and victories where the level of taxes was below the national norm, as in Texas and Idaho. In Michigan, where the reliance on property taxes was relatively heavy, a Proposition 13-like measure to cut property taxes failed. But a Gann-like spending limit simultaneously passed, even though the overall level of taxes was moderate. In Colorado, however, even a moderate "spending cap" proposal failed in 1977.

We have already emphasized that the inflation of real estate values in the late 1970s was unusually severe in California and that this produced the very high property taxes targeted by Proposition 13. Most other states did, however, share at least the shift in the overall property tax burden from business onto individual homeowners, and a variety of specific mechanisms were proposed to meet homeowners' complaints. For example, in addition to property tax cuts or limits, many states have legislated or are considering indexation of income taxes, "truth-in-taxation" procedures, property tax circuitbreakers, postponement of property taxes for senior citizens, and the functional reassignment of expenditures from local to state government. In addition to legislation, popular initiatives were a frequent response to rising taxes, especially in the western and mountain states where Populist and Progressive traditions have firmly implanted the institutions of direct democracy and the inclination to resort to them.

One tentative conclusion about the onset of grass-roots tax protests is that they occur when visible taxes rise rapidly *and* overall taxes are high.[6] It also appears that after voters impose far-reaching tax or spending cuts they adopt a wait-and-see attitude, as their concern about the delivery of services mounts. The cycle of anger-protest-caution observed in California has also been displayed in such dissimilar states as Connecticut, Colorado, and Michigan.[7] What seems clear too is that the dynamics of each election campaign and the way officials respond to public concern about taxes are important determinants of the outcomes of anti-public-sector referenda. This can be illustrated by a brief look at selected recent contests outside California.[8]

Idaho. Although Idaho's taxes ranked thirty-third in the nation in 1977, the Jarvisite approach to property tax reform found fertile soil there. State-ordered reassessments in several counties had resulted in increases of as much as 75 percent in the property tax bills of homeowners. Proposition 1, a Jarvis-Gann imitation limiting property taxes to 1 percent a year and restricting increases in assessments to 2 percent a year, qualified for the ballot with the largest total of signatures of any initiative in Idaho history.[9]

State action to alleviate the tax burden was belated and much less far-reaching than the initiative would provide. The rhetoric of the campaign and the alignment of forces in Idaho followed the California pattern. The pro-initiative arguments criticized bureaucracy, governmental waste, and the threat of high taxes to besieged homeowners. The opposition, led once again by the education lobby and public employee unions, warned of the threat to educational programs and the likelihood that other taxes would be raised should property taxes be cut so sharply. In Idaho, as in Oregon and Michigan, there was a tendency to downplay the general threat to public services; mindful of the California experience, the anti-initiative forces felt this scare tactic would be counterproductive.

As in California, the Idaho property tax initiative took an early lead in the polls and then slipped in popular favor. By late October, the *Boise Statesman* reported that among those who had decided to vote 34 percent were in favor and an equal proportion opposed. This galvanized the advocates of tax relief into a renewed effort in the media that emphasized how much property tax bills would rise should Proposition 1 fail. The fact that an earlier supreme court decision required homeowners' reassessments to "catch up to those of business" by 1977–1978 dramatized the growing tax burden; success at drawing attention to this led to a surge of anti-tax feeling in the late stages of the campaign, and the initiative ultimately won with 59 percent of the vote.

Massachusetts. The victory of a Jarvisite measure in liberal Massachusetts – Taxachusetts to some cynics – again shows how, as in California a decade or so earlier, political reform in the name of equality under the law can fuel the tax revolt. Although taxes were high in both California and Massachusetts, the distribution of the tax load was much more progressive in the former state. Massachusetts depended more heavily on the property tax so an individual's overall state and local tax rate tended to fall as income rose.[10] But as in California before the late 1960s, a "political" form of tax relief had traditionally eased discontent: local tax assessors usually assessed homes far below their actual market value.

Trouble began because some neighborhoods suffered as a result of this discretionary procedure. They sued for equity. In 1975 the state supreme court's Sudbury decision required the state to assess all properties at 100 percent of their market value. This set in motion what Kuttner describes as a tax revolt of the "left" – a homeowners' movement for relief that was aimed as much against the tax advantages of businesses as against government. In November 1978 the Classification Initiative qualified for the ballot, providing lower property tax assessments for homeowners than for business. At the behest of Mayor Kevin White, the organizers of this measure, Fair Share, received a million dollars from the city of Boston. The initiative passed easily.

But this populist victory was short-lived. In March 1979 the state supreme court ruled that business and residential property had to be assessed at the same rate. Massachusetts had shown no inclination to cut public services, so the demise of preferential assessments for homeowners set off a search for alternative sources of revenue. Efforts to impose new taxes on business failed to garner sufficient support, and as property taxes continued to rise Proposition 2½ emerged. The initiative was so named because it provided that the property tax be limited to 2.5 percent of a property's market value and that the total annual growth of property tax levies be restricted to the same proportion. In addition, the state's high auto excise tax would be cut in half. Proposition 2½, unlike its local predecessor, the Classification Initiative, was not hostile to business. Like California's Proposition 13 it was a constitutional amendment that cut revenues drastically without indicating how they could be replaced. And Massachusetts had no state surplus to fall back on. Thus when the measure passed in November 1980, even as Ronald Reagan carried the only state that had gone for McGovern in 1972, the prognosis was clear. Massachusetts would have to impose new state taxes or else cut current levels of staff and services.

Michigan. In November 1978 Michigan had a complicated set of measures on the ballot related to limiting taxes and public spending. One proposal, sponsored by Robert Tisch, a little-known drain commissioner and the leader of a "people's organization" of local taxpayers' groups, was to slash property taxes by cutting assessments in half and limiting annual increases in assessment to 2.5 percent. Theoretically, the state could step in and replace these lost revenues, but this was thought to be politically unfeasible. Tisch's movement resembled Jarvis's in the early stages of the campaign over Proposition 13, but it never progressed in comparable fashion beyond that.

The more moderate Headlee Proposal was more directly designed to curtail public spending, and proposed that state revenues in Michigan be "capped" at 9.5 percent of personal income. Like California's Proposition 4, which was to pass a year later, this measure was an outgrowth of the activity of the National Tax Limitation Committee. Their guiding idea was not so much that government is bad per se but rather that any further growth in the public sector would be excessive. A precursor of the Headlee amendment had been defeated in 1976; this time its backers assuaged the fears of the pro-public-sector elements by raising the allowable limit of revenues and by including a limit on local taxes to prevent the shift of taxes from the state to the localities. Opposition to Headlee among elected officials and major interest groups was muted, in part because it was viewed as a "responsible" alternative to the Jarvis-like Tisch amendment.

Polls showed that voters believed that the Tisch amendment would be more effective than Headlee in reducing their overall tax burden. But Tisch was also perceived as more likely to reduce revenues available for services, particularly the local schools. This concern became the focus of the opposition's campaign. Without a charismatic leader, a reassessment mess, or a supreme court decision to help, and facing a well-prepared alternative measure to act as a lightning rod for discontent, the Tisch amendment failed by a 63 percent to 37 percent margin. Headlee passed with 52 percent of the vote.

Oregon. In Oregon, both a Jarvis-Gann facsimile (Ballot Measure 6) and an establishment alternative (Ballot Measure 11) were on the ballot in November 1978. At first it appeared that the California scenario would be replayed. With Howard Jarvis on hand, Ballot Measure 6 qualified for the ballot soon after Proposition 13's victory and held a wide early lead in the polls.

Oregon's counterpart to Jarvis, Jimmy Dale Wittenburg, proposed to cut property taxes by 40 percent, and the same anti-government, anti-spending themes evoked by Jarvis characterized his campaign. The Democratic governor and legislature, backed by a coalition of teachers and other public-employee organizations, proposed an alternative consisting of a one-year freeze on assessed values, a state rebate of up to $1500 of property taxes, and a limit to the allowable increase in state spending. Renters were also guaranteed a rebate. After some hesitation, the Republican candidate for governor endorsed the more radical plan, and the partisan battle lines were drawn.

Property taxes had grown in Oregon along with rising real estate values, but overall taxes were below the national norm, in part because there was no state sales tax.[11] As this campaign progressed, the "people's proposal" lost ground to the "establishment" alternative, but ultimately neither measure passed. Concern over the availability of government services and the recognition, as in Michigan, that there was no California-like state surplus to compensate for the loss of property tax revenues seemingly prevailed over the desire to cut taxes. As in California, the defeat of the more moderate tax reform suggests that once two such measures are portrayed as antagonists people find it hard to vote for both.

Overview. To recapitulate, inflation, a rise in the property tax burden of homeowners, judicial decisions that are less sensitive to homeowners' plights than to ensuring equal treatment under the tax laws, and legislative delay, are the ingredients of explosive protests against the growing size and cost of the public sector. Yet despite the intensity of public concern about high taxes, drastic remedies are not always adopted. The tax revolt has not swept all before it. Jarvis-like amendments won in Idaho and Massachusetts but lost in Michigan and Oregon. They lost in part because people also continue to want government to provide a high level of service, and in part because political elites, like college administrators a decade earlier, are learning how to cope with rebellious constituents. With the example of California's failure to sidetrack Jarvis-Gann in mind, they attempt to provide some tax relief to head off more far-reaching reforms, and they avoid the doomsday predictions that seem to anger voters rather than intimidate them. Local factors such as the nature of tax laws and assessment practices, the availability of mechanisms to alleviate painful tax increases, partisan infighting, and intangible elements of campaigning are important influences on the outcomes of anti-tax referenda. These shape public perceptions of the need for a proposed tax cut, the likelihood of obtaining it, and the consequences of implementing it.

Despite the differences in the fiscal climate of states in which tax and spending limitation referenda have recently occurred and their varied outcomes, the pattern of public opinion in these diverse locales is strikingly similar. To be sure, inconsistencies in the timing of polls and the wording of questions make precise comparisons difficult. And there are inevitable differences in the absolute level of discontent expressed. For instance, during the peak years of recent protest, 1977–78, voters in western states were more likely than their counterparts elsewhere to single out the property tax as particularly burdensome.[12] In Idaho a survey at the time of the vote on Proposition 1 found that 76 percent felt that taxes were too high relative to their ability to pay.[13] Before the vote on Proposition 13 the California Poll found that 62 percent of Californians felt that property taxes were unfairly high, whereas a Florida Poll conducted in 1979 reported that only 27 percent of that state's residents felt that way. Parenthetically, there is little variation among states in the degree of antipathy to the federal tax burden.[14]

What is even more regular from state to state is the persistent support for continued government services. In Michigan, for example, people expressed a preference for maintaining or increasing government services in every area of policy except welfare. Local expenditures, which the Tisch amendment addressed, were more popular than programs paid for by the state, whose expenditures the Headlee amendment sought to control. And a substantial minority of Michigan's voters said they would be willing to pay more in taxes for the services they desired. For example, 38 percent reported a desire for more spending on local schools and 32 percent of this group were willing to bear a heavier tax load for this purpose. At a more general level, on the eve of the vote on Tisch and Headlee a majority of Michigan's residents said they preferred the status quo to either a reduction or an increase in *both* spending and taxes.[15] And the smattering of data available from other state polls shows a similar preference for maintaining existing levels of state services, which, it should be remembered, had been growing in the 1970s.

Anti-government sentiments were also widespread outside California. The pervasiveness of political cynicism in Massachusetts is legendary. In Idaho a November 1978 poll found that 83 percent of the public believed "government wastes a lot of our tax money."[16] In Florida a year later, only 27 percent felt that the government could be trusted to do what is right most of the time.[17] In sum, the combination of beliefs we found to be most prevalent in California reappeared in states with widely varying fiscal and political conditions: taxes were too high, public spending was excessive, and government was wasteful and inefficient, but the flow of public services should continue at least at their current level.

Nor was California unusual in the nature of the demographic, political, or attitudinal factors that accounted for support for anti-tax or anti-spending measures. Opinions about the tax burden and preferences for public spending correlate in the predicted fashion. In Michigan, Oregon, and Idaho, surveys indicated a crude rationality among voters; that is, their choices tended to conform to their preferences about the impact of a ballot measure on their tax bills and the supply of services.[18] Beliefs that the government was wasteful were also associated with support for the tax revolt in these states.

With some departures, other findings are similar to our own. A high level of education tended to reduce support for the Jarvis-like property tax reforms proposed in Michigan, Oregon, and Idaho, but not for the Gann-like Headlee amendment or Ballot Measure 11, Oregon's establishment alternative.[19] Blacks were more likely to oppose the proposed tax cuts in other states. Income was positively associated with support for Headlee but not for Tisch in Michigan. Men were more likely than women to favor the more drastic initiatives in Oregon and Idaho, although this difference did not emerge in Michigan; Democrats were more likely to oppose the tax- or spending-limitation measures in every case except the Tisch proposal, whose following conformed most closely to the "middle mass" described by Wilensky.[20]

There are numerous other nuances we might note, but the thrust of the data is clear enough. Symbolic attitudes invariably play an important role, and self-interest tends to assume greater explanatory importance when a ballot measure provides a clear, calculable and substantial cash benefit. When respondents are asked about cutting taxes in the abstract or about a hypothetical proposal, the tendency of personal circumstances and social background to predict choices weakens and responses are governed most heavily by symbolic predispositions of long standing.[21]

The Tax Revolt Goes to Washington

At the national level, the opportunity for citizens to take direct electoral action on taxing and spending issues does not exist. But after the presidential election of 1980 the tax rebels enjoyed a much more potent weapon than the ability to mount initiative drives: the White House was in their corner. We have already noted that the Republican party had made cuts in the federal budget, reduced taxes, and made "smaller" government the centerpiece of their domestic political program. In Ronald Reagan these Jarvisite themes had an eloquent spokesman. In Chapter 3 we cited surveys that show that public attitudes were favorable toward these elements of the president's program. The federal income tax was viewed as too high by more than 70 percent of the public in polls conducted at intervals throughout 1979 and 1980. Inflation was viewed as the most important national problem, and government spending was often regarded as its principal cause. Polls suggested that inflation was eroding expectations of personal financial progress and that people blamed "bracket creep" and the resultant rise in effective tax rates for the deterioration of their real after-tax incomes.[22] Calls for a balanced federal budget won overwhelming approval in the polls, and this objective was given higher priority than a cut in taxes. Finally, perceptions of bureaucratic waste and governmental inefficiency showed no sign of slackening.

At the same time, there was little evidence as President Reagan took office that the public's preferences concerning the government's activities in the economic and social domains had substantially changed. Indeed, the available data consistently point to strong majorities for the maintenance or expansion of social security benefits, health care programs, aid to education, crime prevention, and even the problems of big cities.[23] There is no obvious mandate for the emasculation of the New Deal.

Although President Carter recognized the drift of public opinion about the size and cost of government and proposed substantial reductions in his last budget, it seems obvious that the Democratically controlled Congress throughout the 1970s was in feeling and action attached to the idea of expanding the scope of entitlements from government rather than curtailing the flow of benefits. How much President Reagan owed his electoral triumph to a shift toward conservatism among the public rather than to frustration and disappointment with the performance of the Carter regime, particularly in the realm of economic management, is still being debated. There can be no doubt, however, that President Reagan has taken the line that his election constituted a mandate for his program of tax and spending cuts. With the Republicans in control of the Senate, the renascent conservative coalition able to provide a majority in the House, and the liberal leadership of the Democrats in disarray, an unprecedented set of budgetary reductions and then major tax cuts were passed into law by August 1981. In both legislative battles, the Democratic opposition felt the need to present an alternative program tailored to fit the preferences of their own constituents. Even so, their program accepted the basic premises that cuts in taxes and public spending were imperative. To oppose the idea of cuts altogether was regarded as politically unfeasible.

This is not the place for a detailed description of the recently mandated cuts in federal spending and taxation. Our concern rather is the interplay between the president's proposals and mass opinion. It should be stressed that the Reagan administration's proposed cuts in government spending recognized the popularity of the so-called safety net programs: social security retirement benefits, veterans' compensation, Medicare benefits, supplemental security income for the disabled, and educational assistance for low-income families. This bow to political reality is conveniently part of the "supply-side" economic doctrine that the administration has adopted. This doctrine holds that the basic infrastructure of the welfare state is an entrenched feature of modern economies, and that under these circumstances, tamping down inflationary forces by reducing the overall level of economic activity is unlikely to work. People have access to a wide range of costly benefits and the budget deficit therefore widens rather than shrinks during recessions, further feeding inflation. The best that can be done, therefore, is to hold the flow of benefits to a reasonable level.

President Reagan's budget cuts therefore aimed mainly at the long list of entitlements provided by Congress in the 1970s, leaving the core of the New Deal and even some major elements of the Great Society, such as Head Start, relatively intact. A Harris Survey conducted in February 1981 showed that 81 percent approved of the president's call for a $41 billion cut in the federal budget. However, 92 percent favored the president's exemption of the safety net programs listed above from the budgetary axe, and majorities ranging from 74 percent to 59 percent approved reducing expenditures on welfare, free school lunches to children from families able to pay, food stamps, and unemployment compensation. Only the proposed cuts in federal aid to primary and secondary education, a program that benefits the middle class, and Medicaid were opposed by more than half of those polled. In sum, the president's initial program of budgetary reductions was tailored to fit the contours of public preferences on government spending. By demanding a single vote on the entire package rather than accepting a series of votes on separate expenditure programs, the president also made the level of spending per se the salient issue. And on this there is no mistaking the massive symbolic attachment to cutting back government. The polls did record doubts about whether the impact of the budgetary cuts would fall equitably, but these voices were overwhelmed by the pervasive agreement that government spending should be limited.

Somewhat ironically, in view of the evidence of sustained antagonism toward high taxes, many observers believed the president's proposed reduction of individual income taxes by 30 percent over a three-year period would have a more difficult time in Congress. This prediction was based on polls that indicated the public feared reduced taxes would stimulate additional inflation and that a reduced federal deficit was regarded as more important than a personal tax rebate.[24] And as the Democratic leadership of the House Ways and Means Committee prepared its own package of tax cuts that were more favorable to families earning under $50,000 a year than the administration's plan, the Harris Survey found that this enjoyed a wide degree of support. Nevertheless, the president ultimately had his way. At the national level of American politics the tax revolt is no longer an opposition movement seeking change; at least temporarily, its central tenets have redefined the political status quo.

A Successful Protest

In American politics, Proposition 13 stands out as a watershed event whose national repercussions amount to a reversal in the direction of domestic public policy. President Reagan's program places economic growth at the top of the nation's priorities and shifts the balance of responsibility for individual welfare away from the state toward private institutions. His message to the public is, "Ask not what your government can do for you. Ask what you can do for yourself."

In California, the tax revolt began as a grass-roots protest against the cost of programs which had grown over the years partly because of pressures from the less well-off segments of the electorate. Now the institutions of direct democracy have forced political elites to attend to a different set of popular grievances, if only in self-protection.

The victory of Proposition 13 legitimized Jarvis's credo as majoritarian sentiment. To propose new activities for government and to impose new taxes, even on the wealthy or on corporations, was, in the new political climate, to flout the popular will. The Republican party seized on the opportunity to expand its national following, and the mass upheaval that Jarvis had sparked became institutionalized. With the liberal political forces that had dominated American politics since 1932 in silent retreat, the populist hostility toward large institutions was harnessed to conservative policies favorable to business interests.

Proposition 13 therefore was successful on several fronts. It did achieve its overt purpose, providing property owners in California with a sizeable reduction in their taxes. Before the passage of Proposition 13, the per capita burden of state and local taxes in California ranked behind only Alaska, New York, and Wyoming. But by 1980, it had fallen to twenty-second among the fifty states. As we have shown, the electorate is now generally satisfied with the state's property tax structure, indicating that substantive reforms can defuse public anger. The symbolic outcry against the government's size and insensitivity to popular needs also has had tangible results. The growth of public spending has been slowed and legislators are now keenly attuned to the ebb and flow of concerns about high taxes and can be expected to act quickly to head off accumulating resentments. The initiative process remains as a potential outlet for popular frustrations, however, and as familiarity with the sophisticated new techniques for soliciting signatures and financial support spreads, we must anticipate new efforts on the part of citizen groups to change the ground rules for fiscal policy in California.

The Fiscal Crunch

While property owners continue to enjoy the benefits of Proposition 13, state and local officials are now confronting a gloomy fiscal future. The state's surplus has run out, and the 1981–82 state budget reflected the reduced revenues available to state and local governments. Indeed, in early October 1981 Governor Brown was forced by the lack of state funds to order an additional 2 percent cut in the expenditures of all state agencies. He warned of the need to raise local fees and hinted at the possibility of amending the state's constitution to allow a split roll that would tax owners of business property at a higher rate than homeowners.

Thus a wide variety of interest groups, public employees, welfare recipients, school officials, and so on, are starting to squabble over a smaller fiscal pie. And as the impact of budget cuts at both the federal and state levels, and the redistribution of the tax burden, become clear, it is likely that conflicts will intensify among groups that have gained and groups that have suffered, and that cracks will appear in the consensual support for the prevailing anti-government mood.

Social Conflict in the Tax Revolt

Although our analysis emphasized the mass character of the protests against high taxes and government spending and the absence of strong differences in social background between those who supported and opposed the tax revolt, some elements of class politics do appear. In California, the amount of money one expected to gain from a proposed tax cut was an important factor in determining how one voted. And on balance support for the tax revolt rose steadily with income. Moreover, although corporate interests were sometimes cautious about supporting anti-tax referenda and for the most part opposed Proposition 13, it is clear that the main beneficiaries of the recent changes in the state and national tax structure have been business and the relatively wealthy. The tax revolt thus is likely to redistribute income upward.

In California, Proposition 13 is a catalyst for several conflicts of interest. The continuing shift in the share of the local property tax burden away from owners of commercial property toward homeowners is one source of future controversy. Without a surplus in the state treasury, there is no avoiding the incompatibility between the public's desire to maintain extensive government services and its unwillingness to provide additional revenues. In this fiscal crunch the revival of proposals to increase taxes on business and to institute the split roll is predictable, particularly since these taxes are more likely to win popular endorsement than are levies that fall on individuals. For example, the California Poll conducted in February 1980 found that two-thirds of the public favored increasing taxes on business property and corporate income if Proposition 9 had passed and the loss in revenue threatened services. Less than 15 percent preferred cutting education, health, or emergency services to imposing these new taxes.

Another emergent conflict would pit owners of homes purchased after July 1, 1975, against those who bought their homes earlier, for Proposition 13 gives an advantage to the early buyers. Clearly, every time a home changes hands at the high current prices, the new owner will have a higher tax bill than the person next door who will be paying either 1 percent of the 1975–76 assessed value or of the post-1975 purchase price plus an annual increment of only 2 percent. How neighborly relations will stand the test of this inequity remains to be seen.

The conflict between landlords and renters has already erupted. Although Howard Jarvis promised that landlords would pass on their property tax savings to renters, few actually did so. On the contrary, the continuing strong demand for housing in California both pushed rents up and stimulated the conversion of many rental units into condominiums. At the same time, the high price of homes and rising mortgage interest rates have made it increasingly difficult for people, particularly young people, to enter the housing market.

Rent control in various forms has been passed in many cities including Los Angeles, San Francisco, Santa Monica, Berkeley, and Santa Barbara, and initiative drives are under way in other communities, too. Banning condominium conversion is also on the agenda in many locales. The battle lines between renters and landlords, who sought but failed to emasculate local rent control ordinances by means of a statewide initiative in 1980, are clearly drawn and carry strong overtones of generational conflict.

The demands of public employees are another source of potential political turmoil. Understandably, public employees resist the layoffs that result from cuts in public spending. More important perhaps is that in seeking increased pay and benefits, government workers are now contending for a share of a fixed, if not shrinking, pie. Throughout the 1970s the salaries of public employees rose more rapidly than salaries in the private sector; a highly mobilized bloc of voters, public employees also obtained generous retirement and other fringe benefits. Today, however, public employees are at a double disadvantage. Public opinion is hostile to their claims; as the California Tax Revolt Survey showed, there is widespread sentiment that government workers are overpaid. And political leaders are far less sympathetic, if not out of conviction, as in the cases of Ronald Reagan and Jerry Brown, then out of necessity. And with the normal budgetary process closed as an avenue for achieving their demands, it is to be expected that public employees will resort to "industrial" action. The wave of strikes among teachers, firemen, police, and other public employees that has followed in the wake of the tax revolt is likely to continue. Such strikes appear to be very unpopular, even among unionized workers in the private sector. This cleavage between the taxpayers in the private sector, whether they have white-collar or blue-collar occupations, on the one hand, and the tax-receiving employees in the public sector on the other hand, was already evident in our analysis of support for Proposition 13. This may well become a dominant line of division in American politics in the coming years.

As this suggests, we should expect sharpened conflict between the clienteles of government programs and the taxpayers who support reduced public spending. While it is too early to gauge the full impact of the tax revolt on the provision of public services, either in California or nationally, there is no doubt that the next several years will witness reductions in transfer payments and in programs varying from inoculations to basic scientific research. Moreover, the fact that public revenues and expenditures are shrinking simultaneously at local, state and national levels is bound to tighten the fiscal vise for the public sector. In the absence of a major upsurge in the private economy, those dependent on the state for their economic well-being are bound to suffer some personal deprivation. Most experts agree that the state surplus has run out. And as cuts in services have to be made, the recent political successes of conservatives in local, state, and national elections make it likely that these cuts will fall most heavily on economically disadvantaged groups. In Los Angeles County, for example, the Board of Supervisors has reacted to a diminution of state aid by closing regional health centers and pharmacies that served ghetto residents.

How much the "truly needy" are affected will doubtless be established soon enough. That the upper middle class will survive the loss of low-interest loans to their college-student offspring is certain. But it is also clear that the low-income and black citizens who have been heavy consumers of government services will be deprived of some assistance. Blacks have consistently opposed the tax revolt, viewing government as the principal agency of their collective economic and social progress. To a considerable extent, the proliferation of government programs in the middle and late 1960s was a reaction to black demands, sometimes expressed in violent protests such as the Watts riot. Racial polarization leading to similar outbreaks may be an unfortunate consequence of the tax revolt, particularly should the promised economic recovery not occur. For blacks are on the disadvantaged side of each cleavage engendered by fiscal limitation: they are more likely to be renters, public employees, and recipients of government services.

The tax revolt is likely to have unfortunate symbolic as well as practical effects upon the black community. Blacks are, not surprisingly, quite sensitive to the political winds as they blow from the white majority. Many blacks expected that one of the major consequences of the ghetto riots would be more attention from whites to blacks' problems. And they hoped it would be sympathetic attention.[25] In retrospect, it seems to us that such attention was indeed one of the major consequences of the riots, though clearly interwoven with fear, anger, and other less sympathetic feelings. Many of the civil rights gains of the past decade, especially those carried out by governmental institutions, began as responses to such events. And those gains had great symbolic as well as practical value, as expressions of whites' concern for blacks. However blacks have sensed a fading momentum behind such efforts, not without some reason. We find symbolic racism to be a major factor in whites' support for the tax revolt. Should this finding be replicated in other research on other political choices being made by whites, it would bode ill for race relations, and for continued progress toward a more racially egalitarian society, at least in the near future.

Whither the Tax Revolt?

Any assessment of the staying power of the tax revolt must at this stage be somewhat speculative. The historical forces underlying the steady growth of government in advanced industrial societies are strong. Whether the constraints imposed by the recent fiscal reforms are more than a temporary check probably depends in large part on whether ideological changes take place to overcome the demographic push toward more public spending on old age pensions and health care.

The tax revolt also expressed a negative reaction against social and cultural changes that had been endorsed if not always promoted by liberal governments. The unsettling changes in race relations, the declining role of institutional religion, the increased permissiveness of personal behavior, and the challenge to traditional patterns of family that the feminist movement posed are an important part of the background to the electoral changes of recent years. The sense that things had gone too far, that freedom had become license, that government had overstepped its bounds in regulating economic and social relationships ran deep among supporters of the tax revolt and President Reagan. The impulse to call a halt and revive traditional values, including patriotism, broadened the base of the tax revolt and provided much of its fervor. The combination of economic discontent and cultural revivalism interrupted the long era of liberal political dominance in America. But it should be noted that belief in the traditional virtues of frugality and individual effort are weakened in the younger cohorts of the population.[26] So demographic trends, at least, are unlikely to reinforce the recent move to the political right.

Whether the events of 1978–1980 signal the beginning of a long period in which government no longer grows must depend on the interplay of events with popular values. There is as yet no compelling evidence of a slackening in the public's attachment to the government programs that make up the welfare state. Indeed, a CBS/New York Times Poll conducted in June 1981 found that 66 percent of the public favored increasing social security taxes if necessary to keep the social security system solvent. This is not to underplay the ability of political leadership to reshape public opinion, but merely to repeat that enduring public preferences place political limits on the pace and extent of fiscal retrenchment.

A subject that still requires investigation is the degree to which people's expectations about their economic circumstances are changing and the influence of such expectations on attitudes toward government. The prolonged economic difficulties of the late 1970s seem to have spread pessimism about the future. Respondents are now telling polltakers that they expect their children to have a harder time economically than they themselves have had, for example, to be less likely to own a home.[27] Earlier we reported the somewhat puzzling finding that worries about inflation and pessimism about the economy had no appreciable influence on attitudes toward the tax revolt. It is unclear whether, when people revise their long-run economic expectations downward, they want more or less governmental activity on their behalf. Should a prolonged period of sluggish economic growth limit chances for upward mobility, demands that the government expand its activities to redistribute income and soften the blow of macroeconomic misfortune may well increase.

Longer-term demographic changes may also influence the demand for public services. As middle-class white parents become a smaller portion of the electorate, the constituency for increased spending on public education may weaken. At the same time, the aging of the population is a major potential force in favor of increased government spending on both social security and health care. The net result of these changes varies from one level of government to another, but on balance they suggest that the current pattern of preferences for government activity will persist.

The Tax Revolt and American Political Culture

The recent tax revolt, particularly in its national incarnation, exemplifies a number of features that have historically distinguished American political culture from those of other countries. Most obviously, the size of the public sector in America, as measured by the proportion of the gross national product that is accounted for by public expenditures, is much smaller in America than in other industrialized countries. The tax revolt aims at keeping this so. Americans seemingly expect fewer entitlements from government than do their European counterparts. This is true even among the lower-class clienteles of the public sector, who also have a lesser symbolic attachment to class-oriented ideologies and a lower rate of political participation.

The popular disdain for public officials that contributed to the success of the tax revolt has been an important aspect of American political life from the very beginning. The nation's political tradition legitimates attacks against authority, whereas those defending the growth of the public sector lack equivalent institutionalized symbolic support to draw upon.

The fragility of political party organizations, particularly in California, has often made established programs vulnerable to sudden upheavals in the public mood. In the absence of organized channels of political communication and persuasion, political leaders are less able to contain expressions of discontent. The Townsend plan for the elderly in the 1930s and the temperance movement are but two examples of single-issue protest movements whose appeals drew adherents over the opposition of both established parties. The availability of the initiative process clearly enhances the political reach of fringe elements. And the expanded role of the mass media in transmitting political information also tends to inflate the impact of dramatic events.

Finally, one can see in the ideological defense of the tax revolt, particularly as articulated by President Reagan, an attempt to reassert the validity of the ethos of economic individualism that is a predominant element in the historical political culture in this country. Restricting the growth of government, in the president's view, is an essential step toward restoring the virtue of Americans and the power of America. In broad perspective, then, the tax revolt is a challenge to recent political history, in which the growth of government was a deeply embedded and rarely challenged aspect of public policy.

At the more mundane level of the costs and benefits of government, the questions of what services to supply and how to pay for them, the issues the tax revolt raises are permanent dilemmas in political life. Recent events have altered the political tide on these matters and elicited new conflicts. These promise to be intense; not only are there differences in interest and ideology among groups, but, as we have tried to show, there are often competing impulses within the same individual.

Underneath the illusion that we can get something for nothing lies the reality that there is no such thing as a free lunch. Voters in California, indeed all American citizens and politicians, are going to have to face up to this. Since we have become habituated to the steady growth of government, to expecting government to do more, adjustment to an era of fiscal limitation cannot be easy. Is the American pie now limited? And if it is, how is it to be divided? The tax revolt has posed these questions. The struggle over the answers is the political agenda for the 1980s.

12

The Legacy of the Tax Revolt

The tax revolt of the late 1970s was a historical milestone that separates an era of steady growth in government from an era of fiscal retrenchment. The most dramatic eruption was Proposition 13 in California—a state that had been a leader in providing public services—whose electorate thereby placed state and local officials in a budgetary straitjacket. The revolt then spread to many other states and localities, and finally to the federal government.

The tax revolt was a grass-roots protest against government. Its message was "Taxes, No! Big Government, No! Services, Yes!" Five years of budgetary history have now passed since the implementation of Proposition 13, and it is timely to assess the impact of the tax revolt and ask what its legacy will be. This chapter begins by summarizing the fiscal and political developments since then, with particular attention to changes in the tax burden and the size of government. The impact of the revolt in California really raises two separate questions. First, how successfully did the popular protest influence governmental policy? Did state and local government in fact accommodate to the protesters' wishes? To what extent does the pattern of fiscal adjustment to the tax revolt represent a successful translation of public opinion into public policy? As will be seen, we believe that government in California did make important adjustments in response to the tax revolt.

Second, did public opinion then reflect these changes in public policy? That is, to what extent did fiscal realities influence public preferences about taxes and spending? Did the public follow a sort of "reality principle," adjusting opinion to reflect actual political and economic changes? Here the data indicate a fairly accurate perception of changes in policy, but also continued adherence to what we earlier described as a wish for "something for nothing." In the post-Proposition 13 era, there is evidence of a political feedback loop in which protest led to reform, which in turn assuaged discontent by more closely aligning opinion and policy.

We will take a look in this chapter at the influence of the California tax revolt upon similar efforts in other states, and upon federal policies. In the first edition we suggested that the California tax revolt was the precursor and model for numerous other state-level revolts, and set the stage for similar actions by the newly arrived Reagan administration in Washington in 1981. That seems even more clearly true now. So we will briefly examine what has happened to taxes and government spending since that time in the nation as a whole, and especially in Washington, and how these changes too have been reflected in public opinion. We continue to view these changes as placing major constraints upon growth of the welfare state, probably for some time to come, though with some built-in contradictions of the sort highlighted by the book's subtitle.

The Aftermath of the Tax Revolt in California

The objectives of the tax revolt were to reduce taxes, curb the growth of government, and enhance the accountability of budgetary decisions to the voters. Plebiscitary action was the principal tactic the tax rebels employed to achieve these interrelated goals. By formally restricting the authority of elected officials to tax and spend, people would pay less and government, perforce, do less. The passage of Proposition 13 in particular confronted public officials with an acute dilemma: how to meet the electorate's demand for lower taxes yet satisfy the intense organized pressures for maintaining public services and employment. This task was complicated, in California and other states where the tax revolt succeeded, by the national economic recession of 1981-82 and the sharp reduction in federal aid.[1]

After Proposition 13 passed, official opposition to new proposals to cut taxes was more limited and restrained. Indeed, the tax rebels increasingly found allies in high places, particularly in the Republican party. Soon after Proposition 13 passed, the California state legislature, burdened with an embarassingly large surplus, cut state taxes by more than $1 billion by providing a one-time tax credit, increasing tax relief for renters, reducing certain business taxes, and partially indexing state income taxes to the rate of inflation. After the passage of the Gann Amendment in 1979, which constitutionally limited state and local spending, and the defeat of Jarvis II in 1980, tax-cutting activity temporarily subsided.

In the summer of 1982 the voters passed, by a two-to-one margin, an initiative that fully and permanently indexed the state's personal income tax. This plebiscitary action, taken at a time of sharp deterioration in the state's fiscal health, overrode then-Governor Brown's veto of similar legislation. The voters also repealed the state's inheritance tax, going beyond the reductions previously enacted by the legislature.

The election of conservative Republican George Deukmejian as governor in November 1982 was another victory for fiscal conservatives. This was quickly apparent in the governor's handling of his first budget, for fiscal year 1983-84. It was prepared in the context of a cash shortage so severe that the state had to resort to issuing warrants (IOUs) to some creditors. Yet Deukmejian was adamant that taxes not be raised, choosing instead to cut spending sharply and to run a one-year deficit. He prevailed over a strong and hostile Democratic legislature.

A number of state Supreme Court decisions through this period mitigated the fiscal impact of Proposition 13. Principally they have permitted the imposition of new local revenue-raising devices without obtaining a two-thirds majority of the relevant electorate. A number of localities have accordingly resorted to an array of user fees, exactions, and leaseback arrangements. In addition, the state enhanced its revenues by changing its accounting and collection procedures.

Howard Jarvis's reaction to these Supreme Court decisions and to the wide-ranging use of fees by local government was to qualify a new initiative for the November 1984 ballot. This measure, Proposition 36, the so-called Jarvis 4, had two main provisions. First, it would reverse a Supreme Court decision that allowed a 2 percent annual inflationary increase (for the 1975-1979 period) in assessed value on homes purchased before July 1, 1975. This one-time tax rebate to "early homeowners" would cost $1.3 billion, according to the Legislative Analyst, about one-third of which would be borne by the state. Second, it would subject all new or increased taxes and fees to a two-thirds majority vote of legislators or electorate. This would limit the imposition of user fees as revenue-raising devices. Jarvis 4 attracted the widest coalition of opposition yet, even including such erstwhile allies as the California Tax Foundation. After a highly controversial campaign managed by the Butcher-Forde firm, Jarvis 4 lost, taking but 45 percent of the vote.

One consequence of Proposition 13 was to force local governments to search assiduously for sources of revenue other than the property tax. In addition to resorting to fees and charges, local officials could also appeal to the voters to approve taxes earmarked for special purposes, such as libraries, transit, fire protection, or police services. Indeed, one indicator of the continuing strength of the tax revolt is that most such special levies have been rejected by the voters; the California Tax Foundation has reported that from 1978 until the end of 1983, 60 percent of the almost 100 proposed "special" taxes have been defeated. Community colleges, correction departments, and even the police have been spurned. As a result, supporters of specific services, such as the community colleges, are looking to the statewide initiative as a device for securing guaranteed levels of revenues for their programs. This, of course, would take budgeting by plebiscite one long step further.

Changes in the Public Sector in California

Public opinion had held that state and local taxes were too burdensome and government too large, inefficient, and unresponsive to the popular will, but also that the level of spending for virtually every category of public service should be sustained or even increased. The proponents of the tax revolt argued that the widespread desire to reduce taxes yet maintain services could be realized through the elimination of bureaucratic waste and the growth in economic activity that lower taxes would stimulate. Meanwhile, their opponents scoffed at these claims and warned that slashing government revenues would inevitably result in significant cuts in essential programs. What changes have in fact occurred?

Lower Taxes

The tax revolt in California clearly succeeded in sharply cutting taxes. The State Department of Finance estimated that between 1978-79 and 1983-84 the property tax cuts embodied in Proposition 13 alone saved taxpayers (and cost local treasuries) almost $51 billion.[2] This amounts to about $10,000 for every home-owning household, or more than $2500 for every man, woman, and child in the state.

The Legislative Analyst estimated that the combined effects of the legislation to index the state income tax between 1978 and 1982, and the 1982 initiative to index fully, has reduced California's personal income tax revenues by $12.1 billion over the period 1978 and 1984, or more than 22 percent of what would otherwise have been collected.[3] And it should be remembered that the effect of indexing, like that of freezing assessments, is cumulative, so its impact on revenues increases over time.

The combined effect of various tax cuts enacted in the late 1970s and early 1980s was to lower the overall state and local tax burden for Californians by more than 31 percent between 1978 and 1983, or by $48 per $1000 of personal income.[4] In 1978 California's taxes were 24 percent above the national average; by 1982 its state and local tax burden stood at about the mean for all other states.[5] Whatever the unanticipated consequences of the tax revolt in California, then, the promise to slash taxes was kept. Indeed, California differed from many other states in refusing to raise taxes during the worst of the recession, even after its surplus had been spent. The apparent electoral strength of the tax rebels made the avoidance of new taxes on individuals integral to the politics of coping with fiscal stress in California.

The distributional consequences of these changes in California's tax structure are yet to be fully disentangled. Every taxpayer in California gained from the lower rates mandated by the voters, in the sense that government would have extracted a larger share of his or her income in the absence of these cuts. Yet some groups have clearly benefited more than others. Proposition 13 helped homeowners much more than renters in two ways — by sharply reducing their tax bills and increasing the market value of their property. Among homeowners, those who had bought their current residences before July 1, 1975, stood to gain the most. This meant the elderly benefited more than the young, since people over sixty are 10 percent more likely to own homes than are younger Californians and four times less likely to have moved. Despite predictions to the contrary, the homeowners' share of the property tax burden has not grown relative to that carried by businesses, landlords, and owners of agricultural property.[6] Indexing, in the California tax structure, has a mildly progressive effect because wealthy taxpayers have a larger share of their total income in the maximum tax bracket and are therefore unaffected by inflation-induced "creep." On the other hand, user fees and the property taxes imposed by Proposition 13 are regressive in their effect. It seems likely, therefore, that the tax revolt increased economic inequality. Of course a more egalitarian distribution of income was never among the stated goals of the tax revolt.

A Smaller Government?

Complaints about the "bloated" public sector figured prominently in the rhetoric of Howard Jarvis, and polls repeatedly showed that in the abstract at least voters wanted a smaller government. How one characterizes the subsequent trends in the size of government depends on the yardstick employed.

In absolute terms, state and local governments are larger: more dollars are collected and spent today than in 1978. Relative to the size of the state's economy, however, both state and local spending have declined, since personal income has risen substantially in California during this period. And total per capita state and local spending adjusted for inflation actually *fell* by an average of 1 percent a year in California between 1978 and 1982 after registering an average annual real increase of 4.1 percent between 1957 and 1978.[7] Whether voters troubled by the size of government think in real or nominal terms is unknown. But when one adjusts for growth of inflation, compares recent trends to the past, or asks what would have happened in the absence of Proposition 13 and income tax indexing, the inescapable conclusion is that government spending in California has receded.

There have been three distinct phases in California's adjustment to fiscal constraint. The first was the immediate afterwash of Proposition 13, from 1978 to 1981, when accumulated reserves, a strong state economy, and a wide array of user fees and charges enabled spending to rise, despite yearly current deficits. Officials strove to mitigate the impact of Proposition 13 on their activities, and public spending declined less than the amount "lost" by government through the tax revolt. Then, during 1981 and into 1983, reserves were exhausted and the recession emasculated incoming revenues. After 1981 the fiscal noose truly squeezed.

Still, nothing is forever; the picture has changed once again. The economic upsurge that began in mid-1983 is swelling public treasuries in California. The final state budget for 1984-85 appropriated $31 billion, an increase of 15 percent in General Fund Expenditures over the previous year, providing for a "rainy day fund" of $950 million. Indeed, in preparing this fiscal plan politicians faced a happy trade-off decision: whether to increase spending even more or to rebate taxes.

Another measure of the size of the public sector is the number of public employees. When Proposition 13 had passed, public employees understandably feared for their jobs. After all, Governor Brown had warned before the election that tens of thousands of government workers would have to be laid off. In fact, the tax revolt made only limited inroads into the size of the public work force, fueling complaints that the bureaucracy once more had evaded the guillotine. The number of public employees relative to the state's population fell by 6 percent between 1978 and 1983, but this resulted mostly from the elimination of CETA positions and administrators charged with the operation of federal programs that were being cut back.[8] Attrition and hiring freezes were the tactics employed to protect the jobs of those already on the public payroll. Government workers might well have felt that Proposition 13 had made the public sector a less interesting place to work, that they had lost the capacity to do good by doing more; but most could be relatively sanguine about keeping their jobs even as the rate of unemployment in the state soared. And, although the rate of increase in the salaries of public employees in California was considerably slower after 1978 than in the previous decade, their earnings continue to be much higher than the national norm.

The Mix of Public Services

Did the tax revolt influence the shape as well as the size of government in California? At the state level, there were few changes in the mix of services provided. The main change was a modest growth in the relative share of expenditures devoted to health, welfare, and education. This occurred in the first two years of the new fiscal era, resulting from the assumption of the bulk of the cost of elementary and secondary (K–12) education by the state.[9]

Within the health and welfare area, a significant recent change concerns the costs of medical aid to the poor, called "Medi-Cal." Between 1978 and 1982, Medi-Cal costs steadily increased in dollar terms and consistently took up approximately 35 percent of total state spending on health and welfare. However, a dramatic change took place in 1983-84, when medically indigent adults (the non-elderly poor) were made ineligible for Medi-Cal benefits, various other reductions in benefits took place, and hospital reimbursement rates were established on the basis of negotiated contracts: Medi-Cal spending actually declined.[10] The fiscal restraint imposed by these reforms, which many state officials long desired but despaired of being able to implement, should continue to curb state spending for health.

Changes in the pattern of public spending at the local level have been more pronounced. Fees and state aid could not entirely fill the revenue gap faced by the localities, so cuts had to be made. The reallocation of local expenditures reflected the strong influence of political constraints. Cognizant of the public desire to retain existing services, officials disproportionately reduced maintenance, capital spending, and overhead to shore up activities that touch citizens in more directly visible ways. Thus, cuts were not made across-the-board. Rather, the budgetary axe tended to spare departments whose activities had large and vocal constituencies. Obeisance to public opinion polls and the organized power and police and firemen's unions were notable. For example, real per capita operating expenditures for the police actually rose by 9 percent from 1978 to 1982, and for fire departments they fell by only 2 percent, whereas parks and recreation were cut by 10 percent, and streets and roads by over 16 percent. These figures match well the profile of public preferences across service areas at the time Proposition 13 passed (see Table 3.2).[11] The popularity of services as revealed by the polls was rather closely related to the amount their spending was reduced.

Strategies of Governance

From the very beginning, political considerations dominated California's adjustment to the new fiscal regime resulting from Proposition 13 and subsequent tax reforms. Electoral considerations required that new taxes be avoided, that local government be kept afloat by state aid, and that cuts in services should be tailored to the demands of public opinion. More generally, the guiding principle in budgetary strategy was to minimize disruption to existing processes, in other words to preserve the status quo defined in political as much as in programmatic terms. Within this broad constraint, partisan differences have made themselves felt, particularly at the state level. When the state's fiscal circumstances truly worsened, Republicans pushed harder for cuts in spending, while the Democrats were even willing to contemplate selective new taxes in order to sustain social programs.

The commitment to maintain existing levels of services and staffing made searching for secure financial resources the order of the day for all levels of government in California. At the state level, this concern focused on cash management. As the surplus began to run out, increasing effort was directed to accelerating tax collections, levying new penalties on delinquent payments, and improved forecasting of future revenues. The state had no choice but to rescue local governments from the loss of tax revenues, but here too the rules governing state aid were conservative in design. The formula adopted in the so-called bailout plan apportioned relief on a *pro rata* basis rather than allocating funds on the basis of need. And the state adopted conservative targets for the level of future assistance to localities, hoping to protect its own programs in the event that an economic downturn reduced available reserves.

For their part, local governments lobbied for guaranteed levels of state aid. And when the recession did emasculate state funds, the political imperative to provide a reasonably steady flow of local services prevailed. The notorious "deflator" clause in the state's bailout law, which would have automatically required draconian reductions in state assistance from 1982 to 1984, was suspended.

But at the local level too, innovations in organizational structure and budgeting procedure were rare. Immediately after Proposition 13 passed,

Governor Brown appointed the Post Commission to recommend changes in California government; its report was stillborn. Local agencies did improve record-keeping and experimented with contracting selected services out to private organizations. Most of all, however, they searched for new sources of revenue—from the state as well as from local residents and businesses.

In short, public officials sought to conduct business as usual during straitened fiscal circumstances. There was little systematic review of the long-run effectiveness of current programs. Instead, government was preoccupied with survival in the short run, with making ends meet while hoping that time—and economic growth—would soon ease the pain.

Despite official efforts to mitigate the impact of the tax revolt on prevailing practices, significant changes have occurred. Local governments have become more financially dependent on the state; as a result, their capability to plan in an orderly fashion was reduced and the possibility of external control over the content of policy was enhanced. More significantly, perhaps, the dominant political style in California was transformed by Proposition 13. Austerity and self-reliance replaced planning and social reform as symbols of legitimacy. Politicians increasingly came to speak the language of trade-offs and constraints rather than growth and progress. In the pre-Proposition 13 era, policy-makers could think first of what programs they wanted to expand and feel confident that revenues would be available. After 1978, the dominant mood forced officials to revise spending priorities to fit fixed revenues. New programs had to be "marketed," not merely announced, since they took money away from ongoing activities or necessitated raising fees or taxes.

As the Economy Goes...

One important consequence of the tax revolt was to couple the expansion of government in California more tightly than ever to the fortunes of the private economy. Vulnerability of government services to macroeconomic revenues became painfully apparent in 1981 when the impact of the national recession forced the state, already denuded of reserves, to make significant cutbacks. Yet the ability to increase expenditures massively in 1984-85 shows that even under the prevailing fiscal limits government can grow at least as fast as the private economy.

California is so large and rich and its tax structure so potent that the revenues "lost" by the tax revolt could have been absorbed without reducing government spending *in real terms* if the economic growth of the late 1970s had continued. By the same token, the public sector would have weathered the recession of 1981-83 had Proposition 13 and the tax reforms it spawned been defeated. It required *both* — major tax reductions and a severe recession — to create a fiscal crisis in California. The state's fiscal resources are less stable, but it is hardly enfeebled.

An interesting sidelight concerns the new relation of inflation to the growth of government. We have explained above that inflation stimulated the tax revolt, and it helped to provide the wherewithal to mitigate its immediate impact on government. But the electorate's decision in 1982 to index permanently and fully California's personal income taxes and to repeal gift and inheritance taxes has drastically changed the impact of inflation on public revenues, and therefore the relation of personal income to tax liabilities. For example, in 1982-83 General Fund revenues grew less in percentage terms than did personal income, and the Legislative Analyst estimates that this will be true even for income tax liabilities in 1985.[12] In the past, when inflation exceeded economic growth, government benefited. To transform inflation into the enemy of government may be a most significant long-term effect of the tax revolt on the political process.

The Mandate Confirmed

From the perspective of the mandate theory of elections, the tax revolt in California was a successful protest. The fiscal changes, whether adopted out of conviction, electoral prudence or financial necessity, moved policy in the direction of the aggregate preferences of the public at the time of the vote on Proposition 13. The most striking example, of course, is the sharp reduction of taxes, especially property taxes. Dominant opinion also favored a "smaller" government, in terms of cost and of the number of government workers. The Tax Revolt Survey showed that public employees were perceived as overpaid, and polls conducted by the Field Institute found that voters unhappy about the implementation of Proposition 13 frequently complained that too few "high paid administrators" had lost their jobs. The public was apparently more willing to accept layoffs of government workers than the officials who would have had to write the pink slips. Notwithstanding this possible disappointment, the slowdown in the growth of government after 1978 does match the dominant mood.

As to changes in the delivery of public services, we have argued that even among those who voted for Proposition 13 there was little appetite for massive cuts. To the contrary, the public desired most existing government programs to be sustained, or even increased. The strenuous effort to mitigate the impact of lost revenues on services thus followed the public's wishes. Moreover, the manner in which budgetary reductions were allocated mirrored well the public's expressed priorities. The same might be said of the increases in expenditure embodied in Governor Deukmejian's 1984-85 budget.

Polls had consistently indicated widespread concern about the deterioration of public education, the rise in crime, and the sorry condition of public roads. It is hardly surprising, then, that the main beneficiaries of renewed growth in public spending were the public schools, the University of California, and prison and highway construction programs — all services with a large middle-class constituency.

The People's Verdict

How has the public responded to the shifting fiscal realities?

Changes in Taxes and Services

The most dramatic manifestation of change is the diminished resentment about the property tax burden. In late 1977, 60 percent of homeowners in California had complained that their property taxes were excessively high, but only 15 percent did so by March 1983. And 75 percent of homeowners credited Proposition 13 with lowering their property taxes.[13] Opinion toward the overall level of taxation in California also has softened, although less dramatically than have feelings about property taxes alone. Prior to Proposition 13, 39 percent of the public believed that the state and local taxes paid by the average person in California were "much too high"; this dropped to 28 percent by March 1983, and the modal response dropped from "somewhat too high" to "about right" (see Table 3.1).[14]

On the other hand, many people expressed concern about deteriorating public services, to some extent speaking for themselves but most of all for the public as a whole. In March 1983, 31 percent of the public reported that Proposition 13 had had an unfavorable effect on the services their family received; 50 percent reported no unfavorable effect. However, at the same time 42 percent of the California public stated that the overall quality of state and local government services they received had declined over the past five years (only 6 percent perceived improvement), with education, street maintenance, recreation facilities, and libraries singled out as the most salient areas of decay. Interestingly, these services actually did experience disproportionate cutbacks in spending, indicating another fit between "reality" and opinion.

Satisfaction with Proposition 13

Despite the growing acknowledgement that Proposition 13 had brought problems in its wake, few doubt that the voters in California would, if given the chance, affirm their decision of 1978. We noted above that between 1978 and 1980 the polls that asked Californians how they would vote on 13 consistently found that it continued to enjoy an approximate 60 percent in favor. After 1981, the California Poll only asked the voters how satisfied they were with Proposition 13 rather than how they would cast their ballot. As problems in the public sector mounted, and the tax relief receded more into the past, the dissatisfied began virtually to equal the satisfied in number by March 1983. This question about satisfaction with Proposition 13 may understate the continued electoral support for this measure, since some original supporters are dissatisfied in the sense that it did not go far enough in its implementation, but its margin of advantage does seem to have diminished since 1978.

Who is satisfied, and who is dissatisfied, with the outcome of the tax revolt at this juncture? In Chapter 10 we elaborated a statistical model to account for differences in individuals' support for the tax revolt in California. The model outlined a causal chain in which social background and current social circumstances embodied differences in self-interest and symbolic predispositions that in turn promoted the beliefs about the tax burden, spending priorities, and governmental performance that were the proximate influences on how one voted. To examine the forces underlying satisfaction with Proposition 13 in March 1983, five years after its passage, we retain the same theoretical structure, with one set of modifications. Since our concern is to explain retrospective rather than prospective support for Proposition 13, we introduce beliefs about the impact of this tax reform as a potentially important causal factor. Once again we distinguish between the *direct* effect of a hypothesized cause, which refers to its relation to the dependent variable after the influence of all other predictors has been controlled, and its total effect, which includes that portion of its influence that is funneled through intermediate points in the explanatory chain. The total effect is measured by the regression coefficients in an equation that excludes the predictors regarded (by assumption) as more proximate. In presenting these results, we will also examine group cleavages in relation to satisfaction with Proposition 13, by comparing the responses of demographic subgroups to questions about the tax burden, spending, and the impact of Proposition 13.

The model, shown in Table 12.1, clearly identifies the continuing connection between self-interest and feelings about Proposition 13. There is a highly significant influence of perceptions of the favorable impact of Proposition

TABLE 12.1 Model for predicting satisfaction with Proposition 13 in 1983.

Independent variable	Total Effect	Direct Effect
Demographics		
Race (white/black)	− .01	.01
Ethnicity (white/hispanic)	.08	.06
Age	.19*	.00
Education (no college/college)	− .09*	.01
Income	.05	.04
Symbolic predispositions and objective self-interest		
Liberalism/conservatism	.13*	.05
Party identification (D/R)	.09*	− .01
Rent/pre-1976 home ownership	.21*	.06
Rent/post-1976 home ownership	.10*	.03
Employment sector (private/public)	− .08*	− .04
Child in public school?	− .02	.03
Household member in public college?	− .03	− .01
Value priorities		
Spending preference index	.06	− .05
Preferred size of gov't (lrg./small)	.04	.01
Sociotropic judgments		
State financial condition (worse/better)	.10*	.07*
Local financial condition (worse/better)	.04	.00
User fees index	.02	.01
Impact of Proposition 13		
Service quality index	.11*	.10*
Impact of 13 on own household's taxes	.22*	.17*
Impact of 13 on own household's services	.28*	.23*
Impact of 13 on own household's wages/jobs	.10*	.05
Support for new taxes index	− .06	− .05
Immediate personal situation		
Overall evaluation of 13's impact on own household	.23*	.21*
Tax burden	.04	.04
Number of Cases	412	
R-square	.35	

Source: California Poll, March 1983.

Note: The entries are standardized coefficients. The dependent variable is scored from dissatisfied to satisfied. The personal impact variables are scored from unfavorable to favorable; the overall impact variable is scored from worse off to better off. For scoring of other indices, see Citrin and Green, "Living with the Tax Revolt."

*Statistically significant at the p≤.05 level.

13 on taxes paid on support for it (beta = .17). The main beneficiaries of the tax revolt in California are people who have owned their current residences since before 1976. Indeed, being an "early" homeowner has a residual influence on favorable attitudes toward Proposition 13 even after the mediating role of beliefs about the favorable tax consequences of the initiative is taken into account. This distinction between "early" and "late" homeowners had not emerged even a year and a half after the vote on Proposition 13 at the time of the Tax Revolt Survey (see Chapter 6), so it appears that experience has clarified the precise connections between self-interest and the mandated reductions in property taxes. These "early homeowners" are of course disproportionately elderly, so not surprisingly homeowners in the over-60 age group have emerged as the strongest partisans of Proposition 13. By 1983 they were considerably more likely than their younger counterparts to say that it had had a very favorable impact on their own taxes (57 percent to 36 percent). And, paralleling our earlier finding of the relative lack of correlation between self-interest and support for income tax reductions (see Chapter 6), we do not find that middle or upper income groups adopt a more favorable view of the state's tax burden, whatever the actual incidence of their personal gains due to income tax indexing. Nor do feelings about the amount of taxes paid "by the average person like yourself" have any causal influence on satisfaction with Proposition 13 (placing the Tax Burden variable earlier in the causal sequence does not change this result). Once again, then, the self-interested effect of taxation on support for the tax revolt focuses first and foremost on the property tax, whose inflation-driven escalation was at the heart of its initial appeal.

Both party identification and ideological self-designation strongly influenced assessments of Proposition 13, replicating our earlier results (see Chapter 8). The debate over how California should cope with fiscal stress became increasingly partisan and ideological after 1980. Most elected politicians, Democrats and Republicans alike, originally opposed Proposition 13 and then, following its great electoral success, rushed to embrace it. But once difficult budgetary choices could no longer be avoided, Republicans and Democrats, conservatives and liberals, most often came down on opposite sides when deciding how to trade off taxes against services. The preferences of the general public have also become more ideologically polarized, largely because liberals have become more insistent on maintaining services, even at the expense of higher taxes. When presented with the standard trade-off choice between services and tax cuts, the opinions of self-identified conservatives changed hardly at all between 1980 and 1983. However, the proportion of moderate liberals opting for higher taxes and more services rose from 40 to 59 percent, and the proportion of strong liberals making this choice grew from 58 to 71 percent.

The voter's belief that services in his community had declined, which we view as at least in part a sociotropically oriented response merging concern with one's community with one's own circumstances, promoted dissatisfaction with Proposition 13 (beta = .11). The voter's conviction that Proposition 13 had negatively affected the particular services his own family uses had an independent and even stronger causal effect (beta = .23).[15] And these dual indices of concern for the quality of public services wholly account for the influences of party identification and ideology on satisfaction with Proposition 13. Similarly, the belief that the financial condition of state government had worsened over the past year enhanced dissatisfaction with Proposition 13, which seemingly was blamed for reducing the government's resources. Interestingly, though, preferences for a smaller (or larger) government and for reduced (or enhanced) spending on specific services were severed from Proposition 13 itself, contrary to our earlier findings reported in Chapter 10. Evidently evaluation of Proposition 13 has shifted by this time to both the more abstract level of the ideological disputes in Sacramento, and to the very concrete level of local services.

It is widely believed that the post-Proposition 13 cutbacks in government services and the imposition of new user fees to replace some of the lost tax revenues have burdened racial minorities more than whites. Yet throughout the period under study whites, blacks, and Hispanics in California assessed the impact of Proposition 13 on services in a virtually identical manner. Moreover, older respondents were actually *less* likely to say that the services they received had been unfavorably affected, which seems to belie the conventional wisdom that recent budgetary cutbacks have caused disproportionate suffering among the elderly.

Other trends give uneven support to the claim that opinions changed to conform to "reality." In 1978 and also in 1983 parents of children in public schools were more likely than the rest of the public to attribute negative consequences to Proposition 13. Both groups expressed greater anxiety about the impact of 13 as time passed, but the gap remained intact. Between 1978 and 1983, public employees did become less worried about the potential consequences of Proposition 13 for their jobs. Expectations about Proposition 13's impact on one's job have only a limited influence on support for it among the population as a whole, but this variable (Impact on Job) does interpret the tendency of public employees to be more dissatisfied with it, as shown in Table 12.1.

Finally, the 1983 California Poll included a question about whether, on the whole, Proposition 13 has made one's family better or worse off. This item apparently captures an evaluative dimension that is separate from the judgments about services, taxes, or job. The Overall Impact variable has a highly significant beta of .21, though it is admittedly close in meaning to the dependent variable itself.

One unanticipated finding from analysis of recent surveys is that growing doubts about Proposition 13 are expressed by the college-educated voters. If the elderly have become the pro-13 loyalists, the college-educated, also a politically active group, may be viewed as an opposition faction. They are much more likely to have shifted to the position that the level of state and local taxation was now satisfacatory, that Proposition 13 had unfavorably affected public services, and that taxes should be raised if this were necessary to maintain existing services. Whether this is because of their higher expectations of government, greater awareness of a decline in public services, of diffuse antipathy to the blunt approach of the tax rebels we cannot say, but the college-educated emerge as the staunch defenders of the public sector.

To summarize, these findings confirm that both self-interest and general political orientations remain determinants of support for Proposition 13. But these generic causes course through separate streams of influence. Beliefs about its consequences for taxes are more firmly grounded in self-interest, perhaps because the savings involved are so large and visible and therefore either directly felt by, or widely known to, large segments of the public. Personal experience appears to have less relevance to beliefs about how Proposition 13 has harmed government services. One possible reason for this is success of the official effort to limit cutbacks in services. Another is that the level of utilization of public facilities and programs varies widely according to groups and types of services. If the public parks are now dirtier but one visits them only rarely, the negative impact of Proposition 13 might be noticed yet carry little weight. In general, for many respondents the answer to how government services have been affected by Proposition 13 is ambiguous or unknown. In these fluid circumstances, voters' expectations of what government should do, which their partisan and ideological orientations embody, more strongly influence assessments of what has occurred. More drastic, highly visible changes in the delivery of government services are required if a wider spectrum of self-interest reactions is to be expected.

Whither Something for Nothing?

In attempting to establish the precise intentions of the citizenry who supported Proposition 13, we found (Chapter 4) a widespread desire for a smaller, cheaper government that somehow delivers more services, the paradox that Lipset and

Ladd refer to as ideological conservatism combined with programmatic liberalism[16] and that we have labeled the "something for nothing" syndrome. Some people who favored a smaller government that costs less, nonetheless demanded more spending on many expensive programs. Many who complained about an excessively high tax burden expressed a similar desire for an enlarged public sector. And there were also citizens who advocated a smaller government in the abstract yet said that government in California should respond to its current fiscal crisis by raising taxes rather than cutting services.

Five years later, there was much evidence that this apparent inconsistency persisted, at least in the aggregate. When asked about a variety of specific service areas, California's electorate favored maintaining or increasing current levels of spending in almost every area. Respondents who favored cutting back were always a small minority. There are interesting nuances in the trends for specific policy domains, suggesting that when political elites focus attention on a particular problem such as crime or the quality of public education, mass preferences for increased spending in that area tend to grow. But the important datum is the pervasive expectation that government should contrive to engage in a wide variety of expensive activities. Officials therefore continue to inhabit a minefield bounded by opposition to higher taxes on one side and pressures for maintaining services on the other.

On the other hand, a clear majority continues to prefer, in the abstract, "a smaller government that provides fewer services": 64 percent of the California public in 1983, as compared to 61 percent in 1979. Perceptions of waste seem even less likely than before to explain this contrast, in view of reduced criticism of waste in government. In late May 1978, fully 49 percent of Californians believed that the budgets of state and local governments could be cut by 20 percent or more without having to reduce services. By August 1982, only 22 percent felt that there was this much "fat" in California government.

What accounts for the inconsistencies in individual's thinking about taxes and spending?[17] Many observers believe that ignorance or confusion about the specific content of government programs, their cost, and how they are financed often underlie the compartmentalization of political attitudes. That many citizens lack awareness of the trade-offs inherent in government policy is hardly surprising, of course, since politicians do their best to spread the illusion of costless progress.

Still, it is reasonable to expect that the more politically involved and better-informed citizens and those for whom taxing and spending issues are highly salient would be more likely to organize their beliefs in a logical way. Learning about the actual consequences of a given policy, in some cases through direct personal experience, as many Californians did after the passage of Proposition 13, also should lead to a more consistent set of preferences.

We tested this assumption in two ways. First we investigated whether beliefs about taxation and spending were more consistent among those with most information and personal experience with these issues than among those more distant from them. Second, we tested whether or not the passage of time in and of itself, by increasing awareness of the fiscal consequences of Proposition 13, also increased the consistency of the public's responses to these questions about taxes and spending. To make a long story short, analysis along this line produced uniformly negative results. The level of consistency among opinions is unrelated to any of the putative indicators of awareness employed.[12]

There is then a striking invariance in the disjunction between opinions about taxing and spending. The desire to get something for nothing is well entrenched among a substantial portion of the citizenry in all segments of society. There remain tiny extremes whose general attitudes about the role of government are tightly bound to reactions to one specific effort to harness the public sector. But for most people the connections are loose. The staying power of the something-for-nothing mentality indicates a volatile electorate and suggests that the outcome of initiatives on taxing and spending can be shaped by the dynamics of the campaign; for example, by whether the responsibilities or the efficiency of government become salient symbols. Obviously, the balance of perceived benefits and risks associated with a particular measure is also crucial.

Resistance to Increased Property Taxes

One of the primary legacies of the tax revolt is a strong resistance to increases in the property tax. As we indicated in Chapter 4, responses to trade-off questions forcing the respondent to choose between tax increases and service cuts depended greatly upon how concretely the services are described. People generally preferred cuts in "spending" in the abstract to tax increases, though they were not so willing to support cuts in concrete services. This pattern persisted even though the state's financial situation steadily worsened between 1980 and 1983, resulting in a growing threat to popular services. The proportion of the public that opted for "reduced spending" in the abstract as a way out of the budgetary dilemma fell only slightly, from 60 to 56 percent. When asked what should be done if taxes absolutely had to be raised, only 14 percent of those polled, and virtually no homeowners, said they could support the policy of reversing Proposition 13 and imposing higher residential property taxes. Increasing taxes on alcohol, cigarettes, gasoline, crude oil, or

business was more acceptable as a response to fiscal emergency, so here too
state policy has followed public opinion.[19] Although the appetite for service
reductions is limited, the notion of increasing property taxes has virtually no
constituency.

The Tax Revolt in Other States

Officials outside California interpreted the passage of Proposition 13 as a
message to cut back on taxes and spending. The result was an unprecedented
rash of legislated tax cuts. The effort to lower taxes was concentrated on the
levy on property, at least in the short run. State officials hastened to use accumulated reserves to expand programs of property tax relief for local governments. Indeed, between 1978 and 1980 fully 43 states adopted new limitations
on local property taxes or new property tax relief plans, either on official initiative or as a result of the electorate's decision.[20] Spending caps were also
adopted in many states during this period. In eighteen states, the constitutional or statutory limits on either the taxing or spending authority of state
government now in place were adopted in 1978 or later. Statistics compiled
by the Advisory Commission on Intergovernmental Relations (ACIR) also
show that these post-1978 formal restrictions are more varied and comprehensive than their historical antecedents.[21]

It is apparent that the intensity of the tax revolt diminished after 1980,
following much the same trajectory nationally as in California. In 1978 and
1979 twenty-six fiscal limitation measures were put before the voters, and 65
percent passed. In the next four years, during which there were two general
elections, scattered state electorates considered only 41 such proposals, and
the success rate dropped to 54 percent. This decline was especially notable in
the case of the initiatives that imitated Proposition 13; after November 1978,
only 1 of 8, Proposition 2½ of Massachusetts, won approval. Moreover, the
relative severity of a fiscal limitation proposal strongly influenced its chances
of success. Moderate restrictions tended to pass, but drastic reductions in taxes
usually were rejected. So, for example, only 4 of 13 of the property tax reforms
closely modeled after Proposition 13 passed, compared to 7 of 8 relatively
minor property tax relief measures. Reductions in income taxes and other state
levies were approved on 11 of 19 occasions, whereas the proposal to impose
a global limit on state of local expenditures, which typically had no immediate
consequences, passed 8 of 10 tests.[22]

When the 1981-82 recession eroded reserves, a substantial and rapid retrenchment at the state and local levels was inevitable. After 1982 the felt need
to shore up services and public employment led to tax increases. To some ex-

tent, increases in state and local spending also resulted from the reduction of federal aid for domestic programs by the Reagan administration. In the face of the ideological challenge from Washington to reduce the size of government, officials at lower levels of government felt constrained to respond to their constituents' continued preference for a wide range of public services. As in California, the subsequent economic recovery may usher in a new phase of governmental growth at the state and local level.

Conditions for Successful Revolts

What conditions promoted success for the tax rebels? It is generally assumed that popular approval of tax cuts is more likely where taxes are high, although the critical factor has been variously hypothesized to be the absolute amount of taxes, the amount of visible taxes such as the property tax, or the rate of increase in taxes. At any rate, individuals with higher perceived tax burdens, or greater anticipated tax savings, generally vote for reduced state and local taxes in any given jurisdiction more than do those with lower tax burdens, according to surveys in California, Massachusetts, and Michigan.[23] Similarly, homeowners at all income levels have consistently favored the property tax cuts more often than renters, and the relatively affluent are the strongest supporters of cuts in income taxes, also presumably because they would benefit more.

But the relative tax burdens in different jurisdictions within a state do not predict support for tax cuts in any simple fashion. For example, in Massachusetts a locality's property tax rate was positively related, as expected, to its aggregate vote for Proposition 2½, whereas in California, by contrast, Proposition 13 fared *worse* in counties with a high or rising property tax rate.[24] Moreover, neither a state's relative tax burden nor its level of public spending influenced the likelihood that it would adopt a proposal to place a ceiling on state or local government expenditures or to provide minor property tax relief. These types of fiscal restrictions almost always passed, and were as likely to appear on the ballot in states with a tax burden well below the national average as in the highly taxed states. This also holds true for proposals to reduce state income or sales taxes.

High statewide property tax burdens were important in *spawning* Proposition 13-like initiatives: in 10 of the 13 cases (7 of 9 states) where votes were taken, the local property tax burden in the fiscal year immediately before the election was higher than the national average—and in 7 cases, more than 20 percent higher. The role of high property taxes in particular in energizing property tax cuts is underscored by the fact that a state's *overall* tax burden was substantially higher than the national average in only 5 of the 13 tests for the "Jarvis clones."

A close look at the three states that ultimately passed grass-roots proposals to drastically reduce property taxes — California, Massachusetts, and Idaho — does suggest some pattern of fiscal pressures that enhances support for the more drastic proposals of the tax revolt. This complex of conditions, however, is rare, underscoring the point made in Chapter 9 above about the peculiar nature of the campaign for Proposition 13. In California before the passage of Proposition 13, both local property taxes and the overall state and local tax burdens were far above the national average, and property taxes were escalating rapidly. In Massachusetts, property taxes in 1980 were virtually double the national average, and several weeks before the vote on Proposition 2½, property owners received the news that their 1981 taxes would go up by 11.5 percent over what they had to pay in 1980.[25] When Idaho voted on its "Jarvis clone" in November 1978, its property taxes were low compared to other states, but residential property taxes had risen sharply over the previous decade because of a state Supreme Court decision that caused the homeowners' share of the property tax burden to leap from 24 percent in 1969 to 44 percent in 1978.[26] Even where taxes are relatively low, then, a steep rise in visible exactions can fuel a revolt, particularly if the trend toward higher taxes is perceived as uncontrollable.

In short, a high overall tax burden in a jurisdiction was not sufficient by itself to produce success for the tax revolt there. Rather, with public cynicism about government prevalent, failure of the elected officials to meet burgeoning complaints about high taxes at least partway was critical to the success of the tax revolt. The rebels won their greatest victories in California and Massachusetts, where the political system was unresponsive to an obvious problem — in other words, where democratic processes broke down. That is, success for "revolution" rather than "reform" appears most likely when taxes are rising and many voters come to believe that relief is unlikely under the prevailing political practices.

The relative skill and resources of the opposing forces also has influenced the outcome of campaigns to impose fiscal restrictions. For example, the success of Proposition 13 brought recruits, enthusiasm, and political allies to the tax rebels in other states, who sometimes rode to victory on Howard Jarvis' coat-tails. On the other hand, the attempt to repeal Ohio's 90 percent increase in state income taxes was badly defeated in November 1983, in part because of the superior campaign of the opposition coalition led by the state's governor.

New State Taxes

The tax cuts adopted between 1978 and 1980 resulted in a decline in the state tax burden in 44 of the 50 states between 1978 and 1982. This era of tax cuts abruptly ended in the 1981 and 1982 legislative sessions when 34 states raised at least one tax, and in 1983 this happened in 38 states.[27] This growth in revenues represented less than 5 percent of state tax collections nationally, but in 19 states the tax revenues for fiscal year 1984 were more than 5 percent above their collections for 1982.[28]

The rash of increases in state taxes does not necessarily mean that we have embarked on a new phase of steady growth in government or that the spirit of the tax revolt has faded away forever. Most states raised their taxes out of fiscal desperation, not choice. The deep economic recession sharply eroded revenues, and states were forced to confront this shortfall with reserves spent, commitments to provide aid to local governments firmly entrenched, and little hope of federal assistance. Taxes were typically raised in order to sustain existing levels of services in a context of shrinking resources rather than to fund new programs, usually as part of a broader strategy to balance the state budget that also included a wide variety of belt-tightening measures and cuts in expenditures. For example, a 1983 survey found that 41 states had placed limits on hiring, 37 had cut selected programs, 32 had restricted travel for their employees, 14 delayed making payments, 22 adopted or proposed plans to lay off workers, and 7 put workers on unpaid furlough.[29]

Officials proceeded warily, first increasing taxes the polls showed to be most politically acceptable—those on gasoline, cigarettes, and alcohol. Increases in income or general sales taxes were adopted only when the fiscal crisis was truly severe. Of the ten states that increased either their personal income or general sales tax rates in 1981 and 1982, all but two had heavier-than-average unemployment rates and were dependent on the ailing heavy manufacturing and construction industries.[30] As Shannon and Calkins put it, "a state government now extracts a major transfusion from its citizenry only when it is clearly apparent that the state is suffering a severe fiscal hemorrhage—due to the economic recession."[31]

The public appears willing to tolerate enhanced spending on "infrastructure," a category that was severely cut back in the recent retrenchment, and on public education, a widely used service whose quality is widely thought to be in decline. Beyond this, however, there is a rough consensus that the growth of government should correspond to the growth of the economy as a whole. Because people are willing to pay more in taxes when their own incomes are rising, a robust economy gives the public sector room to grow. The tax rebels flourished in the late 1970s when stagflation squeezed personal incomes while government treasuries swelled, and are poised to resist recurrence of this pattern.

For state officials, the lessons of the past five years are clear. If large surpluses accumulate, share government's wealth with the taxpayers. Justify a strong surge in spending by necessity, and if taxes must go up, start by closing loopholes and taxing first "sin" and then business, rather than voters directly. Having learned to cope with adversity in hard times, develop a political strategy for managing prosperity. It is noteworthy that governors of several states, including the formerly beleaguered Illinois, Ohio, and Pennsylvania are proposing tax rebates and reductions for 1985.[32] Thus, although the tax rebels may lose electoral battles, their brooding presence remains a force for fiscal restraint.

Living with 2½ in Massachusetts[33]

The case of Massachusetts' Proposition 2½ is most comparable to California's Proposition 13. In both states, the tax rebels struck against a background of abnormally high and rising property taxes and triumphed over a liberal political coalition that had presided over more than a decade of sustained growth in government spending. Property taxes were rolled back, and their future growth severely limited. Officials in Massachusetts appeared to be in a weaker position to cope with the shock to its fiscal system, because the nation was in the midst of a deepening recession, and they lacked the advantage of a highly professionalized system of public administration, a well-diversified tax structure and, most important, a large surplus in the state treasury. Yet Massachusetts has seemingly adjusted to fiscal constraint without significant disruption to the operations of state or most local governments.[34]

Massachusetts managed to absorb major tax reductions and avoid drastic cuts in public spending in much the same way California had. Moreover, Massachusetts escaped the brunt of the national recession; indeed, officials there were able to increase state spending and state aid to localities. Officials strove to protect the budgetary base, preserving core services and avoiding layoffs. The allocation of cuts was governed not by quantitative criteria such as across-the-board reductions, but a more explicitly political approach that preserved public safety programs at the expense of education, recreation and public works, and capital projects. And in Massachusetts the tax revolt also resulted in the centralization of budgetary decision-making.

Proposition 2½ succeeded in lowering the tax burden in Massachusetts. Statewide, the property tax, including the motor vehicle tax, had taken a $58.30 bite out of every $1000 of personal income in 1980, and this fell to $46.60 in 1982.[35] Yet, as in California, cuts in public spending have been smaller than the amount of tax "revenues" lost as a result of Proposition 2½. Since its passage, state expenditures have risen 5 percent in real terms, and the 1984-85 budget proposes an 8 percent real increase.[36] Drastic cuts in local services could be avoided in Massachusetts because several sources replaced the revenues lost to Proposition 2½. Revaluation of existing property, new construction, and increased fees added to local resources. Just as in California, however, the increase of state aid was the critical factor. Although Governor King originally proposed that the state bail out in 1981-82 be limited to a trivial $8 million, the final amount of assistance for that year was $252 million, to rise to a proposed $550 million for fiscal year 1984.[37]

In deference to public opinion, police and fire departments were cut substantially less than other areas of government service, despite evidence that they were staffed at higher levels than their counterparts in other states.[38] Supporters of the public schools have complained that education departments were unfairly treated in the post-Proposition 2½ budgetary process. Others claim that the decline in spending on schools merely reflects a long overdue restructuring that would tie expenditures on education to enrollment. From 1974 to 1982, per pupil spending in Massachusetts rose by 133.7 percent, while enrollment declined by 20.7 percent.[39] Even in 1982, when overall spending in schools declined, per-pupil expenditures rose due to the loss in enrollments. Moreover, in Massachusetts, as in California, schools officials tended to eliminate only peripheral programs such as adult education and summer programs.

Most politicians in Massachusetts awaited the implementation of Proposition 2½ with fear and trembling. Now that they have survived the initial threat to basic services and personnel so well, many local officials are finding unanticipated virtues in the initiative. They have undertaken a variety of management reforms in the effort to increase their productivity. Among these are inter-local arrangements to share overhead, the contracting out of services, the adoption of self-insurance programs, computerized record-keeping, and more modern cash management policies. It is too early to assess the net effect of these innovations, but at least one dramatic example must be reported. After Proposition 2½ passed, the city of Boston decided to "decriminalize" minor traffic violations and dispose of them through the administrative process rather than in the courts. The result was to increase the amount collected in penalties from $2 million to $30 million in the first year. One senior Boston official acknowledged that Proposition 2½ should be praised for "nudging an antiquated system of government onto the road to modernity."[40]

Frustration with Proposition 2½ seems most pronounced among officials at the state level. True, Proposition 2½ furnishes besieged legislators with a convenient excuse for saying no to incessant demands for more spending. But the diversion of revenues to localities is a barrier to the expansion of programs to which the liberal Democrats who control state government, and their electoral constituencies, are deeply committed. This has intensified concern about enlarging the state's fiscal base. In 1983 Governor Dukakis appointed a state tax study commission with a mandate to recommend changes in the existing tax structure. The tax rebels may find that one consequence of their success is tax reform, including a possible increase in the state's sales taxes, which are relatively low in Massachusetts.

The Tax Revolt and the Reagan Record

President Reagan has based his policies on a simple diagnosis of the nation's ailments and a clear vision of how to cure them. In his own words, "The most important cause of our economic problems has been the government itself": its excessive spending promoted inflation, burdensome regulation of business sapped productivity, and high marginal tax rates discouraged the investment, innovation, and hard work required for sustained growth.[41]

Reducing the size and influence of government therefore was the cornerstone of the Reagan administration's economic program, although its other commitments — to strengthening the nation's military capabilities and reinforcing traditional moral values — implied an expanded role for government. In the economic realm, the President proposed a two-pronged strategy. On the one hand, tax cuts and regulatory reform would stimulate economic growth by facilitating a more efficient use of resources. On the other, the elimination of waste and fraud in government programs, cuts in domestic spending, and a restrictive monetary policy would relieve inflation. Taken together, the revenues generated by sustained growth and the savings resulting from reduced domestic spending would enable the federal government to balance its budget (eventually) even as expenditures on defense grew.

This set of ideas diverge sharply from the liberal consensus that had dominated American politics since the New Deal. As he clearly articulated during his campaign for office, President Reagan intended to redirect the public agenda. As we wrote in the first edition of this book, the President's particular blend of fiscal conservatism with populist arraignment of government as arrogant and inefficient echoed the sentiments expressed by the tax rebels in California. Mr. Reagan's success is a vindicatory "I told you so" for Howard Jarvis, until 1978 a neglected, if shrill, voice in the political wilderness.

The Mandate of 1980

Despite the clarity and consistency with which Ronald Reagan proclaimed his doctrinal attachments, it is generally believed that his victory represented a repudiation of Jimmy Carter more than an embrace of the conservative political agenda espoused by the new president.[42] There was no notable increase between 1976 and 1980 in the number of people who identified themselves as Republicans or conservatives, and the apparent shift in that direction recorded by some 1981 surveys proved ephemeral. And while people complained about their tax burden and by an overwhelming margin claimed to favor a smaller government that both spent and taxed less, they continued to support maintaining or increasing spending in most domains of policy, as shown in Table 12.2. Similar support for the Reagan program in the abstract, but not in more concrete form, was expressed in opinions about regulatory policy. While a plurality of the public agreed (in a series of 1978 and 1979 polls) that "in general" there was too much government regulation of business, large majorities

TABLE 12.2   National spending preferences.

Service Domain	1976	1980	1983
Rising crime	+ 57	+ 63	+ 62
Drug addiction	+ 51	+ 52	+ 54
Education	+ 41	+ 42	+ 54
Health	+ 55	+ 47	+ 54
Environmental protection	+ 45	+ 32	+ 46
Problems of big cities	+ 23	+ 19	+ 26
Condition of blacks	+ 2	0	+ 11
Military; arms and defense	− 3	+ 45	− 8
Welfare	− 46	− 43	− 25
Space exploration	− 51	− 21	− 26
Foreign aid	− 72	− 65	− 72

Source: General Social Survey, 1983, National Opinion Research Center.

Note: Entries and PDI values were obtained by subtracting "spend less" from "spend more" responses.

simultaneously, if inconsistently, opposed weakening the regulation of banks, the oil industry, advertising, or the drug and automobile industries.[43] And on so-called "social issues" such as women's rights or abortion, the public in the aggregate actually had moved in the liberal direction.

Moreover, the "average" citizen was not uniformly closer to Reagan than to Carter on issues related to the themes of the tax revolt: although closer to Reagan on the proposed 30 percent cut in federal income taxes, and on the question of whether the federal government should guarantee everyone a job and "good" standard of living, the average citizen perceived himself or herself as closer to Carter on the issue of whether government should continue to provide existing services even if this meant no cuts in spending. Only 48 percent of the electorate expressed a personal opinion and at the same time accurately perceived the nature of the difference between the candidates on this latter issue, and only 32 percent did so on Reagan's proposal to cut income taxes.[44] Hence the net contribution of the tax-revolt issues *per se* to President Reagan's victory appears quite limited.

What is clear is that voters whose principal concern was the state of the economy resoundingly favored the Republican candidate. The survey evidence indicates that President Reagan won a mandate to cure the economy and reduce inflation, but the electorate was more interested in success than in the specific policies that would bring it about.

The people certainly would accept something — a tax cut — while hoping it would cost nothing in services. Thus, when the Reagan administration started to put its policies into practice, it faced the same dilemma that confronted state and local officials stripped of revenues by revolt and recession. The federal government, however, possesses one escape route denied to lower levels of government — deficit financing. Indeed, the federal budget's annual deficit grew from 79 billion dollars in 1981 to an estimate of approximately 200 billion in 1984 because the loss in revenues due to tax cuts and the recession of 1981-82 was not matched by a public willingness to cut expensive, but popular programs. In the end even the Reagan administration itself acknowledged there was no mandate to greatly reduce what government provides for its citizens.

The Record

Whatever the ambiguities in the electorate's message, President Reagan began by acting as if there was a public consensus in favor of an ideological transformation of national economic policy. What have been the accomplishments? First, the federal tax burden has indeed declined dramatically. During the

Carter administration federal revenues rose from 19.1 to 20.8 percent of GNP.[45] According to the Office of Management and Budget, as a result of President Reagan's Economic Recovery Tax Act of 1981, federal revenues are expected to shrink by 1985 to 18.7 percent of GNP, despite the revenue-raising measure enacted in 1982. In addition, beginning in 1983, federal income taxes are indexed against inflation, depriving the public sector nationally (as in California) of another source of funds.[46] President Reagan's policies have therefore contributed significantly to the success of the tax-cutting component of the Jarvisites' programs. In fact, it is estimated that the average family's combined federal, state, and local tax payments will be 2.6 percent less in 1984 than in 1979.

As to the size of government, federal spending as a share of GNP actually is bigger (an estimated 24.1 percent in FY 1985) than when President Reagan took office (23.5 percent in FY 1981). The rate of growth in government was substantially slowed, however, and the budget priorities shifted away from domestic programs toward defense and the interest on the national debt. Federal spending on all social programs as a percentage of GNP is expected to have declined marginally between FY 1981 and FY 1985, after reaching a peak during the recession in 1982. Clearly, though, the changes proposed by Reagan and enacted by Congress have reversed three decades of growth in the public sector. Indeed, the Urban Institute estimates that federal spending on domestic programs in FY 1985 will be 10 percent less than it would have been under prior policies. And this reduction would have been half again greater had Congress granted all the President sought.[47]

The Reagan administration has swung its budgetary axe unevenly. The idea of reducing social security benefits was broached in 1981 but quickly abandoned in the face of immediate and intense political opposition. Thus, universalistic social insurance programs, which account for two-thirds of all social spending and have a large, socioeconomically diverse, and mainly elderly constituency, received only a glancing blow. Changes originally proposed in Medicare payments would have cut spending by an estimated 11.2 percent of the $80 billion in previously projected outlays for FY 1985; the reforms ultimately approved by Congress limited the reduction to 6.8 percent.[48]

By contrast, the poor and minorities have been hurt disproportionately. The tax structure has become more regressive, since it now relies more heavily on payroll and excise taxes. Indeed, the tax burden for a family of four at the poverty line rose from 4 to 10 percent of income between 1978 and 1984.[49] Like Jarvis's version of the tax revolt, the tax policies of the Reagan administration were designed to promote savings and investment rather than equity. Service cuts have also fallen disproportionately on the poor. The cumulative effect of the administration's proposed cuts for means-tested assistance, the programs frequently lumped together under the unpopular symbol of "welfare," amount to 28 percent of projected outlays. And the discretionary grant programs that help fund the delivery of health, education, and social services by state and local governments received even deeper cuts. Changes actually enacted have reduced federal spending in this category for FY 1985 by 42 percent of the outlays projected under the Carter administration. It might be said that President Reagan's policies for domestic spending spared the New Deal while amputating the Great Society.

The administration did succeed in cutting categorical grants to states and localities. As already indicated, state and local governments imposed new taxes in 1982 and 1983 and used these funds to replace some or all the lost federal dollars. The focus of this effort, however, was to sustain assistance to high-need populations at prior levels. Increasing benefits or developing new enterprises was extremely rare. The policy of the Reagan administration thus reinforced the fiscal restraint initiated by the tax revolt policy. The withdrawal of federal aid also reversed the trends toward greater financial interdependence and the nationalization of standards of public services that many observers had thought to be inexorable.[50]

We can only make a passing reference to the Reagan administration's record in other important facets of economic policy. Consumer price inflation, a paramount concern to voters in 1980, dropped from more than 12 percent in 1980 to under 4 percent in 1984. This success was obtained at the price of rising unemployment, which rose to a post-Depression high of 11 percent in 1982 before subsiding to pre-1980 levels. An economic turnabout began in 1983, and by 1984 the *real* income of the average family was 3.5 percent higher than it was in 1980, although this aggregate gain was concentrated at the upper end of the income distribution.[51] A snapshot of the American economy at the end of 1984 indicates real growth in the darkening shadow of the large structural budget deficit.

The Court of Public Opinion

Between 1980 and 1984, the Reagan administration sought and substantially achieved a historic reversal in the size of government. The pattern of fiscal change that occurred — lower taxes accompanied by a more limited reduction in public expenditures, particularly for the generally accessible safety-net programs — reflected the majority's viewpoint prior to the 1980 election. Public approval of the Reagan administration's performance in managing the economy predictably followed in the wake of the macroeconomic indicators. It peaked at 61 percent in April 1981, following the assassination attempt, then fell with the economy to a low of 29 percent in January 1983. As the economy revived, it rose to 55 percent in August 1984.[52]

However, changes in economic reality had little impact on the inconsistency, noted repeatedly above, in opinions about the proper responsibilities of government. As in California, national surveys recorded an ideological preference for smaller government and the ethic of self-reliance. For example, a *Los Angeles Times* poll conducted in December 1983 found that 59 percent of the public felt that "people are responsible for their own well-being and taxes must be as low as possible" compared to 32 percent who took the opposite view that "government is responsible for the well-being of all its citizens and taxes must be high enough to provide these services." And the 1982 National Election Study found that 65 percent agreed that the federal government had become involved in deciding issues which are "not its business" compared to just 16 percent who disagreed. But as Table 12.2 indicates, the desire for government to spend more, rather than less, in most areas of social policy remained as strong as ever in 1983, notwithstanding the administration's unremitting rhetorical attack against this outlook.

Despite the Reagan administration's crusade against bureaucratic inefficiency, the public's image of government as profligate remained intact. While 55 percent of the public in 1983 agreed that President Reagan was cutting waste, 74 percent still believed that people in government waste "a lot of the money we pay in taxes."[53] Rampant inefficiency was perceived to prevail in both domestic and military spending. The *Los Angeles Times* poll found that 53 percent of Americans believed the government wasted *more* than 30 percent of what it spent on domestic programs, whereas only 7 percent felt that the amount of waste was less than 10 percent of spending. The corresponding figures for opinions about waste in military spending are almost identical: 36 percent felt more than 30 percent of the military budget was misspent and only 6 percent regarded waste as minimal.

Opposition to any general increase of taxes on individuals continues. Between 1980 and 1982, a constant two-thirds of the public complained that the federal income taxes they paid were too high. Substantial doubt about the fairness of the tax system persisted; for example, an April 1983 CBS News/*New York Times* survey found that 30 percent of the adult population perceived the present income tax system as "quite unfair," while only seven percent regarded it as "quite fair" to people like themselves. President Reagan's proposal to cut income taxes by 30 percent over three years remained popular with a majority of the electorate as it wended its way through Congress and ultimately was implemented in a slightly modified form. Surprisingly, though, the recognition that the federal tax burden had been lowered was quite limited. An April 1984 CBS/*New York Times* poll found that 40 percent of the public actually believed the amount their family paid to the federal government in taxes had gone up. Another 40 percent perceived no change in their tax burden, and only 15 percent reported a decline.

Polls repeatedly find that the public considers the large federal deficit to be a serious threat to the nation's economy. For example, a June 1983 *Los Angeles Times* national survey found that 69 percent felt the most important thing for the federal government to do was balance the budget, while only 14 percent believed that cutting taxes was the paramount task. Responses to differently worded questions found that creating jobs was viewed as much more important than balancing the budget, with lower taxes even further down the ladder.[54] And by a significant majority people expressed support for a constitutional amendment to require a balanced federal budget.

Nevertheless, the opposition to tax hikes is such that even when warned that the federal deficit was approaching $200 billion and was now the largest in history, 70 percent of the public told a January 1984 ABC/*Washington Post* survey that the government should *not* increase taxes to reduce the deficit. And a February 1984 CBS/*New York Times* poll found that by an astounding margin of 82 to 8 percent, reduced spending was preferred to higher taxes as a means of balancing the budget.

Despite this apparent concern about the deficit, there is at best a limited willingness to sacrifice in order to reduce it. Only 20 percent of the public would cut social programs to balance the budget, and a majority opposes reducing any element in the current package of social security benefits. More were willing to cut military spending, but in most polls there was still a majority unwilling to cut that. In mid-1982, 50 percent said they were willing to have taxes on gas, liquor, or cigarettes raised to help reduce the deficit.[55] A Harris survey conducted in December 1983 showed that the public, by a large majority, consistently opposed proposals to raise personal income or consumer taxes, while indicating a willingness to impose new levies on business. At bottom, the public hopes to avoid both higher taxes and cuts in spending. The confusing welter of responses to queries about the budget deficit amply testify to the prevalence of the something-for-nothing mentality and the reluctance to face the trade-off between taxes and services.

In sum, there is a lack of popular consensus about the proper course for budgetary policy. Given the size of the structural deficit however, fiscal austerity is bound to be the watchword of any national administration whether liberal or conservative in ideology. For the rest of the 1980s, there will be little room for government to grow. The era of doing good by doing more is past, and the accountant's mentality, not the planner's, dominates official thinking at all levels of government. This is the triumphant legacy of the tax revolt.

A Successful Protest

We would conclude, then, as we did three years ago, that the tax revolt has in many ways been a successful protest. In particular, it checked the growth of property taxes and even rolled them back in many areas, at a time when inflation in the real estate market was throwing long-established arrangements out of balance. When the lesson of California was interpreted in Washington, D.C., it helped check the growth of taxes at the federal level. Public policy responded to the "message" of the protest, and the public has responded in turn, through the operation of a "reality principle."

Not all of the problems have been solved and some new ones have been created. Plebiscitary budgeting is a little like carving a turkey with an ax. It remains to be seen if such inequities as service cutbacks for the poor and minorities, and special tax rebates for long-time homeowners, ultimately create further social discontents and protest. At this writing the huge federal deficit created in large part by the Reagan administration's tax cuts remains, its consequences and cure difficult to decipher. Nevertheless the tax revolt must be seen as a successful protest from the perspective of the tax rebels.

Although the first edition was focused first and foremost on the tax revolt as an effort to change public policy, we had also introduced a number of other themes from a more political-psychological perspective. One was the clear but relatively limited and narrow role of self-interest in producing political preferences. Our later data re-emphasize that clear and generous financial benefits do affect the public's preferences, as in the special attraction for Proposition 13 shown by the "early homeowners," who benefited most. But this updating again emphasizes the limits of self-interest, for instance, in its continued weak effects upon parents of children in the public schools. The continuing power of basic symbolic predispositions such as ideology and party identification was also apparent. So was the continued support of the majority for the status quo in concrete services, in tandem with the seemingly contradictory but fairly highly correlated desire for lower taxes and smaller government. We hope that these findings will contribute to an enlarged perspective on mass political behavior in general.

Our research, like others in this field, has touched on but not fully explored the many effects of what we earlier called "the American political culture." The tax revolt evoked some core values in Americans, matters they feel deeply about, such as equity, the importance of hard work, its role in determining success, and the relative roles of the individual and the government. Future research on policy and opinion might well explore the way protests such as the tax revolt express these underlying values together with the tensions among them.

Appendix
Notes
Index

Appendix

The main data bases for this book are the California Tax Revolt Survey and various California Polls. The latter are statewide surveys conducted by the Field Institute from four to eight times a year. Typically their sample contains at least a thousand cases and represents adults 18 and over throughout the state, and the survey is conducted by telephone. Specific surveys are referenced in the tables and notes in our chapters according to a code that describes their year and ordinal position: for example, California Poll 7807 was the seventh survey done in 1978. All the California Polls referred to in this book are archived by the State Data Program, Survey Research Center, University of California, Berkeley, and codebooks, raw data (usually in SPSS file form), and other information can be obtained there.

The California Tax Revolt Survey was conducted in November and December 1979, beginning immediately after the special election that offered the Gann amendment and other ballot propositions. It was conducted by the Survey Research Center, University of California, Berkeley, using a computer-assisted telephone interviewing (CATI) technique. The sample was drawn using a random digit-dialing procedure, and the resulting 1788 respondents are treated as representative of California adults. This study is also archived by the State Data Program, which distributes codebooks, data, and any further information.

By and large, the specific measures are described when first introduced in the book. But since they are scattered throughout the book, we summarize them here. The following briefly elaborates the treatment of our main variables as they appear in our summary analysis (table 10.1). The exact documentation details can also be obtained from the State Data Program.

Dependent Variables

1. Tax rebel index: the sum of attitudes toward the three Jarvis-Gann ballot propositions as of the interview date, each on a three-point scale where undecideds were given the middle position. This yielded a scale running from 3 to 9. To illustrate our general method of handling data, the following shows the exact question wording and coding decisions:

	Item Score		
Question	1	2	3
Proposition 13: Do you feel passing Prop 13 turned out to be mostly:	A bad thing	Undecided, Mixed	A good thing
Gann amendment: How did you vote [or, for nonvoters, how would you have voted] on Prop 4, which placed a limit on the state government's spending?	Against	Never heard of it Don't remember Don't know	In favor
Jarvis II: Howard Jarvis, one of the authors of Prop 13, is proposing a new initiative that would cut state income taxes paid by Californians by about one half . . . People supporting Jarvis's plan say that even *after* Prop 13, state and local taxes are still too high and government spending hasn't been cut. People who are against it say that cutting taxes again would make it impossible for state and local governments to carry out needed activities. If you had to vote today, would you vote for or against Jarvis's plan to greatly cut state income taxes?	Against	Don't know Undecided	For

2. Tax activism: the number of overt actions on tax- and spending-limitation proposals (talked to friends, wrote letters, gave money, or signed petitions).

3. Vote frequency: number of votes cast on Propositions 13 and 4.

4. Opinionation: how many of the three ballot propositions the respondent had a definite opinion toward.

Tax Revolt Schema

1. Size of government: choice between "a smaller government providing fewer services" and "a larger government providing more services" with a "same as now" response allowed if mentioned spontaneously.

2. Service spending: the sum of eight three-point items, each asking for a separate service area (see table 3.2) whether "state and local governments should spend more, the same, or less than they do now on [e.g.] police."

3. Waste: the sum of items asking whether "the public schools in your area could spend less without hurting the quality of education which they provide," "local government in your area could spend less and still provide the same level of services," "state government could spend less and still provide the same level of services," and two items following these last two items asking for a percentage estimate: for example, "how much could local government cut its spending without reducing services, only 10 percent or less, between 10 percent and 20 percent, between 20 percent and 30 percent, or more than 30 percent?"

4. Overpaid government workers: a single item, "compared to what people in the same job get paid outside government, do people working for state and local government get paid more than they should, [then, a lot more or somewhat more?] the right amount, or less than they should?"

Demographic Variables

In general, Chapter 5 provides adequate detail on how the demographic variables were coded. In our last analyses, "race" contrasted blacks with everyone else, "region" contrasted the seven counties south of the Tehachapi Mountains with the rest of the state, and a dummy variable was created contrasting people 65 and over with everyone else.

Self-Interest Variables

Chapters 6 and 7 present the specific self-interest variables and their marginals. In table 10.1, "Homeownership" contrasts all homeowners with renters and "public employees" contrasts those who worked for "state or local government, a state university or college, or a public school" with everyone else.

Symbolic Predispositions

1. Party identification: the standard seven-point scale used in the University of Michigan's election studies; people are asked first "Do you think of yourself as a Democrat, Republican, Independent, or what?" This is followed by asking for strength of feeling among partisans and "leanings" toward either party among Independents.

2. Ideology: a five-point scale based on "generally speaking, in politics do you think of yourself more as conservative or more as liberal?" "Would you say strongly or just moderately?"

3. Symbolic racism: the sum of two items: "The government should *not* make any special effort to help blacks and other racial minorities because they should help themselves; do you agree strongly, agree somewhat, [etc.]," and "First let's talk about Proposition 1, which limits the use of forced busing to produce racial integration in the schools. Did you vote [or, for nonvoters, would you have voted] yes on Proposition 1, that is *against* forced busing, or did you vote no (or in favor of allowing forced busing)?"

4. Cynicism: the sum of two standard items used in the University of Michigan's National Election Studies: "How much of the time do you think you can trust the government to do what is right?" and "In general would you say that the government is mainly run for the benefit of special interest groups, or is it run for the benefit of all the people?" One innovation was to offer "almost none of the time" as an explicit response alternative to the first item, rather than just accepting it if volunteered, as is the Michigan practice. In our sample, 11 percent leapt upon this opportunity to crush any vestige of respectability left in government's reputation; by comparison, only 4 percent volunteered this response in the last prior national study (1978) conducted by Michigan.

5. Incumbent disapproval: the sum of two job-approval items, on Governor Brown and on the state legislature, with "don't know" responses placed in the middle.

Notes

1. Introduction

1. Even if all that is paid is sales tax. See T. C. Schelling, "Economic Reasoning and the Ethics of Policy," *The Public Interest*, 63 (Spring 1981):37–38.

2. G. Peterson, "Voter Demand for Public School Expenditures," in *Public Needs and Private Behavior in Metropolitan Areas*, ed. J. E. Jackson (Cambridge, Mass.: Ballinger, 1974).

3. M. J. Boskin, "Some Neglected Factors behind Recent Tax and Spending Limitation Movements," *National Tax Journal*, 32 (June 1979):37–42.

4. H. I. Wilensky, *The New Corporatism, Centralization and the Welfare State* (Beverly Hills: Sage Publications, 1976).

5. G. Break, "Interpreting Proposition 13: A Comment," *National Tax Journal*, 32 (June 1979):43–46.

6. For a summary of these measures and the outcomes see "1978, The Year of the New Populism," *Intergovernmental Perspective*, 5 (Winter 1979):14.

7. *Public Opinion*, 4, no. 1 (1981):40.

8. Ibid. and "1978, The Year of the New Populism."

9. Advisory Commission on Intergovernmental Relations (ACIR), *Significant Features of Fiscal Federalism* (Washington, D.C., 1979). This represented an annual growth rate in real terms of 4.5 percent for state government spending, 3.7 percent for local governments, and 2.5 percent for the federal government.

10. A. H. Pascal, M. Menchik, J. M. Chaiken, P.L. Ellickson, W. E. Walker, D. N. DeTray, and A. E. Wise, *Fiscal Containment of Local and State Government* (Santa Monica: Rand Corporation, 1979).

11. ACIR, *Significant Features of Fiscal Federalism*.

12. Pascal et al., *Fiscal Containment*.

13. For this point of view, see R. Novak, "What's Happening Out There?," *Public Opinion*,1, no. 4 (1978):2–7. For a recent summary of the decline in trust in government, see J. Citrin, "The Changing American Electorate" in *Politics and the Oval Office*, ed. A. Meltsner (San Francisco: Institute of Contemporary Studies, 1981).

14. J. Citrin, "The Political Relevance of Trust in Government," *American Political Science Review*, 67 (Sept. 1974) and "The Changing American Electorate."

15. "Gratuitous" because Proposition 13 would have prevailed if both measures

had passed and voting for both would have maximized the chance for some cut in taxes.

16. See S. M. Lipset and E. Ladd, "Public Opinion and Public Policy," in *The United States in the 1980s*, ed. P. Duignan and A. Rabushka (Palo Alto: Hoover Institution, 1980); W. E. Miller, A. H. Miller, and E. J. Schneider, *American National Election Studies Data Sourcebook: 1952–1978* (Cambridge, Mass.: Harvard University Press, 1980).

17. W. Heller and A. Burns, "Tax Revolt: The Lady or the Tiger?," *Public Opinion*, 1, no. 3 (1978):3–4.

18. J. Q. Wilson, "Reaganism," *Commentary*, October 1980.

19. D. P. Moynihan has argued that the tax revolt embodies a broader sense of outrage against the "new class" of liberal professionals who thrive on the expansion of government.

20. The California Tax Revolt Survey employed a cross-sectional sample of California residents over age 18 and was administered by the staff of the Survey Research Center, University of California, Berkeley. The main national surveys we analyze are the National Election Studies of the Center for Political Studies, University of Michigan, (CPS/NES) and the General Social Survey of the National Opinion Research Center (NORC).

21. S. E. Taylor and J. Crocker, "Schematic Bases of Social Information Processing," in *Social Cognition: The Ontario Symposium*, vol. 1, ed. E. T. Higgins, C. P. Herman, and M. P. Zanna (Hillsdale, N.J.: Lawrence Erlbaum, 1981). The notion of schema describes beliefs about a more restricted set of objects than do the terms "belief system" and "ideology," which are frequently used by political scientists in a similar fashion.

22. See for example P. E. Converse, "Public Opinion and Voting Behavior," in *Handbook of Political Science*, vol. 4, ed. N. W. Polsby and F. I. Greenstein (Reading, Mass.: Addison-Wesley, 1975).

23. S. J. DeCanio, "Proposition 13 and the Failure of Economic Politics," *National Tax Journal*, 32 (June 1979).

24. M. Fiorina, *Retrospective Voting in American National Elections* (New Haven: Yale University Press, 1981).

25. P. E. Meehl, "The Selfish Voter Paradox and the Thrown-Away Vote Argument," *American Political Science Review*, 71 (March 1977):11–30.

26. D. O. Sears, C. P. Hensler, and L. K. Speer, "Whites' Opposition to 'Busing': Self-Interest or Symbolic Politics," *American Political Science Review*, 73 (1979):369–384; D. R. Kinder and D. O. Sears, "Prejudice and Politics: Symbolic Racism versus Racial Threats to the Good Life," *Journal of Personality and Social Psychology*, 40 (1981):414–431.

27. D. R. Kinder and D. R. Kiewiet, "Economic Discontent and Political Behavior: The Role of Personal Grievances and Collective Economic Judgments in Congressional Voting," *American Journal of Political Science*, 23 (1979):495–527, and D. O. Sears, R. R. Lau, T. R. Tyler, and H. M. Allen, Jr., "Self-Interest vs. Symbolic Politics in Policy Attitudes and Presidential Voting," *American Political Science Review*, 74 (1980):670–684.

28. See A. Campbell, P. E. Converse, W. E. Miller, and D. E. Stokes, *The American Voter* (New York: John Wiley & Sons, 1960); Kinder and Sears, "Prejudice and Politics"; and D. O. Sears and J. B. McConahay, *The Politics of Violence: The New Urban Blacks and the Watts Riot* (Boston: Houghton Mifflin, 1973).

29. Sears et al., "Self-Interest vs. Symbolic Politics."

30. R. Hofstadter, *The Paranoid Style in American Politics* (New York: Knopf, 1965).

31. The term "primordial loyalties" is well explained in C. Geertz, ed., *Old Societies and New States: The Quest for Modernity in Asia and Africa* (New York: Free Press of Glencoe, 1963).

32. L. Hartz, *The Liberal Tradition in America* (New York: Harcourt, Brace, 1955).

33. H. Wilensky, *The Welfare State and Equality* (Berkeley: University of California Press, 1975), pp. 32–34.

2. The History of the California Tax Revolt

1. This discussion draws heavily from J. Citrin and F. Levy, "From 13 to 4 and Beyond: The Political Meaning of the Ongoing Tax Revolt in California" (Paper delivered at the annual meeting of the American Economic Association, 1979); and F. Levy, "On Understanding Proposition 13," *The Public Interest*, 56 (Summer 1979):66–89.

2. D. Paul, *The Politics of the Property Tax* (Lexington, Mass.: D. C. Heath, 1975).

3. M. Levin, "How Property Tax Reform in the Sixties Fueled the Tax Revolt of the Seventies," *Taxing and Spending*, 2 (1979):14.

4. The costs of these reforms were met by an increase in the state's sales tax.

5. California Roundtable, *California Tax Study* (Burlingame: California Roundtable Task Force Publications, 1979), p. 9.

6. It is important to note that the sharp rise in real estate values was concentrated in the market for single-family housing. According to estimates made by the State Board of Equalization, the value of all owner-occupied single-family homes rose by an average annual rate of 12.8 percent between 1973 and 1976, while the average annual growth rate in the value of all other (mainly commercial) property on the rolls was approximately 7.6 percent. Because different kinds of property are taxed at the same rate, this differential rise in assessed valuation meant that the homeowner's share of the property tax burden grew—from 31.6 percent of total property tax receipts in 1973–74 to 41 percent in 1977–78. W. H. Oakland, "Proposition 13: Genesis and Consequences," *National Tax Journal*, 32 (June 1979):387–407. An unintended consequence of the passage of Proposition 13 was to accentuate this trend toward transferring a part of the local tax burden from business to homeowners.

7. Levy, "On Understanding Proposition 13."

8. Oakland, "Proposition 13: Genesis and Consequences," p. 393.

9. *California Tax Study*, pp. 11–13.

10. See J. Citrin, "Do People Want Something for Nothing?" *National Tax Journal*, 32 (June 1979):114.

11. *California Tax Study*, pp. 20–21.

12. A. H. Pascal, M. Menchik, J. M. Chaiken, P. L. Ellickson, W. E. Walker, D. N. DeTray, and A. E. Wise, *Fiscal Containment of Local and State Government* (Santa Monica: Rand Corporation, 1979); and *California Tax Study*.

13. For a fuller discussion of this material see J. Citrin, "The Changing American Electorate," in *Politics and the Oval Office*, ed. A. Meltsner (San Francisco: Institute of Contemporary Studies, 1981), pp. 48–51.

14. L. J. Kimbell and D. Shulman, "The Impact of Proposition 13 on the Rates of Return for California Intensive Firms" (paper presented at the Annual Meeting of the Financial Management Association, 1979).

15. Oakland, "Proposition 13: Genesis and Consequences," p. 397.

16. M. Fitzgerald, "Living with Proposition 13," *Tax Revolt Digest* (November 1979).

17. Oakland, "Proposition 13: Genesis and Consequences," p. 397.

18. Ibid., p. 394.

19. Fitzgerald, "Living with Proposition 13" provides a useful summary of many of the user fees.

20. Oakland, "Proposition 13: Genesis and Consequences," p. 391.

21. Personal communication from the Secretary of State's office.

22. Remarks made by Harvey Englander of the Butcher-Forde firm at a conference on Proposition 9 held on April 14, 1980.

23. *Los Angeles Times*, Feb. 10, 1980, p. 28.

24. Ibid., pt. II, p. 4.

25. Jarvis was using official figures provided by the State Franchise Tax Board.

26. *Los Angeles Times*, Feb. 10, 1980, pt. II, p. 5.

27. J. Citrin and M. Baker, "The Public Mood and the California Tax Revolt: Some Recent Evidence," State Data Program, Research Report no. 3 (Berkeley: University of California, April 1980). The California Poll frequently asked respondents their vote intentions twice in an interview, especially early in a campaign, interposing either a description of the proposition or items measuring agreement with the campaigners' pro and con arguments. The idea was to simulate the effects of the information to which the voter would probably later be exposed. While this procedure presumably has some value in anticipating later developments, we rely in the text on the first choice posed to the respondent in the interview unless stated otherwise.

28. *Los Angeles Times*, May 30, 1980, p. 1.

29. Ibid., May 28, 1980, pt. I, p. 3.

3. Opinions about Taxes and Spending

1. See *Public Opinion* 1, no. 3 (1978):23, and 2, no. 4 (1979):34. Nationally, attitudes contrasting the relative unfairness of various kinds of taxes have remained rather stable, except that the property tax is cited less and less (dropping from 45 percent in 1972 to 25 percent in 1980), and the federal income tax more and more (increasing from 19 percent to 36 percent), no doubt reflecting the joint effects of the property tax reductions and federal income tax increases in recent years. *Public Opinion*, 3, no. 4 (1980):15.

2. *Los Angeles Times*, May 24, 1981, pt. VII, p. 16.

3. *Public Opinion*, 2, no. 6 (1979):20.

4. The sample for the California Poll just prior to the vote on Proposition 13 (interviewed May 29–31, 1978, a week before election day) consisted of registered voters who planned to vote, whereas the other samples presented in table 3.2 consisted of unselected adults. The former group is generally less in favor of services than the general population, but not by enough to explain the marked drop in mid-1978 in support for spending on services. The full Tax Revolt Survey sample had a mean PDI on the composite service spending scale of + 60 percent, but the narrower subgroup of respondents who both were registered voters and reported voting on Proposition 13 had a mean PDI of + 26 percent. Based on the same service areas, the mean PDI for the service spending scale in the May 1978 California Poll was − 5 percent.

5. This index does not weight each service area by actual expenditures, but if it did, the results would be very similar. The most costly of these items are education, public health, and the safety services, which are popular, and welfare, which is not.

6. Our treatment of attitudes about taxation and government spending in this chapter is not intended to consider explicitly their personal impact on the respondent.

Chapters 6 and 7 will introduce such personal impacts into the analysis. However, the only taxation item available to us, shown in table 3.4, does focus on *personal* tax burden, and is therefore a little less appropriate for the present purpose than the more impersonal one shown in table 3.1 would have been.

7. Another way to describe this inconsistency, or asymmetry, is to make the preferred size of government the dependent variable. In every cell but one, the overwhelming majority prefers "smaller government." In the extreme case — those who feel they pay much too much and who want more service areas cut than increased — 95 percent prefer smaller government. The only exception is the other extreme case — those who want a net increase in service spending, and who feel their taxes are "about right." Even here, though, 47 percent want smaller government.

8. D. O. Sears, "Political Behavior," in *Handbook of Social Psychology*, 2nd ed., vol. 5, ed. G. Lindzey and E. Aronson (Reading, Mass.: Addison-Wesley, 1969), pp. 315–458. P. E. Converse, "Public Opinion and Voting Behavior," in *Handbook of Political Science*, vol. 4, ed. F. I. Greenstein and N. W. Polsby (Reading: Addison-Wesley, 1975), pp. 75–170.

9. Four California Polls done in the two years after the passage of Proposition 13 found a very stable majority (about 60 percent) feeling service cuts had been made in the "wrong places." They complained especially about cuts in the schools and in police and fire departments. Few (about 15 percent) felt they had been made in the right places.

10. Fully 49 percent gave an unqualified affirmative response, another 4 percent specified that they were willing to suffer a small increase in taxes, and 20 percent said they would pay more if they could designate what programs it would be used for.

11. These data are from California Polls 7803, 7807, and 7902.

12. Specifically, in a February 1978 survey, support for Proposition 13 fell by 13 percent after these tradeoffs were made salient; in three surveys that spring, support for the legislature's "safe and sane" alternative, Proposition 8, rose by 24 percent, 20 percent, and 11 percent; and in 1980, support for Jarvis II fell by 18 percent. These data come from California Polls 7802, 7804–06, and 8001.

13. R. Rose, "The Makings of a Do-It-Yourself Tax Revolt," *Public Opinion*, 3, no. 4 (1980):13–18. This is not an isolated finding when taxes and services are pitted against each other explicitly. A 1980 NORC survey asked, "Some people think the government should provide fewer services, even in areas such as health and education, in order to reduce spending. Other people feel it is important for the government to consider the services it now provides, even if it means no reduction in spending." By 43 percent to 31 percent, respondents wanted to continue services. See *Public Opinion*, 3, no. 5 (1980):24. The 1973 survey conducted by Katz and others yields the same finding: asked "Should government do less, if it means lower taxes," 65 percent said no, 35 percent said yes. D. Katz, B. Gutek, R. L. Kahn, and E. Barton, *Bureaucratic Encounters: A Pilot Study in the Evaluation of Government Services* (Ann Arbor: Institute for Social Research, University of Michigan, 1975), p. 138.

14. These data come from "Opinion Roundup," in *Public Opinion*, 1, no. 2 (1978):21–40, and the January 1981 CBS/*New York Times* Poll.

15. Some later elections have offered simpler tradeoffs. As indicated in Chapter 2, in the November 1980 elections, California voters approved only fourteen of fifty-four local proposals that would have required higher property taxes to fund additional police, fire, or paramedical services (see *Newsweek*, 6/15/81). However, across the nation, ballot propositions reducing property taxes passed in only one (Massachusetts) of eight states. As we will see in Chapter 6, the property tax was a particularly sore point for Californians, and remains a point of considerable sensitivity if no longer quite so painful.

16. Again the level of perceived waste could logically explain the inconsistencies, but again it turns out not to. It could be that people would be willing to accept the same or added taxation only if they perceived government as free of waste. Those who feel that government is very wasteful, however, might want it to clean up its act before asking for any more money from taxpayers. But in fact people made almost exactly the same tradeoffs no matter what their perceptions of waste. More perceived waste decreased their willingness to absorb higher taxes, or increased their desire for tax rebates, by a trivial 3 percent in each case. Nor does this effect of perceived waste get any more impressive when value priorities about the size of government are taken into account. One might think that willingness to pay more taxes or willingness to forgo tax rebates for larger government would be especially dependent on perceiving "clean" government for those who want government to provide a lot of service. But no such interactions occur (the effect of perceived waste on tradeoff decisions only increases to 6 percent among those who want net service increases).

17. One possible caveat is that these tradeoff items asked the respondent to trade taxes off against the *specific* services he or she wanted changed, not against the public sector in general. However, other analyses show that this distinction is unimportant—the tradeoffs are made in exactly the same service-protecting way even by the anti-public-sector respondents, no matter whether they are identified by their support of specific service cuts or of "smaller government" in general.

18. C. E. Osgood and P. Tannenbaum, "The Principle of Congruity and the Prediction of Attitude Change," *Psychological Review*, 62 (1955):42–55. N. H. Anderson, "Information Integration Theory: A Brief Summary" (manuscript, University of California, San Diego, 1972).

19. Katz, et al., *Bureaucratic Encounters*.

20. Ibid.

21. Ibid., p. 178.

22. This is analogous to the argument often made by social psychologists that specific behaviors are "real" while general attitudes may not be, and therefore are often inconsistent with them. See R. T. LaPiere, "Attitudes versus Actions," *Social Forces*, 13 (1934):230–237; A. W. Wicker, "Attitudes versus Action: The Relationship of Verbal and Overt Behavior Responses to Attitude Objects," *Journal of Social Issues*, 25, no. 4 (1969):41–78.

23. See, inter alia, R. E. Lane, "The Politics of Consensus in an Age of Affluence," *American Political Science Review*, 59 (1965):874–895.

24. J. Citrin, "Comment: The Political Relevance of Trust in Government," *American Political Science Review*, 68, no. 3 (1974):973–988; D. O. Sears, "The Person-Positivity Bias" (manuscript, University of California, Los Angeles, 1981).

25. D. O. Sears and J. B. McConahay, *The Politics of Violence: The New Urban Blacks and the Watts Riot* (Boston: Houghton-Mifflin, 1973).

26. This might seem contrary to our general point, since the public most enthusiastically supports spending on safety services. But it should be remembered that the Katz comparison is not parallel. The gratitude of a welfare-check recipient should not be compared with the anger of someone given a ticket for going through a red light. It should be compared, instead, with the gratitude of an onlooking law-abiding citizen who wants to be protected from such cowboys of the highway.

27. S. E. Asch, "Studies in the Principles of Judgments and Attitudes: II. Determination of Judgments by Group and Ego Standards," *Journal of Social Psychology*, 12 (1940):433–465; Sears, "The Person-Positivity Bias."

28. Though we might note a growing literature asserting a stronger relationship between attitudes and behavior when the former are based in direct experience. See R.

H. Fazio and M. P. Zanna, "Attitudinal Qualities Relating to the Strength of the Attitude-Behavior Relationship," *Journal of Experimental Social Psychology*, 14 (1978):398-408.

4. The Vote and the Tax Revolt Schema

1. For one thing, the rules of psychological implication are different from the rules of logical implication. See R. P. Abelson, "Psychological Implication," in *Theories of Cognitive Consistency: A Sourcebook*, ed. R. P. Abelson, E. Aronson, W. J. McGuire, T. M. Newcomb, M. J. Rosenberg, and P. H. Tannenbaum (Chicago: Rand McNally, 1968).

2. P. E. Converse, "Public Opinion and Voting Behavior," in *Handbook of Political Science*, vol. 4, ed. F. I. Greenstein and N. W. Polsby (Reading, Mass.: Addison-Wesley, 1975), pp. 75-170. D. O. Sears, "Political Behavior," in *Handbook of Social Psychology*, 2nd ed., vol. 5, ed. G. Lindzey and E. Aronson (Reading, Mass.: Addison-Wesley, 1969), pp. 315-458.

3. One cautionary note: our analysis relies mainly on the Tax Revolt Survey, which somewhat overestimated support for these propositions. Like most postelection surveys, it somewhat overestimated voters' recalled support for winning propositions (by 6 percent and 8 percent, respectively, for Propositions 13 and 4, excluding voters who could not remember how they had voted). And it was conducted at an early, rather sympathetic point for Jarvis II, and thus overestimated its final support by 14 percent. These differences are not of a magnitude to distort our findings significantly. But it should be borne in mind that the support for the tax revolt we describe is a little "softer" than the opposition, relative to actual voting behavior — a bias that fortunately works against rather than in favor of one of our main conclusions, which is that the tax rebels were politically firmer, as well as more numerous, than the public-sector defenders.

4. By this index, 30 percent supported all three propositions; another 12 percent supported two but had no opinion on the third; yet another 19 percent fell on the pro-revolt side of neutral but were less committed. This yields the 61 percent we describe as "tax rebels" in the analyses to follow. In contrast, only 15 percent opposed all three or opposed two but had no opinion on the third.

5. S. T. Fiske and P. W. Linville, "What Does the Schema Concept Buy Us?," *Personality and Social Psychology Bulletin*, 6 (1980):543-557; S. E. Taylor and J. Crocker, "Schematic Bases of Social Information Processing," in *Social Cognition: The Ontario Symposium*, vol. 1, ed. E. T. Higgins, C. P. Herman, and M. P. Zanna (Hillsdale, N.J.: Lawrence Erlbaum, 1981).

6. In this sense our use of schema treats it as an extension of the consistency theory literature; for example, *Theories of Cognitive Consistency: A Sourcebook*, ed. Abelson et al. Those were generally called "cognitive consistency" theories, in our view quite incorrectly, since all were concerned with reconciling affective inconsistencies rather than with cognitive process: for example, inconsistencies between valences placed upon source and advocated position (congruity theory), or upon another person and some third entity (balance theory), or between one's own real underlying attitude and the overt expression of it (dissonance theory). Hence we do not regard this extension to more highly affective contents as discontinuous or distorting, rather as a small corrective to the tendency for laboratory psychologists working with college student subjects to characterize human behavior in general as more cognitive than it really is. Also see R. B. Zajonc, "Feeling and Thinking: Preferences Need No In-

ferences" *American Psychologist*, 35 (1980):151–175.

7. P. E. Converse, "The Nature of Belief Systems in Mass Publics," in *Ideology and Discontent*, ed. D. E. Apter (New York: Free Press of Glencoe, 1964) pp. 206–261; Sears, "Political Behavior"; J. E. Mueller, *War, Presidents, and Public Opinion* (New York: John Wiley and Sons, 1973).

8. For example, see the 1976 CPS/NES study.

9. All of this is well established in social psychology generally, and in work on consistency theories and schemas in particular. See, for example, Abelson et al., eds., *Theories of Cognitive Consistency: A Sourcebook*; J. L. Freedman, D. O. Sears, and J. M. Carlsmith, *Social Psychology*, 4th ed. (Englewood Cliffs, N.J.: Prentice-Hall, 1981); Taylor and Crocker, "Schematic Bases of Social Information Processing."

10. See D. O. Sears and M. T. Gahart, "Stability of Racial Prejudice and Other Symbolic Attitudes" (paper presented at the annual meeting of the American Psychological Association, Montreal, 1980); D. O. Sears and J. B. McConahay, *The Politics of Violence: The New Urban Blacks and the Watts Riot* (Boston: Houghton-Mifflin, 1973); P. Converse, "Public Opinion and Voting Behavior"; Sears, "Political Behavior."

11. Converse, "The Nature of Belief Systems in Mass Publics."

12. Gammas are more appropriate for the latter relationships because all cells have substantial numbers of cases. But the choice of statistic does not affect the outcome: the average correlation among the propositions was higher than that among elements of the tax revolt schema whether gamma (.60 to .34) or Pearson (.36 to .22) was used.

13. E.g., N. H. Anderson, "Information Integration Theory as Applied to Attitudes about U. S. Presidents," *Journal of Educational Psychology*, 64 (1973):1–8.

14. Similarly, among college graduates the median intercorrelation is .33, whereas among those with no college education at all it is .19. This is evidence of more schematic thinking among the college educated, though the difference is of modest scope. Interestingly, and perhaps counterintuitively, the anti-government theme seems to have been more dominant among the best educated, while value priorities were the stronger organizing principle for the less educated. When the varimax rotations were repeated for persons high and low in education, the first factor was more clearly the anti-government factor for the college educated, and the value-priorities factor for the less educated (loadings averaged .30 and .31 higher, respectively). In both cases "tax rebel" loaded by far the most heavily on the first factor.

15. These three separate factors are very unlikely to reflect more method variance, since the items used to measure the six input dimensions were all quite different in format and wording.

16. Obviously, the size of the blocs derived by thus classifying voters depends on the nature of the particular ballot measures. Crossclassifying votes made on a series of mild proposals would produce a much larger group of seemingly committed tax rebels than if radical measures that threatened drastic and immediate changes in the fiscal status quo were also included in the set.

17. The tax rebels retain a substantial numerical advantage after adjustment to account for the fact that approval of Proposition 9 in the Tax Revolt Survey surpassed the proportion of votes it ultimately received. Even on the extreme assumption that the excess support was located entirely among the tax rebels and should be moved into the "enough is enough" group, we are left with 38 percent (of those respondents who had definite opinions on all three measures) as consistently in favor of the tax revolt.

18. One shortcoming of this empirical test is that the variance on the other dimen-

sions of the tax revolt schema is severely constricted within these two extreme groups on the tax rebel index. This should bias the correlations among these other dimensions (and their factor loadings), usually underestimating them. Hence we developed an index of variability of each respondent's attitudes across the several dimensions of the tax revolt schema. To take into account the gross differences across dimensions in type of scale, we used standardized scores. So this new "tax revolt consistency" index equaled the variance across the respondent's standardized scores for the several dimensions of the tax revolt schema. Parallel techniques have been developed independently by A. H. Barton and R. W. Parsons, "Measuring Belief System Structure," *Public Opinion Quarterly*, 41 (1977):159–180, and M. L. Wyckoff, "Belief System Constraint and Policy Voting: A Test of the Unidimensional Consistency Model," *Political Behavior*, 2 (1980):115–146.

Since we wanted to compare supporters and opponents of the tax revolt, we excluded the tax rebel index; and since we wanted to use this index to test the effects of self-interest, or personal impact, on schematic thinking in Chapter 6, we excluded the taxation item also. To validate that the index did pick up differences in schematic thinking, we first tested for difference between college-educated respondents and those who had no college background. It was huge; the mean score was almost half again as large in the latter group, where large scores reflect inconsistency and thus less schematic thinking. However, variability within educational groups was also large, so the difference was barely statistically significant (F = 4.88; 1, 1275df; p © .03). Then we obtained similar consistency scores for the four quartiles on our tax rebel scale. Indeed the strongest tax rebels showed the highest consistency, but the differences were quite small, and not statistically significant. Hence this may have some promise as a technique for measuring schematic thinking, or the level of structure in an individual's belief system, but it seems to have been insensitive in our data. It probably would be more reliable were the component dimensions measured on more comparable scales.

19. By way of comparison, in the 1976 presidential campaign only about a third of the public talked to or were talked to by someone about whom to vote for, and 21 percent had signed a petition for or against any action by local government in the previous two or three years, according to the National Election Studies.

20. It must be noted that the data we report were collected before the effective campaign against Jarvis II mounted by public employees got under way.

21. These are actually weighted rather than simple averaging theories; the valences placed on different symbols may be weighted somewhat differently when they are combined. See C. E. Osgood and P. Tannenbaum, "The Principle of Congruity and the Prediction of Attitude Change," *Psychological Review*, 62 (1955):42–55; Anderson, "Information Integration Theory: A Brief Summary." The usual finding is that heavier weights are given to more extreme affects, and to negative ones. Our data are not refined enough to permit these added fillips.

22. S. M. Lipset and E. Raab, *The Politics of Unreason*, 2nd ed. (Chicago: University of Chicago Press, 1978). P. E. Converse, W. E. Miller, J. G. Rusk, and A. C. Wolfe, "Continuity and Change in American Politics: Parties and Issues in the 1968 Election," *American Political Science Review*, 63 (1969):1083–1105.

23. J. E. Mueller, "Voting on the Propositions: Ballot Patterns and Historical Trends in California," *American Political Science Review*, 63 (1969):1197–1212.

24. D. E. Stokes and G. R. Iverson, "On the Existence of Forces Restoring Party Competition," *Public Opinion Quarterly*, 26 (1962):159–171.

25. P. E. Converse, A. R. Clausen, and W. E. Miller, "Electoral Myth and Reality: The 1964 Election," *American Political Science Review*, 59 (1965):321–336.

5. The Social Base

1. For the notion of a "middle mass" and its consequences, see H. L. Wilensky, *The Welfare State and Equality* (Berkeley: University of California Press, 1975); and for the "public-regarding" affluent, see J. Q. Wilson and E. C. Banfield, *City Politics* (Cambridge, Mass.: Harvard University Press, 1963).

2. These parallels between the May 1978 California Poll data and the recalled-vote data from the Tax Revolt Survey reassure us somewhat about the validity of the latter. For example, when income and education are cross-tabulated on these two measures, the median difference in support for Proposition 13 is only 5 percent (over nineteen cells); the mean is 8 percent.

3. This was tested simply by crosstabulating income and education by support for Proposition 13 in the four surveys shown in table 5.1, and by "tax rebel." The mean value of tax-revolt support across the six middle-mass cells (education at least high school graduate but no college degree, income $11,000–$25,000) was then compared to each sample-wide value. The differences were 0, +1 percent, 0, −3 percent, and +2 percent for the five comparisons. Raising the income threshold for the middle mass makes it consistently more pro-revolt than the full samples (the difference ranges from +3 percent to +5 percent), but this is because of greater support among higher-income people, not a middle-mass phenomenon, and anyway the differences remain small.

4. M. P. Rogin and J. L. Shover, *Political Change in California: Critical Elections and Social Movements, 1890–1966* (Westport, Conn.: Greenwood, 1970); and R. E. Wolfinger and F. I. Greenstein, "The Political Regions of California," *American Political Science Review*, 63 (1969):73–85.

5. Nor does race account for the income effect. When whites only are considered, support for the tax revolt among those earning less than $10,000 increases just slightly, from 52 percent to 56 percent.

6. The zeal among the college-educated for smaller government and for cutting services holds up with income controlled. For example, the well-educated affluent were by far the most interested in cutting government services: 80 percent of those with college degrees and incomes over $25,000 wanted less government. Moreover the tendency for the college-educated to be *more* liberal in younger generations, found by Angus Campbell in *White Attitudes toward Black People* (Ann Arbor: Institute for Social Research, University of Michigan, 1971) regarding racial prejudice, and by Ronald Inglehart in "The Silent Revolution in Europe: Intergenerational Change in Post-Industrial Societies," *American Political Science Review*, 65 (Dec. 1971):991–1017 regarding lifestyle issues, has no parallel here. Within each age-group, more education is associated with wanting less government. Additional evidence against the middle-mass hypothesis is the fact that the middle mass was almost identical to the sample as a whole in this respect: 67 percent of the middle mass and 68 percent of the sample as a whole wanted less as opposed to more government (see note 3 for our definition of the middle mass).

7. This literature is usefully reviewed by R. E. Lane, *Political Life* (New York: Free Press of Glencoe, 1959) and by L. W. Milbrath and M. L. Goel, *Political Participation* (Chicago: Rand McNally, 1977). The best recent studies are: of voting frequency, R. E. Wolfinger and S. J. Rosenstone, *Who Votes?* (New Haven: Yale University Press, 1980), and of other forms of participation, S. Verba and N. H. Nie, *Participation in America: Political Democracy and Social Equality* (New York: Harper and Row, 1972).

8. The elderly generally do not slip much in participation, and actually increase

somewhat in voting turnout, aside from these incidental correlates of age. To test this, we treated age up to 65 as one variable, and then added a dummy variable for being over 65. Both influenced voting frequency, as shown in table 5.3, proving that it actually kept rising after retirement age, with other demographic factors considered. Age increased activism in general up to retirement age, when it leveled off.

9. This is not an unusual result. Wolfinger and Rosenstone (*Who Votes?*), in their careful study, found that voters in national elections do not differ very much from nonvoters in party identification or in the liberalism of their issue positions, despite the clear differences in demographic status.

6. The Pro-Revolt Interests

1. P. E. Converse, "The Nature of Belief Systems in Mass Publics," in *Ideology and Discontent*, ed. D. E. Apter (New York: Free Press of Glencoe, 1964) pp. 206–261.

2. R. R. Lau, T. A. Brown, and D. O. Sears, "Self-Interest and Civilians' Attitudes toward the War in Vietnam," *Public Opinion Quarterly*, 42 (1978); D. O. Sears, R. R. Lau, T. R. Tyler, and H. M. Allen, Jr., "Self-Interest vs. Symbolic Politics in Policy Attitudes and Presidential Voting," *American Political Science Review*, 74 (1980):670–684.

3. These are the same demographics as those discussed in the previous chapter: income, education, race, age, sex, and region. They increase the R^2 for vote frequency to .289, and for tax activism, to .174; but for the tax rebel index, only to .157, and for service spending, to .133.

4. ACIR; R. Rose, "The Makings of a Do-It-Yourself Tax Revolt," *Public Opinion*, 3, no. 4 (1980):13–18.

5. The *San Francisco Chronicle*, May 22, 1978; S. J. DeCanio, "Proposition 13 and the Failure of Economic Politics," *National Tax Journal*, 32 (June 1978).

6. Southern California was a special case, because the housing inflation there had hit most intensely. Some estimates based on regular home appraisals done for the real estate industry make the point. Home prices in Southern California had been close to the national average in 1974, but mid-1978 they were almost 50 percent higher, and were over 200 percent of that earlier price. At the time of Proposition 13, the average home price in Southern California was $83,200. Without Proposition 13, the tax rate on this home would have remained at about 2.6 percent, yielding a tax of $2163. But its assessed value would have kept on rapidly inflating. By October 1978 it would have been worth $91,500, which at the old tax rate would have yielded an obligation of $2379. By contrast, Proposition 13, by cutting the rate to 1 percent, would have reduced the tax to $832, then by limiting the rise of its assessed value, would have contained it at that level, and then, if the home had been purchased before mid-1975 (as most had been), would have rolled back its assessed value to the 1975 level, which would have been $43,600. The tax on that would have been about $436 (ignoring some other minor clauses in Proposition 13 which generally had a small impact; see Chapter 2). In other words, for the average home in the seven-county Southern California area, Proposition 13 cut the 1978 tax bill from $2379 to $436, or $1943. Since these estimates of home prices are based on appraisals done for the real estate industry, they are probably a little higher than assessed value as ascertained by county tax assessors, but they are close; see the *Los Angeles Times*, May 24, 1981, pt. VIII, p. 16.

7. Indeed in Chapter 3 we saw that subjective property tax burden already, by November 1979, was being affected by this factor. Its potential magnitude may be shown as follows. The average home price in Southern California rose from $43,600 to

$129,900 from 1975 to 1981 (see note 6). The long-time owner of a typical tract home might then pay about $450 in property taxes, while his new neighbor would pay about $1300 on its identical twin.

8. However, the owner-renter difference in current support for Proposition 13 (that is, at the time of our survey) was somewhat more closely based on their differential incomes; controlling income reduces the owner-renter difference from 20 percent to 13 percent, on the average. As the independent effect of homeownership declined, that of income increased. Hence with homeownership controlled, income has no residual effect (less than 1 percent) on recalled vote for Proposition 13, but it retains a large effect on current opinion about 13 (an average difference of 16 percent between those earning under $15,000 and those earning over $25,000).

9. Among those who felt they paid "much more" than they should, 74 percent supported Jarvis II; 53 percent supported it among those feeling their property taxes were no worse than "about right." But only 15 percent of the sample felt they paid "much more."

10. In our survey, homeownership yielded an average 11 percent increase in support for Jarvis II with income controlled, though in the last pre-election California Poll, in May 1980, this had dropped to 4 percent.

11. An obvious hazard in our use of subjective indicators of tax burden as predictors of support for the tax revolt should be acknowledged here. Expressing the feeling of paying much more in taxes than one should, or even claiming to expect a very large dollar return from tax cuts, could simply be a rationalization for supporting tax-cutting propositions: "Why am I for Proposition 13? Well, because my property taxes are too high" sounds better than "Why . . .? Well, I dunno, because my buddy is, I guess." To the extent that this is true, we err in placing tax burden causally prior to support for the tax revolt. Presumably the dollar estimates shown in table 6.2, being more concrete, are somewhat less subject to this ambiguity, and homeownership, being a factual matter, is subject to it very little. Thus to the extent that the results are the same across these three sets of indicators, our treatment of them would seem to be justifiable. If subjective tax burden had much stronger effects than did homeownership, the rationalization possibility would seem to be more plausible. But in fact most of the findings are parallel, as can be seen in table 6.1. For a discussion of some of these problems, and an experimental test on them, see D. O. Sears and R. R. Lau, "Inducing Apparently Self-Interested Political Preferences: An Experiment" (manuscript, University of California, Los Angeles, 1981).

12. This estimate of $40,000 uses the 1980 tax tables, and assumes nonitemized deductions. Indeed, only 22 percent reported the $30,000 or more annual income that would be required to generate $1000 in state income tax liability, and hence a potential savings of even a new color TV. Since the demographic profile of "the taxpayers" closely resembles that of the "tax rebels," possible confounds are important. Property taxpayers, relative to renters, tend to be more white, middle-aged (especially 50–64), and high-income. Those aggrieved about income taxes have a similar demographic profile though less distinctively so. But these self-interest effects on support for the tax revolt were not artifacts of these demographic correlates. Adding the demographic variables to the first regression equation shown in table 6.1 scarcely alters the effects of self-interest at all, though the multiple correlation increases from .34 to .40. So the self-interested support for the tax revolt among "the taxpayers" stands as an unambiguous finding of this chapter.

13. The b-weights for the tax burden fell from .42 to .23, while those for homeownership fell only from .67 to .43. We also tested the effects of self-interest on the tax revolt consistency index (see note 18, Chapter 4), which measures the variance of the re-

spondents' attitudes across the several dimensions of the tax revolt schema. The results are about the same: homeowners and the tax-burdened did not show significantly more consistent attitudes than their more disinterested counterparts (indeed, they were actually a little less consistent).

14. By themselves, the self-interest terms collectively account for 11.6 percent of the variance in vote frequency and 7.4 percent in tax activism. But the demographics contribute 29.0 and 15.6 percent, respectively, and adding the self-interest variables to the equation only increases this to 31.4 and 18.5 percent, respectively, meaning that self-interest adds less than 13 percent in each case. The betas for homeownership and subjective tax burden range from .02 to .10 with the demographics included.

15. Of course in California the property tax is a county and city tax, not a state tax. But in a pre-election California Poll (7803), the proportion who thought Proposition 13 was a "good idea" rose almost as much among those aggrieved by state taxes (37 percent among those who felt they were "about right"; 60 percent among those who felt they were "much too high") as among those aggrieved by county and city taxes (29 percent to 64 percent).

16. See note 11 for another way to make the same point. If subjective tax burden were just a rationalization for supporting the tax revolt, it would, in these terms, have symbolic meaning rather than reflecting dollars-and-cents concerns.

17. The retrospective voting hypothesis is most clearly laid out by G. H. Kramer, "Short-Term Fluctuations in U.S. Voting Behavior, 1896–1964," *American Political Science Review*, 65 (1971):131–143; E. R. Tufte, *Political Control of the Economy* (Princeton, Princeton University Press, 1978); and M. P. Fiorina, *Retrospective Voting in American National Elections* (New Haven: Yale University Press, 1981). In earlier eras, the same idea cropped up in findings that incumbents in agricultural areas suffered electoral losses in drought years and that southern blacks were more likely to be lynched when cotton prices fell in the single-crop Deep South. For a useful review of this literature, see K. R. Monroe, "Econometric Analysis of Electoral Behavior: A Critical Review," *Political Behavior*, 1 (1979):137–176. The classic study of lynching and cotton prices is by C. I. Hovland and R. R. Sears, "Minor Studies of Aggression: Correlation of Lynchings with Economic Indices," *Journal of Psychology*, 9 (1940): 301–310.

18. See B. I. Page, "Elections and Social Choice: The State of the Evidence," *American Journal of Political Science*, 21 (1977):639–668; and M. Fishbein and I. Ajzen, *Belief, Attitude, Intention, and Behavior* (Reading, Mass.: Addison-Wesley, 1975) for useful reviews of this idea, though from quite different traditions.

19. See, inter alia, Monroe, "Econometric Analysis," and such more recent studies as Fiorina, *Retrospective Voting*; D. R. Kiewiet, "Policy-Oriented Voting in Response to Economic Issues," *American Political Science Review*, 75 (1981):448–459; D. R. Kinder, "Presidents, Prosperity, and Public Opinion," *Public Opinion Quarterly*, 45 (1981):1–21; J. H. Kuklinski and D. M. West, "Economic Expectations and Voting Behavior in United States House and Senate Elections," *American Political Science Review*, 75 (1981):436–447; and Sears and Lau, "Inducing Apparently Self-Interested Political Preferences."

20. The California data come from the Tax Revolt Survey and California Polls 7801, 7902, 7904, and 8003. See Kiewiet, "Policy-Oriented Voting," for national over-time data.

21. R. Kuttner, *The Revolt of the Haves* (New York: Simon and Schuster, 1980).

22. In general, the results here for the individual propositions are very similar to those for the tax rebel index. The one exception seems to be a modest (9 percent) association between current support for Proposition 13 and feeling one's finances had *im-*

proved; and as we have seen, for most homeowners that was no doubt true.

23. These analyses used California Polls 7904, 8001, and 8003. Because of the importance in many social theories of the role of inflation in producing political upheavals, we gave this interaction hypothesis even more extensive tests. Separate regressions were run of the self-interest variables on the tax rebel scale for people who mentioned inflation as a major problem and for those who did not. The only major difference (that is, where the unstandardized regression coefficient was more than twice its standard error) was in an increased negative effect of past employment problems. Also, the bivariate relationships of homeownership and tax burden to support for each of the propositions were assessed for people who mentioned inflation as the most important problem or who felt especially hurt by it, as opposed to those less concerned about it. No shred of evidence any stronger than that presented in the text turned up.

7. The Anti-Revolt Interests

1. Tax Revolt Survey; California Poll 7904.

2. These data are from California Polls 7807, 8001, 8004, and 8005. The next most frequently mentioned were libraries and the police, at 14 percent each.

3. These data are from California Polls 7807, 7901, 7904, 8001, and 8005. It might be tempting to interpret these responses as reflecting the self-interested grievances of parents of public school children, since the number of parents (a little under 30 percent of the adult public) so closely resembles the number of people aggrieved about the tax revolt's impact on the schools, by these various indicators (usually a little over 30 percent). But, as will be seen, the similar sizes of these two groups is mere coincidence; parents and nonparents differed very little in their responses to these questions.

4. And 5 percent received three or more, while 46 percent received at least one. These figures reflect the 17 percent receiving unemployment compensation, 18 percent on a state or local government pension, 12 percent receiving direct public assistance, and 30 percent receiving public financial aid for medical costs. But even this actually overestimates dependency on state or local government somewhat in that the most common form of assistance in our survey is for medical care. Much of this is handled by the federal government, and our item did not screen that out – unlike the other programs, which were described specifically as state or local.

5. While perceptions that the tax revolt would cut government were quite widespread, as we shall see in Chapter 9, the public generally believed neither the doomsday forecasts of massive recession put forward by the public sector nor the Jarvisites' contentions that it would stimulate the economy. Only 13 percent thought the Gann amendment would help economic growth and development in California (and 9 percent that it would slow it), and only 21 percent thought it "very" likely that Jarvis II would stimulate growth. See the Tax Revolt Survey and California Poll 8001.

6. Parents of public school children voted against Proposition 13 only 1 percent less than nonparents, supported it in August 1978 by 2 percent less and in November 1979 by 1 percent more, and supported Jarvis II by 2 percent less (Tax Revolt Survey and California Polls 7807 and 7904).

7. Forty-two percent of the enrollees were opposed to Jarvis II, compared to 30 percent of the rest of the sample. One caution is that this poll was conducted four months before the election, so the campaign had not really gotten heated up yet. Self-interest might have had a greater yield later, though of course in this case we are talking about the presumably best educated, most perceptive, and most forward-looking citizens of the state.

8. These three groups did not overlap very much: only one respondent (of 1788)

met all three criteria, and only 38 (2 percent of the sample) met at least two. But if we included anybody who met *just one* of these criteria, the distressed group is enlarged to 17 percent of the sample, of whom 52 percent were tax rebels, not dramatically below the sample-wide level of 61 percent.

9. See R. Kuttner, *The Revolt of the Haves* (New York: Simon and Schuster, 1980). Nevertheless, in the period of the tax revolt there is little evidence of severe erosion in the constituency for public education. The number of people with children in the public schools dropped considerably, especially among homeowners. But support for school spending remained intact, as shown in table 3.2.

10. Though the hostility toward the symbol "welfare" is so widespread in American society that the PDI value for welfare is − 8 percent even among those on some public assistance program; even welfare recipients, on balance, want to cut welfare.

11. With one exception. Parents of public school children did not differ from nonparents in support of Proposition 13, but were more supportive of spending on the public schools, as we have seen. We therefore thought that some self-interest effect might emerge if this difference in spending preferences were taken into account; specifically, the preferences about school spending might have more leverage over attitudes toward Proposition 13 for parents than for nonparents, for whom the issue presumably was more peripheral. It did, but only slightly. The difference in support for Proposition 13 between those wanting increased and those wanting decreased spending on schools was only slightly (11 percent) greater among parents than among nonparents. This indicates limited cognitive effects even of this narrow version of self-interest.

12. R. R. Lau and D. O. Sears, "Cognitive Links between Economic Grievances and Political Responses," *Political Behavior*, 4 (1982): in press.

13. The question elicits somewhat different answers depending on how it is put. In three surveys, 9 percent, 8 percent, and 10 percent of the respondents themselves worked for "state or local government," and in another survey 12 percent worked for "federal, state, or local government" (Tax Revolt Survey and California Polls 8001, 8002, 7807). The "household" contained a government worker in 18 percent and 17 percent of the cases (8001 and 8002), while the "immediate family" did in 24 percent of the cases (Tax Revolt Survey).

14. ‚For tax rebel, the b for the public employee term falls from .56 to .52; for vote frequency, from .18 to .15, and for tax activism, from .13 to .10 when the demographic variables are included.

15. R. E. Wolfinger and S. J. Rosenstone, *Who Votes?* (New Haven: Yale University Press, 1980).

16. All these findings hold even with the public employees' relatively favored demographic status considered. The public-employee effects on the elements of the tax revolt schema — no impact on value priorities, a weak one on perceptions of waste, and a strong one on "overpaid government workers" — are utterly unchanged with demographics considered.

17. In the face of all these negative results, it is surprising that this is the one place the "tax revolt consistency" index does show a difference; public employees showed significantly less variance across the elements of the tax revolt schema than did other respondents (F = 6.02, 1/1714 df, p © .02). See note 18 in Chapter 4 for a description of this index.

18. M. Ross and F. Sicoly, "Egocentric Biases in Availability and Attribution," *Journal of Personality and Social Psychology*, 37 (1979):322–336; and J. L. Freedman, D. O. Sears, and J. M. Carlsmith, *Social Psychology*, 4th ed. (Englewood Cliffs, N.J.: Prentice-Hall, 1981).

19. Kuttner, *Revolt of the Haves.*

8. Symbolic Predispositions

1. A. Campbell, P. E. Converse, W. E. Miller, and D. E. Stokes, *The American Voter* (New York: Wiley, 1960); W. E. Miller and T. E. Levitan, *Leadership and Change: Presidential Elections from 1952–1976* (Cambridge, Mass.: Winthrop, 1976).

2. D. O. Sears and J. B. McConahay, *The Politics of Violence: The New Urban Blacks and the Watts Riot* (Boston: Houghton Mifflin, 1973); D. R. Kinder and D. O. Sears, "Prejudice and Politics: Symbolic Racism versus Racial Threats to the Good Life," *Journal of Personality and Social Psychology*, 40 (1981):414–431; J. B. McConahay and J. C. Hough, Jr., "Symbolic Racism," *Journal of Social Issues*, 32, no. 2 (1976):23–45; D. O. Sears, C. P. Hensler, and L. K. Speer, "Whites' Opposition to 'Busing': Self-Interest or Symbolic Politics," *American Political Science Review*, 73 (1979):369–384.

3. For the recent political impact of race and racism in California, see the studies cited in note 2; also, R. E. Wolfinger and F. I. Greenstein, "The Repeal of Fair Housing in California: An Analysis of Referendum Voting," *American Political Science Review*, 62 (1968):753–769.

4. J. Citrin, "Political Alienation as a Social Indicator: Attitudes and Action," *Social Indicators Research*, 4 (1977):381–419.

5. The two items are correlated but far from perfectly (r = .31). Only 5 percent describe themselves as liberal Republicans. The other residual groups are also small: moderate Democrats or liberal Independents (7 percent), moderate Independents (2 percent), moderate Republicans or conservative Independents (7 percent). All this classifies "leaning Independents" into the party they prefer, based on much evidence that many of them are in fact closet partisans. And it excludes the 3 percent who refused to classify themselves.

6. The surveys referred to are the Tax Revolt Survey, and California Polls done just before and after the passage of Proposition 13 (7806 and 7807) and in the middle of the campaign for Jarvis II (8002 and 8003). One other exception: in the May California Poll (7806), the ideology effect was much larger than in the other surveys (31 percent) probably because the sample included only registered voters likely to vote, which is a more ideological crowd than is the public as a whole.

7. Since this second, aid-to-minorities, item also measured strength of agreement or disagreement, and the busing item took into account whether or not the respondent had actually voted, adding these two four-point items together yielded a seven-point scale, with 47 percent of the full sample on the anti-minority side of the midpoint, and 27 percent on the pro-minority side. The main empirical justifications for describing this scale as measuring symbolic racism are contained in other reports; see especially McConahay and Hough, "Symbolic Racism"; Sears et al., "Whites' Opposition to 'Busing' "; Kinder and Sears, "Prejudice and Politics." Basically, the argument is that attitudes toward matters of current racial policy, such as opposition to busing or affirmative action, are a joint function of racial prejudice as expressed more generally regarding a wide variety of racial issues, and of general political conservatism. They are not demonstrably tied to any personal consequences such policies have had or might have had for white respondents.

8. The beta for symbolic racism drops from .23 to .20, while the R^2 increases only from 13.0 percent to 15.7 percent. When column 2 of table 8.2 is run for whites only, the results are almost identical; the beta for symbolic racism is .23, and the R^2 is 12.8.

9. Comparisons of table 5.3 (column 1), with table 8.1 (columns 3 and 4) shows that the racial difference in support for the tax revolt is due mostly to symbolic predispositions, and to a lesser extent to racial differences in value priorities more specifically.

10. Homeownership had a significant but modest effect upon each predisposition (betas of .07, .08, and .13), but with the demographics entered, it remained significant only on ideology (beta of .06). Tax burden also had significant effects on ideology and symbolic racism which remained significant with demographics considered (betas of .07 and .13). Our indices of economic malaise, public-sector employment, and service recipience were almost completely unrelated to these predispositions: only 3 relationships of 21 were significant, and 2 of these dropped out with demographics controlled. These weak relationships parallel those found between self-interest and these symbolic predispositions in several other studies. See Sears et al., "Whites' Opposition to 'Busing' "; D. O. Sears, R. R. Lau, T. R. Tyler, and H. M. Allen, Jr., "Self-Interest vs. Symbolic Politics in Policy Attitudes and Presidential Voting," *American Political Science Review*, 74 (1980):670–684.

11. When the two separate service-recipient items are replaced with the two composite variables – the government assistance scale and the employment index – the self-interest relationships are almost all statistically significant, presumably because of greater reliability and more balanced distributions, but in general remain quite weak. The pooled R^2 contributed by self-interest when it is indexed by the composite variables rather than the individual items is actually smaller, averaging 2.7 percent rather than 3.5 percent.

12. These differences cannot be attributed to educational level, since the two groups were almost equal in education: 25 percent of the strong ideologues were college graduates, against 23 percent of the others. In this context, as in Chapters 4 and 6, the tax revolt consistency index, of variance within respondents across items of the tax revolt schema, proved less sensitive than other indicators. Extreme ideologues showed less variance but not significantly so ($F = 1.36$). However, the few people (6 percent) who volunteered that they were "neither" liberal nor conservative showed markedly less consistency in their attitudes – that is, about twice as much variance in their attitudes ($F = 6.90$; 4, 1969 df, p © .001).

We wanted also to test whether symbolic racism created more schematic thinking, as ideology had. But it would be inappropriate to compare extreme respondents on the symbolic racism scale with moderates, using techniques to assess schematic thinking that rely on affective consistency, since the extremes had already been preselected for high consistency – on the two items measuring racial attitudes. Should other attitudes held by such respondents also turn out to be especially consistent, it would only indicate that consistency goes with consistency, with only ambiguous implications for schematic thinking. So neither constraint nor factor analysis would be appropriate in this context.

13. For this literature, see J. Citrin, "Comment: The Political Relevance of Trust in Government," *American Political Science Review*, 68 (1974):973–988; D. Easton and J. Dennis, *Children in the Political System: Origins of Political Legitimacy* (New York: McGraw Hill, 1969); A. Miller, "Political Issues and Trust in Government: 1964–1970," *American Political Science Review*, 68 (1974):951–972.

14. Governor Brown's approval ratings had undergone some considerable changes over time. His initial popularity after he was elected in 1974 was extremely high. It was eroded somewhat by his opposition to Proposition 13, though it still stood at 54 percent approval and 39 percent disapproval in the last pre-election *Los Angeles Times* Poll in May 1978. Then it came roaring back following his post-13 change of heart, to the point that by August 45 percent felt he had done an "excellent" or "good" job, and

only 18 percent a "poor" or "very poor" job, regarding Proposition 13. His popularity then resumed its downward trek, as reflected in our survey results. Evaluations of the state legislature tended to be slightly on the positive side throughout the tax revolt period; for example, in the same May *Los Angeles Times* poll, 42 percent approved, and 40 percent disapproved, of its performance.

15. These results are very similar to national survey results taken in that period; in the 1978 Michigan National Election Study, 70 percent and 73 percent were negative on these two items, respectively.

16. The unique variance contributed by mistrust is computed here by subtracting the R^2 accounted for by the three value-priority predispositions, considered alone (12.6 percent; see table 8.1, column 2) from that accounted for by both categories considered together (13.1 percent; see table 8.2, column 1); the unique variance accounted for by the value priorities, by subtracting the mistrust R^2 (1.8 percent; table 8.1, column 5) from the same combined total (again 13.1 percent).

17. Our other tests for schematic thinking are again inappropriate in this context; see note 12.

18. The incumbent-disapproval scale, on the other hand, is correlated both with the two partisan predispositions and with cynicism. In a regression analysis, the three variables yielded $R^2 = 13.2$ percent on the measure of incumbent support, with the two partisan predispositions (combined beta = .20) and cynicism (beta = .29) both contributing. Not surprisingly, then, its role in support for the tax revolt is fully accounted for by these more basic predispositions (table 8.2, column 1).

19. D. Katz, B. Gutek, R. L. Kahn, and E. Barton, *Bureaucratic Encounters: A Pilot Study in the Evaluation of Government Services* (Ann Arbor: Institute for Social Research, University of Michigan, 1975); M. K. Jennings and G. B. Markus, "The Effect of Military Service on Political Attitudes: A Panel Study," *American Political Science Review*, 71 (1977):131–147; J. B. McConahay and W. D. Hawley, "Is It the Buses or the Blacks? Self-Interest versus Symbolic Racism as Predictors of Opposition to Busing in Louisville" (Paper presented at the annual meeting of the American Psychological Association, San Francisco, 1977). A Harris Survey release of March 26, 1981, shows 48 percent of white respondents feeling busing of their children had been very satisfactory, and 13 percent "not satisfactory."

20. D. O. Sears, "Positivity Biases in Evaluations of Public Figures" (Paper presented at the annual meeting of the American Psychological Association, Washington, D.C., 1976); and D. O. Sears, "The Person-Positivity Bias" (manuscript, University of California, Los Angeles, 1981).

21. See note 16 for the procedure by which these estimates were derived.

22. Symbolic racism retained a strong effect (beta = .15) on turnout, but mainly because the anti-busing amendment on the ballot with the Gann amendment attracted voters especially concerned about busing. The other symbolic racism item, concerning aid to minorities, was not closely related to turnout for either Proposition 13 or 4.

23. When the same analysis is done using all the individual items rather than combining them, the results are lower, but strikingly similar to each other; for example, the loadings in a principal components analysis for party identification and ideology are .39 and .45; for size of government and service spending, .52 and .67; for waste and overpaid government workers, .34 and .33.

24. This, it should be noted, is contrary to Murray Edelman's contention that feelings of personal threat are essential to the success of symbolic appeals. See his *Politics as Symbolic Action* (Chicago: Markham, 1971).

25. E. C. Ladd, Jr., and S. M. Lipset, "Anatomy of a Decade," *Public Opinion*, 3, no. 1 (1980):2–9.

26. This is most readily seen in varimax rotations, which attempt to maximize independent dimensions. For example, analyses of the tax revolt schema paired them; see table 4.2. A number of factor analyses not presented here using the symbolic predispositions did as well. These were analogous to those depicted in table 8.3 but using individual items rather than combining them. The value priorities versus malaise contrast occurs reasonably consistently, with size of government and service spending showing similar loadings on each factor, whether high or low.

27. See the Harris Survey release of March 2, 1981, for public reactions to some specific budget cuts proposed by the Reagan administration.

28. Miller, "Political Issues and Trust in Government."

29. The contrast between these two separate mediational processes can readily be seen in table 8.1. Value priorities mediated much of the effects of ideology, party identification, and symbolic racism (compare columns 3, 4, and 7), while the antigovernment themes mediated all of the effect of cynicism (compare columns 5, 6, and 7).

9. Proposition 13: The Peculiar Election

1. The data tracking Proposition 13's popularity over time were shown in table 2.1.

2. For example, during the period of Proposition 13's surge in popularity, the *Los Angeles Times* and the *San Francisco Chronicle* published few explicit references to the state surplus, and those were in all cases incidental and inconspicuous references. In the *Times*, the state surplus was not mentioned on the front page, or in a headline, or as the major focus of any article, letter, or editorial. When it was mentioned at all, it was an afterthought, and buried so deep in the newspaper that mass attention must have been very weak.

3. This conceivably could have occurred because renters were afraid of being forever priced out of the homeownership market, and so still reflect a self-interested response. However, as we saw in Chapter 6, there is little evidence that many renters responded to Proposition 13 as if they were prospective homeowners; they responded as renters, and did not expect it to reduce their rents (see table 6.4).

4. N. J. Smelser, *Theory of Collective Behavior* (New York: The Free Press, 1962).

5. D. Katz, B. Gutek, R. L. Kahn, and E. Barton, *Bureaucratic Encounters* (Ann Arbor: Institute for Social Research, University of Michigan, 1975); D. O. Sears, "The Person-Positivity Bias" (manuscript, University of California, Los Angeles, 1981).

6. Again we repeat the qualification noted in Chapter 3 (note 4), that the latter survey only included registered voters who planned to vote, who are markedly less pro-services than the general population, but this factor accounts for at most half the difference.

7. In the calmer period of our Tax Revolt Survey, this reverted more to normal: the college-educated showed a higher relationship between service-spending and support for Proposition 13 (gammas of .61 and .52, respectively).

8. Another possibility is that some other pre-existing regional difference was triggered by the campaign. To test this, we compared the Bay Area, traditionally the most liberal region of the state, either with Los Angeles County alone or with both Los Angeles and Orange counties (which together make up the main body of the metropolitan area and the media market) on all the variables used in earlier analyses of the Tax Revolt Survey. This comparison revealed virtually no regional differences. For example, 56 percent were homeowners in both areas, and 53 percent were conservatives in both.

A regression equation using all these variables was run on the tax rebel index in Los Angeles County separately from the rest of the state, but almost no variables proved to interact with region, and the R^2 was almost identical (.27 and .28, respectively). Yet support for the tax revolt was markedly higher in the Los Angeles area: 66 percent to 53 percent, on the tax rebel index. As will be seen in the next chapter, that difference holds with everything else controlled. In short, there was considerably more support in Los Angeles for the tax revolt, but it was not based on any other demographic or attitudinal variables we have measured.

9. But more formally, expectancy and value ought to have multiplicative rather than additive effects upon vote intention, as would be expected from expectancy-value models of decisionmaking. See W. Edwards, "The Theory of Decision-Making," *Psychological Bulletin*, 51 (1954):380–417; M. Fishbein and I. Ajzen, *Belief, Attitude, Intention, and Behavior* (Reading, Mass.: Addison-Wesley, 1975); and many others.

10. This earlier material included over-time data from the California Poll as well as comparisons using the Tax Revolt Survey. The proximal attitudes toward taxation and spending were shown in table 4.1; the demographics in table 5.3; the main self-interest variables in tables 6.3, 6.5, and 7.3; and the symbolic predispositions in Chapter 8. The California Poll did not include measures of symbolic racism, so no comparable over-time data exist on that variable. However, within the Tax Revolt Survey it retained the same pre-eminent status among the three partisan predispositions no matter which proposition was at issue.

11. These data come from the Tax Revolt Survey and California Polls 7806, 7807, 7904, 8001, 8002, and 8003.

12. These were the Tax Revolt Survey and California Polls 7806, 7807, and 7904.

13. The similarities among the predictive structures for the several propositions can be emphasized yet one further way. Factor analyses earlier showed that the tax rebel scale loaded heavily on a value priorities factor, and scarcely at all on a malaise factor (table 8.4). Very similar patterns emerged from similar factor analyses done separately on support for each of these propositions.

14. The Tax Revolt Survey asked: "What about the effect of Proposition 13 on government services for your family? Has there been a change for the better, a change for the worse, or has there been no real change?" and found 16 percent reporting an unfavorable *overall* change in service levels. California Polls 7807, 7901, 8001 report 24, 28, and 24 percent respectively experiencing *any* unfavorable effect on themselves or their immediate family "in regard to the government services you receive."

15. D. R. Kinder and D. R. Kiewiet, "Economic Discontent and Political Behavior: The Role of Personal Grievances and Collective Economic Judgments in Congressional Voting," *American Journal of Political Science*, 23 (1979):495–527.

16. Some other minor differences across these propositions turned up in the regressions done at different time points, and should be noted here, though they seem not to have contributed in a major way to the diverse outcomes of these elections. Men were especially attracted to the two "hot," angry, protest-filled campaigns waged by Howard Jarvis, for Propositions 13 and 9. Hence sex differences were significant on virtually all surveys regarding those two, but men and women barely differed (and not significantly) on the tame, uncontroversial, low-key Gann amendment. Educational level was most strongly related to opposition to the revolt when the proposals seemed most radical and their consequences most uncertain. Hence it had a strong relationship to vote intention and vote on Proposition 13, but very little in the aftermath, when it had been safely implemented. It was strongly negatively related to Gann right after Proposition 13 passed, when its further consequences were potentially threatening – but little after it passed, when it too seemed safe. And education was strongly negatively related

to Jarvis II throughout that campaign; as we have seen, that proposition never came to be regarded as safe.

10. Putting the Pieces Together

1. H. M. Blalock, Jr., ed., *Causal Models in the Social Sciences* (Chicago: Aldine, 1971). This model is, of course, based on a particular causal sequence. The ordering of categories of variables such that demographics enter first and the proximal attitudes last is probably not controversial. It is implausible in the present context that the symbolic predispositions are caused by self-interest, since as we have indicated (Chapter 8) they are so weakly related. And within each category of variables shown in table 10.1, the ordering of variables is quite arbitrary and probably does not make an enormous difference. The two areas of most potential difficulty, to us, are the possibilities that subjective tax burden and the four proximal attitudes are consequences rather than causes of attitudes toward the tax revolt propositions. The use of homeownership as a clearly prior parallel measure of self-interest protects us somewhat in the first case, as we have seen in Chapter 6. For the second, we have simply tried to be somewhat cautious in asserting a definitively causal role of these proximal attitudes; they no doubt were influenced to some degree by the tax revolt campaigns themselves, though the proximal attitudes sometimes changed over time in a direction contrary to the change in success of the tax revolt (see tables 3.2 and 3.3). Alternative placements of variables in the causal chain were tested but, in our view, fit the data less well in addition to being less plausible on theoretical grounds.

2. We are indebted to J. Merrill Shanks for providing this analysis.

3. Aside from demographic variables, public employee status and incumbent disapproval both contributed to greater participation on both indices, and a few other scattered minor findings were significant, as discussed earlier. But the main finding is that demographic variables accounted for virtually all the participation findings, as they have in many other political situations.

4. D. E. Kanouse and L. R. Hanson, Jr., "Negativity in Evaluations," in *Attribution: Perceiving the Causes of Behavior* (Morristown, N.J.: General Learning Press, 1972), pp. 47–62.

5. The effect of age also drops markedly with symbolic predispositions considered, suggesting a fairly powerful generational difference reflected in older people's greater conservative Republicanism. One other age effect could be resolved here. We speculated that the slight drop in support for the tax revolt among those over retirement age might be due to their greater dependency on services. That turns out to be true, at least to some extent. The elderly who are dependent on no government service programs are actually 3 percent more likely to be tax rebels than the middle-aged (50–64), whereas those dependent on one or more services are 7 percent less likely.

6. The betas for education were − .20 and .02, respectively, and − .07 and − .10 on Gann and Jarvis II, with all other variables shown in table 10.1 included in the equation.

7. It should be noted that we did not include the attitudinal variables most often used in analyzing behavioral participation in politics, such as citizen duty, political efficacy, and so on. The main thing added to the explanation of participation by including these other variables is that public employees were especially active in the revolt, quite aside from all their demographic and attitudinal characteristics. Their special activation in the revolt perhaps presages a special role for them in defending the public sector in years to come; this needs to be monitored carefully.

8. These are from California Polls 7806, 7904, 8001, 8002, and 8003, and the Tax Revolt Survey.

11. Comparisons and Implications

1. For findings about Western Europe see S. Barnes et al., *Political Action: Mass Participation in Five Western Democracies* (Beverly Hills: Sage, 1979).

2. See this discussion in R. Rose, "The Nature of the Challenge," in *Challenge to Governance*, ed. R. Rose (Beverly Hills: Sage, 1980).

3. R. Rose and G. Peters, *Can Government Go Bankrupt?* (London: MacMillan, 1979).

4. See R. Rose, "Ordinary People in Extraordinary Circumstances," in *Challenge to Governance*.

5. See Chapter 2 and *Intergovernmental Perspective* (Winter 1979).

6. The experience of California and Massachusetts, where the two most radical tax-cutting proposals passed, in particular, corroborates this conclusion of Wilensky's comparative studies of advanced industrial societies. See H. L. Wilensky, *The Welfare State and Equality* (Berkeley: University of California Press, 1975).

7. For a good summary of the events in these states see R. Kuttner, *The Revolt of The Haves* (New York: Simon and Schuster, 1980).

8. This discussion of ballot measures and public opinion in states other than California relies heavily on R. Palaich, J. Kloss, and M. F. Williams, *Tax and Expenditure Limitation Referenda: An Analysis of Public Opinion, Voting Behavior, and Campaigns in Four States* (Denver: Education Commission of the States, 1980); and for Massachusetts on Kuttner, *Revolt of the Haves*.

9. The increase in the burden of property taxes on homeowners was the result of a state supreme court decision in 1967 that forbade different assessment ratios for different types of property. This caused the familiar shift in the tax burden toward the individual homeowners — that is, toward voters.

10. Kuttner, *Revolt of the Haves*, p. 310.

11. Palaich et al., *Tax and Expenditure Limitation Referenda*, p. 43.

12. Advisory Commission on InterGovernmental Relations, *Changing Public Attitudes on Government and Taxes* (Washington, D.C., 1978).

13. Palaich et al., *Tax and Expenditure Limitation Referenda*, p. 50.

14. See P. A. Beck and T. Dye, "Sources of Public Opinion on Taxes" (manuscript, Florida State University, 1980).

15. P. Courant, E. M. Gramlich, and D. L. Rubinfeld, "The Tax Limitation Movement: Conservative Drift or the Search for a Free Lunch," Institute of Public Policy Studies Paper no. 141 (Ann Arbor: University of Michigan, 1979).

16. Palaich et al., *Tax and Expenditure Limitation Referenda*, p. 50.

17. Beck and Dye, "Sources of Public Opinion," p. 22.

18. See the summary in Palaich et al., *Tax and Expenditure Limitation Referenda*, p. 56.

19. Ibid., pp. 20–23; and Courant et al., "The Tax Limitation Movement."

20. See Wilensky, *The Welfare State and Equality*, ch. 1.

21. This emerges clearly from an analysis of responses in a national survey conducted after the 1978 national elections by the University of Michigan's Center for Political Studies. Support for a measure like Proposition 13 "in your community" had no relationship to demographic variables at all: even blacks were as likely to support it. The only significant predictors were indicators of generalized malaise and mistrust of

government. In the absence of a concrete measure whose costs and benefits are being debated, symbolic attitudes dominate completely.

22. See "Why the Middle Class Supports Reagan," *U.S. News and World Report*, May 19, 1981.

23. For a summary see J. Citrin, "The Changing American Electorate," In A. J. Meltsner, ed., *Politics and the Oval Office* (San Francisco: Institute for Contemporary Studies, 1981).

24. For example, see L. Harris, "Americans Oppose a Federal Tax Cut," ABC News — Harris Survey Release, December 1, 1980.

25. D. O. Sears and J. B. McConahay, *The Politics of Violence: The New Urban Blacks and the Watts Riot* (Boston: Houghton Mifflin, 1973).

26. D. Yankelovich, *The New Morality: A Profile of American Youth in the '70's* (New York: McGraw-Hill, 1974).

27. See "Opinion Roundup" in *Public Opinion*, 4, no. 2 (1981).

12. Legacy of the Tax Revolt

1. For additional detail on the material covered in this section see J. Citrin, "The Legacy of Proposition 13," in *California and the American Tax Revolt*, ed. T. Schwadron (Berkeley: University of California Press, 1984); and J. Citrin and D. Green, "Living with the Tax Revolt: Public Opinion and Public Policy in California" (paper delivered at the convention of the American Political Science Association, 1984).

2. See State of California, *Fiscal Year 1983 Budget Summary*. This is probably a conservative estimate of the revenues lost to local governments, calculated on the basis that in the first year after the passage of Proposition 13, 1978-79, property tax collections fell by $6.6 billion and that this shortfall, modified slightly by a factor that takes account of growth and inflation, occurs annually. If Proposition 13 had failed, and tax rates had remained unchanged, and assessments had continued to rise — probably a politically unrealistic scenario — the hypothetical loss to local governments in 1982-83 alone would have amounted to a staggering $24 billion, according to David Doerr, Chief Consultant to the California State Assembly Revenue and Taxation Committee.

3. California Legislative Analyst, *The 1983-84 Budget: Perspectives and Issues*, p. 81.

4. California Legislative Analyst, *The 1984-85 Budget: Perspectives and Issues*, p. 140.

5. Advisory Commission on Intergovernmental Relations, *Significant Features of Fiscal Federalism, 1981-82 Edition* (Washington, D.C.: 1983). The fall in property taxes was much more precipitous. In 1978, just before the passage of the Jarvis-Gann Initiative, property taxes in California were 50 percent above the national average; in 1981 they were 22 percent below, according to C. Jamison, *Taxes and Other Revenue of State and Local Government,* (Security Pacific Bank, 1982), p. A-4."

6. On both these points, see Citrin, "The Legacy of Proposition 13."

7. The fact that expenditures from the State's General Fund increased between 1978 and 1984 by about $11 billion, an average annual rate of 12 percent, is often cited as proof that Proposition 13 failed to stop the tide of governmental expansion. But adjusting for inflation reduces the above-mentioned rise in nominal *state* expenditures to about $2 billion, spread over six fiscal years, and even this increase was devoted almost entirely to replacing the property taxes lost by *local* entities. Spending on ser-

vices provided by the state government itself actually dropped by 12 percent in real terms. See *The 1984-85 Budget* p. 27, and *Significant Features of Fiscal Federalism,* p. 2.

8. F. Levy, D. Shimasaki, and B. Berk, "Sources of Growth in California Public Employment: 1964-78," *American Economic Review,* 72, no. 2, (May 1982): 282.

9. Expenditures on K-12 education rose from 22 percent of the 1977-78 General Fund to 36 percent in 1983-84. See *The 1984-85 Budget,* pp. 48-50.

10. Ibid., p. 51.

11. K. Bacon, "The Los Angeles Times Survey of Local Government Responses to Proposition 13 of 1978," in Schwadron, *California and the American Tax Revolt.*

12. See *The 1984-85 Budget,* p. 86.

13. The Field Institute, *California Opinion Index* (April 1983): 3-4.

14. Perhaps more important, but harder to measure, is that the tax revolt protected against future inflation in taxes. Proposition 13 produced permanent insurance against inflationary increases in the assessed valuation of property. Indexing constructed a shield against uncertainty in the other main component of the state and local tax burden, and the elimination of the inheritance tax spares heirs from the impact of inflation on the value of what they are left.

15. Having to pay more fees for local services also failed to boost unhappiness with Proposition 13. As other surveys have indicated, user charges are not considered truly burdensome. See R. Cline and J. Shannon, "Municipal Revenue Behavior after Proposition 13," *Intergovernmental Perspective,* 8, no. 3, (Fall 1982): 22.

16. S.M. Lipset and E. Ladd, "Public Opinion and Public Policy," in *The United States in the 1980s,* ed. P. Duignan and A. Rabushka (Palo Alto, Calif.: Hoover Institution, 1980).

17. It might be objected, with some justice, that to pair one's beliefs in this manner is not necessarily illogical. For example, people could rationalize their simultaneous advocacy of lower taxes and increased public services by arguing that surplus revenues exist, that the loss in tax revenues could be absorbed by eliminating bureaucratic waste, or, along with supply-side economists, that lower tax rates would generate a higher total amount to spend. Similarly, a voter may feel that at some point a smaller government would be preferable, but that at present there is still room for the public sector to grow. One might demand a little more spending in a variety of areas but be willing to compensate by emasculating a narrower set of programs, a possibility that surveys generally ignore. Finally, the voter may be persuaded that specific emergencies justify a temporary departure from the path of fiscal austerity. In Chapter 3 we tested and rejected most of these possibilities.

From a methodological perspective, it might be legitimate to complain that the standard survey questions about preferences on taxing and spending policies simply compile a "wish list" without enabling respondents to say how intensely they desire more spending, precisely how much more money they think is involved, whether they would agree to postponing proposed increases or cuts, and so on. On the other hand, the survey questions we employed did explicitly remind respondents that to provide more services government must collect taxes and that a smaller government means fewer services. Despite these reminders, the something-for-nothing mentality was widespread, even among those who do not employ the rationalization that cutting the "fat" in government would allow for the delivery of more for less.

18. See Citrin and Green, "Living with the Tax Revolt."

19. J. Shannon and S. E. Calkins, "Federal and State-Local Spending Go Their Separate Ways," *Intergovernmental Perspective,* 8, no. 4/9, no. 1 (Winter 1983): 21-25.

20. For an excellent review, see G. E. Petersen, "The State and Local Sector," in *The Reagan Record,* ed. J. L. Palmer and I.V. Sawhill (Washington, D.C.: The Urban Institute Press, 1984).

21. See Cline and Shannon, "Municipal Revenue Behavior," p. 23.

22. These statistics were obtained from results compiled by Sue Thomas of the National Center for Initiative Review, Denver, Colorado, and from *Public Opinion,* Nov./Dec., 1978, Nov./Dec., 1980, and Feb./March, 1983. The less stringent restrictions not only were less controversial but also had enough official support to come before the electorate as referenda rather than popular initiatives. All the "Jarvis clones" and 17 of the 19 proposals to cut state taxes were placed on the ballot as a result of grass-roots petitions. That they passed less often than the officially sponsored referenda is further evidence that the tax rebels frequently could succeed in wresting concessions from the established order while failing to prevail when more fundamental transformations of the fiscal system were at issue.

Compiling a comprehensive box-score for the tax revolt is complicated because it is not always clear what counts as a win or loss. For example, it seems reasonable to score as a defeat for the tax rebels their failure to obtain enough signatures to place an initiative on the ballot. But what if this occurs or their proposal is defeated largely because politicians reacted to popular pressure by cutting taxes on their own? Yet if one credits the tax rebels with a victory for every instance of a tax reduction after 1978, should not the recent proliferation of increases in state taxes be entered in the loss column? Our tabulation of the results of statewide initiatives and referenda that actually were voted upon between 1978 and the end of 1983 should be considered in the light of such ambiguities.

23. This, of course, was true of the results we report above. See also P. Courant, E. Gramlich, and D. Rubinfeld, "Why Voters Support Tax Limitation Amendments: The Michigan Case," *National Tax Journal,* 33, no. 1 (March 1980): 1-20.

24. See E. P. Morgan, "Public Preferences and Policy Realities: Proposition 2½ in Massachusetts" (paper presented at the meeting of the Northeastern Political Science Association, (1982) p. 11; R. Attiyeh and R. F. Engle, "Testing Some Propositions about Proposition 13," *National Tax Journal,* 32, no. 2 (June 1979): 131-146.

25. See S. Gold, "State Tax Increases of 1983: Prelude to Another Tax Revolt," in National Conference of State Legislatures, *Legislative Finance Paper,* 40: 20; also personal communication from Edward Collins, Deputy Commissioner, Department of Revenue, State of Massachusetts.

26. See R. Palaich, J. Kloss, and M. Williams, *Tax and Expenditure Limitation Referenda* (Denver: Education Commission of the States, Report F80-2, 1980), pp. 50-51.

27. S. Gold, "Recent Developments in State Finance," *National Tax Journal,* 36, no. 1 (March 1983): 21.

28. Ibid., p. 12

29. G. H. Miller, "Remarks," *National Tax Journal,* 36, no. 3 (September 1983): 392.

30. Petersen, "State and Local Sector," p. 191.

31. Shannon and Calkins, "Federal and State-Local Spending," p. 191.

32. See G. E. Petersen, "Federalism and the States," in *The Reagan Record*, ed. Palmer and Sawhill.

33. This account owes much to L. Susskind, ed., *Proposition 2½, Its Impact on Massachusetts* (Cambridge, Mass.: Oegleschloger, Gunn and Hain, 1983).

34. L. Susskind and C. Horan, "How the Most Drastic Cuts Were Avoided," in *Proposition 2½*, ed. Susskind, p. 263. This is a summary conclusion that masks the obvious differences in the amount of suffering across communities.

35. Massachusetts Tax Foundation, *A Massachusetts Primer: Economics and Public Finance* (Boston, Mass:, 1983), p. 28.

36. Massachusetts Tax Foundation, *State Budget Trends, 1975-84* (Boston, Mass.: 1983), p. 4.

37. Massachusetts Municipal Association, *The Governor's Budget for Fiscal Year 1983,* Table IV (Unpublished report, Boston, 1983).

38. *A Massachusetts Primer,* p. 18.

39. D. Soyer, "The Quality of Public Services," in *State-Local Fiscal Relations After Proposition 2½* (unpublished report of the Institute for Governmental Studies, University of Massachusetts, Boston, 1983), p. 61.

40. This incident was vividly described in interviews with several members of then-Mayor White's staff. The huge increase, of course, is a one-time gain. The more general comment is reference to the multiplicity of small units of government in Massachusetts and to the domination of administration by politics.

41. President Reagan's remarks appear in *America's New Beginning: A Program for Economic Recovery* (Washington, D.C.: Government Printing Office, Feb. 18, 1981), p. 4.

42. See, for example, the analysis in P. Abramson, J. Aldrich, and D. Rohde, *Change and Continuity in the 1980 Elections* (Washington, D.C.: Congressional Quarterly Press, 1982).

43. J. Citrin, "Change in the American Electorate" in A. Meltsner, ed., *Politics and the Oval Office* (San Francisco, Calif.: Institute for Contemporary Studies, 1981).

44. Abramson et al., *Change and Continuity,* pp. 125, 132-133.

45. J. Palmer and I. Sawhill, "Overview," in *The Reagan Record,* p. 8. This section draws heavily on this excellent volume.

46. These data were prepared by the Office of Management and Budget, and are reprinted in *The Reagan Record,* p. 110.

47. *The Reagan Record,* p. 13.

48. G. B. Mills, "The Budget," in *The Reagan Record*, pp. 121-122.

49. F. Levy and R.C. Michel, "The Way We'll be in 1984: Recent Changes in the Level and Distribution of Income" (unpublished discussion paper, Washington, D.C., Urban Institute, 1983).

50. Petersen, "Federalism and the States," pp. 242, 257-258.

51. *The Reagan Record,* p. 358.

52. These are Gallup Poll results.

53. Polls between 1980 and 1983 showed very similar levels of cynicism. In this poll another 21 percent felt that "some" money was wasted.

54. The proportion mentioning reducing the budget deficit as the best way of improving the economy grew slightly toward the end of 1983. The polls were conducted by Penn and Schoen Associates.

55. This result was obtained by a Roper organization poll.

Index

Activism: of factions, 90-91, 95;
demographic variables and, 107, 108-110,
211-212, 220-221; self-interest and, 113,
115, 130, 139, 141, 221; of taxpayers, 130;
of service recipients, 151; of public
employees, 154, 158; and symbolic
predispositions, 178-179
Affective consistency: tax-service tradeoff
and, 60-64, 216-218; concreteness and,
69-70, 77, 93-94; tax revolt schema and,
73-74, 76, 79-82, 87-89, 91-93, 95;
symbolic predispositions and, 165. See
also Cognitive psychology
Affirmative action, 164, 214
Age (as demographic variable), 101, 105,
208, 214, 241; activism and, 109, 110; sale
of houses and, 125-126; self-interest and,
220. See also Elderly; Young people
Alcohol, tax on, 260, 264
Anti-government attitudes, see Government,
mistrust of
Assembly Revenue and Taxation Committee,
118

Bailout bill, 33, 196-197, 250. See also
Surplus
Balanced budget, 6, 41, 63, 204-205, 233
Behr bill, 25, 27. See also Proposition 8
"Big government," see Government, size of
Blacks, 214, 232; oppose revolt, 100, 106,
167-168, 220; activism of, 109, consume
services, 165, 168, 239, 257. See also
Racism; Whites
Brown, Edmund G. "Pat," 163
Brown, Jerry, 175, 245; on small
government, 9, 236, 238; in Prop. 13
campaign, 25, 26, 27, 165, 248; cuts after

Prop. 13, 31, 37, 188, 196-197, 204-205,
251; on Prop. 9, 37, 38; on federal
budget, 41, 204-205. See also Incumbents,
disapproval of
Budget, balanced, 6, 41, 63, 204-205, 233,
267, 273; centralized control, 265; by
plebiscite, 246
Business interests: commercial property
owners, 5, 19, 25, 228, 237, 247; Prop. 13
and, 5, 26-27, 31-32, 34; A.B. 80 and, 19;
Prop. 14 and, 20; Prop. 4 and, 36; Prop.
9 and, 36, 37, 38, 205-206; tax on oil
companies, 40. See also Split roll
Busing, 14, 164, 168, 177-178, 214

California Federation of Labor, 38
California Poll, data collection of, 11
Carter, Jimmy, 268
Cash savings, 130-132; of Prop. 13, 118,
120, 140, 190, 201, 205; of Prop. 9, 127,
201, 204; self-interest and, 140-141, 160,
212, 213, 221, 232
Cigarette tax, 260, 264
Civil rights movement, 164, 239
Class differences, 97-100, 125, 236-239;
history of, 15-18; Prop. 9 and, 37, 38;
Prop. 13 and, 106; spending and, 107-108;
activism and, 109, 211-212; "revolt of the
haves," 121-122, 123-124, 140, 162,
220-221; and self-interest, 207; in nation,
232. See also Income; Lower class;
Middle class; Upper class
Cognitive psychology, 76, 93, 112, 151,
212-213. See also Affective consistency;
Schematic thinking; Social psychology
Colorado, 226, 227
Community colleges, see Education, higher

Connecticut, 227
Conservatism: in government, 163, 226; as symbolic predisposition, 165, 166, 208, 214, 220, 256, 268; Jarvis's, 166; Prop. 13 and, 198, 205; in nation, 219-220, 233, 239. *See also* Political ideology; Republicans
Cranston, Alan, 188
Cynicism, 164, 166, 175-176, 211, 231; origins of, 176-178, 185-186; activism and, 178; malaise schema and, 181, 214-215. *See also* Government, mistrust of; Incumbents, disapproval of; Symbolic predispositions

Deficit financing, 245, 248, 269
Democrats: national party, 2, 9, 230, 232, 233, 235, 245, 267; party philosophy, 9, 72, 163; California party, 21, 25, 36, 38, 165, 256; as respondents, 166-167, 185. *See also* Liberalism; Party identification; Political ideology
Demographic variables, 200, 208-212, 224, 241; self-interest and, 13, 133; activism and, 211-212; urban residence, 214. *See also* individual variables
Deukmejian, George, 26, 245, 253
Distribution of income, 247
Dukakis, Michael, 267

Economic individualism, 16, 183, 242. *See also* Values
Economic malaise, 240; and self-interest, 112, 115, 132, 134-136; effects of, 140, 193, 212; in larger schema, 214, 218-219. *See also* Inflation; Malaise schema
Economy, California: voters' perceptions of, 4, 132, 135-138, 177; Prop. 13 and, 31-32; Prop. 9 and, 37, 38, 39-40
Education (as demographic variable): tax revolt schema and, 83-84; as index of class, 97, 258; and lack of support for revolt, 98-100, 106, 208, 211, 220, 232; and other variables, 103, 105, 107-108; activism and, 109; self-interest and, 143-144, 145-146, 150, 151, 227; and service preferences, 195-196; Prop. 9 and, 200-201
Education, higher, 7, 227, 233, 241; Prop. 9 and, 37, 145-146, 151, 200-201; self-interest and, 143, 145-147, 150; spending and, 143, 147, 150, 233, 234, 237, 246, 249, 266. *See also* Schools; University of California
Elderly, 122, 140, 145, 150, 208, 241, 247, 256, 257, 270. *See also* Age

Employment: public vs. private, 23, 52; Prop. 13 and, 27; Prop. 9 and, 37; self-interest and, 144, 146, 151. *See also* Economy, California; Public employees; Unemployment

Factions, 76-77, 85-89
Federal budget: balancing of, 6, 41, 63, 233, 235; Jerry Brown on, 41, 204-205; cuts and services, 47-48, 72, 94, 232, 234
Federal government, 6, 8, 38, 232, 235
Fees for service, 33, 38, 40, 236; Supreme Court decision, 245
Fire services, 23, 33; valued as safety services, 58-60, 218, 237, 249, 266; opinions on, 49, 62, 198
Florida, 231
Food stamps, 48, 234
Friedman, Milton, 38

Gann, Paul, 2, 8, 21, 34
Gann amendment, *see* Proposition 4
Gasoline tax, 260, 264
Government, mistrust of, 52-53, 166, 178, 219, 267; in nation, 8, 24-25, 67, 226, 231; as opposed to value priorities, 80, 84, 110, 181; tax burden and, 132; self-interest and, 141; as symbolic predisposition, 164, 174-178, 185-186; activism and, 179; Prop. 13 and, 193-196, 197, 198, 205, 224, 236. *See also* Incumbents, disapproval of; Malaise schema; Tax revolt schema
Government, role of, 18, 187, 219-220, 236, 250; in world, 1-2, 225; services and, 58; blacks and whites on, 168; symbolic predispositions and, 172; activism and, 221. *See also* Tax revolt schema; Value priorities
Government, size of, 6, 46-47, 74-87, 211, 232; Prop. 1 and, 21; Prop. 13 and, 23-24, 194, 197, 223, 243, 248; concreteness and, 60, 65; tax-service tradeoff and, 63-64, 184-185, 217; demographics and, 107-108, 110; linked to economy, 251, 264; service recipients on, 147-148; public employees on, 157; symbolic predispositions and, 170, 172, 210-211. *See also* Tax revolt schema; Value priorities
Government, waste in, 35-36, 107, 148, 211, 267; Prop. 13 and, 27, 194; commission on, 31; tax-service tradeoff and, 50-53, 55-57, 217-218; in schemas, 74-87, 214; public employees on, 157, 210; symbolic predispositions and, 170, 176; Prop. 9

and, 201, 205; in nation, 232, 233. *See
also* Malaise schema; Tax revolt schema
Government spending, *see* Services;
   Government, size of; Tax-service tradeoff
Government workers, *see* Public employees
Great Britain, 1, 226
Great Society, 267

Hahn, Kenneth, 194
Headlee amendment, 229, 231, 232
Health care, spending on, 48-50, 149-150,
   172-173, 234, 239, 249
Heilbroner, Robert, 9
Heller, Walter, 9
Higher education, *see* Education, higher
Highway construction, 253
Homeowners, 122, 125, 208; tax burden of,
   5, 22, 226, 237; Prop. 13 and, 18, 26,
   196, 200; A.B. 80 and, 19; in Los
   Angeles, 30, 205; "early vs. late buyers,"
   46, 120-121, 125-126, 161, 237, 256; self-
   interest of, 113-114, 117-126, 140, 160, 212,
   247; for tax reform, 129; on schools,
   148-149; Prop. 9 and, 200; homeownership as symbol, 215; in nation, 228, 230.
   See also Property assessment; "Taxpayers"
Housing, 223, 237, 238. *See also* Real
   estate; Renters

Idaho, 6, 226, 227-228, 230, 231, 232
Income (as demographic variable), 5, 97,
   237; education and, 98-100, 107-108; and
   other variables, 105, 212; Prop. 13 and,
   106; activism and, 109; self-interest and,
   220; in nation, 232; in future, 239, 241.
   See also Class differences; Lower class;
   Middle class; Upper class
Income tax: in Denmark, 1; Prop. 9 and, 3,
   5, 36, 126-127, 200, 201, 204; corporate,
   20; inflation and, 22-23; indexing of, 37,
   41, 226, 246; Prop. 13 and, 41, 45-46;
   federal, 117, 233, 234, 269; self-interest
   and, 140, 160, 262, 263; in nation,
   226-227; state, 245
Incumbents, disapproval of, 174-179, 185,
   214, 241. *See also* Brown, Jerry;
   Legislature, California; Malaise schema;
   Political cynicism
Independents, 166, 185
Inflation, 4, 7, 53, 62-63, 212; personal
   income and, 21-23, 126, 161-162; surplus
   and, 32; Prop. 4 and, 35; in nation, 41,
   230, 233-235; economic climate and, 112,
   122, 132-139, 177; in Southern California,
   223; in world, 225, 234. *See also*
   Economic malaise; Malaise schema

Inheritance tax, 245
Initiatives: in nation, 5-6, 227; in
   California, 19, 21, 40, 44, 189; as political
   process, 25, 53, 236, 242; on rent control,
   238. *See also* Populism; individual ballot
   measures and propositions
International trends, 1, 225, 241
Issue public: defined, 11; extent of, 106-108,
   110, 218-219; self-interest and, 112, 115,
   140; "taxpayers" as, 127-130; economic
   malaise and, 139; service recipients as,
   146-147, 151; public employees as, 155;
   symbolic predispositions and, 165, 170,
   176, 214. *See also* Opinionation; Political
   activism; Schematic thinking; Tax revolt
   schema
Issue salience, *see* Opinionation

Jarvis, Howard: Prop. 13 and, 2, 8, 10, 26,
   27, 31, 174, 270; and Paul Gann, 2, 8, 34;
   Prop. 9 and, 3, 36, 37, 39; Prop. 8 and,
   25; beliefs compared to public's, 55, 76,
   87, 94, 198, 219; broader schema of, 166,
   181; in nation, 188, 229, 235; belligerence
   of, 222
Jarvis-Gann amendment, *see* Proposition 13
Jarvis II, *see* Proposition 9
Jarvis IV, *see* Proposition 36

King, Edward, 266
Kuttner, Robert, 135-136, 138, 162, 228

Landlords, 27, 121, 125, 237-238. *See also*
   Rent control; Renters
Legislative Analyst, 31, 37, 39
Legislature, California, 6, 8, 25, 175, 178,
   196-197, 204. *See also* Incumbents,
   disapproval of
Liberalism, 163, 166, 211, 235, 240, 256,
   265, 267. *See also* Conservatism; Political
   ideology; Symbolic predispositions
Local government: services of, 6, 197,
   201-202; state funds, 33, 37, 226-227, 236;
   Prop. 4 and, 34-35; opinions on, 35-36;
   Prop. 9 and, 38
Los Angeles: County tax assessor, 20-21;
   homeowners in, 22, 205; as supportive
   region, 30, 102, 105, 118, 208, 223;
   County administrator, 30, 191; services in,
   40, 239; racial conflict in, 164; rent
   control in, 238
Los Angeles reassessment controversy, 10,
   28-30, 190-194; role of officials in, 191,
   196; mass reactions to, 219, 223, 224
Los Angeles Times, 30, 74, 118, 191
Lower class, 139, 140, 150, 234, 241. *See
   also* Class differences; Income; Minorities

McCarthy, Leo, 26, 165
Maddy, Ken, 26
Malaise schema, 181-182, 187, 214-215, 219; Prop. 13 and, 193, 194-196, 197; Prop. 9 and, 202
Management reform, 266
Massachusetts, 6, 42, 230, 265-267
Mass behavior, 196, 222-223, 224; Prop. 13 and, 193, 219; Prop. 9 and, 204-205. *See also* Los Angeles reassessment controversy
Media, 215-216, 227-228, 242; and Prop. 13, 26, 32, 40, 188, 191
Medicare, 234. *See also* Health care
Michigan, 6, 226, 230; tax revolt in, 229; services in, 227, 231, 232
Middle class, 139, 234, 239, 241; "middle mass" theory, 97, 99-100, 232. *See also* Class differences; Income
Minorities: ghetto residents, 68; Hispanic voters, 100, 257; government assistance programs, 143, 144, 146, 149-150, 151; as service recipients, 49, 145, 257, 270; disabled, 234. *See also* Blacks; Elderly; Lower class; Racism
Moynihan, Daniel, 158-159

National Election Studies, 8, 24, 40-41, 52, 96, 175
National trends, 5-6, 40-42, 52, 62, 63, 226-235
Nevada, 6
New Deal, 267
Northern California, 102, 105, 108, 118, 223

Opinionation, 139, 147, 155, 176; self-interest and, 113, 128-129, 161, 213. *See also* Issue public; Tax revolt schema
Oregon, 6, 227, 229-230, 232; ballot measures, 229-230, 232

Parents, 148-149, 150; self-interest of, 115, 143, 146, 160, 211, 257, 274; demographic breakdown of, 145, 241; on Prop. 4, 151. *See also* Schools
Participation, *see* Activism
Party identification, 14, 77, 163, 165, 166-167, 210; racism and, 169; cynicism and, 176, 177; Prop. 9 and, 200. *See also* Democrats; Independents; Political ideology; Republicans
Pensioners, 144, 150. *See also* Service recipients
Plebiscites, 245; budgeting by, 274
Police services, 23, 40, 49, 58, 198, 233, 245, 246, 266

Political culture, 102, 241-242
Political ideology, 8-9, 14, 67, 163, 166-167, 210, 250; strength of attitudes and, 70; schematic thinking and, 76, 174; demographic variables and, 110; racism and, 169; cynicism and, 176, 177; Prop. 9 and, 200. *See also* Conservatism; Liberalism; Party identification; Symbolic predispositions
Political sophistication, 55, 57-58, 105, 217-218, 223
Poor, hurt by Reagan, 270
Pope, Alexander, 28-29, 191-192, 205
Populism, 8, 15, 226, 235; Prop. 13 and, 16, 25, 26, 30-31, 205; Watson initiative as, 20; Prop. 9 as, 39; in nation, 227, 228, 242
Post, A. Alan, 31
Post Commission, 251
Prison construction, 253
Property assessment: A.B. 80 and, 19-20; residential vs. commercial, 19-20, 25, 34, 228, 236, 237; S.B. 90 on, 21; inflation and, 21-22; reassessment cycle, 22, 32, 124, 266; Prop. 13 and, 31, 34, 118; in Massachusetts, 228. *See also* Homeowners; Los Angeles reassessment controversy; Real estate
Property tax: Prop. 13 and, 2, 22, 31, 118, 190, 198; in nation, 5, 94, 226, 228, 231, 256, 262; other referenda on, 19-20, 40, 226-231, 260, 261; inflation and, 21-23; unfairness of, 23, 45, 117; circuitbreakers, 41, 226; self-interest and, 117-126, 140; as symbol, 193; resentment diminished, 253; seeds for tax revolts, 262. *See also* Cash savings; individual propositions
Property values: boom in, 21-22; after Prop. 13, 32, 124; "early buyers" and, 46, 121; self-interest and, 120-121, 133, 161; in Southern California, 123; in Oregon, 230. *See also* Homeowners
Proposition 1 (California), 21
Proposition 1 (Idaho), 227-228, 231
Proposition 2½ (Massachusetts), 5, 42, 228-229, 261, 265-267
Proposition 4 (Gann Amendment): campaign for, 34-36, 198-199, 244; activism and, 90, 109; homeowners and, 132; service cuts of, 151, 198-199, 216, 217; public employees and, 155, 158; party identification and, 167; sex differences and, 222
Proposition 8: rejection of, 2, 8, 26, 30; Behr bill and, 25, 27; campaign for, 27, 28, 189, 190

Proposition 9 (Jarvis II), 125, 167, 224; rejection of, 3, 5, 188, 200-206; campaign for, 36-40, 143-144; tax-service tradeoff and, 50, 216; activism and, 90, 109; cash savings from, 117, 126-127, 140, 160, 221; homeowners and, 132; economic effects of, 135, 139, 143; education and, 147, 151; public employees on, 153, 155-158

Proposition 13: 135, 138, 185, 224, 243, 244, 245; reasons for, 4, 5, 205; historical context of, 2, 19-26; homeowners and, 22, 45, 46, 140, 160, 161; campaign for, 26-31, 165, 188-198, 237; economic effects of, 31-34, 124-126; in nation, 40-42, 226, 229, 235; services and, 49, 62, 152, 216; activism and, 90, 109, 221; cash savings from, 117-118, 127; public employees on, 153, 155, 157-158; Prop. 9 and, 200, 201-212; schools and, 143, 145, 149; as revolt of "the haves," 220, 221; satisfaction with, 254-258; demographic variables and, 220, 222

Proposition 36 (Jarvis IV), 245

Public employees, 23-24, 210, 211; Prop. 1 and, 21; California State Employees Association, 27, effect of Prop. 13 on, 27-28, 31, 33, 143; Prop. 4 and, 36, 154; Prop. 9 and, 38, 200, 201; self-interest of, 112, 115-116, 152-159, 213; Prop. 13 and, 153; demographic breakdown of, 154; schematic thinking of, 218-219; in nation, 227, 230, 238

Public employees, salaries of, 52, 74-87, 176, 211, 238, 248, 257; demographic variables and, 107; parents on, 148; public employees on, 155, 160, 210; liberals and conservatives on, 170. See also Government, waste in; Malaise schema; Tax revolt schema

Public schools, see Schools; Teachers

Public services, see Services

Public transportation, see Services

Race (as demographic variable), 100, 103, 105, 109, 145, 208. See also Blacks; Minorities; Whites

Racism, 77, 163-165, 208, 211, 220, 239; symbolic, 9, 14-15, 49, 163-164, 167-174, 185, 214; in value priorities schema, 166, 176, 177, 210; defined, 167-169; schematic thinking and, 170-172. See also Blacks; Symbolic predispositions; Whites

Reagan, Ronald, 41, 71-72, 222, 238, 262, 268-269; on government, 2, 55-56, 226, 232-234; "reaganism," 9-10; as governor, 20, 21, 163; public and, 94, 187; Congress and, 189, 233-234; economic individualism of, 235, 242; as president, 269-271

Real estate, see Property values

Recession, 244, 248, 261

Referenda, see Initiatives

Region (as demographic variable), 102, 105, 108, 118, 223

Rent control, 34, 238

Renters, 33-34, 37, 237-238; Prop. 13 and, 121, 122, 125, 205; in Oregon, 230

Republicans: national party, 2, 230, 232, 235, 244, 245, 256; philosophy of, 8-9, 71, 163, 181; California party, 25, 26-27, 36, 38, 165, 190; as respondents, 166-167, 178, 185, 208, 214. See also Conservatism; Party identification; Political ideology

"Retrospective voting," 133, 134, 135, 136, 137

Revaluation, 266

Risk aversion, 133, 135, 136-137, 138

San Francisco, 22, 118, 164, 238; Bay Area, 102, 105, 223

Saxon, David, 144

Schematic thinking, 95, 187, 218-220; schema defined, 12, 74, 75-78; self-interest and, 113, 212; symbolic predispositions and, 165-166, 170-174, 179-185. See also Affective consistency; Cognitive psychology; Tax revolt schema

Schools, 6, 147, 150, 152, 234; Prop. 4 and, 20; Prop. 13 and, 27, 143; Prop. 9 and, 37, 38, 143; spending on, 49, 62, 148-149, 157, 197, 198; self-interest and, 70, 143, 148-149, 173; in nation, 229, 231. See also Education, higher; Parents; Teachers; University of California

Self-interest, 4, 5, 70, 106, 274; defined, 13-14, 111-112; class and, 18, 97, 100, 217, 220; tax-service tradeoff and, 58-60, 217, 256; demographic variables and, 101, 103, 221-222; schematic thinking and, 112-113, 217, 218-219; activism and, 113, 115, 130, 139, 141, 221; in overall model, 113-116, 208, 212-213; of "taxpayers," 117-132, 254; economic malaise and, 132-139; of service recipients, 142-152; narrowness of, 146-152, 155-162; of public employees, 152-159, 211; symbolic predispositions and, 165, 169-170, 172-173, 177, 182, 214, 258; Prop. 9 and, 200, 201; in nation, 232

Service recipients, 112, 142-152, 211, 212; defined, 115, 116; government assistance programs, 143, 146, 149-150; activism of,

159-162; schematic thinking of, 218-219;
in future, 238-239
Services, 4-5, 6-7, 68, 194-195, 197-198, 249,
253; Prop. 1 and, 21; Prop. 13 and, 32,
152, 243, 257, 273; Prop. 9 and, 37, 38,
40, 202; opinions on, 47-50; safety
services, 58-59; social services, 58-59, 68,
150, 233, 234; concreteness of description
of, 64-68, 71-72; in tax revolt schema,
74-87, 181, 211; demographic variables
and, 107-108, 241; self-interest and, 150,
213; Prop. 4 and, 151; symbolic
predispositions and, 172, 210-211; in
nation, 213, 238-239; reduction, 269. *See
also* Education, higher; Fees; Fire
services; Health care; Police services;
Schools; Service recipients; Surplus; Tax-
service tradeoff; Unemployment; Welfare
Sex (as demographic variable), 103, 105,
208; women and services, 122, 211; Prop.
9 and, 200-201; explanation of
differences, 221-222; in nation, 232
Socialization, 14-15, 18, 175, 185-186
Social psychology, 161-162, 165; schematic
thinking and, 12, 76, 93; self-interest and,
204, 213. *See also* Mass behavior
Social security, 233, 234, 240, 241
Something-for-nothing syndrome, 259
Southern California, 102, 105, 108, 118, 223
Split roll, 25, 34, 40, 236, 237. *See also*
Property assessments
"Stagflation," 135-136, 137-138, 265. *See
also* Economic malaise; Inflation
State colleges, *see* Education, higher
State government: budget, 6, 31, 32, 33;
Prop. 1 and, 23. *See also* Legislature,
California; Local government;
Proposition 8; Proposition 9
"Status" politics, 15-16
"Supply-side" economics, 234
Supreme Court, 245
Surplus, 265; California state, 23, 62, 204,
216, 236, 239; size of, 25, 32-33; in
Prop. 13 campaign, 27, 32-33, 190;
bailout plan, 32-33, 106, 196-197; Prop. 4
and, 34; Prop. 9 and, 36-37, 202; schools
and, 143, 147
Symbolic predispositions, 64-65, 69-70, 193,
274; in overall model, 14-15, 18, 208, 210,
211, 214-216; schematic thinking and, 76,
179-182, 219; class and, 97, 207, 220;
activism and, 178-179, Prop. 9 and, 201;
sex and, 222; in nation, 232. *See also*
Cynicism; Party identification; Political
ideology; Racism

Symbols, 82, 92, 165, 179, 193, 217; "big
government" and welfare, 60;
concreteness of, 64-72, 94, 183-185, 187,
215; taxes as, 130-132, 140, 215, 232, 236;
racism and, 239

Tax burden, 5, 41, 44-46, 63-64, 80, 243;
tax-service tradeoff and, 58-59; self-
interest and, 113-115, 140; taxes as
symbol, 130-132; cynicism and, 177;
demographic variables and, 208, 220;
federal, 231; perceptions of, 273
Tax cut, 5, 25, 41, 61, 69, 244, 247; Prop. 4
and, 35; Prop. 9 and, 36; surplus and,
36-37; Prop. 13 and, 230; in nation, 233,
235. *See also* Tax-service tradeoff
Taxes: economic theories and, 4-7; visibility
of, 5, 227; local, 5, 6, 21, 40; state, 6, 21,
22, 61; federal, 6, 231; liquor, 20; luxury,
20; corporate income tax, 20; sales tax,
20, 22, 230; inheritance tax, 22; rated as
problem, 23, 53, 89; on business
inventory, 37; on oil companies, 40;
withholding tax, 126, 127, 201; as
political symbol, 130-132, 140, 215, 232,
236; justification of, 159; personal
resistance to, 225-226; in nation, 226-235;
auto excise tax, 228; regressive, 247;
rebates, 248, 265; sales, 267. *See also*
Income tax; Property tax; Tax-service
tradeoff; Withholding tax
Tax limitation organizations, 13, 26, 229
"Taxpayers," 112, 113-115, 117-130,
159-162, 208, 218. *See also* Homeowners;
Self-interest; Tax burden
"Tax rebels," 75, 87-95. *See also* Tax revolt
schema
Tax revolt schema, 92-93, 95; defined,
74-84, 262-263; demographic variables
and, 108; self-interest and, 113, 128-130,
139, 140, 161; of service recipients, 147,
151; of public employees, 155, 158;
symbolic predispositions and, 165-166,
174, 176, 181-182; and larger schemas,
180-182, 187, 219. *See also* Issue public;
Schematic thinking; Value priorities;
individual issues
Tax Revolt Survey, data collection of, 11,
252
Tax shift, 5, 20, 33, 40, 226, 230. *See also*
Split roll
Tax-service tradeoff, 12, 40, 54-64, 87, 198,
216-218; concreteness of symbols in,
69-70; value priorities and, 182-185;
Prop. 13 and, 195-196; Prop. 4 and, 199;

Prop. 9 and, 202-204; tax revolt schema and, 219; in nation, 231-232; in future, 237, 242

Teachers, 20-21, 27-28, 31, 230. *See also* Education, higher; Schools

Texas, 226

Thatcher, Margaret, 1, 226

Tisch amendment, 6, 229, 231, 232

UCLA Business Forecasting Project, 27, 31, 191

Unemployment, 4, 115, 143; compensation, 48, 144, 149-150, 234. *See also* Employment

University of California, 27, 150, 157-158, 253; Prop. 9 and, 37, 38, 143-144; graduates as self-interested group, 144, 145-146

University of Michigan National Election Studies, 8, 24, 40-41, 52, 96, 175

Upper class, 97-98, 208, 213, 237. *See also* Class differences; Income

Value priorities, 64, 110, 220; anti-government attitudes and, 80, 84, 176; self-interest and, 129, 159; of public employees, 157; conservative vs. liberal, 163, 170; party identification and, 166, 214; racism and, 168, 169; concreteness of symbols and, 187; in Los Angeles reassessment controversy, 194; of men and women, 222. *See also* Government, size of; Services

Value priorities schema, 197, 210-211; defined, 181-182, 187, 219; tax-service tradeoff and, 182-185. *See also* Malaise schema

Values, 15, 161-162, 183, 225, 240; Protestant values, 10, 70, 164, 184; economic individualism, 16, 183, 242; sex differences and, 222

Voting behavior, 87-91, 94-95. *See also* Activism; Factions

Waste, *see* Government, waste in

Watson, Philip, 20-21; Watson initiatives, 20-21, 164

Welfare, 23, 234, 249; Prop. 13 and, 33, 144; unpopularity of, 47, 48, 49, 59-60, 195; as symbol of big government, 49, 60, 165, 218; recipients of, 142, 150

Welfare state, 1, 225, 234, 240

Whites, 100, 167-168, 220, 241; activism of, 109, 110; racism of, 168, 208, 239. *See also* Blacks; Race

Wilson, Pete, 26

Wittenburg, Jimmy Dale, 230

Wolden, Russell, 19

Young people, 145, 150, 237, 240. *See also* Age